BATTLE ABBEY

The Eastern Range
and the
Excavations of 1978–80

Plate 1 Air view from the south-east.

HISTORIC BUILDINGS AND MONUMENTS COMMISSION FOR ENGLAND
Archaeological Report no. 2

Battle Abbey

The Eastern Range
and the
Excavations of 1978–80

by J.N. Hare

with contributions by
M. Archibald, R.J. Charleston, J. Geddes, R. Halsey, J. Kerr,
A. Locker, A.D.F. Streeten, R. Warmington,
N.J. Armes, D.R. Atkinson, J. Bayley, J.G. Coad, V.J. Coad, B.M.A. Ellis, M.A. Girling,
M. Hutchinson, B. Knight, C.A. Keepax, G. Lawson, P.J. Paradine

LONDON : HISTORIC BUILDINGS AND
MONUMENTS COMMISSION FOR ENGLAND

First published 1985 by the
Historic Buildings & Monuments Commission for England,
Fortress House, 23 Savile Row,
London, W1X 2HE.

Distributed by Academic Marketing Service, Alan Sutton Publishing
Limited, Brunswick Road, Gloucester, GL1 1JJ.

ISBN 1 85074 062 3

Produced by Alan Sutton Publishing, Gloucester
Printed in Great Britain

Contents

List of Figures

List of Tables

List of plates

Photographs by R. Sheppard and J.N. Hare. Plate 1 is illustrated by permission of Aerofilms Ltd., plate 23 by permission of the Battle Abbey Trustees and plate 24 by permission of the British Library.

Note on references to the abbey records

The obedientary accounts have been referred to in the text by the office concerned and by the closing year of the account. The precise reference to the manuscript may then be found by referring to the list of unpublished sources. Other manuscripts have been given their full reference in the text.

Abbreviations: B.L.   British Library

                 P.R.O.   Public Record Office

                 E.S.R.O.   East Sussex Record Office

                 Cellarers' Accounts   *Accounts of the Cellarers of Battle Abbey*, eds. E. Searle & B. Ross.

                 Chronicle   *The Chronicle of Battle Abbey* ed. E. Searle.

Abstract

Excavations took place in 1978–80 at both ends of the standing eastern or dormitory range at Battle Abbey. The chapter house, which had later undergone a complete rebuilding, and the reredorter were fully excavated. Here and outside these buildings, a sequence of development was established for this part of the site: from the hillside of the battle of Hastings, through the Norman monastery and its additions to the great thirteenth century rebuilding, the continued late-medieval building activity and the post-Dissolution periods of decay, re-use and renewed decay.

Later chapters deal with the wide range of finds that were produced by the excavations. These include important sequences of pottery and roof tile; material that throws light on the design, glazing and flooring of the monastic buildings; and an extensive collection of bone, lead, copper alloy, iron and glass objects from a Dissolution rubbish dump.

An attempt has been made to collate the result of the excavations with the documentary evidence for the abbey and with the surviving monastic buildings. Two appendices deal with an important group of architectural fragments from earlier excavations and clearance, and with the results of work at the abbey since 1980.

Preface

On the site of his decisive victory at the battle of Hastings, William the Conqueror founded what was to be one of the greater monasteries of medieval England. Although very little may still be seen of the buildings of his own time, much survives of the extensive and grandiose rebuilding of the thirteenth century, and this provides a fitting reflection of the abbey's wealth and importance. Despite the wealth and architectural significance of the site, relatively little archaeological excavation has hitherto been carried out, but a new phase in the history of the site began in 1976 when the battlefield and abbey were acquired for the nation by the Department of the Environment. As part of its programme of work, excavations were carried out in 1978–80. They were concentrated on the areas at either end of the surviving dormitory range and saw the full excavation of the monastic chapter house and reredorter range. They have now established a picture of the development of this corner of the site that has significantly modified our understanding of the evolution of the area from the time of the battle onwards. At the same time they have produced a valuable range of finds that will be important for the study of the local ceramics of the area, for the study of the buildings of the abbey and for comparison with other Dissolution groups. The opportunity has also been taken to look again at the buildings themselves, some of the abbey's extensive surviving documentation and at the material from the earlier excavations. It is hoped that our work should thus provide both a summation of what has been done and a basis for further work when eventually finances and priorities permit.

To the author, it has been a privilege to have had the opportunity of studying this great abbey at such close quarters. I am thus very grateful to the Department of the Environment whose project this was, and which in recent years has done so much for the site. Many individuals within the Department have given vital support to the project, but I should particularly like to thank Jonathan Coad, the Inspector with responsibility for the monument, whose continued help has been such an essential element in its completion in difficult times. In the later stages of the revision of the text, responsibility for the monument was transferred from the Department to the Historic Buildings and Monuments Commission, to which successor organisation go our thanks and good wishes.

The success of the excavation is a tribute to the work of the site staff, many of whom were also involved in producing specialist reports. Particular thanks are due to Anthony Streeten, who was assistant director on site, who directed the post-excavation sessions on the finds and who has been a constant source of help both during the excavations and afterwards. The supervision on site was also the work of Susan Davies, Jane Geddes, Martin Oake and Mark Taylor, while Vivienne Coad and Amanda Booth supervised the finds shed. The site and publication drawings are the work of Richard Warmington. The photographic record was the responsibility of Richard Sheppard as well as of myself. He also produced the final publication prints for the excavations. To all of them, I am most grateful.

During the excavations, the volunteers who worked so hard on site were fully supported by the hospitality of the Hurst Court Educational Centre at Hastings and by its successive wardens, the late R.J. Davis, and B. White. On site, the excavation benefitted from the support of G.E. Elliott, R. Coleman and the D.o.E. staff at Battle.

In preparing the report, I have been particularly grateful to the specialists who produced their reports with such promptitude, so enabling the completion of the full report eighteen months after the end of the excavations. Their names are listed, but one name that should have appeared amongst them was that of S.E. Rigold. He was to have produced two of the specialist reports and had begun preliminary work for them. Regretably, death was to deprive Battle in particular, and the world of scholarship in general of his generous learning. I would also like to thank the many scholars whose individual help to contributors is acknowledged in subsequent chapters.

The unexpected quantity of the small finds imposed considerable burdens on the hard-pressed services of the Ancient Monuments' Directorate.

Both the conservation section of the A.M. Laboratory and A.M. Illustrators' Office coped valiantly and superbly with this glorious avalanche of material. The drawings themselves are the work of Judith Dobie of the Illustrators' Office (Chapters V, VIII, IX, & X) and Vivienne Coad (Chapters VI & VII).

My task has been made easier by being able to use the work of others. Mr. O.S. Brakspear generously allowed me to study the records of his father's work at Battle. Like any student of Battle, I am grateful to the work of Professor Eleanor Searle whose writings and editions form an essential basis for the study of the abbey. In studying the buildings, I was granted ready access to the abbots' range by Miss. J. Parker and Mr. D.J. Teall, successive Heads of Battle Abbey School, whose pupils now occupy the monastic west range. Finally, the hospitality of Jonathan and Vivienne Coad during my many visits to Battle has provided a much appreciated addition to the delights of monastic archaeology.

The report was completed and presented in January 1982. It was then revised in the first half of 1984. Standardisation and the final editing were the responsibility of Jane Geddes, not the least of her many contributions to the success of the project.

J.N. Hare
Winchester, July 1984

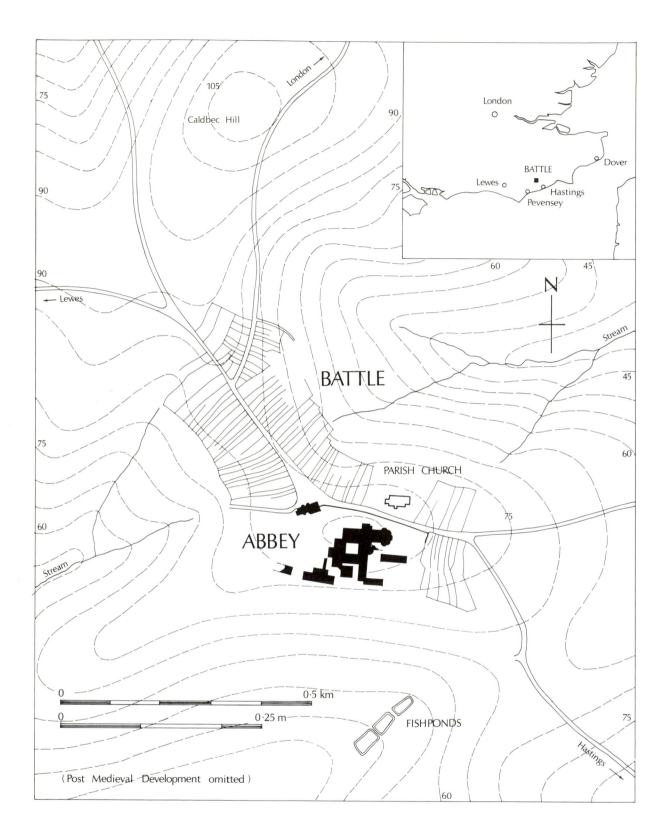

BATTLE ABBEY · LOCATION

RW

Figure 1

Chapter I

The abbey and its buildings:
an historical introduction

Although it is not intended to provide a full account of the history and buildings of Battle Abbey, it seems essential to establish the historical and architectural context against which the results of the excavations should be seen. The history of the abbey has been summarized in the Victoria County History (Salzman 1907) while more recently the work of Professor Searle (especially 1974, *Chronicle* and *Cellarers' Accounts*) has set the history of the abbey and its estates on a newer and sounder footing. Description and discussion of the buildings may be found in the works of Brakspear (1933 and 1937), and in more recent treatments by myself (Hare 1981) and by J.G. Coad (1984).

The abbey was founded by William the Conqueror as a thank-offering for his victory or as an act of penance: a response to the heavy penances imposed on himself and his followers for the death and plunder that had occurred during the conquest (Searle 1980, 20–21; Cowdrey 1969, 233–42). According to the abbey's chronicle, William was adamant that the abbey should be built on the exact site of his own victory over Harold and he prevented the monks from moving the monastery to a more favourable site (*Chronicle*, 42–4). According to monastic tradition, the high altar was placed on the spot where Harold's standard had fallen, and this tradition is reinforced by the archaeological evidence that the altar was on the highest point of the hill (*Chronicle*, 44; Brakspear 1931, 167–8). William's decision placed the monastery on a narrow hilltop site, restricted by the road to the north and with the ground sloping in all other directions, especially towards the south. He had bequeathed his foundation a problem that was to be a dominant influence on the subsequent architecture and archaeology of the site (Hare 1981, 80–2). The abbey seems to have been set up as a royal *eigenkloster* entirely dependant on William himself while free from other outside interference (Searle 1974, 23–6). William seems to have taken a personal interest in the development of the monastery (*Chronicle* 42–6) and from the beginning it was established as a wealthy house, coming fifteenth in order of wealth among the monasteries that figured in Domesday Book (Knowles 1963, 702–3). By 1094 the church itself was consecrated (*Chronicle*, 96 n.3, *Anglo-Saxon Chronicle*, 229) although it was not leaded until later (*Chronicle*, 136). Only a fragment of the south-west corner of the nave and the base of its south wall are now visible, but a substantial amount is known about the east end of the church and is

discussed below (p. 18). As for the conventual buildings, the chronicle tells us little except that they were humble and unostentatious, and that the precinct wall was finished by abbot Ralph (1107–24) who also enlarged the courtyard (presumably the outer court) and surrounded it with new buildings (*Chronicle*, 100, 130). Little survives of the Norman work: parts of the precinct wall, a possible tower that was eventually incorporated into the west wing of the later main gatehouse, and fragments of a Norman building that lie to the east of the later court house. In addition, and on the opposite side of the outer court, Brakspear found a substantial wall that underlay the south wall of the thirteenth century cellarer's range (Brakspear papers, Battle file). It is not clear, however, whether this earlier wall represents part of a building or the precinct wall. Later, under abbot Walter de Luci, the cloisters were rebuilt (*Chronicle*, 262), and finds from the present excavations and from earlier work, have demonstrated the impressive quality of these buildings (*infra* pp. 69, 192). But the practical independence from external authority that had been achieved under William, had to be fought for if it were to be maintained. Much of the abbey's chronicle is therefore concerned with the long twelfth-century struggle between the abbey and the bishops of Chichester over the bishops' rights in the abbey.

For the thirteenth century we lose the helpful chronicle evidence as the main chronicle finishes in 1176 and the brief later ones shed no further light on the buildings (Bodleian Mss. Rawl. B150 ff. 1–4, 48–50, partly printed in Bémont 1884, 372–380; B.L. Cott. Mss. Nero D II). But other sources, both documentary and architectural, show us that this was a century of activity, innovation and expansion, with increased wealth being spent on a grandiose programme of rebuilding. Developments in the early part of the century had increased the abbey's ability to engage in such a programme. In 1211 the abbey bought from King John the right to look after the abbey estates during a vacancy and acquired the right of choosing their new abbot (Searle 1974, 98). Thereafter all the abbots seem to have been monks of Battle or its daughter houses, while continuity of policy could also be maintained during a vacancy. Later, in 1235, a settlement was reached with the bishops of Chichester, thus removing a further source of financial strain (Searle 1974, 97–8). At the same time, and particularly after the accession of abbot Ralph of Coventry in 1235, the abbey's new activity in the land market, and its more active role in estate administration enabled it to profit more fully from the colonisation of the Weald and the rising demand for land that characterised the period (Searle 1974, 136–8, 143, 147–8). Such increased revenue was certainly needed for within a century almost all the monastic buildings had been rebuilt on a lavish and much larger scale.

This transformation of the abbey's buildings began c. 1200 with the rebuilding of the chapter house (*infra* p. 25). This was followed in the first half of the thirteenth century by the construction, west of the cloisters, of a new block of accommodation for the abbot, by the erection of a vast new eastern or dormitory range for the monks and, in the outer court, by the building of a new cellarer's or guest range. Of these, the best surviving are the first two. The abbot's range has been described in detail by Brakspear (1933). It comprised, in its completed early thirteenth-century form, a first floor hall with at one end a chamber with chapel above and at the other end, at right angles to the hall, a large chamber with small adjacent chapel. On the ground floor was a series of undercrofts including an outer parlour, other accommodation, and a large porch. There were also some rooms that have since disappeared. Even today, despite the impact of medieval and post-medieval alterations, Battle provides us with a remarkably complete example of an abbot's house of this date. But the most impressive remains of this period are provided by the dormitory range. This has lost its roof and its northern end, but otherwise survives almost intact and is dealt with in detail below (p. 26).

Both ranges show common characteristics, such as the use of round-headed doorways in buildings that were otherwise clearly Early English in character. Brakespear saw both ranges as belonging to the abbacy of Ralph of Coventry (1235–1261) but there is evidence to suggest that the abbot's range represents the product of two distinct building programmes, although probably without a long intervening period. Thus whereas the porch with its typical water-holding bases and simple hollow-chamfered vault ribs is identical in style to the dormitory range, the undercroft of the abbot's hall shows contrasting and sometimes earlier elements in its columns, bases and in the keel mouldings of its vault ribs. Thus the hall block seems to have been extended at a slightly later date, by which time the design of the eastern range had been fully established. The dating of the latter range is discussed more fully below (p. 34).

In the outer court, a new cellarer's or guest range was constructed. It too should be ascribed to the early thirteenth century, but the paucity of its survival and the simplicity of its architectural character makes it impossible to be more precise. The barrel-vaulted undercrofts were originally at a ground floor level on both sides, but after the Dissolution the ground was built up to the north and the windows and doors were blocked. The new range was two-storeyed. Little survives of its first floor: a fragment of its east wall, and the sill of one of its northern windows was recorded in the 1930s (Brakspear Papers, Battle file). The ground floor, however, is complete and consisted of eight undercrofts or cellars, most of which were entered from the courtyard to the north. At the east end was a distinct group of three rooms, entered from the north by a blocked opening to the second undercroft. The two adjacent chambers each had a doorway leading to this central one and each had a hooded fireplace. They evidently constituted accommodation or offices rather than storage. Vidler also refers to the presence of other vaulted rooms to the north of the range and at its east and west ends (1841, 142), but these would not necessarily have been medieval and could have belonged to the post-Dissolution conversion of the range into the undercroft of Sir Anthony Browne's new wing. In the fourth undercroft from the east, a doorway opens into a later medieval passageway to the abbot's range. This passage was later buried by the raising of the courtyard.

The rebuilding of the monastery continued in the later thirteenth century with the construction of a new frater or refectory and related buildings as well as a new and much larger eastern arm for the church. Unfortunately, the buildings of this major phase have been almost totally destroyed since the Dissolution and we are left with tantalising glimpses of the quality and importance of the work. The west end of the refectory still survives, albeit in a damaged form, and still shows the interior panelling, the fragmentary jambs of the blocked west windows and the battered jamb of one of the side windows. The plan of the rest of the building was established by Brakspear and the large fragmented window discovered by him and still extant should probably be ascribed to this. Adjacent to the frater, we possess the rear panelling of two new bays of the cloister, where they have been preserved against the wall of the abbot's house. They had evidently been designed with stone vaults in mind. Enough survives to show the high quality of their craftsmanship and their similarity to work in the new east end at Bayham Abbey (Sussex), built in about the 1260's (Rigold 1976, 24–5, and pers. com.). A new kitchen was also built; this was pulled down in 1685–8, but Brakspear uncovered its plan, and it would seem to have been a large square building with a central kitchen area and hearths, surrounded by four other lower ranges. Aubrey, in the seventeenth century described it as of great height, open to the top and with four great chimneys one at each corner of the building (*Chronologia Architectonica*, Bodleian Lib. Ms top. gen. C25 f.154r., and *English Romanesque Art*, 370). On the southern side an undercroft had to be constructed in order to create a level platform for the building. This undercroft still survives although it provides no clear dating evidence. Its appearance would, however, be consistent with construction in the thirteenth or fourteenth century. Documentary evidence, moreover, suggests that a new kitchen was being planned in 1279 when timber was being felled for it (*Cellarers' Accounts, 46*).

The new seven-bay eastern arm was 47 m (152 feet) long and would have provided a much needed enlargement to what had hitherto been a small church. The building was destroyed after the Dissolution and our knowledge of it is now restricted to the crypts of three eastern chapels and Brakspear's small-scale excavations (Brakspear 1931 and fig 5). It would seem to have had a *chevet* of five radiating chapels, although two of these have not yet been fully tested for, and the deep buttresses would suggest that the walls were designed to support a stone vault. Unfortunately we have no documentary and little architectural evidence to help date the extension. Although it is traditionally given an early fourteenth-century date (Brakspear 1937, 103) it seems more likely to derive from the preceding half-century. The capitals in the crypt show close similarities to the late thirteenth-century work in the cloisters at Battle. Moreover, this view is supported by the distinctive plan with its eastern chevet such as is likely to have been derived from Henry III's rebuilding of Westminster Abbey, the eastern arm of which was built between 1246 and 1259 (Brown, Colvin and Taylor 1963, 137–144). In the absence of any other example in south-east England and of any evidence in the history of the abbey to suggest any likelihood of continental influences at this time, Westminster seems the most likely source, and this in turn would suggest that the new building at Battle was a product of a period when Henry's great new church was still the focus of architectural interest.

Even considered by themselves such a series of buildings would have been a massive achievement reflecting the power and wealth of the abbey. But two other factors highlight the achievement of the thirteenth century. Although the plan of the monastery was typically Benedictine, this could only be achieved with considerable difficulty. The ambitious plans of the monks had to overcome the problems left by their founder, for the narrowness of the site meant that the new buildings had to expand onto extensive cellarage and involved the creation of considerable earthen platforms (Hare 1981, 80). Moreover, the buildings already mentioned are unlikely to provide a complete survey of the buildings of the period for others have disappeared completely or have left inadequate evidence of dating. A new infirmary range may have belonged to this period (*infra* p. 24) as may various surviving fragments in the outer court, while at sometime in the monastic period a detached bell tower was erected. The latter seems to have lain to the east of the church: in the cemetery and opposite the road to the Little Park (PRO E315/56 f.17r; ESRO BAT 269). For the abbey as a whole, just as for the area of the excavations, the thirteenth century was to be a period of transformation.

Building activity was, however, to continue into the early fourteenth century, particularly in the outer court. Here the major work was the construction of a new gatehouse but there were also extensions made to the abbot's range (Brakspear 1933, 144, 151–2). In 1338 the abbey was granted a licence to crenellate (*Cal. Pat. R1.* 1338–40, 92) and the gatehouse probably dates from soon afterwards. This great tower provides a fitting sign of the domination of the abbey over the town. Above the gateways were the two large chambers on successive floors and the entrance to the south-east turret was strengthened by a portcullis and other defensive features. Although the side wings have been drastically altered or destroyed they probably represent the fourteenth-century plan. The west wing incorporates a rectangular Norman building or tower and was later extended on the first floor. The eastern wing was also remodelled as shown in the east wall of the range, before being pulled down and replaced by the present sixteenth-century court house. The new gatehouse may itself have been built outside the existing precinct wall. This is suggested by the alignment of the later wall, and by the presence of pre-existing buildings immediately to the south of the 'court house', both that against which the gatehouse was built and that represented by a wall recently found by a gas-pipe trench (figure 2). Such buildings would have been difficult to fit with another one immediately to the north. The precinct wall would thus have originally lain along the back of the present gatehouse with the Norman tower projecting at the western corner of the site.

By the middle of the century, so much had been rebuilt on a new and magnificent scale, that it was hardly surprising that the tempo of building slackened. Moreover, the later fourteenth century was a time of financial difficulties and of resultant economies (Searle 1974, 262–5). It is, however, difficult to assess the extent of building operations in the later Middle Ages as modifications to the existing structures may have left no evidence when the original buildings were destroyed after the Dissolution or may have left no marks on the surviving ruins. But building work continued, albeit on a more irregular basis. The major work of the last century and a half of the abbey's existence was the construction of a large new abbot's hall and adjacent rooms (Brakspear 1933, 158–62) and the rebuilding of most of the west cloister walk (Brakspear 1937, 103). But other work was also undertaken. In the outer court a new first floor was added to the accommodation in the wings of the gatehouse range and the stone passage from the cellarer's range to the abbot's quarters was built, possibly in 1366 when £26 was spent on making a passage from the sub-prior's chamber to that of the abbot (Abbey Account, 1366). The excavations themselves have shown the installation of a new drainage system, the construction of a new building as well as substantial refurbishing in the dormitory range and the replacement of the transept apse. The documentary evidence also points to continued activity, thus in the early sixteenth century a new building was constructed by the almoner in 1520 and the sacrist spent over £93 on a new building in 1518 (almoner's account 1521, sacrist's account 1518).

Battle in the later Middle Ages and on the eve of the Dissolution has been described as 'still a tidy, careful, comfortable, burgess household' (Searle 1974, 265). Such a reputation may be a long way from that of the abbey in its early years when for more than a century Battle could be seen as one of the more fortunate abbeys, and when 'more than one able and spiritual abbot helped to keep its first purity untouched' (Knowles 1963, 128), but it was still not a discreditable record. The monastery was generally living within its means (Searle 1974, 266). Although it has been accused of a lack of economic enterprise in the period from the 1380's onwards (Searle 1974, 266), its record on the manors outside the *leuga* suggests that the abbey still possessed a flexible and enterprising estate administration in the fifteenth century (Brandon 1972, 403–20; Hare 1976, 141– 196; & Hare, forthcoming). There were probably now fewer monks than in the thirteenth century but there was no steady decline. In 1347, before the Black Death there were 52 monks and novices. This number dropped sharply as a result of plague down to 34 monks and novices in 1351 or at least 25 monks in 1350. But thereafter there was a recovery and no steady decline. In the later fourteenth century between 1382 and 1394 there were between 27 and 35 choir monks together with the officials. Two elections, in 1404 and 1490, were held by the prior and thirty monks. Between 1503 and 1531 the number was smaller and the ten years for which we have figures show between 21 and 27 choir monks. It was, however, increasingly difficult to find new recruits in the 1530's and by the time of the Dissolution there was only the abbot and 18 monks (Evans 1942, 82–86; Salzman 1907, 54; Searle 1974, 356 and 441). Nor was the household particularly unlearned and at the Dissolution five of the eighteen monks possessed degrees in theology. Such a picture of comfortable well-being contrasts with the picture painted by Cromwell's visitors. Layton was to write in 1538 that, '. . . so beggarly a house I never see, nor so filthy stuff. I assure you I will not [give] 20s for all manner [of] hangings in this house. . . . The revestry is the worst, the baldest and poorest that ever I see . . .' (Cook 1965, 172). He and Gage assured Cromwell that 'the implements off the housholde be the wurste that ever I se in abbay or priorie, the vestymentts so old and so baysse, worne, raggede and torne, as youre lordship wolde not thynke, so that veray smale money can be made off the vestrye' (Searle 1974, 441). But such comments should not be regarded as reflecting general conditions at Battle in the later Middle Ages. Moreover, the sacrists' accounts show that the vestments were kept repaired, and in 1527 a man was employed for seventy-two days to repair the vestments (Evans 1942, 79). It may be that for several years before the Dissolution, Abbot Hammond had stopped replacing household implements, clothing and vestments and had taken the precaution of placing his assets elsewhere (Searle 1974, 440–2).

Such precautions would have proved well-founded for on 27 May 1538, the Conqueror's great foundation was finally surrendered to the officials of Henry VIII (Searle 1974, 441). Later that year (on 15 August) the buildings and site of the monastery, its church, campanile and cemetery were granted to Sir Anthony Browne together with substantial land around (ESRO BAT. 269, Dugdale 1846, 254–6). The following year he acquired further lands in eastern Sussex (*Letters & Papers. Hen VIII*, xiv, pt ii, 619). The new owner succeeded to the abbey's position as the dominant political force in this part of Sussex and it may well be that this was part of a deliberate royal policy. In the latter part of 1538 and the early part of 1539 the international scene looked critically dangerous for Henry's Reformation. France and Spain had buried their differences, albeit temporarily, papal excommunication had been carried out and England seemed threatened by a Catholic invasion. But traditionally the abbey had played an important role as a focus for organising the defence of this vulnerable area (Searle 1974, 341–2). The danger was to be reflected in the major building works at Camber Castle which were begun in 1539 (Colvin 1982, 418–20), and it may well be that the grant of the abbey to Browne was a first and immediate attempt to fill the power vacuum created by the Dissolution. In any case he clearly intended to make Battle the centre of the family fortunes: he built his grand tomb in its parish church and started major building works at the abbey. For although the excavated area saw the destruction of the abbey church and chapter house, and the conversion of other buildings to service use, elsewhere major building programmes were underway. Now the focus of activity on the site shifted from the former claustral area to the old monastic outer court. Here the rubble of the destroyed buildings was dumped to the north of the cellarer's range so that a flat courtyard could be extended up to a range that had originally been built on a sloping hillside. In this way the destruction of the monastery enabled the new owner to overcome the problem of the narrow hilltop site bequeathed to the monks by their founder. A group of architectural fragments from Brakspear's excavations in this build-up (Appendix A) includes material of very high quality including some from the church, the chapter house and the cloisters. At the back of this extended courtyard Browne built a new block, partly on the foundations of the old cellarer's range. Little now survives of this impressive range except its two eastern turrets and illustrations (plate 19 and Brakspear 1933, pl. 29 and pp. 162–6). A local tradition, going back to at least the eighteenth century, associates Battle with Queen or Princess Elizabeth (Torrington Diaries, 362) and the range has been described as having been built for her (e.g. Brakspear 1933, 164). However, there seems to be no supporting evidence and even if it was expected that Elizabeth would come here, it is not clear which building was built for her. The Duchess of Cleveland considered the adjacent south wing of the abbot's range was the one concerned (1877, 234). So, in the absence of any contradictory evidence, it seems more appropriate to see this activity as a product of the new owner's desire to build impressive accommodation, as did so many other beneficiaries of monastic sites. In addition to this range the old abbot's range was extended and modified (Brakspear, 1933).

Although the monastic life had ended, the buildings and site faced a new and active future. Under Sir Anthony and his son Viscount Montague, the Brownes were important influences on national and local politics (Manning 1968). Even after the family's acquisition of Cowdray House (West Sussex),

Battle was to remain an important seat and a focus of its power. This was reflected during the latter part of Elizabeth's reign by Battle's reputation under the Catholic Viscount Montague and his widow, as a hot-bed of Catholic recusancy (Manning 1969, 40, 43, 159, 162–3; Smith 1627, 42–5). At the abbey, the household that had usurped the buildings of the monks continued as a focus of the Catholic faith. Here, we are told by the contemporary biographer of Montague's widow, she maintained three priests and built a chapel with a choir and there were sometimes 120 at the Catholic services that were held here (Smith 1627, 42–3).

It was probably not until the seventeenth century that the abbey ceased to be the regular home of an aristocratic household, a change suggested by the rapid decline and virtual disappearance of recusancy in the town in the early seventeenth century (Fletcher 1975, 98). Deprived of the strengthening patronage of a great Catholic household, recusancy was likely to decline, and the family by now seems to have been based on Cowdray House. Thus during the seventeenth century much rubbish was to accumulate within the area of the chapter house. In the Civil War, the Montagues suffered as did other recusants and in 1643, two-thirds of their estates were sequestered (Thomas-Stamford 1910, 131). What effect this had on the abbey buildings is unclear, although situated in what had by now become a Puritan town (Fletcher 1975, 256), they must surely have been liable to continuing decay or looting.

The decline of the buildings and its owners was to result in large-scale demolition in the later part of the century. In 1685–6 the abbey kitchen and probably other unspecified buildings were destroyed (Steward's Account, ESRO XA 13). Further demolitions are recorded later in the century and in the beginning of the eighteenth century (Cleveland 1877, 192 and 207). In the eighteenth and nineteenth centuries the abbey buildings went through several periods of decay and rehabilitation (Cleveland 1877, 207–23). Many of the alterations were in the area of the abbot's range, into which the accommodation had now shrunk, and have been considered by Brakspear (1933). Developments in the area of the eastern range are considered elsewhere (*infra* p. 45). Such decline and rebuilding is reflected in the topographical drawings and engravings, and particularly in Grimm's 1783 series of illustrations (B.L. Add. Mss. 5670 ff. 37–49, see also *infra* plate 24, Brakspear 1933 plate XXXIX, and Godfrey and Salzman 1951, plate 16). These show both general decay, as in the dormitory range, and the presence of some alterations. Thus the abbot's hall, which had at some time previously been modified by the insertion of a first floor, (as shown, for example, by the marks of its joists) had by now been restored to its original proportions with the removal of this floor. Later, at the beginning of the nineteenth century came the work of Sir Godfrey Webster, who carried out work at many places around the site, and finally that of Sir Henry Vane, Duke of Cleveland, who bought the site in 1858. The latter and his architect, Henry Clutton built the new library wing, to the south of the abbot's range, which was to be the last major building work here. The Duke and Duchess also carried out many small-scale alterations. The twentieth century's contribution has mainly been of consolidation and restoration at various parts of the site, with the largest scale works being those that were necessitated by the gutting of the abbot's range by a fire in 1931 (Brakspear 1933, 145). Such phases of activity were interspersed with periods of decay and lack of care. The Dissolution had begun a new phase in the development of the site. The subsequent centuries were to be a time of fluctuating fortunes for the abbey buildings and they were to leave a considerable mark on the archaeological evidence of both the standing buildings and of the excavated area.

Chapter II

The Eastern Range and the Excavations of 1978–80

Previous archaeological excavations at Battle have been surprisingly limited. In the early nineteenth century the three eastern crypts were uncovered, when they were mistakenly thought to belong to the original Norman church, and then and later in the century trenches were dug on the site of the major range lying east of the parlour (figure 2). The latter range was mistakenly described as the chapter house. Then between 1929 and 1934 excavations were carried out by Sir Harold Brakspear. These were often small-scale trenches that followed the walls, but they enabled him to establish the plan of the original east end of the church and the foundations, subsequently laid out, of the frater, kitchen and parlour. In the chapter house he was able to follow its apse and to find the additional building to the east. He was thus able to establish the plan of the central area of the monastery with considerable economy of effort, although adding to the difficulties of subsequent excavations. He also carried out work in the outer court (see appendix A).

The acquisition of the site by the Department of the Environment in 1976 led the latter to launch a programme of excavation from 1978 to 1980 over a total period, during the three years, of eleven weeks. The aims of these excavations were threefold: to shed light on the archaeological development of the monastery; to provide information as to the survival of the buildings below the ground and thus aid decision-making for further programmes; to reveal additional buildings that could subsequently be displayed to visitors. The unpredictability of possible results led to the adoption of a strategy with maximum flexibility. The chapter house and reredorter were chosen for excavation, as these would both link to the surviving dormitory range, and would provide limited objectives that could be completed. In 1978, work concentrated on the chapter house while trial trenches were cut to establish whether the reredorter range justified large-scale excavation. As a result of this work it was then decided to excavate the reredorter and the area to the east of the parlour. Although the excavations sought to reveal buildings for display, they were carried down to earlier levels in selected areas in order that a full account of the development of the site could be established. The excavations were carried out entirely by hand except for the mechanical clearance of the rubble debris from the destruction of the reredorter and the removal of the eighteenth and nineteenth century accumulations in parts of the area east of the parlour (trenches Q–P). In all cases, this was preceded by the hand-excavation of trial trenches to establish the nature of the layers, and whether machinery could safely be used.

There were two main areas of excavation. On top of the hill, the chapter house was examined together with areas to the east, south-east and a corner of the south transept. Lower down the slope, the reredorter range was excavated. These two distinct areas have been designated the chapter house and reredorter areas, although it should be stressed that the excavations spread beyond the buildings themselves. Trenches A–S were in the chapter house area and trenches R I-IX in the reredorter area. In examining the findings of the excavation, the evidence has been discussed period by period and where possible the two areas have been examined together. Where no clear links can be established between the two areas, they have been treated separately. The standing buildings of the dormitory range have been treated with the archaeological evidence of the relevant periods.

The archaeology of these areas may be divided up into five broad periods. Period A is from the foundation of the abbey until the start of the thirteenth-century rebuilding. The latter constitutes period B and here includes the remodelling of the chapter house and the building of the reredorter and surviving dormitory range. The remaining part of the Middle Ages, with its more limited changes, is period C. Period D covers the Dissolution and subsequent occupation in the sixteenth and seventeenth centuries. Its end is not marked by any particular historical or datable event but by a change in the use of the area. At some time about 1700 major demolition took place and both areas were subsequently largely open space. Period E incorporates these two developments and continues until the beginning of the excavations.

In using this report, it is important to remember the different character of the stratigraphy in the two areas. In the reredorter area there was a considerable accumulation, both of medieval and post-medieval layers, although with a general lack of clear courtyard surfaces. By contrast, there was little medieval stratification in the chapter house area. Here not merely had the ground been kept clean but the surfaces had even been lowered in the medieval and post-medieval periods so that much evidence had been destroyed. Stratigraphic relationships could be established but the lack of a general medieval build-up or of widespread layers posed a severe obstacle to establishing a full sequence of events.

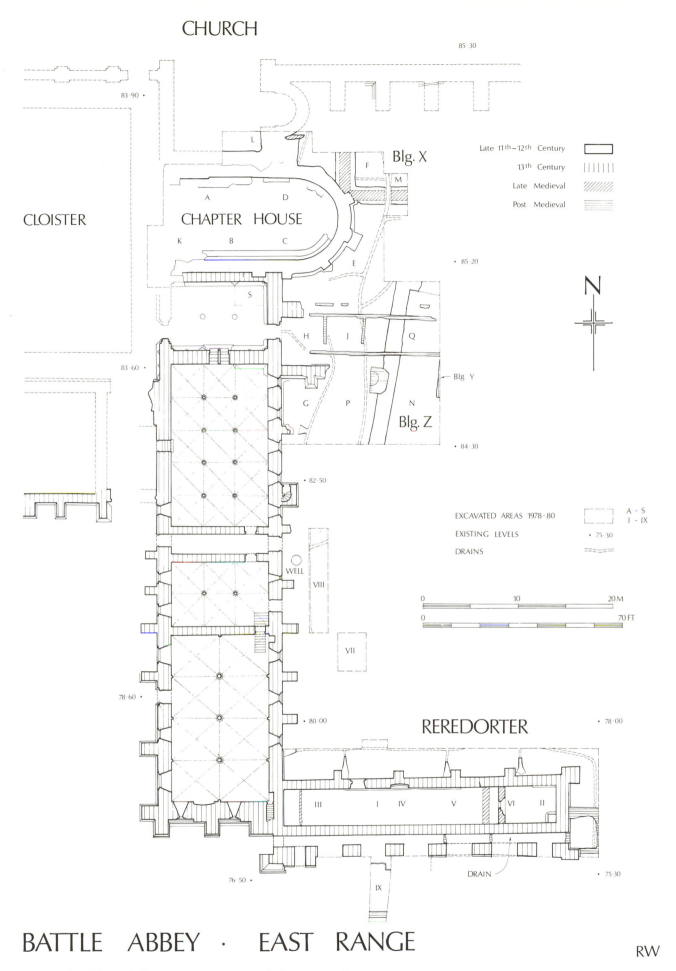

CHURCH

CLOISTER

CHAPTER HOUSE

Blg. X

Blg Y

Blg. Z

WELL

REREDORTER

Late 11th–12th Century
13th Century
Late Medieval
Post Medieval

EXCAVATED AREAS 1978·80
EXISTING LEVELS   · 75·30
DRAINS

A – S
I – IX

0   10   20 M
0   70 FT

DRAIN

BATTLE ABBEY · EAST RANGE

RW

Figure 3   Plan of the eastern range and the excavations.

Before the Monastery

The starting point for the history and archaeology of the site is provided by the battle of Hastings – only the circumstances of the abbey's foundation could account for its construction on such a waterless hill-top site. But while we know a surprising amount about the layout and sequence of the battle (Brown 1981) the excavations have reinforced the evidence of the standing buildings in showing how greatly the topography of the site has changed in the centuries since the battle (Hare 1981, 80–2). In one sense the history of the abbey site may be seen as a continual struggle to overcome the problems imposed by the Conqueror's decision, and a realisation of these changes is essential in order to understand the excavations.

The excavations, together with Brakspear's work in the church, enable us to compare the profile of the hillside now with that before the construction of the monastic buildings. We can now provide an intermittent section from the hill top to its lower portions below the reredorter (fig 4). The transformation of the hillside can most easily be seen by comparing the situation in the church with that in the reredorter area. In the choir of the church the present surface must represent the approximate level of the medieval pavement, for the excavators came across the Norman foundations, where they would have been sealed below the later flooring, only a few inches below the surface (Brakspear 1931, 167). By contrast the area to the north of the reredorter showed an accumulation of 2.4 metres since the battle, both during the Middle Ages and afterwards. The reredorter itself was built on the hillside and considerable levelling was required both inside and outside. Elsewhere in the chapter house area we again find evidence of considerable terracing. East of the chapter house itself the ground seems to have been lowered in the course of the Middle Ages virtually exposing the foundations themselves. Further south, however, the platform was extended by building up an area for a new building (Building Z). Here, in the south-east corner of trench N, the depth of build-up was over 1.2m. Further south the ground sloped gently southwards but in trench RVII the ground dropped suddenly and then more gently up to and underneath the later reredorter. Owing to the great depth, restricted area and lack of time it was impossible to establish the depth of the original ground surface in this trench although probing indicated that it was over 3.3 m. below the present ground surface. This steep drop in part represents a general change in the natural slope of the hill such as is reflected, in an artificially cut-back form, in the drop from the middle room to the novices' quarters and further west in the need for the southern part of the kitchens to be built up on cellarage. But as figure 4 shows, the supposed natural soil seems to slope unexpectedly sharply in trench VII, and to a depth below that to which it would be projected on the basis of the trenches to the north and to the south. A possible explanation of the evidence is that these sharply sloping layers may represent the fill of a ditch that ran from east to west. Such a ditch could have served

as an open sewer for an earlier reredorter, but only further excavation can clarify the situation. In addition to the general slope of the hillside down to the south, the ground level had also dipped eastwards away from the dormitory range.

Period A: the Norman Abbey

The Eastern Arm of the Abbey Church
(figure 5, plate 5)
The abbey church was the first major building constructed on the site. Although in general the recent excavations avoided the church itself, the footings of the south transept were exposed within the adjacent chapter house and a small extension was made to locate the south-east corner of this transept as a check on Brakspear's conjectural plan.

Brakspear's excavations were limited in scale and seem to have involved trial trenching and then wall-following. Although much evidence had already been destroyed by the construction of the foundations of the later and larger eastern arm, and by more recent root disturbance, he was able to establish the position and much of the plan of the Norman work (Brakspear 1931, 166–8). He established that the original structure had an ambulatory and at the east end this led into an apsidal chapel with external pilasters. Clear cut evidence for the expected pair of additional radiating chapels was difficult to establish owing to destruction by the later foundations of the new aisle walls and by the limited area of excavation. An unpublished plan (Brakspear Papers/Battle folder) suggests that the foundations were turning outwards in positions where they could have served the conjectural apses. His excavations also showed that the north transept had an apsidal chapel and an internal chamfered plinth. The latter was presumably similar to that surviving on the south wall of the nave.

The recent excavations have produced additional information on the footings for the church as well as providing confirmation for Brakspear's plan. The lowest course of the wall of the south transept apse was found very close (0.2m) to the present surface and consisted of blocks of ashlar with coarse diagonal tooling of early Norman character and wide joints, such as survive in the remains of the south aisle wall of the nave (plate 5). The three ashlar blocks provided a length of 1.10m and clearly confirmed the curve of the apse. The wall itself was seated on broad stone footings up to 3.6m in width. The foundations were not, however, uniform. The lowest level was revealed in the north-west corner of the chapter house where post-Dissolution activity had destroyed the wall of the chapter house and so exposed the base of the footings. It consisted of large boulders now set in sand and apparently without mortar. Above this were the main footings with much smaller stones set in a pale mortar. The footings were not entirely regular and they were much wider at the south-west and south-east corners of the transept, where they extended beyond the line of the chapter house wall and were revealed in the excavations within the latter building (figure 6). It is not clear whether these extensions should be inter-

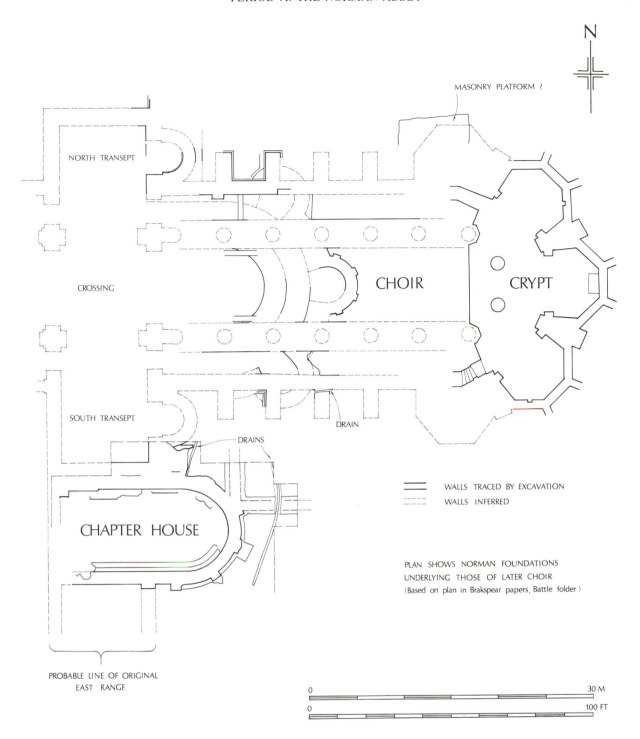

N

MASONRY PLATFORM ?

NORTH TRANSEPT

CHOIR   CRYPT

CROSSING

SOUTH TRANSEPT

DRAIN

DRAINS

—————— WALLS TRACED BY EXCAVATION
- - - - - - WALLS INFERRED

CHAPTER HOUSE

PLAN SHOWS NORMAN FOUNDATIONS
UNDERLYING THOSE OF LATER CHOIR
(Based on plan in Brakspear papers, Battle folder)

PROBABLE LINE OF ORIGINAL
EAST RANGE

0   30 M
0   100 FT

BATTLE ABBEY · EASTERN ARM OF CHURCH

RW

Figure 5 Plan of the eastern arm of the church.

preted as a base for substantial corner buttresses or as indicating the presence of turrets or towers over the transepts. Footings found by Brakspear at the north-east corner of the north transept may indicate a similar situation there.

The eastern arm of the Norman church thus had an ambulatory and radiating chapels, although the precise form of two of these chapels could be subject to argument. The walls were built of quality ashlar and strengthened externally by pilaster buttresses. A visual representation of just such a church is provided by the seal of abbot Odo (1175–1200) which shows the church from the north with a roof line stepped up from the low chapels to the higher aisle roof and then up to the main roof of the choir. It also indicates a regular use of pilaster buttresses (BL LFC vii 4).

The church must have been designed shortly after the Conquest and the foundation of the monastery in 1070–1 (Graham 1929, 188). Its eastern arm was probably in use by 1076 when abbot Gausbert was blessed before the altar of St Martin, the monastery's patron saint, at Battle (*Chronicle* 46, 72), and the church was finally consecrated in 1094 (*Chronicle*, 96 n 3; *Anglo-Saxon Chronicle*, 229). Although the church with its length of 68.6m (225 feet) was small by comparison with the next generation of great churches in England, it was comparable in size to the great contemporary churches of Normandy (Hare 1981, 84; Gem 1981, 45–6). It was also probably the first church in England to incorporate the plan with an ambulatory and radiating chapels such as was to become common among subsequent greater Norman churches as at Bury St Edmund's or St Augustine's Abbey, Canterbury. Such a plan could be found in contemporary Normandy, although it was unusual there (Clapham 1955, 17; Gem 1981, 46). But the design was common in the Loire valley, and this may have been the source, for the chronicle records that William brought over monks from Marmoutier to supervise the work (*Chronicle* 69). The contemporary church at Marmoutier was about to be, or was being rebuilt. We do not know about the plan of its predecessor (Lelong 1977; 1979), but such a design was familiar in the area (Graham 1929, 191). Its early date and the little that we know about the church thus make Battle of considerable architectural interest.

No attempt was made to excavate the layers within the transept as this would merely have served to add to the complications for later archaeologists. The transept and a grave (F404) cut into its footings have been left to our successors. The grave contained iron fittings, perhaps for a coffin.

The Norman Chapter House
(figure 6; plate 6)
A conjectural plan of this building was produced by Brakspear after he had traced part of the outside of the apse, but no other excavation has taken place on the site of this important monastic building. Our excavations confirmed that the chapter house was a substantial apsidal structure with maximum internal dimensions of 8.8 m (28 ft. 10 in.) by 17.8 m (58 ft. 7

in.) and with walls of approx 1.20 m thickness. The west end of the building had completely disappeared as, on this part of the site, the ground level had been lowered in recent centuries, but there remained a shallow cut in the natural clay with its eastern edge on the line of the west wall of the dormitory range. It probably represents all that is left of the lower part of the robbed-out west wall of the building. Its west side would have been completely destroyed as the ground has been lowered more deeply there (see figure 6). The fill was a mixture of clay and soil with no sign of mortar but was clearly distinct from the adjacent natural clay. It should be stressed that because of subsequent lowering of the ground level, we would not expect much evidence of the western wall unless it had unexpectedly deep footings. The walls of the chapter house survived much more substantially on the south side (where they were up to a height of 0.7 m) than on the north side (where they survived up to a height of about 0.35 m on the inside and only 0.1 m on the exterior). The walls were of rubble construction in a cream-coloured mortar. They rested on wider footings and would appear to have been trench-built on the outside and face-built from the bottom on the inside of the building. A shallow construction trench survived on the northern side of the apse and this contained an important group of pottery. To the east of the building such a trench would have been destroyed by the later lowering of the levels as part of the subsequent terracing operations. It should, however, be remembered that the slope of the ground meant that from the beginning this area would have required a less substantial cut than on the upper or north side. Where the building abutted the south transept it overlay the footings of the latter as these can now be seen projecting into the chapter house itself. In order to ascertain the original design of the building it is necessary to disentangle the original structure from the later re-modelling. (*infra* p. 25). There were no indications as to its roofing or internal fittings. The offset and bench are structurally later than the building itself. They overlie one of the graves and are not an original feature. Where the offset and bench had been destroyed as in the north-east they revealed that the wall had been constructed with a proper face. One large block of stone projecting from the south wall may represent the remains of an internal feature in this or a later stage, as may some small projecting blocks on the north side. As for the external arrangements, not all the buttresses would seem to be original. At the east end, F68 with its broad footings keyed into those of the chapter house would appear to belong to the first phase, but the adjacent buttress F69 should probably go with the later remodelling. The latter had no footings of its own, sat on top of the wall footings and over-rode them. Unusually for this building, F69 is constructed with a block of ashlar, and one that lacks evidence of early Norman tooling; it appears to have been constructed with the white mortar characteristic of some of the later alterations. Other buttresses have been concealed by the addition of adjacent buildings so that it has not been possible to

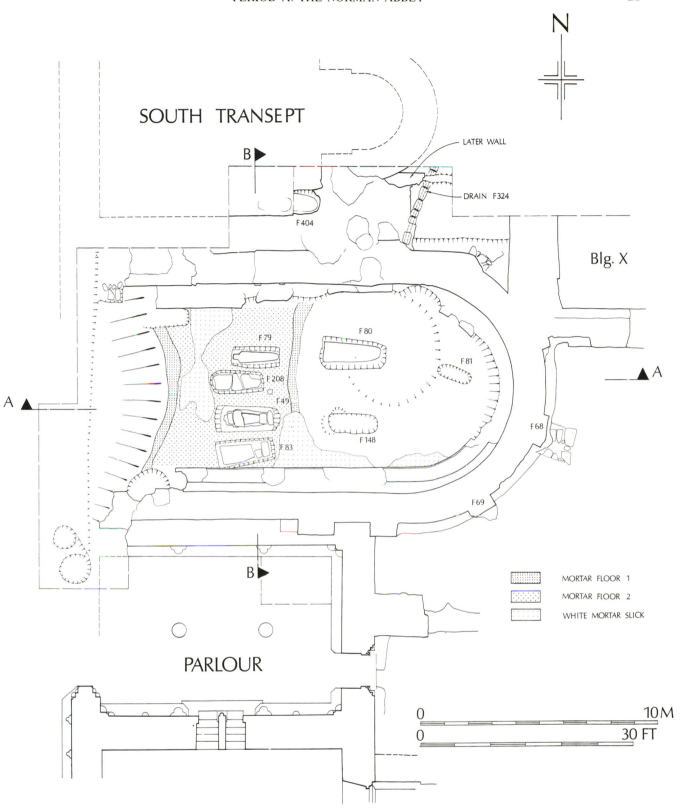

Figure 6   Plan of the chapter house.

examine them fully. It may be suggested that the building possessed two buttresses at the east end, presumably on either side of a window, and probably one at the beginning of the apse, but that it did not show a regular use of pilaster buttresses.

No consistent floor level survived within the building. The latest one was of a white mortar and survived fragmentarily across the chapter house. It overlay a thin yellow slick and the natural clay, except in the south-west corner where the ground dipped away and the floor level had subsequently been raised. Thus sealed below the later mortar layer and up to 0.1 m of make-up was an earlier, yellow-mortar layer which in one area had been reddened by burning. This hard, flat surface was evidently a floor and one which pre-dated the addition of the stone benching as this sat on the make-up above the early floor.

Within the chapter house were six graves. Unfortunately the fragmentary nature of the floors only allows some of these to be phased. They are therefore discussed together here, even though some of them may have belonged to the period after the remodelling of the building. The small size of the group seemed insufficient to justify detailed quantified analysis. The skeletons were therefore examined in situ and the results of this examination have been placed with the site records (Bayley 1979 and 1980). The graves clearly fall into two groups. Four of them contained stone capped coffins where the skeletons remained articulated, while the two eastern ones were shallower, contained no stone coffin, had been completely robbed and disturbed and contained little surviving bone. All were aligned west to east.

The four stone-capped graves lay on a line running across the building from north to south. Three of them were sealed by the later floor level and its build-up, and more fragmentarily by the earlier slick. The other one (F79) was covered with a shattered sandstone slab and while most of the grave was filled with the clean yellow sandy clay that typified the fill of all the graves, its upper layers contained much rubbish and building waste, suggesting a later disturbance. At the bottom of each grave pit was cut a slot for the body or for body and coffin. Once the body had been placed in its final resting place the grave was covered by large slabs of stone and then the pit was refilled with the upcast from the grave shaft. The bases of the graves were between 0.8 and 1.1 m below the level of the later chapter house floor. One of these graves (F49) showed a more sophisticated form of construction, as here the grave itself was stone-lined and was not merely cut into the natural. Each of the graves had a distinct and narrower compartment for the head suggesting that a wooden coffin could not have been placed in the grave itself. Instead the body may have been placed on a plank that was then laid within the grave, as this could account for the dark staining found over parts of the bases of three of the graves and which in places became a very thin fibrous layer. The position of this staining was not constant, occurring under the body and down to the ankles in one

grave (F208) and on the northern half of the grave in another (F79). There were a few nails on the north side of F49 and ten in F79 but no obvious pattern was apparent and there were no nails in the other graves in this group. There were no signs of staining on the sides of the graves. All of this reinforces the view that the bodies were not buried in wood coffins. The decay of the bodies and any supporting plank had caused the skeletons to slump leaving parts of the skulls supported by solid ground at a higher level. None of these graves had any grave goods.

The other two graves were very different in character. They consisted of large rectangular grave pits without a smaller grave being cut into the base and they were shallower, F148 being between 0.6 and 0.5 m in depth. They had both been heavily disturbed and most of the bones had been removed. Those which remained had also been disturbed so that F80 contained parts of two different skulls. In its rubble fill were fragments of painted window glass. The other grave (F148) contained a moulded bone knop from a crozier. It showed signs of staining on its base and north side. These two graves clearly represent a different method of burial and had both been heavily robbed after the Dissolution. It is not clear whether the robbers were merely after grave goods or whether the different character of the graves might represent the use of lead coffins.

Even where the graves had not been robbed out, the preservation of the skeletons was very poor. This and the smallness of the sample render unnecessary much further description. All the skeletons were either of adult males or survived insufficiently for their sex to be determined. None was younger than the age range 25–35. The practice of burying influential members of the monastic community or, as at Lewes, of influential patrons, in the chapter house is well known. At Battle, the custom of burying abbots here was not established early, if ever. Of the seven abbots up to 1200 one was drowned at sea and another retired to Lewes. We can establish the burial places of the remaining five and only one of these was buried in the chapter house (*Chronicle*, 101, 132, 264–6, 109; Dugdale 1846, 235). It was abbot Henry who was buried before the president's seat in the chapter house in 1102. The description would suggest that this was in F208 on the axis of the building (*Chronicle*, 109). To his left was buried Geoffrey who was keeper of the abbey estates during the vacancy after Henry's death (*Chronicle*, 117). No other documentary references to burials within this building have been discovered.

The chapter house at Battle thus provides a design familiar in such buildings during the late eleventh and early twelfth century. During this period they were frequently, although not always, built with an apsidal east end as at Battle. This was the case, for example, at Lewes, Thetford, Castle Acre, Westminster, Durham and Saint Albans (V.C.H. 1940, opp. p. 47; Raby and Baillie Reynolds 1979; Raby and Baillie Reynolds 1952; Gem 1981, 38–9; Pevsner 1953, 111–2; Biddle and Kjølbye-Biddle 1981, 11 & 20). We can, however, be more specific as to the date of the building at Battle. It was not the first building to be constructed as its foundations overlay those of the south transept. During the first few years of the community's existence we should have expected attention to be concentrated on building part of the church while the monks made do with a temporary timber structure, whose evidence has now disappeared. The blessing of Gausbert at the altar of St Martin in 1076 (*Chronicle*, 46) suggests that part of the church was then operational and subsequently the monks would have been able to turn their attention to the conventual buildings and the chapter house. The early form of the building suggests that this was the first permanent chapter house and that it was the one in which abbot Henry was buried in 1102. We may safely, therefore, ascribe the building to the last quarter of the eleventh century.

Little of the chapter house has survived, but a few further comparative comments may be made. It was substantial in size, although much smaller than the great buildings at the cathedral priories of Winchester and Canterbury (V.C.H. 1912 opp. p. 50; Willis 1869, 19). It was comparable in size to the chapter houses of such important monasteries as eleventh-century St. Albans or of Lewes Priory, but was larger than the latter's daughter houses at Castle Acre and Thetford. It was apparently of simple design, and contrasted with the abbey church. Thus the former was built in rubble, whereas the latter was built with ashlar. While the chapter house had some buttresses, it does not seem to have made use of pilasters as a regular feature of the design, as was being done in the church. There was no permanent bench or foot-pace, but the absence of such a feature was not unusual in such buildings of this date.

*The Conventual Buildings before
the Great Rebuilding* (figure 7)
Apart from the chapter house all the conventual buildings around the cloisters seem to have been destroyed in the great rebuilding of the abbey in the thirteenth century. The chronicle tells us little about them except that they were built by Abbot Gausbert (1076–1095) and that it contrasted the humbleness of the buildings with the ostentation shown by builders elsewhere (*Chronicle*, 101). The chronicle leaves us with the impression that these buildings were still in use at the time it was written in the 1180's (Searle 1980, 23). Of the dormitory range, a stub of its east wall probably remains encased in the wall of the later parlour (see figure 7). It was in the same cream-coloured mortar as the chapter house and thus contrasted with the buff-orange mortar of the thirteenth-century stonework that surrounded it. It was wider than the buttresses of the chapter house, and seems more likely to have been the stump of a wall extending at right angles to that building. The later parlour, which lay to the south, was excavated by Brakspear, and a small trench was dug in its north-eastern corner to see whether any evidence remained of the continuation of this early wall. The results were inconclusive. Natural was reached immediately below the turf-line and there was no evidence of any footings or robbing, but the floor

level had probably been lowered during the construction of the parlour and this would have removed any evidence of earlier structures. The evidence of the wall stump suggests, however, that the earlier dormitory range was narrower than its later replacement.

Gausbert's buildings seem to have remained fundamentally intact until the thirteenth-century rebuilding. A few major alterations, however, were carried out. The chronicle records that Abbot Walter de Luci (1139–71) pulled down the existing simple cloisters and rebuilt them with pavements and columns of marble (*Chronicle*, 263). He had also planned to produce a new lavatorium to the same design. Although the cloisters were outside our area, some of the marble capitals had been carried away and were found in the excavations. Stylistic and functional evidence enables them to be asigned to a cloister arcade built in about 1170, and they are thus able to hint at the reality behind the chronicler's comment. They suggest that as with other contemporary cloisters (Webb 1956, 56–8; Blair *et al* 1980, 210–3), it had the open arcade resting on pairs of columns, each pair being set at right angles to the line of the cloister. Further examples of such pairs of capitals came from Brakspear's work in the outer court (appendix A). Like those from the excavations they were in the local Sussex marble, and together show that there were at least three different designs. The excavations also produced a group of contemporary decorated columns and capitals in Purbeck marble. It is not clear whether the two types of marble were used together in the same programme of work or whether we are looking at the product of two near-contemporary campaigns. The excavations have thus been able to shed light on a lavish phase of rebuilding and have produced an important group of carved marble fragments (see Chapter V).

The other major addition in the claustral area has only been revealed by excavation. This was the construction of a major new building (Building Z) to the south-east of the chapter house. The excavations have established its north-west corner and a long section of the footings for its western wall. It was evidently a substantial building for its minimum internal dimensions were 16.3 by 5.8 metres (53.5 by 19 feet) and these dimensions would only have been possible if the building's south-west corner had lain immediately behind our southern section and the east wall immediately behind the south-east corner of the excavations. The building was, therefore, probably substantially larger and we do not even know which was its long side. Of the building itself, only its footings survive. For most of their length, they consisted of a shallow layer of rubble without mortar, but at the southern end where the building was constructed on an artificial platform the footings were mortared and 0.6 m deep. Most of the floor of the building would have been on built-up ground that increased in depth towards the south and east. In the south-west corner of the building it was 1.2 m deep (figure 10). Here there was clear evidence of two stages in construction. The ground was raised, then the wall foundations were built and finally the area within the building was levelled. Associated with the construction of the wall was a thin line of mortar and stone debris which separated the two stages of build-up and which ran to the base of the mortared footings. These deep deposits consisted largely of grey and yellow clays and sealed a dark grey turf or soil-line which itself overlay a small area of charcoal ash and heavily burnt clay of uncertain date. Some of the clay make-up may have come from the area east of the chapter house as the ground was lowered here at some time during the monastic period. Inside the building, the semi-circular area of rubble was clearly distinct from the adjacent wall footings but it might have represented the base for an internal feature. Outside Building Z and probably related to its use were one or probably two graves that were aligned with the building and not strictly to the east. One of these contained a skeleton of an adult (Bayley 1980). Although the other was empty a grave provides a likely explanation for a feature of its size and shape. It contained a fairly clean fill. Its position at the end of the later 'porch' building may provide an explanation as to why there was a change in plan and no skeleton was left. When the building was destroyed, it was levelled to its foundations, but in its north-west corner the footings themselves were robbed out. Within the building (and by contrast to the area to the south) there were patches of a mortar surface which were probably the remnants of its floor.

The major earth-moving efforts associated with the construction of Building Z, show the monks grappling with the problems of the narrow hill-top site. The only way to create space for new building was by substantial terracing. In view of the limited part of the building that has been excavated, attempts at identifying its use must be treated with caution. But in view of its size and its position to the east of the dormitory range a likely identification would seem to be that of the infirmary hall. It is not clear, however, whether our building would have been aligned east-west, as at Canterbury Cathedral Priory (Willis 1869, 13), or north-south as at St Augustine's Abbey, Canterbury (Gilyard–Beer 1958, figure 24). Nor is it clear why the building should have been constructed at an angle to the main axis of the monastery. Topography may have played a role, but it should be remembered that Norman monasteries, as at Lewes, were often not as regularly laid out as their later counterparts. Doubts must also be expressed about any dating of Building Z as the absence of medieval layers post-dating its construction has deprived us of stratigraphic links with the other main phases of activity. It clearly pre-dates the overlying range to the east, but since the latter lies mainly outside the excavation, its own date is subject to doubt. Nor does the make-up material or the later robbing trench provide us with any dating material. A few fragments of information, however, suggest that its construction preceded the thirteenth-century rebuilding. The character of its footings contrasts with those of the later works. Building Z had a layer of mortarless rubble for its shallow footings, but no such layer in its deeper foundations. In the later

work, the situation seems to have been reversed with solid mortared footings in the porch, but with a line of mortarless rubble at the base of the deeper reredorter foundations. The construction technique seems most clearly paralleled by that of the earlier chapter house and church footings. The two graves would also suggest an early date for the building as their alignment would seem more appropriate to a period when Building Z provided the main orientation in the area prior to the construction of the porch. Moreover, the empty grave would have been partly overlain by the east wall of the porch, while the other would have been very close to the wall: an unlikely position in view of the space available further east. It seems more likely that they, and therefore Building Z, predate the construction of the porch. The balance of the evidence suggests that the building pre-dates the main period of rebuilding and, in view of the large amounts of work involved in its levelling, that it was not one of the original monastic buildings. A twelfth-century date would seem most suitable.

Lower down the hillside in the reredorter area, excavation of the early levels was limited by the depth of make-up associated with the thirteenth-century buildings. In general, excavation halted at the surface associated with this new work but the earlier levels were examined in four sections cut through the build up: one within the building and the others to the north. In addition an area was excavated to natural outside the eastern end of the range (RII). Finally earlier levels were excavated in trenches RVII and VIII further up the hillside, although the depth of deposits precluded the completion of the latter trench. The main features shown by the excavations were a series of ditches running down the hillside and presumably serving to drain surface water away from the buildings. Three of these were found in the area excavated outside the north-east corner of the reredorter of which two were cut by the reredorter wall. In addition a ditch was found running down the western side of RVIII.

None of the excavations in the reredorter area produced any evidence of there having been earlier structures and this and the fact that the ditches would be leading surface water into this area suggests that the latter was not being used for buildings. One problem remains that of the position of the thirteenth-century reredorter's predecessor. It seems likely that it catered for a much smaller dormitory and thus would have been further up the slope. Trenches RVII and VIII produced a section down the hillside (figure 4). Although the excavation of the latter trench could not be completed because of the unexpected depth of deposit and consequent considerations of safety, enough could be done to show that the layers dipped down sharply to the south, and to a depth at least level with the natural further south, suggesting that the slope may represent the cut for a substantial east-west ditch, such as could have been associated with a near-by reredorter. The excavations produced no evidence for any buildings in the area of RVII & VIII, suggesting that the early reredorter did not extend far eastwards beyond the line of the later dormitory. If it occupied the site of the later 'middle room' of the eastern range, it would have had both the steeper slope and the ditch below, and adjacent to the south.

Period B: The Great Rebuilding: the Monastery in the Thirteenth Century

The Reconstruction of the Chapter House
(figures 6 and 9, Plate 6)

In the course of its existence, the chapter house underwent major reconstruction, although much of the evidence for this disappeared with the destruction of the building at the Dissolution. The most obvious surviving alterations were internal. Around the inside of the building was added a narrow (0.42 m wide) offset and a broader and low stone step or foot-pace (0.6 m wide). The latter clearly did not belong to the original building for it overlay part of one of the graves as well as the secondary raising of the floor level in the south-west corner. The offset behind the bench was also probably secondary for it was structurally distinct from the original wall and was of a different and poorer quality construction: the offset included the use of tile, although this was not found on any of the earlier work. Both offset and step survived well on the southern side of the building, but elsewhere only vestigal traces remained. The needs of conservation and display precluded any dissection of the structure of the additions but where none of the stonework survived the make-up below could be sectioned. Here, at the eastern end, a bank of grey clay lay against the inner face of the chapter house wall. This would have provided the base for the offset and step, thus reinforcing the view that these were built together.

Although nothing survived *in situ* above the level of the offset, evidence about the later upper levels of the building was found in the destruction debris. This information and that from the surviving structure suggest that the rebuilding was much more extensive than the addition of an offset and step. The addition of an extra buttress (F69) on the southern side of the apse suggests a more regular system of supports. The buttress sits overlapping the footings of the apse and has no footings of its own. In this it clearly contrasts with the adjacent buttresses, which have extensive footings (plate 6, figure 6). That F69 is an additional feature is also suggested by the incorporation of one large block whose tooling would seem unlikely in an eleventh-century context, and the use of flat roof tile in its construction. Here and on some sections of the wall a white mortar has been used and slapped onto the wall surface. This may be a remnant of a plaster dressing applied to the rubble wall. A further indication that rebuilding may have taken place is to be found in the presence of a line of tiles laid and used in the construction of the south wall of the building and now on the surface of the surviving wall. They perhaps mark the junction between the early parts of the wall and its rebuilt upper parts. It should be noted that the tiles are of similar dimensions to those used in the fireplaces of the thirteenth-century dormitory range, that tiles are not used elsewhere in the eleventh-century work and

that the roof tiles used at the earlier period seem to have been of a different form and not flat (*infra* p. 95). Among the stone used in the main south wall was a reused cushion capital. The rebuilding of the walls and the addition of the extra butresses are to be associated with the refenestration of the building. The new windows and the wall arcade which would have rested on the offset, would have been the source of the Caen stone mouldings found in the excavations. For the interior of the building and the area immediately outside produced a substantial quantity of keel mouldings, almost to the exclusion of other types. Some of the former came from Dissolution debris while others came from later layers. Their concentration in this area, and their absence from the other excavated areas and from the standing buildings together suggest that they may safely be ascribed to the chapter house itself. One fragmentary capital also survives from this building. (*infra* p. 73).

Thus although none of these detailed mouldings survived *in situ*, we can discern a very different chapter house emerging from these changes. Substantial rebuilding of the walls had occurred. Around the interior was now a foot-pace and wall arcade. New windows now lit the building. But there is much that we can never know, so that its roofing arrangements must remain a mystery. Although so little survives of this remodelling, there is enough to suggest that this took place in about 1200. The crucial dating is provided by the architectural fragments. The keel mouldings and square foliage capital clearly belong to an earlier period than the details on the standing masonry of the dormitory range. While only some of these fragments are from a clear Dissolution context, their exclusive location in the chapter house or immediately outside it, have allowed us to ascribe them to the chapter house itself. The only other known group of such mouldings at Battle comes significantly from the rubble used after the Dissolution to build up the courtyard in front of the cellarer's range (appendix A), and probably also derives from the chapter house. Such keel mouldings have a longish use as a supplement to other types, but the complete mouldings can be closely paralleled by those from Chichester or Boxgrove in about the 1190's. The one surviving fragment of a capital from the building suggests a date in the late twelfth century and probably not later than about 1200 (*infra* pp. 73–75). The lack of any reference to this building in the abbey's chronicle would suggest, moreover, that such a rebuilding was unlikely to have occurred until towards the end of the twelfth century. The main chronicle ends with a case in 1176, and the last event mentioned is in 1184 (Searle 1980, 9), but it includes a substantial section of praise about Abbot Odo (1175–1200) under whom the chapter house would have been rebuilt. That a writer so imbued with the traditions and corporate identity of the abbey, as was the main chronicler, should have failed to mention such changes in a building so central to the corporate life of the monastery may suggest that the rebuilding had not yet occurred in the early 1180's.

It would thus seem that the chapter house was one of the first of the main monastic buildings to be rebuilt, and this would be appropriate in view of its importance in the life of the monastery. This early dating would also explain one of the surprising features of the reconstruction: its conservatism in plan. For unlike all the later rebuilding at Battle this was a substantial rebuilding and not an enlargement and a new beginning. Elsewhere, such a reconstruction might provide no cause for comment, but it was in marked contrast to the grandiose plans that were undertaken here later in the thirteenth century. Had the chapter house been rebuilt during the latter period we should surely have expected it to be on a larger and grander scale.

Although we have no evidence of any substantial change to the structure of the chapter house, its appearance was changed in the later thirteenth century when its windows were filled with new and high-quality window glass. For the Dissolution debris in the chapter house area included substantial quantities of painted grisaille window glass, and while some of this may conceivably have come from other buildings it is probable that most of it was derived from the chapter house windows at the Dissolution. The glass seems to represent a consistent type and while some was found scattered throughout the building and outside it, several groups were found in concentrations below or near the position of the windows, both on their interior and exterior faces. For although the windows themselves have disappeared, their likely position can be reconstructed from the arrangement of the buttresses. This important group of high quality grisaille glass may be dated on stylistic grounds to the mid to late thirteenth century (*infra* chapter VIII).

The development of the chapter house in this period needs to be seen both in the context of other work at Battle and in that of work elsewhere. Its rebuilding was a prelude to the greatest period of building activity. But subsequently the chapter house seems to have remained structurally intact for there was no evidence of later mouldings that could be ascribed to it. Such an important building was evidently not forgotten while other ranges were rebuilt, as the archaeological evidence of this glazing programme makes clear. On a broader scale, Battle was merely one among the many contemporary abbeys that expanded or remodelled their chapter houses in the thirteenth century, as shown at Newminster, Northumberland (Harbottle and Salway 1964, 130–2), Elstow, Bedfordshire (Baker 1971, 60), Stanley and Malmesbury, Wiltshire (Brakspear 1907, 506–8, *Registrum Malmesburiense* ii, 365) and the examples cited in Bilson (1895, opp. p. 432).

The Rebuilding of the Dormitory Range.
(figures 3 & 4, Plates 8–12)
The rebuilding of the monastery continued on a grander scale with the construction of a new block of accommodation for the abbot (and its subsequent extensions) in the west range, (*supra* p. 13) and of a

new eastern or dormitory range. The latter consisted of the dormitory on the first floor, with four substantial rooms or undercrofts on the floor below, and with two ranges running eastward at either end. Thus at the north end was a room or porch, and at the south end lay the reredorter range. The main dormitory block has lost its northern end and is roofless, but otherwise it is virtually intact and provides what is still the most effective reminder of the wealth and power of Battle Abbey. But its survival contrasts markedly with the porch and reredorter range. Their presence was indicated by evidence remaining on the adjacent dormitory wall and, in the case of the reredorter, by parts of a surviving wall, but otherwise our knowledge is based on the results of the excavation. It would clearly be unwise to examine these peripheral parts of the eastern range in isolation from the standing buildings and the range has therefore been considered as a whole. It is usually extremely difficult to identify such undercroft rooms. Their functions are discussed but their designations must be treated with caution.

Before looking at the individual parts of the range it is necessary to make some general remarks. As has already been mentioned, the dormitory range was built running down a steep hillside. Since the dormitory on the first floor had to be horizontal, this meant that it had to be built on increasingly high undercrofts. The latter thus remind us of the problems produced by the Conqueror's choice of site for his new monastery (figure 4). The new buildings were almost entirely built of the local sandstone although Caen stone was used for some of the detailed mouldings and Sussex marble was used for the bases of the wall arcade and of the door mouldings, for a string course in the dormitory, and for the window transoms, while Purbeck marble was also used for the interior columns. We do not know how it was originally roofed although it was roofed with shingles in 1364–6 (Abbey accounts for 1365 and 1366) and the archaeological evidence suggests that it and the reredorter were roofed with clay tiles at the time of the Dissolution (*infra* p. 42). The building is constructed throughout in the Early English style although an unusual feature which it shares with the west or abbot's range is the use of round-headed doorways in what is otherwise a building of mature Early English character. It will be suggested that a date of around the 1240's or 1250's would be most appropriate. It should be remembered that the buildings have undergone many alterations in the course of the centuries and that rebuilding in the local roughly cut sandstone soon becomes difficult to distinguish from the original.

At the north end of the dormitory range and abutting the chapter house was the parlour. This was cleared for Brakspear in 1933 (see letters from F.G. Jones in Brakspear Papers, Battle files, and especially that of 20.12.33) and consolidated. No flooring had survived, but the walls remain up to a height of about 0.85 m. As in the chapter house, its west wall had been completely destroyed except in the south-west corner next to the dormitory. The room was 10.1 m (33.2 ft) by 7.2 m (23.7 ft) and was three bays in length and two in width. Around its interior ran a stone bench, parts of which still survive and on this rested the wall arcade of which many of the marble bases still survive, either completely or as remnants of the marble block. Each bay was further divided into two by the wall arcade. The bases are of the 'water-holding' variety and are identical in form and material to those of the wall arcade in the rebuilt cloisters, where they have been preserved against the dormitory wall, and those of the porch. They are also paralleled by those in the dormitory itself although the latter are not always of marble. The room appears to be a lobby linking three different areas. To the west the surviving base of a door jamb shows that access to the cloister was through a doorway of three orders. The latter would suggest that this was the most important doorway from the cloisters to the conventual rooms of the eastern range and the area to the east. Eastwards, access was given, through a simpler doorway of two orders, to a porch and so to the infirmary beyond. Finally the parlour gave access through a series of steps and a double-arched entrance to the common room to the south. Here, despite considerable subsequent damage, these arrangements may be reconstructed. In the central bay the wall bench ceased and gave way to the steps and to two doorways divided by a central respond, whose base for five shafts survives and is of the same design and material to the other bases of the parlour. The presence of this base set within the thickness of the wall and below the level of the parlour floor indicates that the stairs would have begun within the parlour itself. The steps then continued within the thickness of the wall and the last few steps would have been within the common room itself. The relieving arch for the doorways may still be seen inside the latter room.

The common room lay adjacent to the south. It was 17 m. (55.9 ft) by 10.3 m. (33.9 ft) in size and its floor level was substantially (approximately 1.90 m.) below that of the parlour. Although it may no longer seem the most impressive of the undercroft chambers, its details suggest that it may have been the most important. Thus in each corner of the room the vault was supported on a corbel carved into the shape of a human head. Of these, two survive completely, one has had its face destroyed while the probable fourth has been completely destroyed. The use of such carved heads is not uncommon in the architecture of the thirteenth century (Whittingham 1979, 5), but this 'extravagance' probably indicates the importance of the room. The room was five bays long and three bays wide. Of the four pairs of marble columns, five of the piers still possess their original bases while the others have at sometime been destroyed and the marble columns reset (Cleveland 1877, 254). Of the surviving bases three are of the water-holding variety while the columns are surmounted by moulded capitals. The room was lit by five lancet windows on the eastern side and one to the west. The main and most elaborate entrance seems to have been from the parlour but there was also access through simple round-headed doorways to the cloisters to the west and to the slype to the

south. In the north eastern corner are remnants of a stone bench. While this only provides evidence for benches on two sides of the room, it seems likely that they continued on all sides. The room does not have a fireplace, but warmth could have been provided by a free-standing brazier. In this position we should expect the chamber to be the common room or warming house of the monastery. I have used the former term, although the absence of a fireplace does not prevent it serving the latter function, as other monasteries show (Brakspear 1937, 103–4). The building still shows signs of later repairs, probably from after the Dissolution for some of the vault ribs show patching, some of the columns have been re-erected and at the north end the capitals and vault springers have been replaced.

Next to the common room lay a vaulted passage or slype, 2 m in width, which provided access from the cloisters and the dormitory undercrofts to the area to the east. To the south of this lay a room 6.8 m (22.4 ft.) in length and lit with windows on both sides. The doorway to the east is of pointed form, unlike the others in this range, but has similar mouldings and seems to be a medieval feature. Its high and deep rere arch would suggest, from comparison with other doorways at Battle, that the doorway originally opened into a building to the east, but no evidence for the latter was found in trench RVIII. The room itself, had two marble columns, one capped by a crocket capital and the other by a moulded one. One of the corbels is in the form of a head although its face has been destroyed. The function of the room is unclear and I have therefore described it merely as the 'middle room'. It was the smallest of the three main rooms but it was not, judging from its details, unimportant. It is not clear whether its size was determined by the distance between the slype and the scarp slope below, or whether its plan may reflect an earlier building on the site, such as the early reredorter.

Of the undercrofts, the most southerly seems now to be the grandest. The ground drops sharply from the adjacent room so that there is a difference of almost 3 m between the two floor levels. The room had to be so high because of the fall of the land and not because of any intrinsic importance of its function. It is thus grander but simpler than the common room. The 17.5 m (57.5 ft) of its length is divided into four bays. Like the other undercrofts it is vaulted throughout, with ribs with hollow chamfers. Its windows seem to have been subject to much change. While several parts of the wall show signs of more recent patching the most southerly window is a replacement for one that may well have existed but was subsequently destroyed. Its stonework shows evidence of recent workmanship and topographical drawings, descriptions of the buildings and the excavations in the reredorter area, agree on showing that a doorway had been inserted here (plate 24; Cleveland 1877, 255). The doorway remained until this century for it still existed on the 1902 sale plan (E.S.R.O./BAT.4511). It must have disappeared shortly afterwards for Brakspear shows the present window in his elevation (Brakspear papers: Battle folder) and the reinsertion in sandstone is out of keeping with his own techniques of conservation. During this earlier reconstruction, the bases of this and the adjacent windows seem to have been lowered substantially (plate 24 and figure 4). On the western side of the room, small lancets are found in the central bays while the south-west window had plate tracery such as is also found in the west range, in the undercroft to the abbot's great chamber (Brakspear 1933, 154–5). Now only a worn marble stump of the base of the central column and small fragments of the plate tracery survive, but the tracery seems to have still been complete at the beginning of the present century, as is shown by a photograph in the same sale catalogue (E.S.R.O. BAT 4511). By contrast to the window in the abbot's range, that in the novices' quarters seems to have had a central circular column with moulded capital and base. The north-west window was presumably of the same design, but the evidence has been destroyed by the later insertion of a window or door. The three medieval doorways to the room still survive. The grandest of the three, with its double set of hollow chamfers, was in the west side. It is evidently an original feature, although in its upper parts it may have been reset. In addition, one door led to the adjoining 'middle room', while that in the south-eastern corner led to a stairway and the latrines. The room itself possessed a hooded fireplace from which the tiled back and the line of the hood still survive against the south wall. The division of the room into two bays in width, with a single line of columns down the centre, makes a break with the design of the other undercrofts and evidently represents a change from the original plan. For at 3.35 m from the southern end of the east wall may be seen signs of a torn-off column and part of the vault (plate 12). It would appear that the original design was for this room to also have three bays in width and that this was changed during construction to the present more harmonious arrangement. On the east wall in the south-east corner are the remains of a typical medieval wall cupboard.

This room has been referred to by its traditional description as the novices' quarters. It should be stressed, however, that rooms in this position served a variety of purposes (Gilyard-Beer 1958, 29) and there is nothing in the structure of this room that can be used to make a convincing identification.

The windows of the ground floor undercrofts did not have glazing grooves. They show, however, rebates and the former presence of tie bars across the openings. They could therefore have been glazed with the glass held within a timber frame, a method of securing the window glass that was frequently used in the thirteenth century.

The monk's dormitory occupied the first floor of the range and was at a uniform level except where it stepped up over the parlour. It thus had an uninterrupted length of 48 m (156 ft) and was lit by nine lancets along the east side and eight along the west side, while at the south gable end there were three tiers of windows: two at the main level, surmounted by a line of three and then by a single lancet at the gable head (plate 9). Many of the windows had subsequently been damaged but they seem to have been of a standard pattern incorporating nook shaft and mouldings (see figure 16) and with each window divided by marble transoms. Above the transom the window was glazed, while below it were shutters that could be opened. The building was decorated with an internal string course at the top of the side walls and another below the level of the windows (Grimm, B.L. Add. Mss. 5670 no.80). The lower one has been completely broken off flush with the wall surface, but it has left its mark in a band of stone of uniform depth that runs round the building. This shows that in the north-east corner the string course was of Sussex marble, but elsewhere was of sandstone. The main entrance to the dormitory was at the northern end of its western wall, where a stairway led up from the cloisters to a finely carved doorway whose battered Caen stone decoration still survives (figure 15). There was also a spiral staircase on the eastern side, which would have provided direct access to the eastern area. The opening to this stairway was of almost identical form to those of the dormitory windows. The stairway was clearly, however, an original feature: its opening from the dormitory lacks the splay found at the head of the window lancets, while the foundations and south wall of the stair turret are contemporary with the adjacent wall of the dormitory range (see also appendix B, p. 195). Nothing is known about the roof structure for that illustrated by Grimm (B.L. Add. Mss. 5670 no. 80) has a distinctly unmedieval appearance and would appear to represent a later replacement. The precise arrangements at the northern end of the range are unclear owing to the destruction of this part. The former would either have lit a chamber off the dormitory or the parlour itself. At the northern end of the east wall one nook shaft of a destroyed window survives and this starts well above the level of those of the other windows. Nothing is known about the original floor or decorations and most of what we know is probably about the alterations of the later Middle Ages and is discussed below (p. 37).

The Porch
(figure 7; plate 17)
Having considered the standing remains, it is necessary to turn to the buildings of this range revealed by excavation. At the north end was a room or porch approximately 5.8 m (19 ft) by 3.8 m (12.5 ft). It has left its traces against the adjacent wall of the dormitory and common room and these reveal that the room was vaulted, that it had a bench against this wall, and a wall arcade with identical bases to those in the parlour. The chamfered plinth of its southern wall was first discovered in 1875 (Cleveland 1877, 253) and this has now been fully excavated. It is keyed into the adjacent dormitory wall and supported the build-up of material that was necessary in order to create a level floor within the building. At its eastern end it was strengthened by a buttress. The northern wall has disappeared, but its footings remained linked with those of the parlour. The foot-

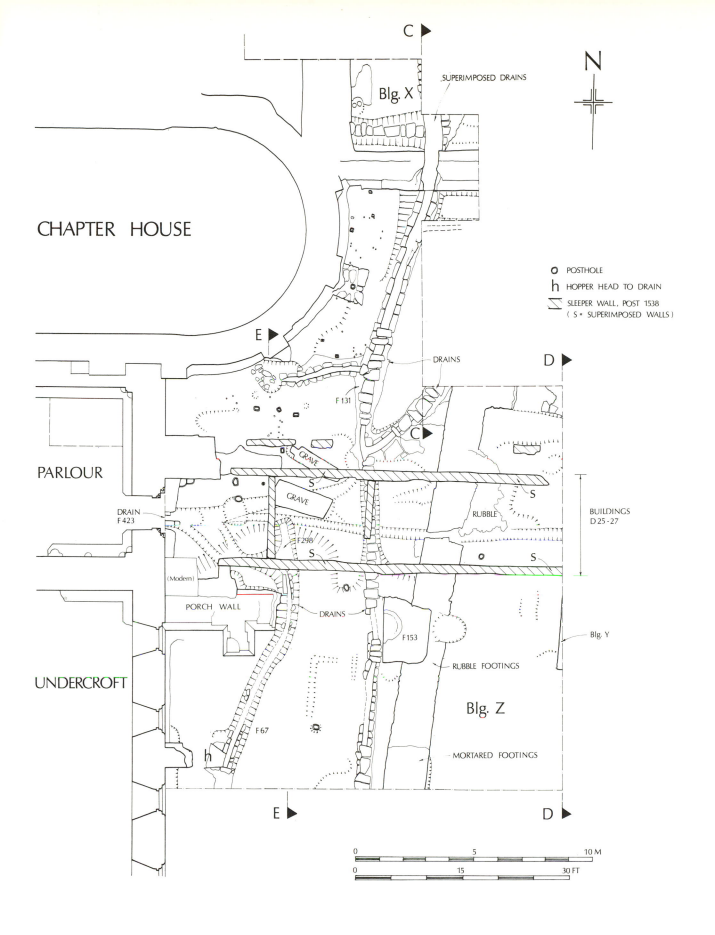

C ▶

N

SUPERIMPOSED DRAINS

Blg. X

CHAPTER HOUSE

○ POSTHOLE
h HOPPER HEAD TO DRAIN
⬛ SLEEPER WALL, POST 1538
(S = SUPERIMPOSED WALLS)

E ▶

D ▶

DRAINS

F 131

C ▶

PARLOUR

GRAVE

S

GRAVE

S

DRAIN
F 423

RUBBLE

S

BUILDINGS
D 25-27

F 298

S

S

(Modern)

PORCH WALL

DRAINS

F 153

Blg. Y

RUBBLE FOOTINGS

UNDERCROFT

Blg. Z

F 67

MORTARED FOOTINGS

h

E ▶

D ▶

0   5   10 M
0   15   30 FT

BATTLE ABBEY · AREA EAST OF CHAPTER HOUSE

RW

Figure 7   Plan of the area east of the chapter house and the parlour.

ings consisted of a broad (1.9 m) base of sandstone in mortar 0.2 m in depth. Even this had been partially robbed in its eastern part, although the robbing revealed the re-use of part of a sandstone column in the foundations. There was, however, no sign of any foundations for the east wall. Since this wall would have had to bear less strain than the others, its footings need not have been so deep and it is clear that later developments have severely damaged the medieval deposits. It is evident, for example, that they have been removed to below the medieval floor level as represented by the bottom of the base of the shafts belonging to the doorway between the parlour and the porch. This development must have occurred after the construction of the stone storm-water drains and it should probably therefore be seen as a post-Dissolution development (on the drains see *infra* p. 38). It seems likely that the building was completed for its wall arcade had at least been begun while a later stone-lined drain curves round its south-eastern corner suggesting that the wall was already known and standing. The builders were less aware of the extent of the footings as these were cut. Terracing was required to create a level surface within the building with the ground having to be built up in the southern half of the room. Part of this was done with redeposited clay and part with domestic refuse. The latter was also used to extend the terrace to the east of the building. While interpretation of this layer has been complicated by its dissection by a stone-lined drain and by the latter's robbing, it seems clear that it represents the levelling infill within the porch and that the undisturbed material is thus coeval with the construction of the dormitory range. The infilling cannot represent the product of any later robbing of the east wall of the porch since its east-west alignment would be unsuitable for the latter, while it does not extend sufficiently far northwards to account for the disappearance of this wall. The association of this layer with the main construction of the dormitory range provides us with important dating evidence for its contents. It contained, in clearly uncontaminated contexts, Rye pottery of a type which can now therefore be pushed back into the mid-thirteenth century. I have described the building as a porch, but it might have functioned as an extension of the parlour, with the two different alignments being caused by the restrictions of the site. Any such eastern extension would have to be set back to the south or it would have deprived one of the chapter house windows of its light.

The Reredorter
(figures 8 & 11, plates 13–16).
At the other end of the dormitory range was the much more substantial reredorter range. This has now been completely excavated. Before the excavations began, evidence for its location could be seen in the doors and marks of vaulting against the dormitory wall, in the blocked remnants of the drain and in a visible fragment of its eastern end. The excavations have revealed the full plan of the range, showing that the building extended 30.6 m (100.2 ft)

(excluding buttresses) from the dormitory range and had a width (excluding buttresses) of 8.3 m (27.2 ft). The building was supported by a series of buttresses along its north and south side, and each corner (except that to the north-west) was provided with angle buttresses. As was usual, the ground floor comprised a long room or undercroft with the main drain behind, while the main area for the latrines was on the first floor with access from the dormitory. In addition at the west end of the drain were two small latrines with access from nearby buildings (*infra* p. 32). Substantial remains of this range have now been revealed with the walls of the ground floor undercroft standing up to 1.7 m above the thirteenth-century floor level. It is only in the north-east corner that the wall, but not the footings, has been robbed away. The wall between the drain and the undercroft survived up to 2.6 m above the drain while parts of the south wall of the drain survived to almost first floor level.

The undercroft had internal dimensions of 28.9 m (95 ft) by 3.9 m (12.8 ft). It was entered by one of three doors. That to the west had a sill 1.0 m above the medieval floor level and had a round-headed doorway with hollowed chamfer and moulded stop such as typified the work of this period at Battle. The sill survives almost completely. In the second bay and at ground floor level were the substantial remains of the main door with a similar design but with a double hollow chamfer for its external moulding. Finally there was a probable third entrance in the fourth bay from the west. All but a fragment of one jamb of the opening had been robbed away, but this shows medieval tooling similar to the rest of the work and it seems likely that it represents the opening for a door. The undercroft was vaulted as shown by the vault rib surviving on the adjacent dormitory wall and the destruction debris which contained blocks of the hollow chamfered ribs, such as are still found in the adjacent dormitory undercrofts. Against the north wall was a contemporary hooded fireplace and substantial quantities of its hood were also recovered from the debris (*infra* p. 78). The surviving window jamb and the cut blocks of window jambs found in the destruction debris show that at least some of the windows were fitted with rebates to hold either a wooden frame, such as could have held window glass, or shutters. The walls were covered with a plain plaster, fragments of which still survive. Nothing survives of the medieval floor although a compacted surface, such as might have provided the base for a floor was found. If so, it was below the level of the offset to the north wall and this may have resulted from the settlement of the constructional make-up within the building.

The main drain of the reredorter was of very unusual design. Although on one side it was enclosed by a solid wall, on its outer or southern side it was open, the outer wall being carried on an arcade of five high (4.5 m) open arches and two smaller ones (2.15 m high). For three of the arches, only the rectangular piers survive, but the arches survived complete until the eighteenth century (Plate 23). Excavations were carried out at two places outside

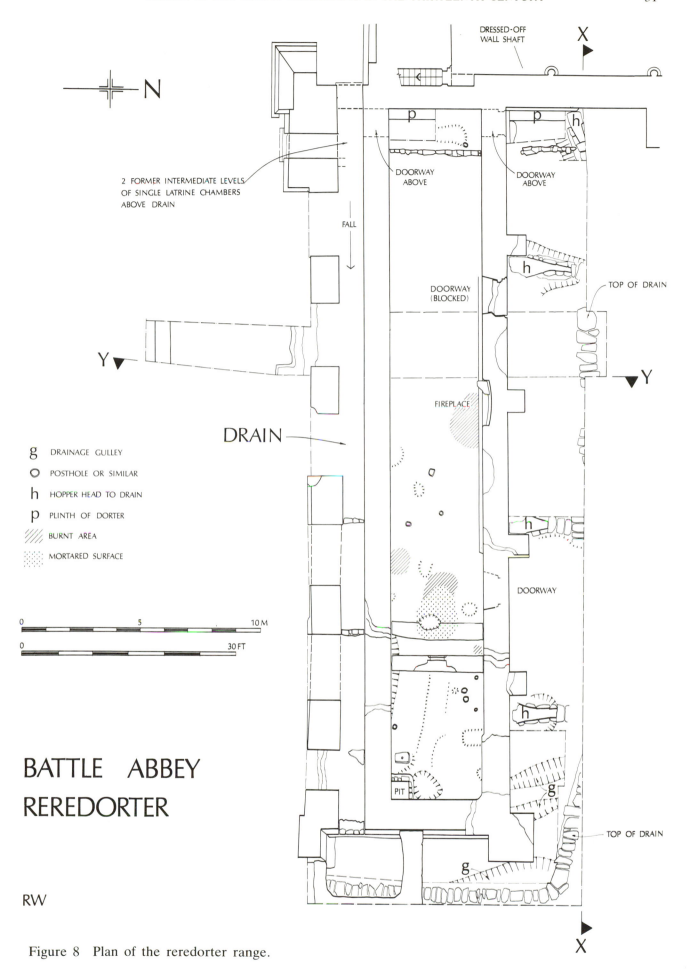

Figure 8   Plan of the reredorter range.

this arcade, and they showed that this outer wall, or at least its footings were heavily buttressed. Above ground the wall had largely been refaced or robbed, probably at various times during the post-Dissolution period, so that most of the above-ground evidence for the buttressing had disappeared. The drain sloped downwards from the west to the east and its floor of large stone slabs still survived almost intact. Within the arches and at about 0.65 m above the pavement level was evidence for a series of pairs of slots about 0.1 m square and 0.05 m deep. Although much of the evidence for these has been removed by destruction and later rebuilding, five of these slots still survive on the arches in the southern wall of the drain, and two survive in its eastern wall. Enough survives to suggest that all the arches of the former wall possessed a slot on each side of the opening and that another pair existed at the eastern end. They all appear to be original features. Such pairs of slots could have provided the means of a supporting removable timber shuttering, such as could have been used across the lower part of the arch to prevent the fill of the drain from spreading out beyond the arcade. No excavation has taken place beyond the western end of the building while at the east end there is no firm evidence of the drain continuing. It is possible, however, that it continued eastwards and was then subsequently removed during the lifetime of the monastery. This could account for a depression east of the building and for the blocking of the drain at the eastern end of the reredorter. (*infra* p. 38).

The drain also contained structural or constructional evidence. A rectangular opening (0.41 m by 0.26 m) at the base of the spine wall was presumably intended to drain moisture from the clay fill of the interior of the range. Putlog holes provided evidence of scaffolding to the full surviving height of the spine wall. Probably to be associated with the construction was a second series of slots in the southern wall. They consisted of rectangular slots of about 0.06 m in width and had a triangular section with a flat base. They occur at the springing line of the curve of the arch. Many of them would have been destroyed by decay and refacing but eight have so far been discovered and these are enough to establish a pattern. Each arch would have had a pair of these slots under each side of the wall. They are to be found under both the large and the small arches and at the western wall as well as with the main arcade. They are also typical of the arches of other buildings of this period at Battle and seem a common feature of buildings of twelfth- or thirteenth-century date elsewhere. The most likely explanation seems to be that they held support for the centring of the arch during its construction.

For the arrangements above the ground floor, we are dependent on the evidence of the surviving west wall of the building (figure 4). At the western end of the drain was a small garderobe tower. The surviving stairway from the novices' quarters provided it with access from there and it had access from the common rooms to the north. The first floor was supported, as we have seen, by a vault over the undercroft and by one over the drain. The main latrine floor was on this level with the lavatories ranged along the south side over the drain. Access was provided from the dormitory through two surviving doorways.

The reredorter range at Battle shows many of the characteristics of those of other thirteenth-century monasteries. This was the time when the arrangements of the medieval English monastery reached their maturity and reredorters of this period, of whatever order, provide a better guide to the arrangements here than do those of Benedictine houses of an earlier period. At the same time, the peculiarities of the abbey's position and the absence of a good flow of surface water made the sewerage arrangements untypical.

It would have clearly been unsuitable for the only lavatories to be on the first floor and with access only from the dormitory, so that monasteries were built with other subsidiary lavatories that were also served by the same main drain. At Battle access was provided at three different levels, each serving different parts of the eastern range. On the ground floor a gallery would seem to have provided access from outside the building through the north-western doorway. This would provide explanation for several of the features at this end of the building. The position of the doorway well above (1.0 m) the level of the external and internal ground levels is unusual. Above the main spine wall between the undercroft and the drain, the damaged springer of an arch still projects slightly from the dormitory wall and this suggests the presence of a doorway in the spine wall at about the same level as the outer doorway. These would also line up with the indications of the existence of a small separate chamber over the west end of the drain, with a window to the south that is below the level of any other possible access points. This chamber was also divided from the drain to the east by a wall represented by the springers of an arch over the drain and by marks of the wall above. Few details of the original gallery that must have linked the doorways and the ground outside have survived, although some of the evidence may have been concealed below later alterations. Joists for the gallery could probably have spanned the distance between the spine wall and the doorway, resting on the walls and thus leaving no surviving evidence. Outside the door, a possible joist hole (0.46 m deep) may indicate support for such a gallery while evidence of support for the other side would have been concealed below the later footings. Its joists cannot, however, have been supported in the reredorter wall, as no evidence survives. There is also evidence of a pentice roof outside this door and against the dormitory wall. The evidence is, however, complicated by later alterations: by the insertion of a post-Dissolution doorway and by the subsequent lowering and refacing of the windows (plate 24, figure 4 and *supra* p. 27). Such a covered gallery would have linked the doorway and the latrine chamber with the ground floor common rooms that lay much higher up the hillside. Although the topography of the site had produced some unusual details, the arrangements echo those of other contemporary monasteries where access from the day-quarters was a regular and necessary feature of the monastic plan, as at Jervaulx, Byland and Eggleston (Durham).

A second latrine was provided with access from the novices' quarters. From there a stairway ran up to the surviving doorway over the drain and to a chamber sandwiched between the ground floor latrine and the vault below the level of the main chamber. Its small window still survives in the west wall. Most monasteries had a smaller eastern range and lacked a large and distinct room such as the novices' quarters at Battle so that it was unnecessary to provide the two subsidiary levels of latrines. But where the range was of comparable size as at Rievaulx (N. Yorks) there were separate latrines for the novices' quarters and for the monk's day quarters each of which was served by the main latrine drain. Such elements were less obvious features of reredorter ranges than the main level of latrines but they were a regular and necessary feature of the monastic plan.

As we have seen the main level of latrines was on the first floor and entered from the monk's dormitory. We know very little about the arrangements of this floor at Battle, for the building has disappeared, but it is clear that the latrines would have been placed as was common, in a single line against one wall.

The ground floor room behind the drain was a typical feature of such ranges at this time, although we know little about its functions. At Battle the fine fireplace and the scale of the building suggest that it was a room of some substance and for a well preserved parallel we may turn to the example in a comparable position at Netley Abbey (Hants). There the importance of the building is suggested by the hooded fireplace and plate tracery but the suggested identification as an infirmary (Hamilton Thompson 1953, 13–16) would seem unsuitable for Battle. For here the buildings on the top of the hill east of the parlour would seem to offer a much more likely candidate. The identification must be left unresolved, but what the study of other reredorters of a comparable date does suggest, is that it was usual for there to be a room in this position that possessed a fireplace. There were exceptions, such as Bayham (Streeten 1983, 12–13), but the generalization remains valid. Where Battle would have differed from the norm, was in the length and particularly the height of the room, a reflection both of the wealth of the monastery and of the difficulties of the site.

It is with the arrangements of the main drain that Battle parts company with most monastic reredorters. Normally this would have been flushed by a permanent stream. So important was the latter that the monastic plan could be transformed to fit in with the availability of such a source of water, as at Kirkham (N. Yorks), where many of the buildings were arranged in a great arc along the stream. But although the site at Battle has wells and additional

water was brought by a leaden conduit pipe (Thorpe 1835; *Cellarers' Accounts, passim*) a regular large-scale source of water was lacking. This absence of water was evident to the early monks (*Chronicle* 42–4) and it must have been clear to the later architects for the reredorter was not designed to be regularly flushed by water. Although the drain was built with a gradient from west to east it effectively only had one side, for its southern side consisted of great arches that were open from the floor of the drain upwards. It should be stressed that such openings were very different from the relatively small ventilation holes found on reredorters such as those of Canterbury Cathedral Priory, Muchelney (Somerset) and Jervaulx, as the latter were both smaller and began well above the level of the drain. Had the monks intended the drain to be flushed by water we should have expected a low retaining wall along the line of the arcade at the very least. Timber shutters would have seemed a very ineffective means of ensuring that the drain was flushed. Nor would the shutters have provided a powerful short-lived flush of water as has been found elsewhere (Tester 1973, 137; Drury 1974, 46). For we seem to have a shutter on the outflow but not one on the intake. The available water after having been used elsewhere, might have been sufficient to flush out the upper or western end of the drain where drain and latrines became closest. Thereafter it and other liquids could find their way through the shutters to the open ground to the south and east, possibly with a small drain in the latter place. The solid material would be retained by the shutters within the drain and periodically would need to be cleaned out (*Cellarers' Accounts, passim*). Such arrangements would be unusual but so too was Battle's position and they seem to provide the most likely explanation for the curiosities of its design. Occasionally elsewhere, awkward sites have led to the construction of what were essentially dry reredorters. Thus, the earlier reredorter at Worcester provides one example (Brakspear 1916a, 197–202), albeit of very different design to that at Battle. There was also a regular digging out of the latrines at the cathedral priory at Canterbury in the twelfth century (Urry 1967, 157).

The excavations have thus revealed a large and important reredorter block. Moreover while much of it has disappeared, enough survives to establish that it was a product of the same building programme as the rest of the dormitory range. The details on the remaining masonry and in the destruction debris all establish this point. The details of the doorways, the vault, the string courses and the window jambs are all paralleled by those in the rest of the range. The excavations have also shown that (*pace* Brakspear 1937, opp. p. 103) the arcade must also be of thirteenth-century date and was not a Norman survival. There is no evidence of any earlier building on what was, until the thirteenth century, a sloping hillside and the arcade is of one build with the drain itself and with the rest of the range. As we have seen it also shares constructional features with the rest of the dormitory range.

The Construction and Dating of the Eastern Range.

Having looked at the buildings themselves, it should be easier to consider what the excavations have revealed about the process of construction. As has already become clear, the builders had to construct their buildings on a steeply sloping site and extensive terracing had, therefore, to take place. Even in the porch area the ground had to be built up behind the chamfered plinth of its southern wall. Much more extensive earth-moving operations were necessary, however, for the new reredorter which was built well below most of the monastic buildings. The cross-section of the building in trench I (figure 11) shows this clearly. The foundations were built in a trench with the lowest layer without mortar and thereafter of mortar and sandstone rubble construction. The ground was levelled after a few courses had been face-built. Within the building considerable make-up was necessary to create a level floor and some of this probably came from terracing by cutting into the hillside immediately above the reredorter. Thus the grey charcoal-flecked clay that formed the surface prior to construction is found within the building and for a short distance outside, but then disappears, while similar material and the yellow clay that would originally have underlain it are to be found as part of the make-up. But the greatest build-up would have been required at the eastern end as the hillside slopes both to the south and to the east. It has not been possible to section the make up within the building at this end but the area outside was taken down to the natural. At the east end the wall seems to have been built free-standing with a broad base that was twice reduced in thickness, the second time with a chamfered plinth. Here the ground was built up outside with a wedge of clay and then with a thick layer of grey-brown clayey silt. This material was very different from the clay and sandstone mixture that was more typical of the build-up on the north, where terracing could occur in the adjacent area. At the east end, the material may have been brought from further away. By the time the building had been finished, the ground level had been raised 0.6 m at the east end and 0.7 m at the south end of trench I. On top of the build-up lay a thin layer of compacted clay and sandstone chips, except at the east end where there was no clear surface.

The construction of the new eastern range and the earth moving that went with it, represented a major undertaking and one that would have taken considerable time to accomplish. We have a few pointers to the sequence of construction, although it should be stressed that we are dealing with a single building programme. The doorway mouldings at the northern end of the eastern range provide what are stylistically the latest features of the original building. It may be that the range was therefore begun on the open ground to the south so that new accommodation could be available before the old was destroyed. At this southern end, excavation showed that the reredorter was begun after the construction of the footings for the dormitory. Here the building of the southern end of the dormitory posed the greatest structural problems because of the great height of the building which today reaches 23 m above the turf-line to the south. It was not therefore surprising that the footings were massive. Excavation in the area between the dormitory and reredorter walls showed that the dormitory walls were constructed initially in a trench and that the reduction in the width of the walls included a hitherto undiscovered chamfer and offset. It was further established that the reredorter was structurally later than this part of the dormitory wall for the north wall of the former overlay one of the plinths of the latter and where it crossed the latter's foundation trench the footings had been broadened out. The plinth itself probably linked up with that still visible on the south face of the dormitory.

It has already been suggested that the eastern range was the product of a single major building programme. Although we have no known documentary evidence for its construction, and accurate dating cannot be expected from the standing remains, the latter would suggest that construction culminated in about the middle of the thirteenth century. The range is built in a mature Early English style, probably towards the end of the lancet phase and, as in the western range, showing some examples of plate tracery. Its extensive mouldings around the doors and windows are enriched with fillets and there are no keel mouldings. In combination, these would suggest that the range could be earlier, but not greatly earlier than about 1240. The bases, on the other hand, with their 'water-holding' design are unlikely to be much later than about the midde of the century. At the north end of the range, the stiff leaf capitals of the main entrance to the dormitory, would suggest a date in the early thirteenth century, while the mouldings of this doorway and of those in the parlour would suggest that they were ultimately derived from the new work at Westminster Abbey (1246–59, *infra* p 75). These latter mouldings come exclusively from the northern end of the range and are the sort of details that could have been later added to the original design, when construction may already have been in progress for some time. A date of about the 1240's or 1250's would seem to fit in with the evidence.

Such a dating would be reinforced by our knowledge of the sequence of rebuilding at Battle in the thirteenth century, in which this eastern range forms part of the second major phase. The three phases differ profoundly in their architectural characteristics and a clear sequence can be established. The first stage saw the remodelling of the chapter house and its characteristics, as far as they can be established, have already been discussed. An intermediate phase between this and the main second phase is represented by the core of the abbots' range. Such work represents the activity of the late twelfth and early thirteenth century. The third phase is not found in the excavated area but is most clearly seen above ground in the refectory and the adjacent bays of the west cloister walk. Such work is to be paralleled at, for example, Westminster Abbey and the cloisters at Salisbury. Attention has been drawn to the particular closeness between the work at Battle and that of the new east end at Bayham Abbey, which itself would seem to be probably not later than the 1260's (Rigold pers. com.; and 1974, 25). Moreover at Battle attention was turning to the new kitchen by 1279 when timber began to be cut down for it (*Cellarers' Accounts*, 46). All this would suggest that this stage of the rebuilding was a product of the third quarter of the thirteenth century. The dormitory range must have come before this and is clearly distinct in style from it. Cautious as any dating must be, the eastern range would thus seem to have been built in about the 1240's and 1250's, and was thus constructed within the abbacy of Ralph of Coventry (1235–1260).

The Range to the East of the Chapter House Excavations (Building Y)

One building which may possibly have belonged to this phase lay on the fringes of the excavation. Just projecting from the eastern end of the excavations in trench N were the mortared footings for a wall that pre-dates the post-Dissolution buildings. They probably belong to the west end of a major range that was discovered in the nineteenth century and of which only a fragment now protrudes from the ground (Building Y) (figure 10). Its position differs slightly from the nineteenth-century records of its location (although the latter may have only been approximations). The footings are at a very slight angle to both the published alignment and to that of the visible fragment, but we have only excavated a short length of their edge and, in the limited area available, it would be difficult to have a separate building. The range (Building Y) would seem to be a medieval replacement for the earlier infirmary (Building Z), as it overlies part of the latter's site. It was evidently a substantial building and was discovered in 1817 when it was thought to be the chapter house (Vidler 1841, 155). It was later trenched by the Duchess of Cleveland and her description and plan form the basis of our knowledge (Cleveland 1877, 249). Its walls survived about a foot below the surface and there were two 'very thick' parallel walls one of which extended to the precinct wall. There were two large chambers about 70 feet by 35 (21.3 m by 10.6 m) with a shorter chamber with winding stairway at the west. Its character was thus very different from the adjacent and later post-medieval timber buildings. We may confidently see it as a monastic building, while the size of its chambers would also suggest a building of importance. Of the two large chambers the most easterly possessed a fireplace whose base and adjacent short length of wall still survive above ground, and at the west end, at least, there seems to have been a two-storeyed building. Probably associated with the latter was a small chamber referred to by both Cleveland and Vidler although with an apparent slight conflict over its exact position (Cleveland 1877, 250, Vidler 1841, 155). It was on the site of the icehouse, so that nothing is now visible. It had a window sill, remnants of vaulting, the steps to a doorway, and an entrance to a small closet. Vidler described it as a subterra-

nean cell, although even in his day the sill was level with the ground outside and the recent excavations would suggest that the monastic ground level would have been about 0.6 m below this. We should probably see the building as a small chamber attached to the main range.

Only further excavation can hope to establish the date of this new range, which in view of its position should probably be seen as a new infirmary together with some private accommodation at the west end. Brakspear placed the range in the fourteenth century (1937 opp. p 103) although it is not clear on what basis. From its scale it clearly belongs to the great reconstruction of the monastic buildings, and there is some evidence to suggest a thirteenth-century date for it. A layer associated with its destruction produced mouldings mainly of this date, although some of the material might possibly have come from the contemporary parlour. In addition several fragments of a chimney were found in trench G, with an identical form to that which belonged to the reredorter. Now the absence of any substantial fireplace in the northern part of the dormitory range means that it is unlikely to have come from there. This new infirmary range (Building Y) would seem the most likely source although it should be added that the chimney comes from a layer below a nineteenth-century disturbance. These parallels between the probable debris of the new infirmary and the dormitory range cannot convincingly demonstrate the date of the new range but they can allow a thirteenth-century date to be suggested tentatively.

Period C: The Monastery in the Later Middle Ages

The rebuilding of the eastern range had produced a transformation of the area, and subsequent changes during the rest of the monastery's existence were to be more in the way of minor adjustments. Only one building programme seems to have affected the whole of the excavated area and this was the installation of a new system of rainwater drainage. For the rest subsequent alterations were essentially local in character and these will be considered area by area.

The New Drainage System.
(figures 3, 7, 8, 11; plates 17–20)

Although the site lacked sources of surface water, there must have been considerable problems with storm water. This would have resulted from the steepness of the hillside, from the clay subsoil and from the concentration of rainwater coming from the roofs of the buildings. We have already seen (p. 24) that in the early phases of the monastery there were a series of ditches, presumably for storm water, running down the hillside. These would have been cut-off by the construction of the reredorter in the thirteenth century, and it is not known what subsequent arrangements were made. There may still have been open ditches if they were diverted to avoid the reredorter and are now outside the excavated area. But the increased size of the buildings in this area and the subsequent extension of the church on the hilltop, must have greatly increased the problem of storm water. This problem was eventually tackled by the construction of a series of stone-lined drains.

Such stone-lined drains have been found in all areas of the excavations although inevitably there are large intervening gaps where excavation has not taken place. This makes it difficult to establish without doubt that they all belong to the same system, and the problem is made more difficult by the lack of any stratigraphic build-up in the chapter house area. What may be concluded, however, is that with the exception of one set of modifications in the chapter house area, all the drains seem to fit into a coherent and unitary scheme designed to drain the rainwater away from the buildings (see figure 3). In the chapter house area we have two main drainage channels. That to the east starts from the church. During his excavations, Brakspear found what appears from his plan to have been a drain in one of the buttresses. Certainly a drain entered the excavations from the north and was joined by tributary drains serving both sides of the chapter house and the infirmary range. A second set of drains lay to the west. This second system would have begun in the claustral area, as it had already passed under the parlour and cut the footings between the parlour and the porch before reaching the excavated area. It then bent south-east across the porch. Here the drain itself was later robbed out and some of the adjacent layers had been removed, but the position of the drain was indicated by a shallow gulley cut into the clay. Just beyond the porch the drain dipped sharply to a lower level where parts of the stone lining still survived. From here it turned southwards but a gulley survived of a short robbed extension such as would have served the east end of the porch building. The drain now ran along the dormitory range, where the roof water poured into a series of rainwater hoppers. Two of these were found, one at either end of the range. Half-way down the hillside, in trench VIII the two drainage systems merged. Here the drain along the dormitory wall was joined by a tributary from the east. Since this side branch would have cut across the line of the eastern system, it seems probable that it provided the link between the two. After this junction the drain continued parallel to the dormitory and along the north side of the reredorter, and was fed from these buildings by a succession of hoppers. The considerable pressure of water should have been enough to keep the system clean. The construction of the drain seems to have varied according to the nature of the adjacent soil. In the area to the south-east of the chapter-house and of the parlour the drains were set into the natural and here the stone lining was set directly into the clay. In trench RVIII where the drain was set in the loose fill of an earlier open ditch, the stone lining was set in mortar. Elsewhere, as in the reredorter area and to the north-east of the chapter-house, a packing of red clay was used. The drains were themselves covered with stone slabs although in some cases these have been robbed.

In the reredorter area, the construction of this new system involved a build-up of soil and the construction of a series of hoppers that have now been excavated. Developments here will therefore be examined more fully. Unfortunately the tendency of drains to underlie the edge of trenches was also found here, and thus the value of the main east-west section (figure 11) was considerably reduced for these phases. In phasing the layers an attempt was made to distinguish those layers that had been laid down in association with the construction of the drains (C14) and those which may have built up in the period between this and the earlier construction of the reredorter (C11). Such a division was not, however, a clear cut one and it may be that the two phases should more appropriately be linked together. The greatest build-up seems to have been at the western part of the excavations and the object would seem to have been to produce a more suitable gradient for the drain so that it sloped from west to east. Altogether the build-up in trench I for these two phases was about 0.5 m at its maximum. It consisted of a variety of soils and clays and there was no sign of a uniform layer, although a layer of heavy clay had been laid down around the drain. Some of the layers contained domestic refuse, animal bone, shell and pottery, and they also contained building debris such as tile and window glass. Incorporated in the make up were two dumps of broken window glass. This consisted mainly of plain glass that had not been fitted into a window and it seems to represent the offcuts from glazing (chapter VIII, p. 137). The glass was mixed with mortar fragments suggesting that it may have been part of a contemporary building programme. In both cases the glass dumps abutted the wall of the reredorter and lay between the buttresses of the latter. The former lay between the second and third buttresses to the east, and the latter between the second buttress and the doorway. It is clear therefore, that they lay below the windows of the reredorter and they may represent debris from glazing operations there. Alternatively they may be the product of glazing elsewhere on the site; the constructional debris being dumped wherever make-up was required. The validity of the latter interpretation is reinforced by the evidence of the adjacent layers. In both cases the layer of glass overlay a wedge of clay that had already been piled against the reredorter wall. Further layers of clay and soil were then added to level the ground, and the drain was then cut into this made-up surface. After the stone-lined drain and capping had been constructed, the cut was sealed with clay. As we have seen, the drain received the storm-water from the buildings on the hillside and hill-top, but it also received that from the reredorter itself. Three rainwater hoppers served the northern half of this range. Each was adjacent to a buttress and would have funnelled the rainwater from a gargoyle or pipe to the drain. One of these (F286) reused in its construction two large pieces of marble column such as may have come from a cloister arcade (Chapter V, nos. 3 & 4). The layers of this phase also included other pieces of Sussex and Purbeck marble shafts.

From the east end of the reredorter, the storm-water was probably carried south, for the drain seems to be aligned approximately with a silted open ditch that runs southward from the terrace and emptied into the fish ponds in the valley bottom. Unfortunately there is no surface trace of the ditch south of the reredorter where modern make-up would have covered the evidence.

This drainage system was probably part of a wider programme. There was evidently a drain on the western side of the dormitory for a small fragment of a similar stone-lined drain was found during the installation of a new drainage system in 1984.

The stratigraphy of the site is of only limited use in establishing the date of the drainage system. It is clear that the latter post-dates the construction of the whole dormitory complex. It has been argued that the system, with the exception of late modifications around Building X, is a unitary one and in two places it can be demonstrated that it post-dates the construction of these buildings. One of the drains makes a detour around the south-eastern corner of the porch although it cuts the foundations of the latter building. This would suggest both that the building was already in existence, and that it was not part of the same building programme, for the footings had already become buried. Secondly in the reredorter, the drain and hoppers are both later than the building for they are added to the latter and built from a higher level. If, as was suggested (p. 36) the drain begins at the new eastern arm of the church then this would imply that the earliest possible date would be in the late thirteenth century. Most of the pottery in the build-up layers is of thirteenth- and fourteenth-century types some of which are known to have continued in use much longer. A sherd of Tudor green ware would suggest a date of after about 1400 and the absence of stonewares would suggest a date before the mid-fifteenth century (infra p. 105). Such a relatively late date is reinforced by the piles of window glass in the build-up levels. This consisted of the waste from reglazing, so that most of the glass had never been in a window. It was of a type for which a date in the fifteenth century, or possibly afterwards, would be expected and one at the end of the fourteenth century would be possible but unlikely. The installation of the drains was not, however, the last phase of monastic activity. The construction of Building X, to the north-east of the chapter house, involved serious alterations to the drainage system. The branch draining the northern part of the chapter house was blocked by the new building, while at the same time a new north-south drain was superimposed on its predecessor. The available evidence would therefore fit with the suggested pottery dating of this phase in the first half of the fifteenth century. Moreover, since one of the hoppers included two large fragments of columns such as may have come from the cloisters, and since fragments of simpler shafts from a similar claustral source were found in the make-up layers of this phase, it seems likely that the drainage system was being installed at a time when the rebuilding of the cloisters was being carried out. As the standing remains show, most of the west range was rebuilt in

the perpendicular style, while the rebuilding of parts of the cloisters was taking place or being planned in 1421 (Brakspear 1937, 103). Such a date would certainly fit the archaeological evidence for the installation of the drainage system. In conclusion a date in the early fifteenth century, possibly around 1420, would seem most likely.

The Dormitory and Reredorter Ranges in the Later Middle Ages.

The new drainage system had been designed to serve these earlier buildings, but substantial repairs or alterations to the existing ranges were also carried out on one or more occasions during the later Middle Ages. The ranges had to be reroofed. In 1364–6 the dormitory was roofed with shingles (Abbey accounts 1365 and 1366). By the Dissolution both ranges were roofed with clay tiles although two different types of tile predominated on each roof, nib tiles on the reredorter and peg tiles on the dormitory (infra p. 99). The archaeological evidence also pointed to a reflooring during this period in the upper levels of these buildings. Large numbers of plain glazed floor tiles of probable fifteenth-century date were found in the Dissolution layers of the reredorter and unlike the decorated tiles which were predominantly found in the rubbish layers to the north of the building, the plain ones were found both there and in the primary fill of the reredorter drain. This would suggest that the plain tiles came from somewhere on the first floor where they could either be disposed of by throwing them outside the building to the north or by dropping them into the drain of the reredorter. For, bearing in mind the location of this building, it would seem improbable that rubbish from the buildings on the hillside would be deliberately carried round to the opposite side of the reredorter, particularly when rubbish was already accumulating on its nearer side. Not all of the floor was destroyed and some of it survived in the dormitory until at least 1811 (Cleveland 1877, 252). A contemporary illustration (reprinted in Behrens 1937 facing p. 30) shows a chequer pattern of apparently plain tiles. It is possible that some decorated tiles may also have been used (infra p. 81). Small-scale excavations within the dormitory floor suggest that nothing of this floor survives. They did not provide any indication of the way in which the room was originally floored, but they showed that the vaults had been filled with mortary mixtures of rubble and soil, over which a layer of reddish clay was added, probably to provide a base for the tiles. By the end of the Middle Ages, and probably before, the walls were decorated with plaster painted white and with coloured masonry joints. Fragments of this still survived in the nineteenth century (Cleveland 1877, 252). Reglazing also seems to have occurred in the first floor windows for plain window glass was found both in the Dissolution layers to the north of the reredorter and in the primary fill of the drain itself. Such reglazing work may possibly have been associated with the construction of the system of storm-water drains, as the two large piles of glass off-cuts and the scatter of such material within the make-up layers (*infra* p. 137) indicates that glazing was taking place somewhere at this time.

During the later Middle Ages, the monastic dormitories were usually divided up into separate cells. The nineteenth-century illustration of the tiled floor (Behrens 1937, facing p. 31) suggests that any such divisions must have been of light timber construction as the floor seems to have been designed for a single room. Such partitions would have been typical of those elsewhere as at Rievaulx and Durham (*Cartularium Abbathiae de Rievalle*, 339; *Rites of Durham*, 72). For Battle the documentary evidence is much less helpful although the treasurer's account of 1501 refers to the repair of beds and desks in the dormitory. One partition is, however, indicated by the structural remains. The addition of a small extra window at the south-west corner of the dormitory together with an adjacent small fireplace suggest that a separate chamber was established at this end of the building. Books were to be found on the first floor at the Dissolution as some of their clasps were to be dumped in the reredorter drain, and not at the end of the drain with access from the ground floor novices' quarters. What cannot be determined, however, is whether this represents books used by the monks in their studies within the dormitory or the conversion of part of the dormitory to book storage.

The reredorter undercroft also showed signs of limited change. A dividing cross-wall was built presumably to provide an additional chamber. The mortared footings of the wall are structurally subsequent to the walls of the building although it is possible that they may simply be a product of a later stage of the building campaign. They were built butt-jointed to the wall and in a similar mortar to that of the east of the building, but subsequent subsidence has opened up a gap between the two. The footings were partially sealed by a patch of mortar (see figure 8). This wall was presumably replaced by the adjacent cross wall. The latter incorporated door-jambs of late fourteenth-century date. The doorway shows some signs of re-use, and it may well represent an early post-Dissolution period of use. Probably linked with this remodelling, is the small latrine shaft in the south-east corner of the undercroft. Both could represent late medieval features, but on balance a post-Dissolution date has been suggested (*infra* p. 44).

At the west end of the undercroft, the gallery which in the Middle Ages provided access from the common rooms to the ground floor latrines (*supra* p. 32) was rebuilt. Both in the interior and outside the door, a line of stone footings was found such as could have served to keep a beam off the ground at a distance of about 1.7 m from the dormitory wall. The blocks seem to have been unmortared although in the interior the gap between this feature and the wall was filled with a loose mortar debris. Make-up of different material also occurred behind the footings outside. These features clearly represent a later modification of the existing structure, being very different in character from the thirteenth-century

work and being built outside on subsequent make-up layers. They also clearly belong to the monastic period as the gallery and doorway would have gone out of use when the area outside became the site of the Dissolution rubbish dump. Unfortunately in the limited area excavated, it was not possible to establish the precise stratigraphic relationship between the footings and the drain phase although both were subsequent to several build-up layers. The appearance of the north end of the footings does not suggest that it has been cut through by the rainwater hopper (F294). A likely explanation would be that the new entrance arrangements should be associated with the construction of the drains for the latter's installation would certainly have required some changes. In this case a date in the first half of the fifteenth century would again be appropriate. One other change may belong to this phase and that was the blocking of the eastern end of the main reredorter drain. This was blocked with a thin rubble wall and west of this a mortar screed was laid over the eastern end of the drain. Such a change may have been associated with the construction of the rainwater drain to the east and it clearly shows that by this stage, at least, the reredorter had ceased to be cleaned by a flow of water.

The Chapter House Area in the Later Middle Ages
(figures 5, 6, 9, 10; plates 7 and 20)
Most of this area saw little change in this period. The building remains betray no evidence of subsequent modifications and the open area to the east of chapter house and parlour saw no new layers or alterations. The only possible changes in this area were those that we have tentatively ascribed to earlier phases: the new infirmary (Building Y) and the lowering of the layers outside the chapter house. In neither case were there any associated layers. We do not therefore know when the layer of soil which developed east of the chapter house began and parts of it were to remain open after the Dissolution. The soil layer was absent in the area to the east of the porch and this may either represent a product of post-Dissolution removal, or it may point to the presence of a paved area between the porch and the infirmary such as would have been robbed out after the Dissolution but could have prevented the earlier development of a soil layer. It may be significant that the stone slabs covering one of the drains (foreground plate 7) extend beyond the area needed to cover the drain itself. It is possible therefore that these slabs may represent the later remnants of such paving. But the drains themselves point to one phase of change within this open area, for the installation of this drainage system was itself a product of the later Middle Ages. Later a new building (Building X), was added to the north-eastern part of the chapter house.

Building X was built abutting the chapter house and its construction involved the partial destruction of one of the latter's buttresses, changes to the drainage system and the disturbance of graves. Although excavations were restricted to one corner of the building a few conclusions can be made. It was constructed with shallow broad (1.7 m) footings of rubble and orange mortar. The wall itself had disappeared but its bottom course had left impressions in the mortar of the footings and these would suggest that the wall itself was about 0.8 m wide. During its construction a new drain was installed running above the earlier drain, set into the new wall and then emptying into the drain outside. The presence of this new drain suggests that the building was freestanding and was not a chapel opening into the church as there must have been an external wall served by the drain between the church and the new building. This is confirmed by a manuscript 'plan of foundations north of parlour next crypt' in the Brakspear papers (Battle folder). This provides a record of his work in the chapter house area where he uncovered the south-western corner of Building X. He seems to have sought to establish its width for he records the presence about 10–15 feet (3–4.5 m) north of its south wall of 'foundation here, no definite line yet found'. This could well represent the remnants of the north wall. But as to the length of the building we have no clue.

The dating and function of the building must also remain a matter of conjecture. It is clearly of monastic date, but post-dates the main drainage phase which has been dated to the early fifteenth century. A date in the mid- or late- fifteenth century or the early sixteenth century would therefore seem appropriate. Given its position just south of the choir, a sacristy would provide a possible identification. In these circumstances, it is tempting to associate the building with that constructed for the sacrist in 1518, when £93 6s 1½d was spent on a new building 'in the cemetery' (Sacrist's Account, 1518). Such an identification would both fit our broad dating and the position of the building in relation to the church and the cemetery. The exact extent of the latter is unknown, but it evidently lay around the eastern arm of the abbey church. Study of the 1429/30 rental and of the properties and abutments there (P.R.O. E315/56 f.17r.) locates the cemetery wall and thus part of the cemetery in what would have been the area to the north of the eastern arm of the church. The burials evidently extended to the south of the latter. Here graves are known from later evidence (Cleveland 1877, 249; Mrs. E. Webster pers. com.) and one or probably two were found east of the parlour in the present excavations (*supra* p. 24). Moreover, two isolated skulls were carefully placed together just west of the footings for the west wall of Building X, suggesting that graves had been disturbed during the building's construction. Further excavation might provide more conclusive evidence, but our present very limited information would fit in with an identification of Building X as the new sacrist's building of 1518.

One other feature may be associated with this phase. Behind the south face of trench M, and only revealed by two winters' erosion, lay the side of a line of blocks set in mortar such as would have belonged to another rainwater drain. Stratigraphically this must be contemporary or later than the main system of drains, but its depth would suggest

that it was associated with the neighbouring higher and later phase of drains that went with the construction of building X. It could have served to drain the south side of the latter building. Finally the two isolated skulls to the west of the building may have resulted from disturbance of graves during the building's construction.

The final phase of activity in this area was to see the replacement of the apsidal chapel in the south transept by a rectangular one. In the limited excavated area all that was uncovered was the stone footings in a crumbly decaying white mortar of a wall running eastwards. It abutted the apse and overlay a stone-lined drain which drained northwards from the chapter house (F324). The replacement of the apsidal chapel was paralleled by a similar development in the north transept (Brakspear 1931, 168, and Brakspear papers/Battle folder) although the two developments may not have been contemporaneous. Here again the absence of a substantive associated layer makes it difficult to date these alterations and we are driven back to the structural sequence. Here the dating of the drain (F324) is crucial as this underlies the wall of the new chapel. This drain seems to have served the north side of the chapter house, although the precise arrangements by which it was filled are unclear. Now the construction of building X had blocked the drain which had hitherto served this purpose and it is suggested that the drain under discussion was its successor and was contemporary with this building programme. This would make the later replacement of the apse one of the latest developments on the site, dating from the late fifteenth or early sixteenth century, or after 1518, if Building X was indeed the sacristry of that date.

Such building works were small by comparison to those of the thirteenth century, but they and the surviving remains in the abbot's range and in the outer court remind us of the works which here, as elsewhere, were to continue in the later Middle Ages and up to the Dissolution (Knowles 1959, 21–4). The changes in and around the eastern range also remind us of how little or no evidence may be left on the standing ruins by substantial programmes of modernization or alteration.

Period D: The Abbey Buildings after the Dissolution. The Sixteenth and Seventeenth Centuries.
The Dissolution of the abbey in May 1538 produced an obvious break in the history and archaeology of the site. But although it began the long process of the destruction and decay of the abbey buildings, it also began a new period of activity. The monks' successor, Sir Anthony Browne, now sought to convert the monastic buildings and site into a residence fit for a nobleman (*supra* p. 14). This conversion was, however, to change dramatically the fortunes of the excavated area. For it was the old outer court of the monastery that was to become the residential focus, while the former claustral area was to decline in importance. In the latter some of the buildings, such as the church and chapter house, were destroyed and there was some new building within the excavated area. But as the Browne fami-

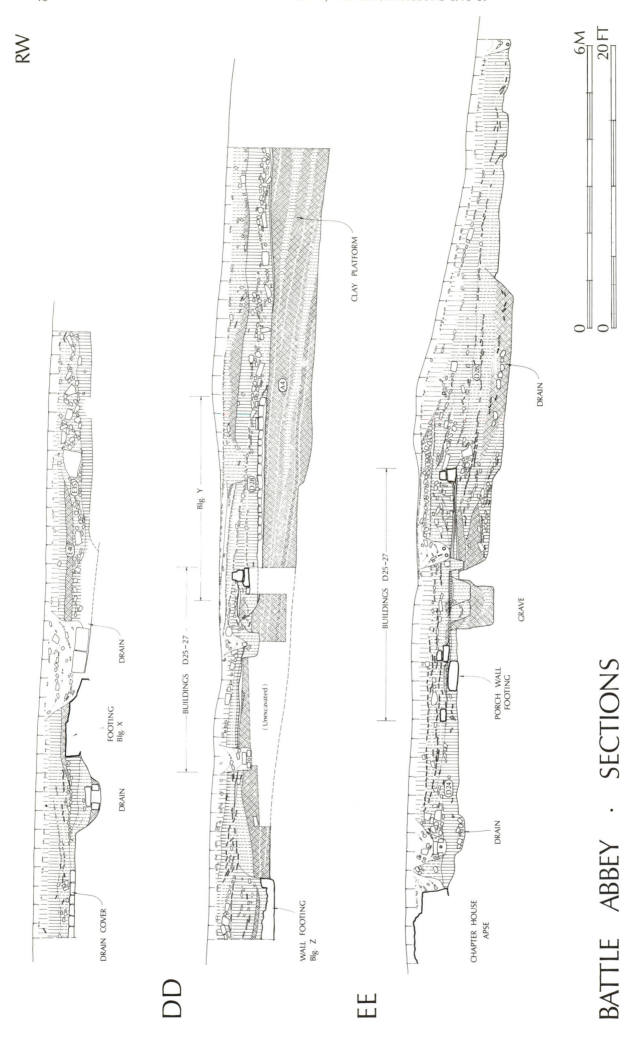

BATTLE ABBEY · SECTIONS

Figure 10 Sections from the area to the east of the chapter house.

ly's interests increasingly centred elsewhere, so Battle declined. Here much of the seventeenth century seems to have been a period of neglect; a period that culminated in wide-spread demolition in the excavated area.

The Chapter House Area after the Dissolution
(figures 6, 7, 9 and 10; plate 20)
The chapter house itself seems to have been one of the first buildings to be destroyed. Any flooring was first robbed, since no evidence of this survived under the destruction debris, and the robbing of the graves probably occurred at the same time. On the north side of the building, the offset and bench were largely destroyed and a bank of mortar debris with some rubble accumulated. This would seem to represent the destruction debris from the walls of both the chapter house and the adjacent transept, the two being destroyed together. As Brakspear's excavations showed, most of the debris from the eastern arm of the church had been carted away so that there was little build-up. In the chapter house the bank of debris was left where otherwise the ground level would have stepped down from the higher level of the church. On the south side of the building destruction took a different form. Here the benching was left and the destruction seems to have been more limited. Mortar debris accumulated to cover the bench and this was to include several fragments of painted window glass. North of the parlour a small bank of large blocks of stone in mortar debris was left, perhaps to help buttress the footings of the dormitory range. Even to-day the south side survives higher and more completely than the north side and it seems likely that the destruction was never so complete as where the building abutted the church and was razed to the ground with it. On the south side some may have been left to buttress the surviving dormitory range. The destruction of the chapter house would thus have left a hollow in the centre of the building with banks of stone or debris around and with fragments of wall projecting on one side. In this hollow a fine dark soil, containing vessel glass and much pottery and bone, gradually accumulated. Most of the pottery was of late sixteenth- and early seventeenth-century date, the vessel glass seems to belong to the same period and the only coin from these layers had a suggested deposition date of about 1600 (*infra* p. 105, 145, 181 no 57). This accumulation therefore seems to belong to a distinct and later stage of the site's existence than that of the Dissolution and the creation of Sir Anthony Browne's new residence. Within this build-up, possible evidence for a small timber structure was provided by a rectangular layer of compacted stone blocks (F77). Also during this stage, the carcass of a pig was buried in a shallow pit that had been cut through the layer that had been accumulating (F81).

Elsewhere there is further evidence of continuing activity in the area around the old chapter house. Building X continued in use. Part of the base of the drain below may have been relined with brick and the bricks themselves would suggest a possible date in the sixteenth or seventeenth century. More importantly, the building's destruction level overlay the soil layer associated with the Dissolution and afterwards. On the surface of this layer was a line of broken medieval floor tiles, laid end to end in a white crumbly mortar and aligned at right angles to Building X (F74). They might have acted as footings for a light timber structure. This layer also contained patches of rubble and fragments of painted window glass but it did not comprise a clear destruction layer. It overlay the main rainwater drain which in this phase had been partially robbed of its capping and gradually filled with a grey sandy soil from the layer above but not with destruction debris. The fish bones found in the drains, suggest that the area was now being used as a dump for some domestic refuse.

Further south, and east of the parlour, the excavations uncovered evidence for three phases of substantial timber buildings (figure 7). Only the footings survived but these would have supported a timber structure. The latter probably linked the parlour to the range further east (Building Y) although the details at either end are unclear. The internal width was 3.6 m. In its first phase its footings consisted of a low stone wall with tile levelling and a neat facing of mortar. A shallow gulley ran down the middle of the range. At its west end the range seems to have used the footings of the north wall of the destroyed porch building. It seems to have been a post-Dissolution and not a late medieval building. It overlies the construction of the drainage system, but also overlies the destruction of two of its branches (F67/423 and F298) and of the porch building. There had also been a substantial accumulation of soil, so uncharacteristic of the monastic phase on this part of the site, between the drain phase and the construction of the range. Later, the range was remodelled, with the long single room being divided up into at least three rooms by additional footings. Then, or afterwards, the floor level was raised with different materials in each room; the drain being filled with the appropriate material, orange clay in one chamber and a sandy mortary soil in the other. This phase would also seem appropriate for the addition of an intermittent line of footings to the north of the building, such as might have served to support a pentice roof. Their foundations seem intermediate in depth between the two other phases and different in character from them, lacking the mortar surface of the first phase and the large rough blocks of the later. Finally, the range was rebuilt with a new set of footings being laid out on top of those of the earlier phases. The new footings consisted of a line of large blocks of stone laid without any mortar. They may have continued right up to the parlour as a line of similar blocks was incorporated into Brakspear's revetment wall east of the parlour and may represent a consolidation of a wall that he had discovered.

To the south of this range lay an open area from which only fragmentary layers of soil survived. During this period the western stone-lined drain (F67) was partially robbed out. It is possible that the stone and mortar raft (F153) which overlay the remains of the early infirmary wall may have belonged to this period and been associated with the adjacent range.

At the western end next to the dormitory (trench G) the stratigraphy was complicated by the activity of the Duchess of Cleveland. By the nineteenth century the ground level had risen outside the common room covering the plinth of the porch and blocking the adjacent window. In 1875 she cleared away the rubble (Cleveland 1877, 253) but in so doing cut a large scoop that in parts reached the natural, and thus destroyed much of the stratigraphy.

The century after the Dissolution thus saw a period of continued activity in this area. The church and porch had been destroyed and the chapter house was in ruins, but the buildings further east (Y and X) and the dormitory continued to survive. They were presumably in use for a new range was built linking the dormitory and Building Y. The character of its construction marks, however, a great contrast with that of the monastic buildings. It is not known precisely what function these buildings performed nor can their dates be established with exactitude. It seems that they were now taking on some of the functions of the old monastic outer court now that the latter was becoming the main centre of importance. Alternatively, they may represent slightly later farm buildings such as might have served part of the Great Park to the south when it was enclosed for agriculture in the seventeenth century (Thorpe, 1835, 157–8).

The Reredorter Area
(figures 8 and 11)
During this period, the reredorter range seems to have been in use, although not for its original purpose and probably not continuously. Outside and to the north, a considerable accumulation of deposits took place, for here building debris, domestic refuse and the unwanted goods that had belonged to the monastery were deposited. These layers and particularly a rubbish dump at the west end, near the junction of reredorter and dormitory, produced a remarkable quantity of finds and much of the specialist reports will be concerned with them. These layers outside the reredorter have been divided into two phases (D21 and D22). This has been done on stratigraphic grounds but it should be pointed out that they represent a similar chronological context and may both be seen as layers belonging to the period immediately after the Dissolution. Thus each of the phases included a distinct layer of tile debris with a concentration of different types of tile in each layer (see chapter VI) but whereas in trench IV they were widely separated by a build up of soil, further west this intervening layer was absent and there was a lack of a clear cut line of division. The two layers also merge towards the east. Moreover, it was the later phase, and particularly layer RIII (230), that was to contain most of the monastic debris.

The first of these layers consisted of large amounts of roof tile in soil and continued along the whole length of the reredorter. This would suggest that it represented debris from the roof of the building itself. Its Dissolution date seems clear. It overlay and blocked the rainwater hoppers (e.g. F285): this both suggests that the drainage system was no longer

of interest and contrasts with the relative cleanliness of the monastic site. At the same time it partially overlay the later medieval footings for the gallery which would have provided access to the ground floor latrine. Finally it showed similarities in its contents to the layer above (RIII 230) that contained so much monastic debris, similarities that included unusual items such as the presence in both layers of bone parchment-prickers and tuning pegs.

On top of the layer and at the west end of the excavations, a large pile of rubbish accumulated. A spread of large blocks of masonry containing five blocks of coping stone and a folded sheet of lead underlay the main build-up of rubbish (Plate 21). The conjunction of the lead with the concentration of coping blocks in such a small area (for only three were found anywhere else in the excavations), together with their location at the dormitory end of the reredorter area would suggest that they may represent the product of stripping the dormitory gutters of their leading. The coping could have been levered off and toppled in order to free the lead. For some reason the lead was forgotten, perhaps rubbish was soon being dumped in the area. The rubbish was dumped on and around the stone blocks and spread beyond them. It included lead strips such as could have been used to hold lead sheets in place (*infra* p. 156). This dump formed phase D22, and comprised an accumulation of up to 0.8 m of fine dark soil. There were distinctive but very local variations within it, and at times the distinction between its main layer, III (230) and the underlying layer of the previous phase, III (264), was almost imperceptible. The extensive and varied character of the finds from this rubbish dump have provided one of the important results of the excavations: a rich survey of the debris of monastic life and culture (see particularly chapter X).

As with the underlying layers, the post-Dissolution date of the accumulation of D22 and RIII (230) is clear. The presence of an obnoxious rubbish dump outside the entrance to the ground floor lavatory indicates that the latter must have gone out of use as had the main doorway to the undercroft where rubbish also accumulated outside. The dump and the previous phase also blocked the rainwater hoppers and would thus have led to the blocking of the drains, not merely for the reredorter but for the main monastic area on the hilltop as this also used the same system. We are therefore dealing with something more than a peripheral building going out of use within the monastic period. This is also made clear by the wide range of material such as was unlikely to have come from a single building or from any normal discarding of unwanted items. But although the post-Dissolution context is clear, the coin evidence suggests a cautionary note in interpreting the date of the material within such deposits. The dump of D22 contained 19 coins, 18 jettons and a currency forgery. Of the coins the latest comes from the second part of Edward IV's reign (1471–83) while seven came from the fourteenth century and the rest are scattered in between. The jettons are generally slightly later, usually of *c.*1500 or possibly early sixteenth century. While a few old coins might be expected in such a group the absence of more recent ones and the general longevity of the material should remind us that we are dealing here with material that was deposited shortly after the Dissolution but that had been produced or accumulated long before. The clear-out of the monastic buildings had presumably uncovered collections of coins that were too old for use (see chapter XI).

Although this was not a layer of building debris, the finds included building materials. In particular, they included a large number of roof tiles. The latter would seem to have come from the dormitory roof as they did not continue along the whole length of the reredorter building. The pile was thickest near the dormitory itself and thinned out eastwards where it lapped over a build up of soil that itself overlay the earlier tile layer. At the west end the tiles were scattered throughout the considerable depth of the layer, and this suggests either a process of gradual decay or that the roof had been destroyed after the dump had accumulated, so that the falling tiles had forced their way into the decaying rubbish below. Although the tiles spread far beyond the dormitory (figure 10) they peter out as a distinct layer. Significantly, they were of a different type from those representing the collapse of the reredorter roof: the former were peg tiles and the latter were nib tiles. Other building material was represented by floor tiles, fragments of moulded stone and window glass. The floor tiles included both plain tiles, which were also found in the reredorter drain and probably came from the first floor of the adjacent ranges (*infra* p. 93) and decorated tiles. The window glass also included both material that had probably come from the adjacent ranges (*infra* p. 133) and the higher quality glass such as woud have come from the more prestigious buildings. The latter glass included both grisaille glass with similar designs to those of the chapter house and other designs. There were also fragments of lead from the windows.

The rubbish also included the products of a monastic culture that had now ended. Evidence of books and writing was found in the bone prickers for marking out the lines on parchment, the fragments from wax tablets, the small lead paint pot, the book clasps and other fragments from book binding. Musical activities were represented by the bone tuning pegs from rebecs and the slate engraved for music. Finally there were objects of artistic value such as the fragment of a Romanesque tau cross (see chapter X).

There were also items of personal and medical use: a comb, toilet sets with tooth picks and ear scoops, urinals of different types, some but not all of which were for uroscopy, and pottery distilling apparatus. Clothes were represented by the metal items, such as buckles, belt stiffeners and chapes, strap ends and studs, hooks and fasteners, and pins. There were a few items of jet, possibly from a rosary. Other items of daily use were the remnants of glass lamps (chapters IX and X).

The pottery included a wide range of different types and fabrics, largely of local provenance but containing some continental types. While much of this pottery came from the monastic period some may have come from the immediately post-Dissolution period when the dump was being used as a place for current refuse. Thus it seems more likely that the bones there should be seen as a product of the successor-household rather than as material left around the buildings by the monks. For substantial quantities of bone were found here from animals, birds and fish. Apart from the more common range of animal meat bones, the variety of bird bones also suggests a range of delicacies and the presence of an opulent household (chapter XI).

Looked at in conjunction with evidence from other parts of Battle and from elsewhere, this corner of the site can tell us much about what happened after the Dissolution. Before the destruction of the buildings, when at Battle much of the rubble was used to level up the outer courtyard, they would be stripped of saleable items. None of the buildings possess surviving floors although tiles had been found in some of the rooms in the monastic period. Probably the explanation lies in the sales of such tiles, as at Reading Abbey (Preston 1935, 119–20) or Bordesley Abbey (Rahtz and Hirst 1976, 22). The roof of the reredorter also seems to have been disposed of. The lead was stripped from the gutters and the coping stone cast to the ground. This process was likely to have been at an early stage after the Dissolution for the lead was the property of the king (Youings 1971, 162; Woodward 1966, 126–7). It would have been smelted on site as the examples cited by Dunning (1952, 200–2) and Bordesley Abbey (Rahtz and Hirst 1976, 22) make clear. The window glass might be taken out, if suitable, for re-use, as at Rievaulx (*Cartularium Abbathiae de Rievalle*, 338–9) but otherwise they could either be used as frit or heated to separate and melt the lead of the cames, as at Monk Bretton (Walker 1926, 103). The rubbish from D22 contained some discarded glass and tile that may have come from the post-Dissolution stripping of the buildings elsewhere. The decorated tiles and high quality painted glass would have been unlikely to have come from the buildings immediately adjacent, and it seems unlikely that they would have been carried great distances just to be discarded. This may suggest that the excavations were on the fringes of an area where sorting or smelting took place. The nearby presence of such destructive activities is also suggested by the presence in D21 and D22 of scraps or off-cuts of copper alloy sheet and wire. The adjacent area, lying as it did east of the dormitory and north of the reredorter would have provided a highly suitable area for such activities, being large, away from the main area of demolition and from the main house, and with easy access to the road. After the saleable assets had been disposed of, the remaining material from some of the adjacent buildings was dumped on the rubbish heap. The perishable items have subsequently disappeared but enough survives to provide a remarkable range of finds such as would suggest that the material came from more than one room. But while all this was going on, a new household was taking shape and some of their current rubbish was added to the growing pile.

The accumulation of such debris outside the reredorter building must have affected the use of the latter. It had lost its roof and the main surviving entrance was blocked by the layers accumulating outside. The building was eventually reused. Its unusable door was left in place so that one of its hinges and many of its nails were uncovered during the excavations, but it was sealed from the outside by faced stone blocking only one block in depth (plate 22). The high entrance to the ground floor latrines must have gone out of use since access would now have been over the rubbish dump. We have no evidence of it ever having been blocked, but it is possible that this could have taken place and that the doorway was re-opened by later antiquaries. Thus, access to the reredorter undercroft would now have been through the third and now robbed-out doorway. Significantly this was at a point where the depth of the build-up was substantially reduced. There was no evidence from the later destruction debris of any reroofing associated with this new use, but it may, like the adjacent dormitory, have been reroofed with wooden shingles.

Inside the reredorter, the areas east and west of the crosswall need to be treated separately. In the western part the picture is relatively simple. If, as seems likely, the undercroft was floored in tile or a similar surface, then this was removed after the Dissolution, but life continued in the building. It may have been at this time that the hearth of the fireplace was narrowed by the addition of a mortared lump of stone and tile which was butted on to the existing fireplace and which projected slightly beyond the offset at the base of the wall. Continued use of the fireplace produced a spread of ash and a burning or reddening of the ground around it. The ash was itself overlain by a layer of loam with tile and some sandstone debris. This layer seems to have accumulated over a considerable period of time. Most of the pottery content was of early sixteenth-century date and was closely paralleled by the contents of the Dissolution layers outside, but it also contained a pipe stem of late seventeenth-century date. It is not known exactly how completely the building survived but as will be discussed in looking at its destruction, it seems to have remained substantially complete with chimney and vaulting still surviving (infra p. 78). We have therefore a further period of use, although probably of a rather shabby sort. Several post holes were found cut into the clay. They do not form any apparent pattern.

In the eastern half the position is more complex. The dividing line would seem to have been provided by the crosswall with doorway. Its door jambs are of medieval date and closely parallel those at Bodiam Castle, the latter being a product of the 1380's (Nairn and Pevsner 1965, 419). They are in greensand. Here the doorway seems to have been reset in a narrow (0.65 m) wall of more recent date, using a white mortar characteristic of later work such as is also found on the destroyed eastern wall of the reredorter. The cross wall butts against the line of

the robbed out north wall of the building and so this wall must still have survived. The wall and doorway were sealed by the rubble and mortar debris of the range itself while the loam layer on its floor seems to have lapped up against both sides of the door sill. The doorway would have opened to the east, and in this eastern room were several features. At an early stage there was a broad shallow gulley running eastwards from the doorway and there were other depressions that failed to form a coherent pattern. A broad mortar-covered depression overlay the gulley itself. The clay level may once have been a flat floor but it had become heavily pock-marked, as if animals had been trampling on wet clay. In the south-east corner, a small rectangular stone-lined shaft (0.8 m by 0.7 m) had been constructed with its two side walls butting onto the walls of the reredorter building. It was excavated to a depth of 1.5 m, when work ceased owing to difficulties of access. The shaft had been cut into the floor levels, and an adjacent feature probably represented the cut for its construction. It seems probable that this was a latrine shaft. Later it had been filled in with a loose yellow-brown sterile clayey soil and then with a brown loam containing numerous blocks of cut stone. The latter contained a large number of pieces of a fireplace hood which, like the loam, had probably come from the undercroft itself. Patches of white lime mortar were also found on the upper part of the east wall of this shaft, above this on the surface of the east wall of the reredorter, where it contrasted strongly with the mortar of the reredorter itself, and on the surviving crosswall. To the south, and adjacent to the heavily damaged wall between the undercroft and the main drain, was a pintle such as would have served a door or gate to the south.

To the east of the reredorter range was a small rectangular building (internally 3.3 m by 2.7 m). Its west wall was provided by the neighbouring reredorter wall and by the rubble blocking of the latter's drain. Part of its south wall was provided by the buttress of the earlier building. Its other walls are now represented by rubble and clay footings or walls, together reaching a height of up to 0.7 m. That to the east would seem to have had two superimposed layers of construction. That to the north included large blocks of sandstone architectural fragments of the same form as material in the undercroft debris and coming therefore from the robbing of the reredorter. These two walls were built on post-Dissolution layers, but in the limited area of excavation it was not possible to establish their date.

It has proved difficult to establish an exact chronological account of developments in this area, but a suggested sequence can be offered. The first phase of these alterations should be associated with the shaft and the crosswall. A medieval date for these seems possible but less likely. The small size of the latrine would have produced difficulties with emptying; it seems unlikely that in a medieval context they would not have somehow made use of the adjacent main drain, while the medieval doorway shows signs of later rebuilding. A post-Dissolution date seems, on balance, more likely, and this would further suggest a new use for part of the reredorter. Eventually this area seems to have changed from human to animal use. The latrine was filled in, before the main destruction of the reredorter, and the building may have remained open for animal use. It is probably with this stage that one should associate the pintle. During the decay of the range, a new building was constructed to the east. Then, or later, white lime mortar was slapped on and around the eastern wall of the latrine, on the east wall of the reredorter and on the reset or heavily repaired crosswall. By this stage the south end of the eastern reredorter wall, at the very least, had been lowered to its present level, as is shown by the white mortar on its surface. Part of the original building had therefore disappeared, but most of the range probably still survived. The loam layer which underlay the main destruction debris trickled over the sill from the west, while after the destruction, the door would have been blocked by a mass of rubble.

The period before the main destruction of the reredorter range was also to see the gradual accumulation of soil and some rubble in the lower parts of the main drain. The latter still possessed its full range of open arches to the south so that such build-up must have spread in front of the arches although this has subsequently been removed by building works or by gardening.

The adjacent dormitory range also underwent a period of new use. At some time after the Dissolution it had, as we have seen, lost its tiled roof. The latter may have been removed for sale or they may have been removed in order to reuse them on one of the new post-Dissolution buildings that were being erected elsewhere on the site. We have no archaeological evidence of reroofing, but this may have been done with wooden shingles. This at any rate was how the building was covered in the eighteenth century (Cleveland 1877, 219). An inserted doorway into the 'novices' quarters' one of whose jambs was found in the north-west corner of the excavations may also have dated from this phase.

Period E: Decline and Revivals. The Eighteenth Century and Afterwards
The declining fortunes of the Brownes and their diminishing involvement at Battle eventually led to a destruction of buildings that had become superfluous, a trend that was to be clearly reflected in the area of excavation. Periodically, however, attempts were made to modernize and rehabilitate the decaying buildings (supra, p. 15). By now, however, the excavated area had largely become an open space: as gardens, park or wasteland.

The period of destruction was represented throughout the excavated area, but it should be stressed that it was not necessarily a single campaign of clearance and may have occurred on different buildings at different times over a period of a generation or more. In the chapter house area and within the site of the chapter house itself a fragment of wall (F62) collapsed on to the earlier soil accumulation, although this may have preceded the main phase of destruction. The hollow within the chapter

house was gradually filled with various dumps of soil, rubble and tiles. To the east a thick layer of rubble in mortar debris was laid down. Its source was probably the destruction of Building X, although some may have come from further demolition of the chapter house ruins. Large quantities of roofing tile were left in the area of the long timber range. Finally a layer of rubble was deposited to the south of this, a layer that included substantial quantities of mouldings. The most likely source of this debris would seem to be the adjacent Building Y. It is probably to this phase that we should ascribe the rubble which was piled outside the windows of the common room until cleared by the Duchess of Cleveland. Her description implies that this rubble included many architectural fragments including carved capitals (Cleveland 1877, 253). The parlour may also have provided a source for such material.

The reredorter was also destroyed, so leaving the dormitory range in splendid, if decaying, isolation. The undercroft, the drain and the area to the north of the building were covered with a layer of large blocks of rubble and mortar debris. This layer included many distinctive blocks of architectural details from the vaults, windows, doorways and fireplace. The presence within it of vault ribs, and more particularly of parts of the chimney itself remind us that the building still survived for much of its height before its final destruction. The demolition debris thinned out towards the east, and this may represent a sign of an earlier and partial destruction at this end or that here part of the rubble had been cleared away. After this demolition, all that was left of the building was that portion where it abutted the dormitory range and the arcade of great arches that had opened into the drain (plate 23).

It remains to establish the date of the demolitions in this area. We have several references to the destruction of buildings at Battle Abbey in the late seventeenth and early eighteenth century. In 1685–6 the steward's accounts record much demolition and the consequent sales of building material. The destruction of the kitchen is specifically referred to although the scale of the operations would suggest that more than this was involved (Steward's Account, 1685–7). The Duchess of Cleveland writing in the nineteenth century (1877, 193 and 207) also refers to the demolition of buildings under the fifth Viscount Montague (in possession 1708–1721) and under Sir Thomas Webster (1721–1751) although confirmatory documentation has not been found. Certainly it was by, or during, the eighteenth century that the monastic buildings were reduced to their present scale. Grimm's illustrations show that by 1783 the dormitory had assumed its present isolated position as the neighbouring buildings had been destroyed (Plate 24). An illustration on an estate map also shows the dormitory in isolation with the reredorter having been totally destroyed except for the series of open arches for the drain (Plate 23). Unfortunately the dating of the drawing is not secure. The map does not have a date although it is probably contemporary with the other maps in the volume, which date from the 1720's. The map itself shows the same buildings in existence as the drawing so that it is unlikely that the latter is substantially later in date. It must, however, pre-date Grimm's drawings for it shows the arches prior to the partial destruction of three of them which was done when the stable block illustrated by Grimm was built (B.L. Add. Mss. 5670/78). Together the topographical and documentary evidence would suggest a likely date for the period of destruction in the late seventeenth or early eighteenth century. Such a date would be supported by the archaeological evidence although fine dating cannot be expected from most of the finds. The limited quantity of tobacco pipes available would suggest dates for the destruction in the chapter house area of the early eighteenth century rather than the 1680's.

After this period of destruction the chapter house area remained open with a layer of loam accumulating throughout the excavated area there and extending into the area of the church, as shown during work associated with the display of its plan. In the reredorter area, there was the construction of a new stable to the south of the old reredorter drain. Grimm shows a brick building here in 1783 (B.L. Add. Ms. 5670/78) and the Duchess of Cleveland records that the stables lay to the south-east of the dormitory until moved to the latter building after 1810 (Cleveland 1877, 219–220) Its south wall was located in the trench south of the reredorter, RIX. These footings consisted of mortared blocks of sandstone with occasional pieces of brick, 0.68 m in depth. The building also left its mark on the standing remains. The three westernmost large arches were destroyed down to the springer level and the soil in their opening was cut back so that stone walls could be built to block off the openings and to provide a continuous back wall for the stable. The blockings were only faced on their outer side. Although the dumps of soil within the arches had had to be cut back, the builders had not taken much trouble so that the loam in the medieval sockets was left sealed behind the new blocking. In addition to the destruction of the arches, new doorways were cut through the reredorter walls providing access to the north, and to the floor inserted into the former 'novices' quarters'.

The dormitory range in the eighteenth century was in a state of decay. This was reflected in Grimm's views of the range with its heavily decaying roof and in a build up of debris within the dormitory itself. The latter included (in trench C) a group of clay pipes, four of which can be given a date between c. 1720 and c. 1750 and ten fragments for which an eighteenth-century date would seem appropriate. The roof continued to suffer and Hooper's engraving of 1785 suggests that by then the roof had been destroyed (reprinted in Behrens 1937).

The next major change in this area came with the decision of Sir Godfrey Webster at the beginning of the nineteenth century to make use of the old dormitory by converting it into first floor stables. Access was provided by a soil ramp from the north. Much of this ramp would have been over the site of the parlour and would have been removed when

Brakspear excavated the latter, but the beginnings of a clay bound ramp were found in the chapter house excavations and the thick clay yard laid onto the earlier loam was also probably a necessary part of this scheme. In the dormitory itself the northern part was taken over for the horses and here a brick floor was laid down. The pattern of the brickwork would suggest that there was a passage down the centre of the building with the stalls lying on either side. Dividing this area from the rest of the building was a brick wall (Cleveland 1877, 252; and Dormitory trench F). The old shingles had been removed and the stables were roofed with slates (Cleveland 1877, 220). When the old stables were destroyed further layers of rubble and tile were produced in the western part of the reredorter. Probably associated with this new use for the dormitory was a group of items of iron horse equipment found in the chapter house area (infra, p. 171).

The unusual arrangement of a first floor stables seems less strange when it is remembered that the building already existed and that the main entrance to the house was then through a large gateway in the precinct wall to the north of the dormitory, where a wide blocked opening may still be seen, and not through the medieval gatehouse (Cleveland 1877, 219). It would have been a more convenient position than that of the old stables on the far side of the precinct and at the bottom of the slope. But its position was no longer so suitable once the main entrance shifted to the gatehouse and the west side of the abbot's range. In about 1818, new access to the stables was provided by cutting the present route to the north of the main house through the destruction debris in the nave of the church. But in 1819, new stables and coach houses were built nearer the house. The horses were now taken from the dormitory and its slates were re-used on the new building (Cleveland 1877, 220; Brent 1973, 11). The dormitory was left roofless and decaying. Illustrations of it in the early twentieth century show it with a lawn on the first floor.

The final move of the stables marked the end of any regular activity in the excavated areas. Thereafter they were to be merely parts of the grounds. In the nineteenth century a series of gravel paths on heavy rubble footings were installed both in the chapter house area and lower down the hillside. Also from this period probably comes the long stone wall running eastwards from the dormitory and revetting a considerable height of soil. Its character and general lack of mortar are untypical of the medieval work and, more crucially, it overlaps the walls of the much later brick and cement-rendered dairy. Further down the slope, further demolition layers accumulated on top of the destruction layer of the reredorter range itself. The former probably represent the destruction of the stables and allied buildings that existed in this area at the end of the eighteenth century. These layers were then cut by a path that ran down the slope. Possibly associated with this were two short north-south walls within the main reredorter drain. They were single-faced and designed to hold back the debris within the drain, thus leaving an open space under the first surviving arch to the west (in RIV). These might have been associated with the construction of a landscaped path passing through the arch, although no evidence was found of the necessary steps leading up to the higher ground. Alternatively they may represent the creation of a shelter or building in the shadow of the arch and extending into the disused drain. At a point subsequent to the main demolition, the remnants and part of the footings of the north-east buttress of the reredorter and the adjacent north wall were robbed out.

The Duke and Duchess of Cleveland who held Battle from 1857–1901 (Brent 1973, 15–16) carried out major works at the abbey and their activities were described by the Duchess. She seems to have done much to tidy up the area to the south of the reredorter arches, clearing away the soil and buildings that had accumulated and establishing a pergola on the sunny side of the monument. Elsewhere she cleared the area east of the monastic common room (Cleveland 1877, 256–7, 253). Signs of her successor's work have already been noted in the removal of a doorway into the novices' quarters, and a substan-

tial sum was spent on repairs by Sir Augustus Webster (Behrens 1937, 117).

Finally from 1929 until his death in 1934, Sir Harold Brakspear was active at Battle. His consolidation of the dormitory range and the restoration of the west range after it had been gutted by fire, were important achievements. His work in the dormitory range may be easily discerned through the use of the distinctive ironstone. At the same time he was able to excavate in several parts of the abbey. In the chapter house area, he was able to expose in its entirety the remains of the parlour, a task which necessitated the end of use of the path that crossed the site of the chapter house and parlour. As the chapter house excavations suggested, much of his concern was to establish a monastic plan and his technique was to follow the wall with a narrow trench (Brakspear 1931, 1933, 1937, Brakspear papers). His work provides a suitable end to this survey for it both produced the last significant features in the excavated area and it marked the last systematic attempt to study and write about this important site until the Department of the Environment launched the present project.

Plate 2   The surviving fragment of the west end of the Norman abbey church.

Plate 3   The later house, showing the rear panelling of the west cloister walk and the remains of the refectory.

Plate 4   The main gatehouse from inside the outer court.

Plate 5   The south transept: the Norman apse with its later replacement in the foreground.

Plate 6   The chapter house from the east.

Plate 7   The wall of the infirmary (building Z) looking south, also showing post-medieval structures and the late
           medieval drains.

Plate 8   The dormitory range from the south-east.

Plate 9   The interior of the dormitory from the north.

Plate 10 The dormitory: window moulding, and evidence for glazing and shuttering.

Plate 12 The novices' quarters: the torn off shaft.

Plate 11 The novices' quarters from the south-west.

Plate 13   The reredorter: excavations from the east.

Plate 14   The reredorter: the hearth and doorway from the south-east.

Plate 15   The reredorter: the footings of its walls overlying those of the dormitory.

Plate 16   The reredorter: the footings, wall and make-up at the north end of RI.

Plate 17   The porch and the adjacent area from the south, with the dark band of the robbed-out drain.

Plate 18   Trenches M and F from the east: the two sets of overlying drains.

Plate 19   Rain-water hopper, RIV F227.

Plate 20   The area east of the parlour from the north-east, showing drains and later structures.

Plate 21   Coping stones, lead and other building debris from the Dissolution (RIII).

Plate 22   Blocking of reredorter doorway overlying Dissolution debris.

Plate 23   Battle Abbey in the early eighteenth century (E.S.R.O. BAT. 4421 f.12)

Plate 24   The dormitory range from the east (1783) by Grimm (B.L. Add. Mss. 5670 no 79)

Plate 25   The blocking of the easternmost arch of the reredorter arcade, viewed from inside,

Chapter III

The Phasing and the Finds: an Introduction

For the purpose of analysis, the archaeology of this area has been divided up into five main periods which themselves have been sub-divided into phases. The pivots of this framework are provided by two episodes that both transformed the whole of the area under excavation. The first of these was the construction of the great new eastern range in the thirteenth century, itself only part of the wider rebuilding of the abbey during this century (period B). The second was the Dissolution of the monastery in 1538 (the start of period D). Period A represents the several constructional phases which precede the great rebuilding. Period C also includes several different programmes of work, all of which post-date the thirteenth-century rebuilding but pre-date the Dissolution. Period D begins with the latter event, but its end is less clear-cut. In some areas there are layers clearly associated with the Dissolution (as in D20–22) but elsewhere there was no such layer, or if there had been, it was later removed. Period D has therefore been given a longer span and represents both the Dissolution and the subsequent period of occupation. Later, in the late seventeenth or early eighteenth century, further demolition occurred in both the chapter house and reredorter areas. These have been taken as the start of period E. The latter was taken up to the beginning of the excavations. The excavations in the floor of the dormitory have also been phased. They have not been incorporated into the main sequence but have been grouped together with the prefix 'F'. Within the periods, the layers have been divided both according to the different building phases and according to their geographical location.

Such an analysis has had, as always, its own problems. The excavation report has already drawn attention to the general absence of clear floor and courtyard levels and the general absence in the chapter house area of medieval build-up and of any extensive stratigraphy. The phasing was compiled on the basis of the stratigraphic relations and was tested against and modified by the dating evidence of coins, pottery and clay pipes. It was finalised in April 1981 and was immediately used for the quantitative analysis of the ceramic material. The remodelling of the chapter house has been left as phase B9 although subsequent analysis of its architectural material showed it to be the earliest of the period B building works. This has enabled the retention of the same numbering scheme in the published report as in the mass of archival analysis.

The phasing is summarised below. Some phases

are represented by structural changes rather than by any finds. References to the discussion of the dating of the main monastic phases have been given; readers using the finds reports may thus readily refer to the range and security of the dating ascribed to a particular phase.

Summary of the Phasing

Pre-monastic

Period A: The Norman Abbey before the thirteenth-century rebuilding.

    A1   the church (late eleventh century, p. 20).

    A2   the construction of the chapter house (late eleventh century, p. 23).

    A3   the chapter house graves – some contain later disturbances.

    A4   trenches H–Q in chapter house area. Build-up of terrace, construction of the 'infirmary' (Building Z), monastic cemetery, miscellaneous features (probably twelfth century, p. 24).

    A5   reredorter area – before the thirteenth century.

Period B: The great rebuilding, the monastery in the thirteenth century.

    B6   the construction of the dormitory and the porch east of the parlour (mid-thirteenth century, p. 34).

    B7   the construction of the reredorter range (dating as B6).

    B8   the fill of the rainwater ditches and the build up in RVII and RVIII (they could extend into period A and the early part of period C).

    B9   the remodelling of the chapter house (chronologically the earliest of the period B phases) (c. 1200, p. 25).

    B10 the medieval layers in RIX (they could extend into period C).

Period C: The monastery in the later Middle Ages.

    C11 reredorter area – before the construction of the drains. There was a lack of clear division between this phase and C14 and subsequent work would suggest that the two phases might more appropriately be seen as part of a single one.

C12 the construction of the drainage system in the chapter house area (early fifteenth century, p. 37).

C13 the construction of the drainage system in RVII and RVIII (dating as C12).

C14 the construction of the drainage system in the reredorter area RI–RVI (dating as C12).

C15 levelled destruction of infirmary and the construction of its replacement, Building Y. This may have belonged in period B (see p. 35).

C16 the construction of Building X to the north-east of the chapter house (late fifteenth or early sixteenth century possibly 1518, p. 39).

C17 the rebuilding of the chapel in the south transept (early sixteenth century, p. 39).

C18 the addition of a cross wall in the reredorter sub-vault.

C19 the remodelled entrance arrangements at the west end of the reredorter.

Period D: The monastic buildings after the Dissolution, the sixteenth and seventeenth centuries.

D20 the Dissolution debris inside the chapter house.

D21 the Dissolution debris outside the reredorter.

D22 the upper Dissolution level to the north of the reredorter, containing the main rubbish dump and the upper tile layer.

D23 the chapter house interior: the build-up to the early nineteenth-century clay yard. The main layer of a fine dark loam was D23a and continued accumulating until the early part of the century. D23b represented subsequent dumping of material.

D24 to the east of the chapter house: soil build up prior to the destruction of Building X (this contains the fragmentary Dissolution debris).

D25 trenches H–Q: the Dissolution and the first phase of stone footings.

D26 trenches H–Q: the first rebuilding of the D25 range.

D27 trenches H–Q: the second rebuilding of this range (subsequently destroyed in E35).

D28 trenches N, P, G: during the sixteenth and seventeenth centuries (subsequently this area becomes part of E35).

D29 trenches RVII and RVIII (extending into parts of period E).

D30 the reredorter drain: primary fill.

D31 occupation of interior of reredorter undercroft.

D32 alterations at east end of reredorter undercroft.

D33 occupation and decay at east end of reredorter undercroft.

D34 post-medieval building to east of reredorter range.

Period E: The second phase of destruction and afterwards, the eighteenth century to the start of the excavations.

E35 the destruction of the Building X and the build-up of soil in the chapter house area (excluding the area within the chapter house walls) (i.e. trenches E to Q).

E36 the destruction of the reredorter.

E37 the stable phase in the reredorter area RIX and RI – III.

E38 the decay of the dormitory in trenches RVII and RVIII.

E39 the final destruction in the reredorter area. The destruction of the stables and the early nineteenth century accumulation.

E40 the clay yard in the chapter house area – the early nineteenth century.

E41 the chapter house area: after the clay yard.

E42 the chapter house area: nineteenth-century paths and gardens.

E43 nineteenth-century paths in RVII and RVIII.

E44 the nineteenth-century gardens and the pergola in RIX.

E45 the chapter house area: Brakspear's excavations and consolidation.

E46 the reredorter area: Brakspear's consolidation.

E47 modern, nineteenth and twentieth century – all other layers not included in phases E39–E46.

Period F: The excavations in the dormitory floor, thirteenth to twentieth centuries.

F48 loose mortar with rubble, sealed by clay surface.

F49 post-Dissolution rubble build up.

F50 early nineteenth-century stables.

F51 Brakspear repairs: mortar rendering and concrete raft.

The Finds

The excavations produced an unexpectedly large and important collection and sequence of finds. These quantities have themselves produced problems of selection and publication. The following chapters deal with different aspects of this material. At the same time the authors have had the opportunity to assess the finds in the context of other material from Battle and that from other sites.

The main importance of the finds from the excavations is essentially threefold. They provided information about some of the destroyed monastic buildings of Battle and of their fittings, through the architectural fragments and mouldings, the painted window glass, the floor tiles and the roofing materials. They provide a valuable addition to the grisaille glass and decorated floor tiles known from this area, as well as more important and problematical fragments of window glass design, and early types of brick and roof tile. Much of the architectural material came from the dormitory range, but some came from the destroyed chapter house and others from the lost twelfth-century cloisters and some from unknown twelfth-century buildings. Secondly, the excavations also produced an important sequence of pottery dating from the eleventh to the nineteenth century, including several phases that possess dating independent of the pottery itself. They are thus able to help clarify the date range of particular pottery types and the sequence should prove of considerable importance for the study of material from other sites in this area. Both the pottery and the ceramic tiles provided extensive and stratified sequences of material that warranted the application of methods of fabric analysis, as a step towards a greater understanding of the patterns of production and marketing. Finally, the excavation of a rich rubbish dump of Dissolution date provided a wide range of material associated with books and writing, music, clothing, medicine and alchemy, and the furnishing of buildings, as well as fragments of medieval art, a substantial group of coins and jettons, pots, bones and building debris. The study of this material has raised questions about, for example, the dating of early sixteenth-century jettons and the typology of urinals, while the coin evidence provides a cautionary warning about the dating of material found in Dissolution contexts. Such a rubbish dump has provided an idea of the range of items present here at the time of the Dissolution, but like much of the excavated material, it has a significance that is much wider than the confines of Battle Abbey itself.

The finds are now in the possession of the Historic Buildings and Monuments' Commission and the excavation records will also be deposited with the Commission. Some of the excavated material will go on display at the proposed site museum. It is anticipated that the architectural material will remain at Battle in the site stone store, that the bone, metal and medieval glass objects and fragments will remain with the Ancient Monuments Laboratory, and that the remaining finds will go to the A.M. archaeological store at Dover Castle, and that copies of the site records will be deposited with the National Monuments' Record.

Those finds that have been dealt with by the A.M. Laboratory have been referred to by the Laboratory's own numbers. The architectural material is referred to by the excavation's cut stone (C.S.) sequence.

Chapter IV

The Building Stone

The surviving monastic buildings were almost exclusively constructed of the local Wealden sandstone. The latter also provided the vast bulk of the worked stone found during the excavations. The abbey lies on the Hastings Beds of the Wealden (Lower Cretacious) series in an area of alternating sandstones and clays and from early days the monks had a local quarry. The chronicler writing about the early difficulties of the monastery recorded that with the aid of a vision a large source of good stone was found not far from the boundary that had been laid out for the church (*Chronicle*, 44). A quarry figures in rentals of the early twelfth century, 1367 and 1433 (*Chronicle*, 64 & 44 note), and in references in the cellarers' accounts in 1386 and 1439 (*Cellarers' Accounts*, 82 & 121). It seems to have lain immediately east of the abbey precinct and behind the street properties (PRO/E315/56 ff. 10r. & 16r.; *Chronicle*, 44, footnote). Throughout the period of the abbey's existence this sandstone was the main building material forming the basis for the Norman nave of the church, the thirteenth-century rebuilding and subsequent work, as in the gate tower itself and the adjacent range to its east. Many of the walls were built with roughly hewn blocks but stone could be worked into a fine ashlar form for architectural features such as the doorways, windows and mouldings.

In view of the known and continued use of the sandstone and the large mass of this stone that was excavated, no further analysis was done. Foreign stones, however, were kept and recorded and a sample series submitted for examination and identification by the late *F.W. Anderson*. The use of such stones was analysed by phases, although it should be pointed out that the archaeological evidence was usually of the material's discarding rather than of its use, so that most of it came from Dissolution and later layers. The evidence of the archaeological finds should therefore be supplemented by the study of the standing buildings, the dating evidence provided by the design of the cut stone, and by documentary evidence in order to establish a reasonably full picture of when particular materials were used. Given its position near the coast, the abbey was able to import stone from considerable distances.

The apparent absence of any good-quality local building stone had been an argument offered by the monks in support of their wish to have an alternative site for the abbey and, according to the monastic tradition, William the Conqueror had already brought stone from Caen to Battle, before the monks had found a local source (*Chronicle*, 44). There seems little reason to doubt this tradition. Battle thus provides an early example of the use of Caen stone in England, for we lack clear evidence of its use in pre-conquest England (Jope 1964, 112). It was also used elsewhere in the late eleventh century in those areas where the lack of a local source of good quality stone was combined with good communications, as in London, at Old St. Paul's cathedral and the Tower of London, and it was increasingly used in the twelfth century (Clifton Taylor 1972, 23 note; Jope 1964, 112). At Battle the destruction of virtually the whole of the Norman church has prevented us assessing the scale of its use, while its virtual absence from the excavated Norman layers need not be significant in view of the very small scale of such areas. But a few fragments of Norman work cut out of this stone have been found. Caen stone was also extensively used for the mouldings of the remodelled Chapter House and chips of it were found in the walls of this building. Later, it was used in select positions in the new dormitory buildings, such as in the main doorways and in the carved heads. The use of this material was characteristic of other buildings of importance with good sea communications in the thirteenth century, as at Beaulieu, Winchester, Westminster and Norwich (Brakspear and St John Hope 1906, 180; Brown, Colvin and Taylor 1972, 858 & 138: Salzman 1952, 135). Most of the excavated Caen stone came from the Dissolution and immediately post-Dissolution phases and from the secondary phase of destruction (E35). The term 'Caen stone' has been used to include similar limestone from Calvados.

The marble used at Battle was of two main types: Purbeck and similar beds and the more shelly Sussex marble. It is not known where the latter was brought from, although it was found locally and it still outcrops nearby in the river Asten (G.A. Elliott pers com). Both types first occur in the excavations in significant numbers in the Dissolution layers. They probably first appear on the site, however, during the construction by abbot Walter de Luci of a new cloister 'with pavement and columns of marble, polished and smooth' (*Chronicle*, 263). This was completed by the time of his death in 1171. A substantial amount of marble survives from this period, although not all from the excavations, but nothing earlier has been found in this material. The fragments which came from the cloister suggests that de Luci's work used Sussex, Purbeck and possibly

Midhurst marble, so that Battle provides an early example of the use of such materials (see also Chapter V, p. 69). The thirteenth-century rebuilding also showed the use of Purbeck marble for some of the main columns and probably for the smaller shafts, and Sussex marble, which was used for bases of the wall arcades, for the transoms of the dormitory windows and in the novices' room for parts of the plate tracery. Battle during this period thus shows the very fashionable use of marble (Drury 1948, 79–80; Salzman 1967, 134). Neither marble seems to have been used in the later refectory or in any subsequent extant building.

Of the other stone types, Greensand was used in some of the later monastic building works, although not on a large scale. It was used in the later thirteenth-century refectory, as reflected in the extant jamb of one of its windows and in the fragments of window tracery, that probably derived from Brakspear's excavations there. The main structure of this building, however, would seem to have been in the local sandstone. Greensand was also used in the later fourteenth-century doorway that was incorporated in the crosswall within the reredorter undercroft, while it would have been stone of this type that was bought from Bourne (Eastbourne) in 1518 for use in the Sacrist's new building (Sacrist's account). But its use in the monastic periods does not seem to have been extensive, and the later monastic buildings still relied on the local sandstone. This limited use was reflected in the excavations, where only two fragments of greensand were found in the Dissolution debris. Most of the examples in the excavated area came from eighteenth- and nineteenth-century contexts. This would seem to reinforce the evidence of the standing buildings which suggest that it was mainly used after the Dissolution, as in the later Court House. A few fragments of red sandstone could be burnt greensand as this was once in great demand for hearths and fireplaces.

Fragments of Purbeck (upper Jurassic) limestone were also found and these may have come from the small inliers of these rocks found to the north of Battle. This material was in use here before the Dissolution, but evidently not on a substantial scale. Two blocks of Portland stone came from contexts of the late eighteenth century or later.

Flint was not a local material and was not used as a building stone, although it was found in thirty different contexts. Most of these flints had been dug directly from the chalk, and most showed signs of burning. They were found in all periods and were probably the offshoots of lime burning. Lime was produced both on site and elsewhere (Salzman 1967, 150) and this may have been the case at Battle. Thus in 1374 some lime was bought from the abbot of Robertsbridge while the abbey also spent money making a lime kiln for itself (Cellarers' Accounts, 70). The finds of chalk probably also represent the by-product of lime production. The largest group came from B7, the phase associated with the construction of the reredorter, and there was a lesser concentration in C14, the phase associated with the

construction of the rainwater drains and with building work elsewhere.

A fragment of brecciated marble, possibly imported from Italy, came from a modern context (E47) and a fragment of graphite came from a late sixteenth- or seventeenth-century context (D26).

Roof Slates

The roof slates were sorted visually into a series of slate types and a sample of each group was later examined and identified by *Professor J.W. Murray* and *Dr E.B. Selwood* of the University of Exeter. Compared with the masses of red clay tile the blue slates were small in quantity, but enough survived to enable useful conclusions to be drawn. They fell into two distinct groups both as far as the source and their archaeological dating were concerned: the earlier Devon slates and the much later Welsh and Lake District ones.

Most of the slates from Devon came from the medieval and the Dissolution phases and therefore represent the remnants of medieval use. Four geological types were represented, all of which came from South Devon deposits: Norden, Kate Brook and Gurrington slates and an unspecified type from this area (Selwood and Durrance, 1982, 15–29). Norden was the most common slate followed in turn by the unspecified, Kate Brook and Gurrington types. All of them were found in every period of deposition except for the Gurrington slate which was not found in period A and only a small fragment in period E. There was relatively little slate from period A, but enough survived from this and from the build-up associated with the construction of the reredorter to suggest that it was being used on part of the monastic buildings before the great rebuilding of the first half of the thirteenth century. Battle thus reinforces the documentary evidence of a wide ranging slate industry in Devon in the late twelfth century as seen in the large-scale royal purchases for building work at Winchester, Portchester and Southampton (Jope and Dunning 1954, 215 and 217). The make-up required to the north of the reredorter for the later medieval drainage system (C11 and C14) provided a much more plentiful source of slate and suggests that somewhere a slate roof was being destroyed or replaced. The largest groups of slate came from the Dissolution phases and the quantity (particularly in D21) would suggest that they had remained in use somewhere on the monastic site despite the apparent dominance of clay tiles in our archaeological record. Most of the slates in period D came from phases which were either wholly or partially Dissolution in date and this would suggest that such roof slates were not used after the monastic phase and that those in later contexts are residual. This use of roofing slates, particularly those from south Devon, was part of a much wider use of this material in south Sussex, around the ports and up the river valleys that led from them (Holden 1965, 68–9; Murray 1965, 79–82). At Battle they were used before the thirteenth century, but it is not clear when they ceased to be used for wholesale roofing. Later clay tiles became common as seen in the backs of the thirteenth-century fireplaces, in the documentary references to the tile kiln, and in the late medieval and Dissolution layers (Chapter VI). If the twelfth-century cloisters were roofed with slate, it might account for the coincidence between the greater frequency of slate finds and the known destruction of portions of the cloister in phases B7, C14 and at the Dissolution. That slates were still needed somewhere in 1370 is suggested by the purchase then of slates and tiles (*Cellarers' Account*, 60).

The slates from North Wales and the Lake District provide a very different picture. As would be expected, bearing in mind the cost of transport, they were not to be found in medieval contexts. One type of Lake District slate occurs in period D but either in contexts which may run well into the eighteenth century or were merely tiny fragments in late layers. None of these groups come from deposits in period D or E that need to be earlier than the end of the eighteenth century, when slates were becoming popular in the south-east as in London (Summerson 1945, 65). The bulk of material post-dates the conversion of the dormitory into a stable block, its new roof and the destruction of the latter. The addition of the new roof for the stable was not before the last few years of the eighteenth century, while its roof was removed to provide material for the new stables in 1819 (*supra* p. 46). The Duchess of Cleveland confirms that the conversion of the dormitory involved the addition of a slate roof and that this was taken down immediately afterwards to provide for the new stables.

There were also a few fragments of limestone slates of uppermost Jurassic 'Purbeckian' age either from the Isle of Purbeck or from the central Weald. None of this came from an uncontaminated medieval context. Most of it came from Dissolution contexts and particularly from the chapter house area. One large slab of slightly calcareous sandstone was probably a roofing slab and could be of Horsham stone. It came from a modern context (E38).

Acknowledgement

I am extremely grateful to the late F.W. Anderson for identifying the stone samples, to Professor J.W. Murray and Dr E.B. Selwood for doing the same with the slate, to G.A. Elliott for his help with the local stone and those used in the standing buildings, to M. Pitts for examining the flint, to A.D.F. Streeten for organizing the analysis of the stone types, and to E.W. Holden for his comments.

Chapter V

Architectural Material

by R. Halsey and J.N. Hare

The large quantity of architectural material that was found during the excavations has posed serious problems of selection. Altogether there were 643 numbered fragments. The Romanesque material had ultimately derived from period A, and consisted of isolated finds from later contexts including several fragments of the late twelfth-century marble cloisters. All the material that can be ascribed to this period has been mentioned or illustrated and discussed (section II). Most of the material, however, derived from the great rebuilding of period B: from the remodelling of the chapter house and more particularly from the reredorter and dormitory ranges. Individually few of the fragments from this period warrant attention, but collectively they can shed light on the buildings that have disappeared. The material was therefore sorted and the results analysed (sections III and IV). In addition to the material from the excavations, some details from the dormitory itself have been recorded before they are further damaged by weathering. The excavations produced few fragments of architectural material that were clearly later than the thirteenth century, and by themselves they did not seem to be of sufficient interest to warrant further study.

Sections I and II were the responsibility of R.H. and sections III and IV that of J.N.H. The exact line of division was by no means so clear cut.

I Synopsis

A few fragments of early Romanesque architectural material were found, namely an impost block or abacus with a quirked chamfer profile, two incomplete blocks of simple twelfth-century chevron, a segment of respond (or possibly a rib) with a triple roll profile (the damaged centre roll being larger than the others), and a cushion capital.

The majority of the illustrated architectural fragments were executed in local Sussex or Purbeck 'marbles' (really polished limestone) and from their style, size and material can fairly certainly be identified with the work of Abbot Walter de Luci, who, according to the Battle Chronicle rebuilt the cloister, 'with pavement and columns of marble, polished and smooth. When that was completed, he had plans to construct a place to wash, of the same material and workmanship, and had hired the artisans. He was outdone by death, but though he could not complete it, he earmarked money for its completion.' (*Chronicle*, 263). His death on 21 June, 1171 (*Chronicle*, 267) was thus in the middle of the building season.

No Romanesque cloister survives in England, but a short piece of the east arcade of the Infirmary Cloister at Canterbury Cathedral (Christ Church Priory) gives some idea of the lavish decoration that was given to such arcades in the late twelfth century. Although the date of this Canterbury work is not known, the stylistic features indicate at least two twelfth-century phases. Elsewhere, double bases and capitals survive on many monastic sites to prove the popularity of this sort of work.

Examples of small marble arcades are much less common, but fragments can be seen at Lewes, Winchester Cathedral and Wolvesey Palace, St Nicholas' Priory at Exeter, Glastonbury, Canterbury and Faversham to demonstrate the use of coloured polished stone for prestigious work (though the original location is rarely certain). The use of such materials in small-scale architectural contexts would seem to develop from church furnishings, tombs and especially shrines, which had long been made of marble or marble substitutes. Initially, architectural pieces, including fonts, were imported from Tournai in southern Belgium. However, local English substitutes were quickly exploited, probably because of the cost of importing foreign stone, but perhaps also because the English stones with their variegated surfaces and colours were more appealing and closer to real marble than the bland Tournai. The early dependence of English craftsmen on Tournai designs has been clearly demonstrated by Martin Biddle in his finds from Wolvesey Palace, Winchester, where the switch is from Tournai to Purbeck (Biddle 1965, 260). Battle would appear to belong to the next generation, for no Tournai pieces that could act as prototypes, have been found here. In the small sample of Purbeck and Sussex marble pieces excavated no stylistic progression can be seen, thus suggesting that they were used together.

The reference to the building of a *lavatorium* in the Chronicle is most interesting in relation to the discovery in 1915 of twinned marble capitals at the Battle dependency, St Nicholas' Priory, Exeter (Brakspear 1916). The Battle Chronicle suggests that such a free-standing structure was planned and indeed, Brakspear searched for it but found nothing 'except some very indefinite foundations' (1937, 103). The Exeter capitals are of different proportions and are more finely finished than the few at Battle. Although the same broad leaf decoration is used (as in most mid-twelfth century marble capitals) there is only a general resemblance between the two groups. St Nicholas' Priory was swept by fire at about this time; the Chronicle does not give a date, but implies that it was during Walter de Luci's period as abbot (1139–71) (*Chronicle*, 258). It is possible that this was during the fire at Exeter recorded in the Annals of Winchester for the year 1161 (*Annales Monastici*, II, 56). Stylistically the Exeter capitals may be dated to the 1160's or 1170's. The sample from each site is too small to suggest a common workshop or source. The awkwardly shaped cluster capital (No 1) may be from the entrance to this *lavatorium* or from somewhere inside it. Further details of English *lavatoria* have been provided by Hope and Fowler (1903, 437–42).

That marble quarrying and carving was a highly specialist trade can be readily assumed from a comparison of surviving examples all over the south of England, (as well as the documentary references that indicate a higher remuneration). There is a remarkable similarity in capital types, perhaps in part dictated by the material and these pieces at Battle (along with two complete pairs of capitals that probably come from Brakspear's excavations in the outer court – appendix A) can be readily paralleled with approximately contemporary work at Winchester and the Temple church in London. Looking at the double base in Purbeck marble amongst Brakspear's finds (plate 27), the striated leaf spur is identical to work in Tournai and Purbeck at Wolvesey Palace, in the Winchester Cathedral triforium collection and to Tournai work at Lewes. The ultimate source of the capital designs is in northern France, for instance in the upper stage of the narthex at St Denis c. 1140; it is not just the Cistercians who introduced the 'waterleaf' capital to this country.

Although it has been strongly argued for some time now, that the architectural use of marble was just one of the innovations William of Sens introduced to England from the Ile-de-France, it is very difficult to find coloured marble used architecturally in France, apart from in Tournai itself, Battle is surely a clearly documented example of the English fashion for coloured architectural marble being popular here long before the re-building of Canterbury choir after the 1174 fire.

The few pieces of sandstone (particularly Nos 9 & 11) and Caen limestone, along with the keeled mouldings of the chapter house, indicate work of some quality being executed in the last decades of the twelfth century, that can be matched stylistically with work in other major local centres – like Chichester Cathedral (retrochoir after the fire of 1187); New Shoreham (St Mary de Haura) and Boxgrove Priory. All these centres were active in the c. 1180 – c. 1220 period, their work owing a general debt to Canterbury choir, though with other French early Gothic features being absorbed too. The florid stiff-leaf capitals of the dormitory stair doorway can be seen in the context of Chichester retrochoir work and the single, simple Caen stone fragment no. 12 may be more directly dependant on Canterbury work. In the dormitory building, the mixed use of marble and ashlar, the round, deeply moulded abaci over deep capitals and water-holding bases can all be seen in these other Sussex 'great' churches and, indeed, one would expect Battle Abbey to be within

this purlieu, just as the marble cloister appears to be paralleled in abbeys in the south of England, c. 1165.

II Catalogue
(Figures 12–16)

The illustrated items are referred to by the number of the illustration. The excavation cut stone number (C.S.) and the phase number of the layer in which it was found are given at the end of each entry.

1. Cluster pier capital, Purbeck marble, *c.* 1170. The most sophisticated piece so far found, both in form and function. There are clearly four seatings for shafts, with the damaged remains of a capital to indicate a fifth. The irregular shape rules out the possibility of a cloister corner support but could well indicate a door jamb location. There are clearly two sets of two capitals at roughly a 45° angle, with the fifth and most damaged capital sitting further forward or backward between them. The capitals are taller and the seatings for the shafts smaller and closer together than the paired (putative) cloister arcade capitals, so a direct use within the cloister arcade seems unlikely. Could this piece have been part of the *lavatorium* that Abbot Walter de Luci left money for, either in the surrounding arcade or as a support for the central bowl?

Though badly damaged at abacus level, each capital appears to have been formed of two simple, thick flat leaves, culminating at each corner in a small, turned-down volute, similar (though not exactly parallel) to some capitals in a five-shaft capital block excavated by Martin Biddle at Wolvesey Palace (Biddle 1965, 260) and similar capital designs can also be seen in the Temple Church rotunda in London.
C.S.261 E36

2. Capital Fragment, Purbeck marble, *c.* 1170. Small fragment of Purbeck, with a smooth curved face shaped like the base of a simple leaf capital near the necking. It may well be part of (1), which it resembles in scale and style.
C.S.426 E36

3. Shaft with knop, Purbeck marble, *c.* 1170. Part of a small shaft of roughly 115 mm diameter, its scale demonstrated by the integral knop – originally a structural device to stabilise detached shafts. This shaft has a well carved spiral moulding, with alternating broad concave and slimmer convex mouldings, separated by quirks. The knop is roughly decorated with shallow diagonal indents, no doubt intended to be read as a spiral. This type of spiral can be seen on many 'marble' shafts of English or Tournai material and is a standard form of decoration. The inclusion of the knop is rare in this material; a decorated band of quatrefoils (not projecting beyond the shaft edge) can be seen on a similar spiral shaft at Canterbury in the Infirmary Cloister, east walk, but they look secondary and are perhaps the remains of an integral knop cut down or broken away.
C.S.589 C14

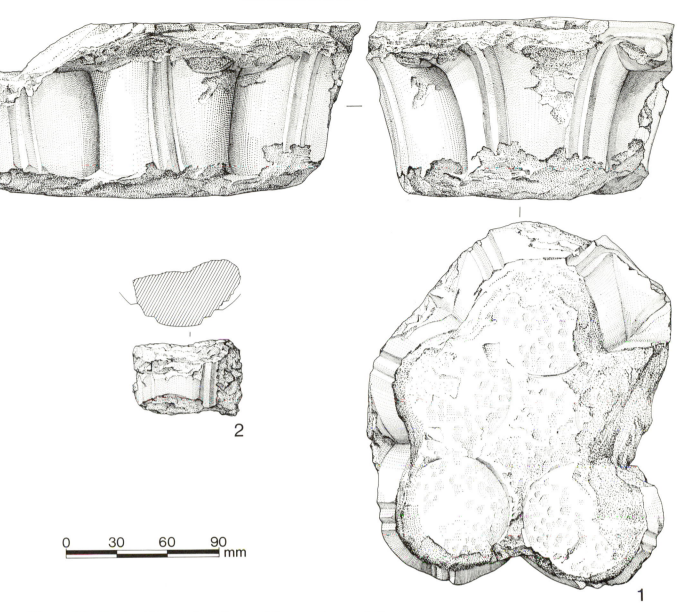

Figure 12   Battle Abbey. Architectural fragments nos 1–2.

4.   Decorated shaft fragment, Purbeck marble, c. 1170.

This piece of shaft is decorated most individually with alternating raised and hollowed irregular 'tonsil'–like shapes. It would seem from the fragment of moulding on one end that there was an integral knop as on no. 3. These two pieces do not fit together, though of very similar size and material and, indeed, with different decoration, one would not expect them to. Is this decoration evolved from a fluted shaft? or is it a peculiar variant of a raised zig-zag?
C.S.643 C14

5.   Capital, Sussex marble, c. 1170
A damaged capital of red veined Sussex marble that from its shape would appear to have been one of a group of three or four capitals joined only at abacus level. If from the cloister arcade, then a doorway or a corner location can be surmised. The simple concave fluted design can be seen on other marble capitals of the second half of the twelfth century, especially on marble fonts and the font at New Shoreham, of Sussex marble, is an excellent parallel. The design may well have originated with the imported Tournai marble fonts, from c. 1140, but can be found in other locations from about the middle of the century.
C.S.104 E42

6.   Capital, Sussex marble, c. 1170.
The classic waterleaf design, with thick-rimmed leaves curling to the top corners, finishing in large, flat reversed volutes, with a raised disc in the centre of the capital between the separating leaves. The square abaci and thick, chamfered necking remain intact, the latter with a slightly flat edge that with the broken fourth side clearly indicates it to be one of a pair. Indeed, there is a pair of capitals of very similar design, in Sussex marble, to be seen on the site,

Figure 13   Battle Abbey. Architectural fragments nos 3–8 (⅓)

perhaps less accomplished and joined at upper capital and abacus level and not at the necking. Such a paired capital also exists at Exeter St Nicholas' Priory, with a similar design in Purbeck marble. However, it has a slightly curved abacus that Sir Harold Brakspear interpreted as coming from a circular *lavatorium* arcade. None of the finds from Battle have curved abaci.
C.S.594 D21

7. Coupled shaft, Purbeck marble, *c.* 1170
Despite the surface of this piece being heavily hacked (and so the overall size significantly reduced?) this coupled shaft would not appear to be capable of any major structural purpose. It would also appear to be unsuitable for supporting the sort of capital found in the excavations – although of approximately the same width as the capital necking diameter. Could there have been two detached shafts of another material placed either side, so making a quatrefoil support like no 8? Such a form would certainly help to explain the otherwise overlarge gap between the shafts.
C.S.600 C14

8. Quatrefoil shaft, Sussex marble, *c.* 1170
A short length of shaft, quatrefoil in section but probably big enough to support one of the excavated capitals with a 'diameter' of *c.* 115 mm at the necking. Shaped shafts are not common in England (though they may well have been) as spirals and fluting motifs seem to have been most favoured. However, it would not be surprising to find this motif in a decorated small arcade, as a variant on spiralling.
C.S.598 C14

9. Capital, sandstone, *c.* 1160–80
Two-thirds of a small, rectangular capital, that from its straight, but uncarved back indicates a wall-arcade location. The long (front) side is decorated with three plain leaves that taper to the (missing) necking and turn over beneath the squared abacus, ending in ovoid, plain knobs. The two outer knobs form corner 'volutes' with the leaves returning onto the short sides. The short sides then have a further half-leaf, terminating in another ovoid knob that must have touched the backing wall.
  Although this is not a very highly finished capital, its shape and the use of indeterminate knobs on plain leaves indicates a date nearer the mid-twelfth century than the marble capitals, though this simplicity could be attributable to a minor location in the abbey. A knob derived from a similar capital was also found.
C.S.500 D30

10. Volute fragment, sandstone
A rather battered volute, broken off from a large capital, possibly of the same size as no. 11. It may well be of the same date too, despite being of a more classical inspiration. However, there is the chance that it could belong to the late eleventh century; the

extensive damage makes a positive identification difficult.
C.S.1 E42

11. Volute fragment, sandstone, *c.* 1160–80
Although only a fragment, this well carved volute is clearly of a pre-stiff leaf date, yet by its sophistication, cannot be much earlier than *c.* 1160. The nearest parallel would be the volutes of the capitals in William of Sens' choir at Canterbury of 1174–9 – or possibly the slightly earlier St Augustine's Abbey, Canterbury choir. More intriguing is the scale and the fact that the volute jutted out from an abacus for almost all its present length. The capital it came from, then, must have been of some size (perhaps about 0.6 m. square) and so is not part of a cloister arcade.
C.S.471 C14

III The Chapter House Material
Although no architectural detail survived *in situ* in the remodelled chapter house, a group of fragments can shed light on the architectural character of this work. Of the Caen stone mouldings in the chapter house area, the largest group was characterised by the use of keel mouldings (type I). Twenty-seven pieces of this moulding were found. These came from within the chapter house itself and in the trenches immediately around and were significantly absent from the southern part of the whole chapter house area, although this was to produce other types of moulding. While these mouldings were scattered through several phases from the Dissolution onwards, over a third of them came from the period immediately or shortly after this cataclysmic event. Such mouldings are not found on any of the standing remains of the abbey. Significantly their only other notable location is in a pile of architectural fragments that seems to have come from Brakspear's excavations in the outer court and from the Dissolution build-up in front of Browne's new range, where the debris of the chapter house could have been added to that of the Church. Taken together, these points suggest that the keel mouldings came from the chapter house itself, from the enrichment of wall arcading, windows and doorways. Two examples have been illustrated: a fragment of a single moulding (no 14) and part of an arch or window moulding (no 13). Although it comes from debris in the reredorter area, the latter closely parallels the less complete fragments in the chapter house area. With its main keel moulding, the shape of the minor mouldings and the deeply cut hollows, it is very similar to those in the presbytery at Chichester and in the tower at Boxgrove (see the drawings in Sharp 1861, 11 and 12). Fortunately the fragment of capital (no 12) came from a demolition context that was clearly associated with the chapter house itself.

12. Fragment of capital, limestone, late twelfth century
The right-hand corner of a small, squared capital with two sprigs of stiff-leaf foliage meeting beyond the angle of the abacus, having a recessed 'spine' and

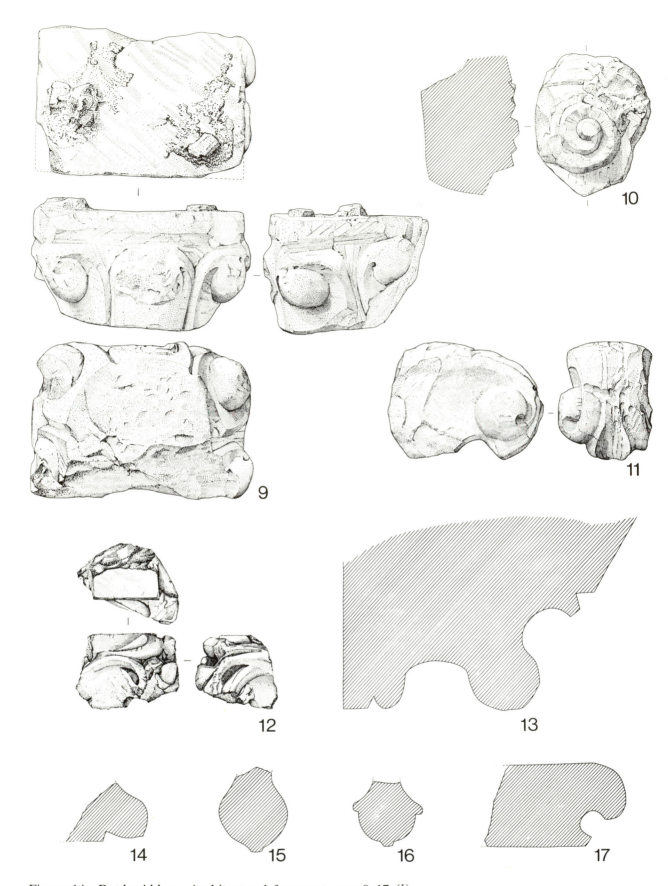

Figure 14   Battle Abbey. Architectural fragments nos 9–17 ($\frac{1}{3}$)

possibly enclosing berries. This type of stiff-leaf capital was extensively used in the rebuilding of Canterbury Cathedral choir after the 1174 fire and with the square abacus, would not be expected in first-class architecture much after 1200. It is certainly earlier in leaf style than the dormitory door capital.
C.S.395 D20

13. Moulding from arch or large window opening. This has a very slight vertical curvature.
C.S.140 D30

14. Type I moulding. Caen stone.
C.S.584 D24

IV The Dormitory Range and Reredorter
The chapter house area had two other types of small mouldings in Caen stone. Both types had much closer affinities to the details on the standing dormitory range and both were concentrated in the southern part of the excavations, at the end furthest from the chapter house. Type II (no 15) consisted of a roll moulding with a single fillet. A group of this type was found associated with the destruction of building Y (and possibly also of the parlour).

Type III, with its central fillet and rounded wing fillets (no 16) produced only six examples, most of which came from the area east of the parlour. Two examples came from the make-up in the reredorter area associated with the construction of the rainwater drains in the early fifteenth century (C11/14) suggesting that a doorway had been altered in connection with the construction of the new drainage system. This moulding is a form that seems to reach England from France in Henry III's work at Westminster Abbey (1246–1259) and then spread from there. At Battle it is found *in situ* on the main entrance to the dormitory and on the doorways of the parlour, and thus should contribute to any discussion about the dating of this northern part of the dormitory (*supra* p. 34 I am grateful to Dr. C. Wilson for commenting on this moulding, see also R.C.H.M. Westminster, 95).

Both types II and III show clear similarities to details in the dormitory range and were probably derived in part from it. Unfortunately, it is not clear as to when the parlour and its fine details were destroyed, the evidence having been removed by the earlier work of the Duchess of Cleveland and Brakspear. The group of fillet mouldings to the west of Building Y may have come from the parlour but in view of their position, and the surrounding debris the former building would provide a likely source.

Type IV (No 17) provided the largest single group. This moulding was always cut in sandstone rather than Caen stone. It consists of a slightly beaked and heavily undercut roll moulding. Extant examples may be seen in situ in the interior mouldings of the dormitory windows, and on a smaller scale in the moulded capitals of these window arches (see nos 22–3). Some of the excavated examples seem to have derived from a string course: this is no longer extant but may be illustrated on Grimm's drawing (B.L. Add. Mss. 5670 no. 80).

15. Type II moulding. Caen stone.
C.S.141 D23

16. Type III moulding. Caen stone.
C.S. 386 E35

17. Type IV moulding. Sandstone.
C.S.368 E39

Most of the architectural materials in this area consisted of such fine mouldings. Four fragments of stone chimney were also discovered. This was of similar diameter to one from the reredorter with a chimney column of about 0.65 m in diameter and approximately 70 mm width. Unlike that in the reredorter, it had been heavily discoloured by heat. Since there is no indication of any chimney close to this in the dormitory range, it may have come from building Y. Unfortunately since it comes from just below the Duchess of Cleveland's clearance work it cannot be convincingly tied to the main layer of destruction. There was also the marble abacus from a capital (no 18).

18. Round abacus, Purbeck marble, early thirteenth century.
A 'disc' of Purbeck marble with a flat side, that is most likely the top moulding of an abacus of a Purbeck capital, similar to those still existing in situ in the east range undercroft. The flat side indicates either a paired capital or attachment to a wall or door jamb. As the edge of the flat side is smooth and certainly not broken, it would seem that the second alternative, a capital against a wall or jamb is most probable.
C.S.377 E35

Within the dormitory itself the capitals were of an identical moulded form with water holding bases although by contrast to the parlour, the bases were of sandstone (nos. 22–3). Many of these have been severely damaged or destroyed since the Dissolution. The main doorway contained much more elaborate workmanship with more detailed mouldings of Caen stone and stiff leaf capitals (nos 19–21). No 24 and plate 10 show the window arrangements with a transom of Sussex marble dividing the window into an upper glazed part and a lower part that was covered with shutters.

Nos 19–21. Capital to dormitory door from main stair. Caen stone, early thirteenth century.
Damaged stiff-leaf capital with a round abacus. Although the heavily undercut leaves have in the main been broken away, the stems remain with some of the background foliage, indicating a rich design of many interlocking fronds. Capitals of this type can be seen in abundance in the retrochoir of Chichester Cathedral, rebuilt after the 1187 fire.

Nos 22–3 Moulded sandstone capital and water holding base from dormitory window.

Many architectural fragments were found among the destruction layers of the reredorter. They contrast

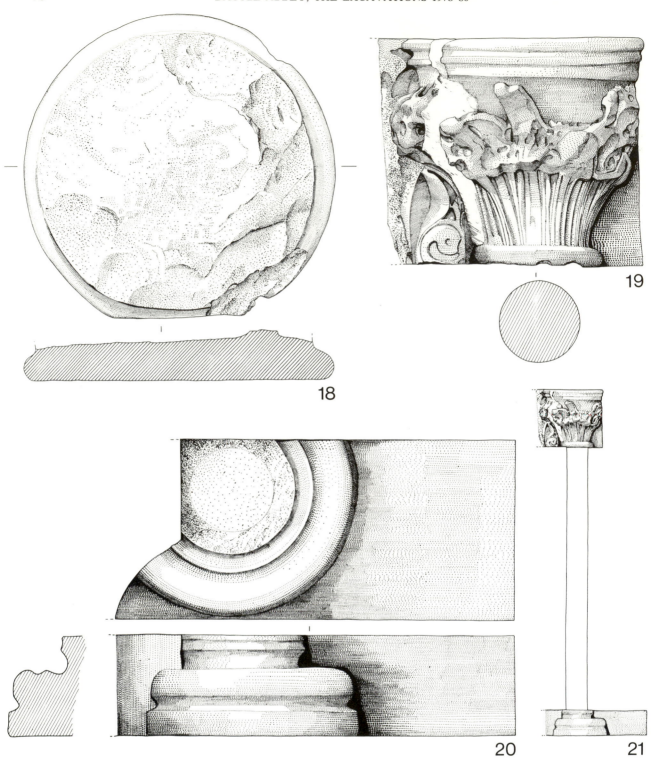

Figure 15   Battle Abbey. Architectural fragment (no. 18), and details of the main entrance to the dormitory
(nos. 19–21) ($\frac{1}{3}$)

with the fine detailed Caen stone mouldings that were found in the chapter house area and consist of simple sandstone architectural details that are paralleled by those that remain in place in the adjacent dormitory range. These excavated items do much to reinforce the evidence of the surviving undercroft walls, in showing that the reredorter block was similar in design to the dormitory range. The large quantity of the material and its distribution show that the bulk of it came from the former range, although some may have come from the dormitory itself. Most of the debris discussed here came from the main destruction phase of the reredorter building (Phase E36), although there were some fragments from most of the post-Dissolution phases in this area. Scattered throughout the length of the buildings were blocks from the vault ribs. They were identical to those still extant in the novices' quarters

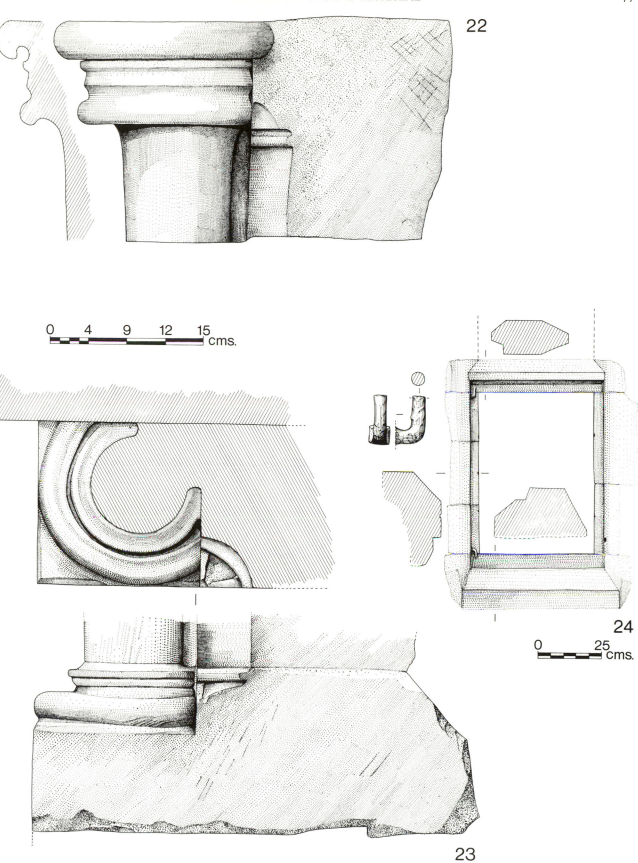

Figure 16   Battle Abbey. Details of the dormitory windows (nos. 22–24) ($\frac{1}{3}$)

and throughout the dormitory undercroft, the only decoration being provided by a hollow chamfer on either side of the rib. At the east end were two blocks cut with a single but otherwise identical hollow chamfer such as would have been needed where the vault met the walls of the building. The blocks of chamfered window jambs, with internal rebates for temporary wooden window frames, are also identical to those found in the adjacent novices' room. They suggest that some at least of the windows were fitted with temporary wooden frames although such a system did not necessarily apply to both floors of the building. Thus in the main eastern range it was not used on the first floor, in the dormitory itself. Two types of chamfered string course were found among the rubble. The most common type consisted of blocks 0.11 m. in depth with a chamfered edge on both top and bottom. Such a string course may be seen in use on the outside of the dormitory range. Two similar-sized blocks with only a single chamfered edge were also found, such as were used internally on this range, as in the slype. The much smaller sandstone roll mouldings found in the excavations, parallel the extant mouldings around the dormitory windows. Some consisted of circular attached shafts, but the largest

group, with many surviving fragments, consisted of a drip mould with slightly beaked profile (No 17). Interestingly, most of these came from Dissolution contexts and not from the later main phase of destruction.

On the north wall of the building, excavation has revealed the lower portion of a fireplace and the architectural debris provided further details of this. At least 79 fragments of the hood of the fireplace were recovered. These would point to the presence of a typical thirteenth-century hooded fireplace, as at Netley Abbey, Hants. The evidence for this is further reinforced by the remains of the fireplace in the novices' room. The fragments of the reredorter hood show that the thin ashlar skin of the hood was held together by mortar-filled grooves and by a series of iron clamps set in lead. Parts of the chimney of the fireplace were also found. The base of the chimney was square with carved scroll decoration. Half of this base survives, and these blocks mark the change from the square shaft below to the circular chimney above. A few fragments of the latter were found and show that this thin-walled stone chimney had circular air vents. Although it is not identical, the chimney from Skenfrith Castle shows some similarities (Wood 1965, 282–3).

Chapter VI

Ceramic Building Materials

by Anthony D.F. Streeten

Introduction

Systematic study of the floor tiles, roof tiles and brick yields interesting information not only about the building materials themselves but also about vanished details and embellishments of the claustral ranges. Some of these finds, however, come from later alterations to the buildings. In this report, therefore, the floor tiles are discussed first, because there is no evidence that tiled floors were laid at Battle after the Dissolution. Much of the roof tile debris is also derived from destruction of the monastic buildings, but there is some indication of post-medieval re-roofing. Most of the brick, on the other hand, dates from after the Dissolution, with the notable exception of early fragments sealed beneath the floor of the reredorter and a group used in the rebuilt drain to the east of the chapter house. Discussion of the evidence for medieval and later manufacture of ceramic building materials both at Battle, and, where relevant, elsewhere in the region, precedes detailed assessment of the individual materials.

Manufacture of Ceramic Building Materials
(Figure 17.)

Many medieval monastic establishments had their own tile kilns. Extensive and well-documented tileries were in operation on the Battle Abbey estates at Wye in Kent (VCH 1932, 392) and on a smaller scale at Alciston in Sussex (Brent 1968, 90; Letters & Papers Henry VIII, 13.1, 396), possibly from the fourteenth century. The first clear reference to a tilery at Battle Abbey itself comes in 1279 (*Cellarers' Accounts*, 46), and thereafter references to it occur intermittently in the cellarers' accounts until 1466. The tilery did not, however, always appear in the account of the same obedientiary. Thus, although there are long periods during the fourteenth and fifteenth centuries when the kiln is not mentioned in the printed cellarers' accounts, this does not necessarily imply that production was intermittent.

It is seldom clear from the documents whether, during the fourteenth century, the tilery was being run directly by the abbey for its own use, or whether, as in the later period, it was leased out. In 1307 the tiler and his boy were paid for six months, and another man was paid for helping in the tilery during the whole year (*Cellarers' Accounts*, 48). Payment for making tiles by taskwork is recorded in the account for 1351–52 (*Cellarers' Accounts*, 57) and there is an entry in 1412–13 for making 14,000 tiles,

for a 'building in the court' (*Cellarers' Accounts*, 107). The cellarer's income for 1319–20 included 26s 8d received from one 'Dom Richard of Battle from tiles sold to him' (*Cellarers' Accounts*, 49) and, while it is conceivable that these were second-hand tiles, the implication must be that the tilery was run directly by the abbey. As in the case of a fifteenth-century kiln at Mayfield (VCH Sussex 2, 1907, 252), tiles were probably made both for use on the estate and for sale outside. Supplies of clay for the kiln at Battle are mentioned in the accounts for 1440–41 and 1442–43 (*Cellarers' Accounts*, 130; 136), from which it might be inferred that tiles were being made specifically for the abbey at this period.

Some of the terminology used in the documents poses problems of interpretation. For example, it cannot be assumed uncritically that the 'kiln' is the tile kiln rather than another type of kiln. Likewise, it is not always certain whether the 'tiler' was a man who *made* tiles or a craftsman who *laid* them on a roof or even on a floor. The same man may sometimes have done both jobs, but positive evidence for the manufacture must be confined to those entries which actually refer to the tiler or to tile-making. Thus, the reference to the tiler's utensils in 1279 (*Cellarers' Accounts*, 45) is ambiguous, and the wages recorded in 1351–52 and 1369–70 (*Cellarers' Accounts*, 57; 64) could have been for building works rather than manufacture. More reliable evidence for actual tile-making does occur at about this time (*Cellarers' Accounts*, 67; 70), but even the references to building a new house at the tilery and to the salary of Robert Tiler in 1359–60 are ambiguous (*Cellarers' Accounts*, 60). These particular wages do not, therefore, necessarily provide conclusive evidence for the important issue of whether or not the tilery was operated directly by the abbey.

Likewise, references to the 'kiln' in the second half of the fourteenth and first decade of the fifteenth century (*Cellarers' Accounts*, 63; 68; 75; 77; 80; 98) are probably related to the tilery, but not necessarily so. Indeed, leaving aside the question of organisation, the printed accounts for the entire period 1275–1513 contain only six specific references to the tilery (*Cellarers' Accounts*, 46; 48; 60; 130; 136; 144). By 1488, however, it was accounted for in the abbey accounts which include payments for making and firing tiles in 1500 and 1509.

In 1521, John Trewe obtained, from the abbot of Battle, a lease of property described as: 'the tile kiln

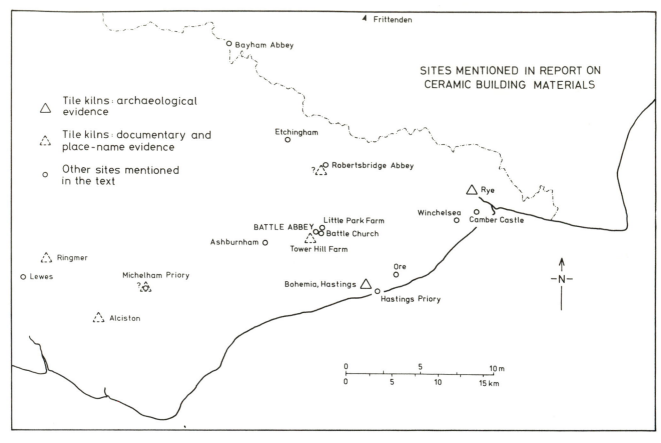

Figure 17   Battle Abbey. Sites mentioned in the report on ceramic building materials.

with all houses and buildings belonging to it with the close called Buttes close, land called Le Launds, land for digging clay and gravel and pasturage for six oxen and two horses or mares' (Thorpe 1835, 136). Again in 1535, receipts of the abbey included 26s 8d 'for rent for a building in Battel called a Tylehouse' (*Valor Eccl.* 1, 346), and these two references provide positive proof that, at least by the second quarter of the sixteenth century, the tilery no longer remained under direct control of the abbey. The grant of Battle Abbey to Sir Anthony Browne in 1539 also included a 'tile house' (Dugdale 1846, 255), and it has been suggested that the site should be identified with archaeological discoveries made in a field named 'Tile Kiln Field' (Richard Budgen's Map of 'Battel Manor', 1724; ESRO: 4421(7)) at Tower Hill Farm, Battle (Lemmon 1961–2; Eames 1980, 735). Some confusion has arisen over this name because the field was identified incorrectly as '*the* kiln field' in a typescript report concerning excavations on the site. Nevertheless, the Webster accounts for 1758 include money paid for grubbing in Tile Kiln Field and around Kilnfield (ESRO: BAT 2751, 4 & 8).

Excavations were concentrated in an area where 'green-glazed bricks' had been ploughed up, and among the finds were two small complete glazed floor tiles; a fragment of slip-decorated floor-tile; and numerous pieces of roof-tile (Lemmon 1961–2, 28). The evidence for workshops arranged around a courtyard is by no means conclusive, and if this was indeed the site of the abbey tile works, then it is surprising that so few tiles were found, even in a small excavation. The name 'Le Launds' mentioned in 1521, however, strongly suggests a site for the tile house either within the Great or Little Park, because 'Laund' is a typical name given to an open area within a park.

Archaeological evidence suggests that other religious houses in the area may also have had their own tileries, in which case specific orders for floor tiles might have been produced by itinerant craftsmen alongside the regular output of roof tiles (Eames 1980, 279). Vidler (1932, 86) recognised a probable association between the Rye kilns and St. Bartholomew's Hospital nearby, and roof-tile wasters found at Michelham Priory suggest that here too there may have been a tilery in the vicinity, perhaps producing floor tiles as well as roof tiles (Barton and Holden 1967, 9–11). The names 'Tylehost Wood' and 'Tylehost fielde' near Robertsbridge Abbey again possibly indicate tile production in the vicinity of another monastic establishment in the area (D'Elboux 1944, 148 no. 366; 149 no. 372).

Medieval kilns which had produced both roof tiles and floor tiles, as well as pottery, were found near Hastings in the nineteenth century (Lower 1859; Ross 1860; Barton 1979, 184–90), but in this instance, there is no positive association with a particular monastic establishment. Other tile kilns are attested from the documentary sources at Telham, near Battle (Cleveland 1877, 3) in the thirteenth century, and at Ashburnham in the mid-fourteenth century (Salzman 1923, 123).

Thus, although there is circumstantial evidence for tile production at other religious houses in the area as well as at Battle, more detailed fieldwork and excavation is needed at kiln sites before the organisation of production in this part of Sussex can be assessed in detail. Nevertheless, it can be inferred from the several known medieval tileries within a radius of some 20 km (12 miles) of Battle that transport of ceramic building materials would have been kept to a minimum. Even so, there would have been opportunities for innovations – particularly in the production of floor tiles – to pass from one workshop to another.

There are abundant supplies of suitable clay for brick and tile manufacture in the locality. However, brick-making on a large scale does not seem to have commenced as early in Sussex as it did in parts of East Anglia and the north, presumably because of the availability of good local building stone. So-called Flemish imported bricks, however, have been found at several sites in E. Sussex. 'Tiles' are listed among the items on which duty was payable at the port of Winchelsea in 1295 (Homan 1940, 64), and shipments of imported bricks are recorded in 1323 and 1327 (Holt 1970, 165). Only two fragments of the typical yellow Flemish-type bricks have been identified at Battle, but pieces of red brick from a thirteenth-century context (p. 34) are of particular interest because hitherto the earliest recorded use of local brick in the county was at Herstmonceux Castle in the early 1440s (Simpson 1942, 110). A few large soft red bricks were found, however, in a fourteenth-century context at Glottenham (D. Martin, pers. com. 1982). Bricks were used in humbler domestic buildings in this part of Sussex from c. 1600 onwards, but they were not in common use until the early eighteenth century (Draper and Martin 1968, 55). Among numerous post-medieval brickworks near Battle, traditional methods of manufacture continued at Ashburnham until 1968 (Leslie 1971; Harmer 1981, 14–21).

Floor tiles

Tiles and floors at Battle Abbey
The very thorough destruction of many of the monastic buildings in the centuries after the Dissolution, combined with surprisingly sparse antiquarian investigation, has hindered serious study of the floor tiles from Battle until now. Compared with the quantity of other finds, the number of complete floor tile designs even from the excavation is disappointing, and many types are only represented by small fragments. Apart from a few (probably relaid) south of Building X, none of the tiles was found *in situ*. Isolated fragments were represented in Periods B and C, but the majority of those illustrated in this report came from debris discarded outside the reredorter shortly after the Dissolution (Period D). Others were found in contemporary deposits in the

chapter house area, and some came from later demolition rubble (Period E).

All the principal rooms of the abbey would probably have been paved either with stone or with tiles, but even in the chapter house where the floor levels had been raised, only slight traces of a thin mortar bed were found, and there were no tile impressions. The excavated floor of the room at ground level in the reredorter was of clay, but it seems improbable that this would have sufficed for such a well-appointed chamber during monastic use of the building. Records show that parts of the abbey had stone floors (p. 66), and although small squared blocks of Caen stone found in the excavation could have been used as flooring materials such a use is unlikely because they are thicker than known examples of stone mosaic. Furthermore, the stone is soft and there are no signs of wear. Stone floors would normally have been of a more durable material.

The tiled floor of the dormitory survived until the early nineteenth century, although a certain degree of ambiguity surrounds antiquarian accounts of the details. Vidler (1841, 151), describing what he thought was the refectory (*i.e.* the dormitory), provides a succinct statement of the discoveries:

'In 1811 some of the original paving tiles were found. They were of excellent material and in good preservation; four inches and a half square; and three quarters of an inch thick; the bottom somewhat less than the top, the colour brown, figured with dull yellow; each one exactly alike, forming part of a pattern which required sixteen of them to shew it entire'.

The Duchess of Cleveland (1877, 252), following Vidler's description, asserts that part of the flooring was still perfect in 1811, and adds that she had been shown one of the tiles in question. Behrens (1936, 130) reminds us that the floor had been covered with earth for many years and maintains that part of the perfect flooring was discovered when the earth was cleared in 1811. In support of this, she publishes a print dated 1826 which shows the chequered floor of the dormitory (Behrens 1937, op. p. 39). The impression conveyed is of a pavement composed of alternate slipped and unslipped tiles with no hint of the patterned types referred to by Vidler and later authorities. Both plain and patterned tiles were found among Dissolution debris excavated outside the reredorter (p. 93), and thus the decorated tiles may have been confined to a small area, perhaps at the south end of the dormitory. However, Vidler, who was writing some thirty years after the alleged date of discovery, does not specify that the tiles were *in situ*; this is an elaboration of the later accounts. It may be, therefore, that the decorated tiles were loose and he assumed that they had come from the dormitory when they may in fact have come from elsewhere. Indeed the Duchess of Cleveland (1877, 220) notes that the church was paved with tiles. Trial trenches excavated in 1979 confirm that the floor of the dormitory does not now survive (p. 195).

Floor Tiles in East Sussex
Although kilns and their products have been investi-

gated and published, tiles from churches and monastic establishments in south-east Sussex have hitherto received little attention. Five tiles displayed in Battle Church were found 'near the Deanery' and are illustrated by Behrens (1937, 129). One of the designs – a figure on horseback – is almost certainly a product of the kilns at Rye (Vidler 1936, 109), but none of the tiles from the church can be paralleled at the abbey. The nearest sizeable group to Battle comes from Robertsbridge Abbey where both excavated material (Salzman 1935, 206–8) and casual finds are represented. Most of these tiles remain at the abbey, but some are dispersed (Martin, MSS notes, Sussex Archaeol. Soc. Library) and others are in the British Museum collection (Eames 1980; Norton 1981, 113–5) and at Battle Museum. Tiles were also found during excavations at Michelham Priory (Barton and Holden 1967 10–11) and at Bodiam Manor (Battle Museum), Camber Castle (Ames 1975), Blackfriars Barn, Winchelsea (Winchelsea Museum); and casual finds are recorded from St Thomas' Church, Winchelsea (Cooper 1850, 127), St Helens (?), Ore and from Wilmington Priory (Barbican House Museum, Lewes). Floor tiles manufactured at the Rye kilns were used in St Mary's Church, Rye (Vidler 1933, 47), and fourteenth-century tiles remain *in situ* at Etchingham Church (Slater 1857, 351). For wider range of earlier designs however, it is necessary to look further afield to Lewes Priory (Boyson 1901; Eames 1980, cat. no. 11247–11276), and to Bayham Abbey where a comprehensive assessment of the tile sequence has recently been undertaken by M. Horton (1983).

The sequence now provided at Bayham Abbey, includes thirteenth-century tile mosaic; a fine series of early slip-decorated tiles; fourteenth-century groups; and late medieval plain tiles many of which have nail holes normally assumed to be distinctive of Flemish manufacture. The chronology is not necessarily applicable to sites nearer the coast, and it is perhaps significant that very few of the tiles from Battle can be paralleled precisely at Bayham. This demonstrates the extent of regional variations in repertoire. Despite similarities with designs at Robertsbridge and Etchingham and two identical designs at Battle, most of the Bayham tiles have closer affinities with those of Kent rather than the coastal regions of Sussex.

In assessing the geographical significance of the tiles found at Battle Abbey it is necessary to consider the date and distribution of known regional groups. A series of thirteenth-century inlaid tiles from Lewes Priory may be derived from 'Wessex' designs, but examples are not recorded elsewhere and the kiln source remains unknown (Eames 1980, 202). Some of the Rye tiles have been assigned to the late thirteenth or very early fourteenth century (Vidler 1932, 95–101; Eames 1980, 741), but again the extent of their distribution is not properly defined. A somewhat later fourteenth-century series was first recognised by Lord Ponsonby who proposed the term 'Lewes group' on the basis of examples from Lewes, Poynings, Wilmington and Winchelsea; with

outliers at Langdon Abbey (Kent) and further afield (Ponsonby 1934, 41). To these should be added two tiles from Horsted Keynes, one of the drawings of which was unfortunately published in reverse (Figg 1850, op. p. 239 (right), no iii; Barbican House Museum, Lewes). More recent discoveries come from Michelham Priory (Barton and Holden 1967, 10), and from as far west as Angmering (Bedwin 1975, 30–1) and Arundel (Evans 1969, 75–6). Eames (1980, 210) suggested the possibility of a French origin for these tiles, and, although the location of the tilery is not known, this suggestion has been confirmed by discoveries in France (Norton 1981, 109).

The distribution of Tyler Hill tiles extends as far as the churches of Romney Marsh (Norton and Horton 1981, 79), and the later mass-produced fourteenth-century Penn-type tiles also reached Sussex (Hohler 1942, 106; 110–12), probably by sea. Thus, although the excavated material from Battle is fragmentary, it does provide an interesting assemblage for comparison not only with the coastal distribution of thirteenth- and fourteenth-century tiles, but also with the earlier inlaid types from Lewes Priory and the ubiquious late medieval plain tiles represented at Bayham Abbey. Situated within 18 km (11 miles) of floor-tile kilns at Rye and Hastings, and with the possibility of production at the abbey itself, the tiles from Battle offer some scope for beginning to understand the organisation of production and distribution in the area.

Classification and Comparison

Method of Classification

The floor tiles have been classified with two distinct, yet related, aims: firstly, to identify groups which were probably made at the same place; and to compare the tiles from Battle with others found elsewhere in the area. Secondly, to identify those tiles which could have been laid together, thereby providing at least some evidence for the appearance of the abbey floors before the Dissolution.

The fabrics have been grouped according to conventional criteria of colour, texture, and inclusions, and the descriptions follow conventions recommended by Peacock (1977, 26–33). Individual tiles have not been examined microscopically, but thin sections have been prepared from selected examples (see below). Despite minor variations in fabric within certain classes, tiles within each group were probably manufactured at the same centre.

Particular production centres may be characterised by details of manufacture. Examination of large kiln assemblages, however, has shown that some traits such as the number, shape, and size of the 'keys' cut into the base of a floor tile may reflect the whim of an individual tile-maker rather than represent a distinctive feature of the output (Eames 1980, 198). Keys have not been found on any of the examples from Battle, but nail holes on the surface of both plain and decorated tiles are indicative of a specific method of manufacture (Eames 1980, 18).

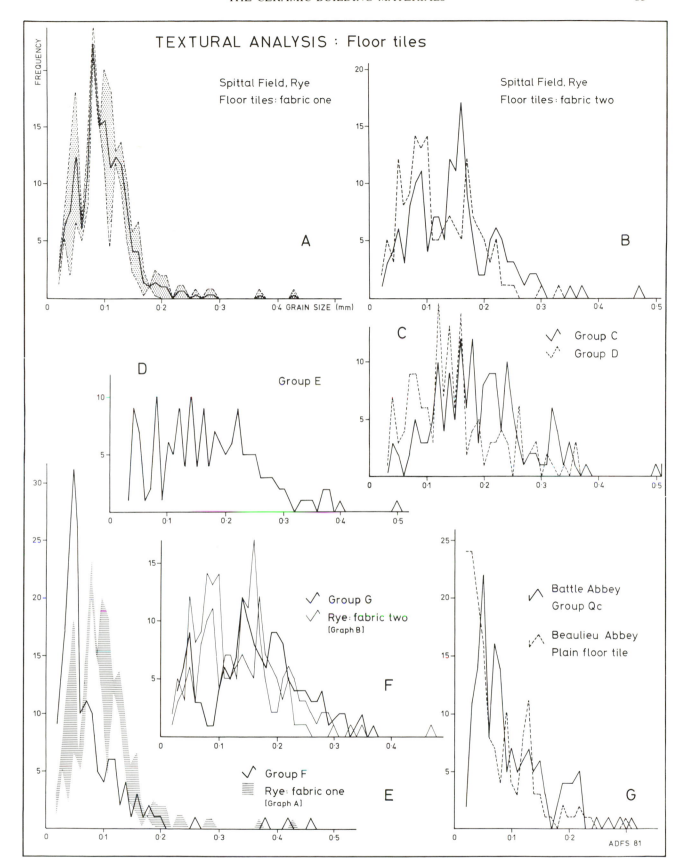

Figure 18 Textural analysis of medieval floor tiles.

The following features have therefore been taken into account in the identification of manufacturing techniques: surface treatment; size and thickness; extent of the bevel; and the presence or absence of nail holes.

Terminology adopted here to describe the surface treatment uses the conventions outlined by Drury (1979, fig 2). In practice, however, it has proved difficult to distinguish between two-colour designs produced by 'slip-over-impression' or 'stamp-on-slip'. Several of the tiles have been underscraped when removing extraneous white slip from their surfaces, and in Group C particularly, the white slip has sometimes smudged beyond the impression of the design (eg. no. 4). Most of the tiles from Battle therefore appear to have been made using the slip-over-impression technique which is widespread in south-east England. One group has designs in counter-relief, and the late medieval plain tiles have been classified according to the combination of white slip and clear or coloured glazes.

Variations in size and thickness due to differential shrinkage of the clay are likely to occur even within the same batch of tiles, and for this reason many surviving medieval pavements have wide mortar 'joints'. It is important, therefore, to distinguish these minor variations from the intentional manufacture of different sizes, and, in view of the broad range of dimensions noted at Battle, the information has been plotted on a graph to illustrate the method of classification. The relationship between size and thickness of all tiles with at least one complete dimension is shown on Figure 21. Thicknesses have been measured on a fracture near the centre of the tile wherever possible, and an average dimension has been taken on complete tiles. Such an approach has the merit not only of defining 'standard' sizes, but it also shows minor variations within each group, and this method of presentation permits objective comparison with tiles from elsewhere.

The edges of tiles with nail holes would have been trimmed with a knife, but the identification of knife trimming has been restricted to tiles with definite evidence of blade strokes. Most of the tiles are at least slightly bevelled, but a few definitely have straight sides. Bevelled or straight-sided tiles of similar thickness could have been laid on the same floor, but variations in the technique of manufacture may indicate alternative sources of production, and the different types have therefore been grouped separately.

A few of the groups are only represented by a single example, and, whereas small decorated fragments can usually be identified, only those plain tiles with at least one complete dimension have been studied in detail. This introduces bias into the quantification, but analysis of thicknesses and surface treatments has been based upon all fragments recovered from the excavation (Figures 21 and 22).

It is not possible to identify where all the tiles were made, and different groups may have been manufactured at the same centre. This method of classification, however, not only offers a reliable means of objective comparison among the tiles from Battle,

but, when a larger sample of kiln material is available in future, it may also be feasible to compare those groups with the range of sizes and traits of manufacture at specific tileries.

Textural Analysis

In the absence of large samples of wasters, similarities between the repertoire of different industries will only become apparent from analysis of marketed tiles. Examination of the fabrics therefore has considerable bearing on the identification of the same stamps used at different production centres, and hence on the interpretation of tile-makers' itineraries.

Like pottery vessels, thin sections prepared from locally-produced floor tiles in South-East England do not contain inclusions which are diagnostic of a particular source. However, the method of textural analysis outlined in the pottery report (p. 107) has been used here for the first time to assess its usefulness in the study of ceramic building materials, and to provide an objective means of comparing the floor tile fabrics from Battle Abbey. Raw materials used in the manufacture of ceramic building materials are seldom as carefully prepared as those required for pottery vessels, and greater variation among tiles from the same kiln must therefore be anticipated. Nevertheless, the range of quartz grain sizes in the floor tiles made at Rye compares closely with the two pottery fabrics identified among the wasters (Figure 18: Graphs A and B; Figure 27: Graphs B and D). The fabric of the Rye floor tiles is also quite different from thin-sections of floor tiles from Tyler Hill, Kent. The minimal preparation of the raw materials (Eames 1980, 18), however, may hinder the identification of marketed tiles where the contrast between the range of quartz grain sizes among wasters from different kilns is less pronounced.

Where possible, one thin-section has been prepared from each group of tiles found at Battle Abbey, although this has not been attempted where it would require disfiguration of the only complete example of a particular type. The slides have been compared visually under a petrological microscope, and the quartz grain size frequency of selected samples has been plotted on a graph (Figure 18). Sample numbers mentioned in the text relate to a reference collection prepared by the writer and stored at the Department of Archaeology, Southampton University.

Detailed analysis of floor tile fabrics thus supplements the information derived from traits of manufacture, but, like the study of pottery, attribution of a whole group of tiles to a particular source on the basis of one identified sample inevitably relies upon less precise visual classification.

Group A (not illustrated)

Fabric Grey core; brown surfaces. Hard, harsh texture; rough fracture. Abundant medium coarse angular flint; sparse ironstone. (TF xii; Sample 1061).
Manufacture Plain, not glazed; straight sides; rough base; no keys.

Figure 19   Medieval slip-decorated floor tiles. 1–23: Battle Abbey; A: Little Park Farm, Battle; B and C: Spittal Field, Rye; D: Tower Hill Farm, Battle ($\frac{1}{4}$).

Size not known *Thickness* 21 mm
Comparison Only one fragment of this type was found (Phase C14), but the thickness suggests that it is a floor tile rather than a roof tile. Similar coarse-gritted unglazed floor tiles were associated with an early/mid-twelfth-century building destroyed before construction of the bailey defences at South Mimms Castle, Hertfordshire (Kent 1968, n.p.). Thin-section analysis of the Battle fabric shows that the range of flint and quartz grain sizes is similar, if not identical, to local twelfth/thirteenth-century pottery types from Pevensey and Newhaven (p. 109). The centre of manufacture is not known.

Group B (Figure 19)

Fabric Red-pink surfaces. Hard, fairly smooth texture.

Fine sand temper. Not thin-sectioned.
Manufacture Inlaid slip decoration; plain tiles. Prominent bevel; fairly smooth base; no keys.
Size 83–85 mm *Thickness* 21 mm
1. Rosette. Phase D30.
Comparison Only one design was found during the excavations but this forms part of a wider repertoire of similar inlaid tiles known elsewhere. A small tile from Little Park Farm, Battle (Battle Museum) shows a unicorn (Figure 19: A), and this is likely to be a stray from the abbey. Another group of similar tiles decorated with a fleur-de-lis or a rosette (without border, unlike Battle) occurs at Robertsbridge Abbey, and the identical methods of manufacture and dimensions indicate that all these tiles are from the same source (Figure 21: Graph A). The designs on larger thirteenth-century inlaid tiles from

Lewes Priory (Boyson 1900, 214–16), although similar in their simplicity, are different from those found at Battle and Robertsbridge. The fabric of the Lewes tiles, which contains specks of shell, is much coarser and indicates a different source of manufacture, but even though the trefoil motif on the border of the example from Battle is also shown on tiles from the kilns at Bohemia, Hastings (Lower 1859, 230), the source of neither the Lewes nor Battle/Robertsbridge group is known. Date: mid–/late thirteenth century?

Group C (Figure 19)

Fabric Red surfaces usually with a thick grey core. Hard, harsh texture; rough fracture. Abundant medium/coarse sand with sparse fragments of siltstone or sandstone. Sparse coarse grains of colourless quartz (up to 2 mm) are visible in the fracture of many fragments, but others are slightly finer. (TF ii and ix; Sample 1024).
Manufacture Slip-over-impression; plain green-glazed tiles. Prominent knife-trimmed bevel; sanded base; no keys.
Size 116–122 mm *Thickness* 18–21 mm
2. Seated human figure wearing a badge; hands clasped. Probably four-tile arrangement. Phase D22.
3. Two-headed eagle. Phase D22.
4. Floral. Four-tile arrangement. Mortar on surface of tile. Phase D22.
5. Birds in foliage. Four-tile arrangement. Phase D22.
6. Two ?eagles facing each other. Four-tile arrangement. Mortar on surface of tile. Phase D21/22.
7. Floral. Triangle cut from a square tile of design no. 8. Phase D22.
8. Repeating floral. Phase D22.
9. Fragment? from sixteen-tile arrangement. Phase D30.
10. ?Floral. Phase D22.
11. Fragment from (?) four-tile arrangement, although possibly similar to no. 2. Phase D21.
12. Fragment; probably the tail of an animal. Phase D22.
13. Fleur-de-lis from four-tile arrangement. Phase D30.
14. Interlocking circles with floral motifs. Possible nail hole indicates that this tile may belong to Group E. Phase E36.
Comparison This is the largest group of tiles, but only one of the designs can be matched elsewhere. No 6 is identical to a tile from Bayham Abbey (Horton 1983, 78: Group F, no. 60) and the treatment of foliage on some of the other tiles has affinities with the same group at Bayham. Devices such as the double-headed eagle and interlocking circles are common amongst fourteenth-century tiles in many areas (Eames 1980, design no. 1728), but M. Horton has identified other designs corresponding with his Group F from Bayham at several sites in Romney Marsh and West Kent, and design no. 6 from Battle also occurs at Frittenden (Anon. 1874, op. p. 203).

In view of the wide range of tiles from Bayham, Mr Horton has argued that the abbey may have been the chief sponsor for production of that group, and he also draws attention to affinities with some of the designs at Rye. Textural analysis of a sample taken from Group C at Battle reveals similarities with tiles of fabric 'two' at Rye, but there is a higher proportion of quartz grains between 0.3 and 0.4 mm in the Battle sample than in the tiles from Rye (Figure 18: Graphs B and C). Likewise, whereas the Bayham tiles (Horton 1983, Group F, size iv) fall within the range of variation among Group C at Battle, products of the Rye kilns are slightly larger (Barbican House Museum, Lewes: Figure 21 Graph A).

Neither the fabric nor the manufacture of this group can therefore be paralleled exactly at Rye, and the source

must remain uncertain. Fragment no. 9 has been assigned to Group C on the basis of its fabric, but similarities with no. 20, which has a nail hole, suggest that Groups C and E may be related. A tile now in Battle Church (Behrens 1937, 129, top right) is of similar dimensions, and perhaps style, to Group C designs from the abbey, but it is framed in modern plaster, and neither the thickness nor the fabric could therefore be examined.

The link with a more extensive range of designs at Bayham suggests that these two groups are contemporary. The Bayham tiles have been assigned to the 1330s on the basis of detailed stylistic analogy, and therefore the Group C tiles from Battle almost certainly belong to the first half of the fourteenth century, although the spirit of no. 2 is somewhat earlier.

Group D (Figure 19)

Fabric Pink core and surfaces. Hard texture; rough fracture. Fairly fine sand temper; sparse fragments of coarse ironstone. Tendency for glaze to flake off from surface. (TF xi; Sample 1063).
Manufacture Slip-over-impression. Slight bevel; sanded base; no keys.
Size 119–122 mm *Thickness* 19–20 mm.
15. Figure in roundel. Either a continuous circle arrangement or a four-tile quartrefoil design. Mortar on surface of tile. Phase D24.
16. Figure with staff probably paddling a boat, in roundel. Arrangement as no. 15. Phase D24.
Comparison These designs cannot be matched precisely either among the published drawings of wasters from Rye, or among the larger collection from Vidler's excavation now stored in Barbican House Museum, Lewes. Several motifs, however, have affinities with the larger size of Rye tiles (Vidler 1932, 99–101: series III). The border circle decorated with lozenges is similar to Rye design III.8; treatment of the figures has much in common with design III.5 at Rye; and the arrangement of facing pairs of birds within a roundel composed of two different tiles (Rye: III.11) is similar to the manner in which the Group D tiles at Battle would have been laid. The fabric of this group is also similar to Rye (Figure 18: Graph C) but, like Group C, the Battle tiles are smaller than the main series from the kilns (Figure 21: Graph A). The source therefore remains uncertain. Date: fourteenth century.

Group E (Figure 19)

Fabric Red core and surfaces. Hard texture: rough fracture. Medium/fine sand temper, with very sparse coarse colourless quartz grains. (TF ii; Sample 1066).
Manufacture Slip-over-impression. Nail holes at corners; slight knife-trimmed bevel; sanded base; no keys.
Size approx. 120 mm *Thickness* 18–20 mm.
17. Angel with halo in floral border. Four-tile arrangement. Thick mortar bed adhering to the base and sides, including impression of the bevel of an adjacent tile. Phase D31.
18. Triangle cut from a square tile of design no. 19. Phase E35.
19. Floral quadrant design forming continuous pattern. Phase E39.
20. Foliage in lattice. Phase D22.
Comparison The size of these tiles is similar to Groups C and D (Figure 21: Graph A), but they are distinguished by the nail holes. No. 19 is similar to a slightly larger tile from Bayham Abbey (Horton 1983, 78: Group F, no. 37) and to another with fairly naturalistic foliage from Faversham Abbey which is considered to be derived from Wessex types (Rigold 1968, 49–50, no. 109). A scaled-down

version of design no. 19 also appears on a hitherto unpublished tile from Rye (Figure 19: B) which would have been divided into sixteen segments if the pattern was complete. No. 20 is again similar to an unpublished example from Rye (Figure 19: C) but, like Groups C and D, there are significant differences between a sample of the Group E fabric at Battle and the wasters from Rye (Figure 18: Graph D).

The decorated floor tile from kiln field at Tower Hill Farm, Battle has the same characteristic nail hole as the Group E tiles found at the abbey (Figure 19: D). Nail holes have not been noted on any of the decorated tiles from Rye, but they do occur on at least two plain ones from there, although the possibility that these were associated with St Bartholomew's hospital rather than with the kilns cannot be ruled out. It must not, therefore, be assumed that nail holes are distinctive of a particular source, but, if the fragment from Tower Hill Farm is indeed a product of the abbey tilery, then the Group E tiles may have been made there. However, the pattern, which includes the paw of an animal, on the fragment from kiln field could also be similar to certain designs at Rye (Vidler 1932, 93, 98). Thus even if this group was manufactured at Battle, there appear to have been marked affinities with the output of the Rye kilns. Date: fourteenth century.

Group F (Figure 19)

Fabric Pink surfaces sometimes with pale grey core. Hard texture; rough fracture. Medium/fine sand temper with very sparse coarse colourless quartz grains. (TF xi; Sample 1026).
Manufacture Slip-over-impression. Little or no bevel; fairly smooth base; no keys.
Size approx. 125 mm *Thickness* 16–18 mm
21. Crowned figure. Four-tile arrangement. Mortar on surface of tile. Phase D24.
22. Griffin, similar to Group G no. 26. Phase D22.
23. Triangle cut from a square floral tile. Reredorter, unstratified.
Comparison 'King' designs occur both on late fourteenth-century tiles from the Nottingham area (Eames 1980, cat. no. 1; 246–8), and on the fourteenth-century mass-produced Penn-type tiles (Hohler 1941, 30, no. P18; Eames 1980, cat. nos. 246–8). It has been suggested that another full-length figure comprising two tiles from Rye may represent King Edward I (Vidler 1932, 96–7, no. III. 1–2), but no. 21 from Battle is slightly smaller than the series III tiles found at Rye (Figure 21: Graph A).

No. 22 is probably from the same stamp as the badly-worn tile no. 28 with nail holes in Group G. These two groups may therefore be related. The fabric of Group F is much finer than the other slip-decorated tiles from Battle, and it is similar, but not identical, to the fabric 'one' tiles at Rye (Figure 18: Graphs A and E). On grounds of both fabric and design there is reason to suppose, therefore, that Groups F and G were made by tilers who had close contact with Rye, even if they were not made there (see below). Date: probably fourteenth century.

Group G (Figure 20)

Fabric Nos. 24–27 are indistinguisable from the fabric of Group F but others are slightly coarser. Red surfaces sometimes with pale grey core. Hard texture; rough fracture. Medium/fine sand temper with sparse fragments of siltstone. (TF ii; Sample 1017).
Manufacture Slip-over-impression; plain tiles. Little or no bevel; fairly smooth base; no keys.
Size approx. 124 mm *Thickness* 17–20 mm

24. Two figures beneath canopy and foliage. Kiln stacking mark on surface of tile. Phase D21.
25. Fragment from four-tile roundel. Phase D21.
26. Griffin, similar to Group F no. 22. Phase E35.
27. Triangular tile cut from square with roundel. Phase D22.
28. Floral. Phase E47.
29. Grotesque. Probably from four-tile arrangement. Phase D22.
Comparison Close similarities between the shape, style and fabric of no. 24 and no. 21 shows that tiles both with nail holes (Group G) and without (Group F) were manufactured at one centre. Nos. 22 and 26 have also apparently been made from the same stamp.

The grotesque on no. 29 occurs on an identical unpublished example (without nail holes) from Rye. The fragments from neither Rye nor Battle are large enough to permit thin-section analysis. A sample taken from a similar plain tile at Battle, however, compares more favourably than any of the other groups with the Rye tiles of fabric 'two', because the graphs showing the quartz grain size frequency have the same distinctive 'double peaks' (Figure 18: Graph F).

The range of wasters found at Rye is reflected at Battle by the presence of both fine and coarser tiles with the same traits of manufacture, and, although the fine fabric of Group F does not correspond precisely with any of the samples from Rye, the distinctive groundmass of small quartz grains appears in most of the wasters. Unlike Groups C-E, the two complete tiles in Groups F and G match the size of series II from Rye, and the combination of all the evidence provides a strong indication that tiles in these two groups were made at Rye.

The motifs and techniques of manufacture are particularly interesting in view of a recent reappraisal of the Corona Chapel at Canterbury Cathedral by E.C. Norton and M.C. Horton (1981). Tyler Hill designs at Canterbury include dragons (?) which are similar to the creatures on the Battle tiles (Norton and Horton 1981, 74), and, perhaps significantly, nail holes occur on the Parisian tiles from which the Canterbury designs are now known to have been derived. The technique of manufacture using nails to secure a template is most unusual for English medieval slip-decorated tiles (Eames 1980, 18) and it is uncommon even in France (Norton and Horton 1981, 76). None of the designs from Battle is identical to the Canterbury tiles, which do not have nail holes, but the distinctive method of manufacture may indeed suggest some contact with foreign tile-makers.

The slip-decorated tiles in the Corona Chapel are now provisionally dated *c.* 1285–90; but the Battle tiles can be ascribed to nothing more specific than the late thirteenth or early fourteenth century.

Group H (Figure 20)

Fabric Red core and surfaces. Hard texture; rough fracture. Medium/fine sand temper with sparse medium-sized fragments of ironstone. Not thin-sectioned.
Manufacture Slip-over-impression; plain tile. Knife-trimmed bevel; sanded base; no keys.
Size approx. 120 mm *Thickness* 24–25 mm
30. Birds with spread wings in foliage which is shown by 'negative' slip decoration. Pattern very worn. Phase D26.
Comparison Tiles in this group are thicker than those in Groups C–G, and the closest parallel in terms of size is a plain green-glazed tile from Tower Hill Farm, Battle (Figure 21: Graph A). The technique of reproducing 'negative' floor-tile designs is more common in France than in England (Lane 1960, 34), and the decoration itself has French affinities (Miss J. Kerr, pers. comm.). The

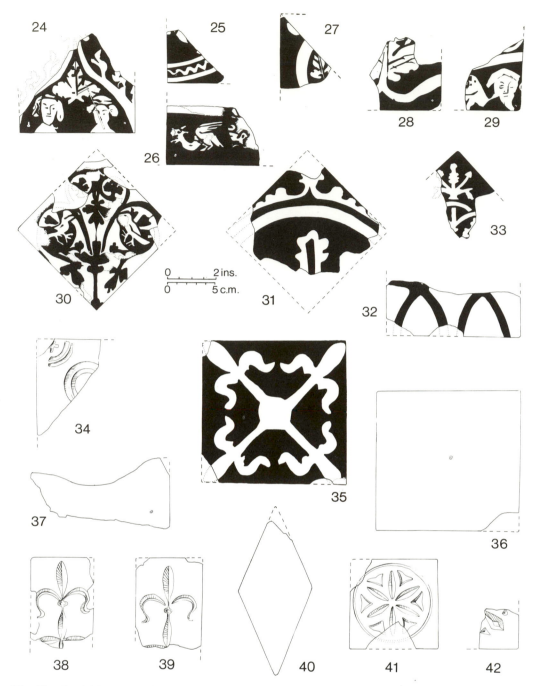

Figure 20 Battle Abbey. Medieval slip-decorated, plain, and counter-relief floor tiles ($\frac{1}{4}$).

decorated example, if not the plain tile, may therefore be an import. Date: probably first half of fourteenth century.

Group J (Figure 20)

Fabric Buff-brown core and surfaces. Fairly soft texture, rough fracture. Medium sand temper with moderate coarse colourless quartz grains. Tendency for glaze to flake from the surface. (TF iv; Sample 1068).
Manufacture Slip-over-impression. Straight knife-trimmed sides; sanded base; no keys.
Size approx. 123 mm *Thickness* approx. 28 mm
31. Floral. Four-tile arrangement. Phase D22.
Comparison The size and thickness is similar to plain tiles in Group Q: size i, and the fabric is the same as

variant (e) in the same group (see below). An identical design from Bayham (Horton 1983, Group G, no. 87) occurs on tiles which are of similar thickness to the Battle example, but slightly smaller (Figure 21: Graph A). Date: probably fifteenth century.

Group K (Figure 20)

Fabric Red-brown core and surfaces. Fairly hard texture; rough fracture. Medium sand temper with moderate coarse colourless quartz grains. Tendency for glaze to flake off from the surface. (TF vi; Sample 1067).
Manufacture ?Slip-over-impression (red pattern against white slip background). Straight knife-trimmed sides; coarsely sanded base; no keys.

Size approx. 142 mm *Thickness* approx. 30 mm
32. Continuous lattice pattern. Phase D21.
Comparison Smaller tiles with red geometric circle patterns showing against a background of white slip are known from Robertsbridge Abbey and Etchingham, but this technique of manufacture is not common among published tiles from Sussex. As noted above, however, the white background did become popular on French tiles from the end of the fifteenth century (Lane 1960, 34). The size is similar to plain tiles of Group Qiii, but it lies just outside the range of variation defined for that group. It is therefore likely to be the lone survivor from a different batch. Date: late fourteenth or fifteenth century.

Group L (Figure 20)

Fabric Thick grey core and red margins. Very hard texture; rough fracture. Fine sand temper with sparse fragments of siltstone and ironstone. (TF v; Sample 1064).
Manufacture Slip-over-impression. Straight or slightly bevelled knife-trimmed sides; irregular sanded base; no keys.
Size not known *Thickness* approx. 32 mm
33. Circle and (?) foliage design. Phase E35.
Comparison The fabric is much harder fired than Group K, but thin-sections show a similar range of quartz grain sizes in these two groups.

Group M (not illustrated)

Fabric Red core and surface. Hard texture; rough fracture. Fine sand temper with moderate medium-sized fragments of ironstone and some siltstone. (TF v; Sample 1020).
Manufacture Plain tiles. Irregular sanded base; no keys.
Size i approx. 100 mm *Size ii* approx. 135 mm.
Thickness 18–21 mm
Comparison The dense groundmass of fine quartz with sparse medium-sized grains seen in thin-section is not matched in the other groups.

Group N (not illustrated)

Fabric Red core and surfaces. Very hard texture; rough fracture. Fine sand temper with streaks of light coloured clay; moderate medium-sized fragments of coarse siltstone (TF i; Sample 1016).
Manufacture Plain tiles. Straight sides; irregular sanded base; no keys.
Size i Square tiles: 143–168 mm; *Size ii* Triangular tiles: approx. 158 mm (base); *Size iii* Triangular tiles: approx. 195 mm (base). *Thickness* 20–24 mm
Comparison These plain tiles are evidently from the same source as the example with counter-relief decoration (Group O). Identification is based principally upon distinctive white streaks in the fabric, and the wide range of sizes may indicate that some of the tiles attributed to this group really represent further fabric variations within Groups Qiii and Qiv (Figure 21: Graph B). White streaks occur in certain Wealden bricks, and they are also found in a few floor tile wasters from Rye. The precise source is not known. Date: probably fifteenth century.

Group O (Figure 20)

Fabric Same as Group N.
Manufacture Counter-relief decoration. Straight sides; irregular sanded base; no keys.
Size not known *Thickness* approx. 21 mm.
34. Circle motifs. Lustrous clear glaze. Phase E35.

Group P (Figure 20)

Fabric Red-brown core and surfaces. Hard texture; rough fracture. Medium sand temper. (TF iv; not thin-sectioned).
Manufacture Slip-over-impression. Slightly bevelled knife-trimmed sides; sanded base; no keys.
Size 151–152 mm *Thickness* 24–26 mm.
35. Four fleur de lys. Phase D21.
Comparison Fifteenth-century tiles with simple slip decoration from Robertsbridge Abbey are larger than those from Battle, and, although there are several examples of no. 35, this is the only design which occurs on tiles over 150 mm square (Figure 21: Graph B). These were almost certainly manufactured with plain tiles of Group Qiii (see below). Date: fifteenth century.

Group Q (Figure 20)

Fabric (a) Red surfaces sometimes with grey core. Hard texture; rough fracture. Medium/coarse sand temper with moderate/sparse fragments of ironstone (TF iii; Sample 1018).
(b) Orange-red core and surfaces. Fairly soft texture; rough fracture. Medium/coarse sand temper with moderate/sparse fragments of ironstone (TF iv; Sample 1019).
(c) Pale purple core and surfaces. Hard texture; rough fracture. Medium sand temper with sparse coarse fragments of siltstone and ironstone. (TF vi; Sample 1021).
(d) Pale purple core and surfaces. Hard texture; rough fracture. Medium sand temper with sparse fragments of ironstone. (TF vii; Sample 1022).
(e) Buff-brown core and surfaces. Soft texture; rough fracture. Medium sand temper with moderate fragments of ironstone and sparse siltstone fragments. (TF viii; Sample 1023).
Fabrics (a)–(d), and probably (e), show a similar range of quartz grain sizes in thin-section and all are apparently from the same source.
Manufacture Plain tiles with unglazed, slipped, and glazed surface treatments. Slight bevel; sanded base; no keys. There are nail holes either at the centre or in the corners of some tiles, and a few have five nail holes. The presence or absence of these holes can only therefore be demonstrated if over half of the tile has survived, and it is impossible to assess the exact proportion of tiles which had been trimmed using a wooden template secured by nails. The proportion of different surface treatments in each size group is shown in Figure 22: Graph B.
Size i 115–123 mm *Size ii* 133–140 mm
Size iii 145–160 mm *Size iv* 163–177 mm
Thickness 22–29 mm
36. Plain green-glazed tile with central nail hole. Group Qiii. Phase D21.
37. Plain tile with eroded green glaze and nail hole at corner. Deliberately shaped after firing, probably to fit around the base of a pillar. Group Q or S. Phase E42.
Comparison Nail holes are thought to be distinctive of tiles imported from Flanders (Norton 1974, 25), but the evidence from Group G at Battle shows that this technique was probably used on two-colour tiles made at Rye as early as the fourteenth century. Another plain green-glazed tile from Rye also has nail holes (Barbican House Museum, Lewes), and it is of similar size, if slightly thinner than Group Qiii at Battle (Figure 21: Graph B). It is possible that the tile from Rye is a stray from St Bartholomew's Hospital. The importation of 'Flanders tiles' is certainly well documented (evidence summarised by Keen and Thackray 1974, 147–8), but in this instance

the presence of nail holes cannot be accepted as a conclusive indication of Flemish manufacture.

Some of the plain tiles at Winchester College belong to a specific batch imported from Flanders and mentioned in the College Accounts for 1397 (Norton 1974, 25, Type A). The dimensions of these tiles (c. 127 mm) fall between Groups Qi and Qii at Battle, but one type of plain tile with nail holes from Bayham Abbey (Horton 1983, 82, Group J: no. 92) just comes within the size range of Group Qi. Dimensions of the somewhat later tiles from the deliberate infill of the north bastion at Camber Castle, dated to c. 1570 (Wilson and Hurst 1964, 259–60), range from 114 mm to 129 mm, but most are slightly larger than Group Qi from Battle (Figure 21: Graph B). Undue emphasis should not be placed upon minor variations in size, but it is perhaps significant that Groups Qiii and Qiv which comprise the largest number of plain tiles from Battle are not paralleled among the considerable quantity of comparable material from Bayham.

Thin-section analysis of plain tiles, similar to those from Winchester, found at Beaulieu Abbey, Hants. did not provide conclusive evidence for their source, and the range of inclusions would even have been consistent with local manufacture (Hinton 1977, 51). Samples from Battle have therefore been compared with the Beaulieu fabric, and the range of quartz grain sizes is strikingly similar (Figure 18: Graph G).

The size of this albeit small sample of plain tiles with nail holes found at sites within reach of south coast ports does not show any marked degree of uniformity. Flanders tiles were certainly available in different sizes (Norton 1974, 32), but other variations between imports not necessarily made at the same place, and spanning a period of a century or more, must be anticipated. However, the presence of nail holes at Rye and the contrast between most of the sizes at Battle and Bayham might indicate that at least some of these bulky products were manufactured locally.

Group R (Figure 20)

Fabric Similar range of colours and inclusions to Group Q, but slightly coarser (TF v; Sample 1065).
Manufacture Plain, mosaic, and counter-relief tiles. Slight bevel; sanded base; no keys.
Size i Plain lozenge *Size ii* Plain mosaic approx. 56 mm
Size iii Counter relief: 67–72 mm wide *Size iv* Counter relief: 93–95 mm *Size v* Plain mosaic: same size as R iv *Size vi* Triangular tiles: 115 m (base)
Thickness 29–34 mm.
38. Fleur-de-lis. Plain green glaze. Group Riii. Phase D22.
39. Fleur-de-lis, same stamp as no. 38. White slip with clear glaze. Group Riii. Phase D24.
40. Plain lozenge. Streaky white slip and green glaze. Group Ri. Phase D23.
41. Roundel. Streaky white slip and green glaze. Group Riv. Phase D22/E36.
42. Roundel; different stamp from no. 41. Plain green glaze. Group Riv. Phase D26.
Comparison Counter-relief tiles were sometimes produced from the same stamp as those decorated with inlaid white slip (Ward-Perkins 1937, 128). However, similarities between the surface treatment of these and the green-glazed or white-slipped plain tiles of Groups Q and S suggests that all three groups are contemporary, if not manufactured at the same centre. This type was not found at Bayham Abbey, but the thickness of the counter-relief tiles from Battle is the same as Group S. It has been observed that the practice of glazing relief-decorated tiles

in contrasting colours for laying alternatively on the pavement appears to have been abandoned by the late fifteenth century (Eames 1980, 45), but there is no independent dating for this type at Battle. Date: probably fifteenth century.

Group S (not illustrated)

Fabric Similar to Groups Q and R.
Manufacture Plain tiles with similar range of surface treatments to Group Q; some unglazed. Slight bevel; sanded base; no keys. Nail holes are represented in Groups Siii and Siv, but not among the limited sample of smaller tiles.
Size i approx. 129 mm *Size ii* 180–191 mm *Size iii* 200–205 mm *Size iv* 216–228 mm
Thickness 28 mm and over.
Comparison Most of the Group S tiles are both larger and thicker than those in Group Q (Figure 21: Graph B). They have a similar range of surface treatments, but, like Groups Qii and Qiv, a higher proportion of the Group S tiles are unglazed than those in the large collection of Group Qiii tiles (Figure 22: Graphs B and C). The paw print of a dog on the *under* side of a fragment from phase D30 suggests that some of the tiles were probably laid out to dry face downwards at the tilery. The white slip is therefore likely to have been applied after the tiles had dried.

Some of the dimensions are akin to plain tiles from Bayham Abbey which are thought to be of local manufacture (Horton 1983, 82: Group H). The largest size, however, corresponds very closely with the 9 in x 9 in tiles from Winchester College which have been identified as probable Flemish imports laid in 1397 (Norton 1974, 39). Like Group Q the presence of nail holes alone is not necessarily distinctive of imported tiles and the source therefore remains uncertain. Date: probably fifteenth century.

Group T (not illustrated)

Fabric Pink core and surfaces. Hard, fairly smooth texture; slightly laminated fracture. Moderate fine sand temper with streaks of white clay and moderate fragments of siltstone. (TF x; Sample 1025).
Manufacture Plain tiles, sometimes with white slip or patchy glaze. Very rough base.
Size not known *Thickness* 26–29 mm
Comparison This small group of fragments may be from floor tiles, but the prominent mould lines and eroded surface of the type sample suggests that it could be a broken 'Roman-type' roof tile in a finer fabric than the main series (p. 95).

Discussion and Conclusions

Floor Tiles and the Monastic Buildings
A small patch of broken plain tiles set in hard white mortar was found adjacent to the north-east buttress outside the chapter house (p. 81), but these have certainly been re-laid. Another row of tiles, including those of Group D, was set on the surface of loam make-up representing late medieval/early post-medieval ground level south of Building X, outside the chapter house. Like many other tiles with mortar on their decorated surfaces, these have also been re-used, possibly even as the packing beneath a light timber-framed structure of late sixteenth- or seventeenth-century date. Thus the only archaeological evidence for the appearance of the floors at

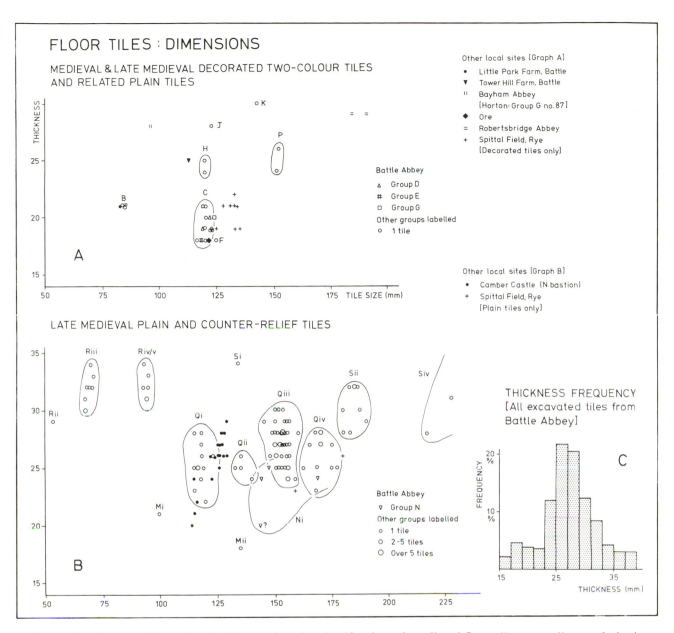

Figure 21   Battle Abbey. Graphs illustrating the classification of medieval floor tiles according to their size and thickness.

Battle Abbey before the Dissolution comes from the scattered collection of loose tiles found in the destruction debris of Periods D and E.

General conclusions must remain speculative because surviving tile arrangements elsewhere are often irregular, and extensive patching or repair would probably have been undertaken during the life of a pavement. Furthermore, the excavated areas may not be typical, because the wide variety of metalwork and other finds from a dump outside the reredorter (Phase D21/22) suggests that items may have been collected from different parts of the abbey. The large number of tiles found here may therefore have come from more than one place. Nevertheless there are significant differences between tiles from different areas of the excavation, and the overwhelming predominance of late medieval plain and glazed tiles indicates extensive re-

flooring in the late fourteenth, or probably in the fifteenth century (Figure 22: Graph A). Only three tiles (Groups A and B) can definitely be dated earlier than the fourteenth century, and the appearance of the original floors which accompanied the thirteenth-century re-building is not known.

Fragments of plain green-glazed floor tiles were found in make-up associated with alterations to the reredorter drainage system (Phase C14), and two examples of the most numerous type represented in the destruction debris (Group Qiii) occur in Period C (Phases C11 and C14). Whether or not this particular group was imported, documentary references to the trade in Flemish tiles confirm that pavements of large plain green-glazed tiles were being laid elsewhere at least from the late fourteenth century onwards.

Classification of tile sizes remains to a certain

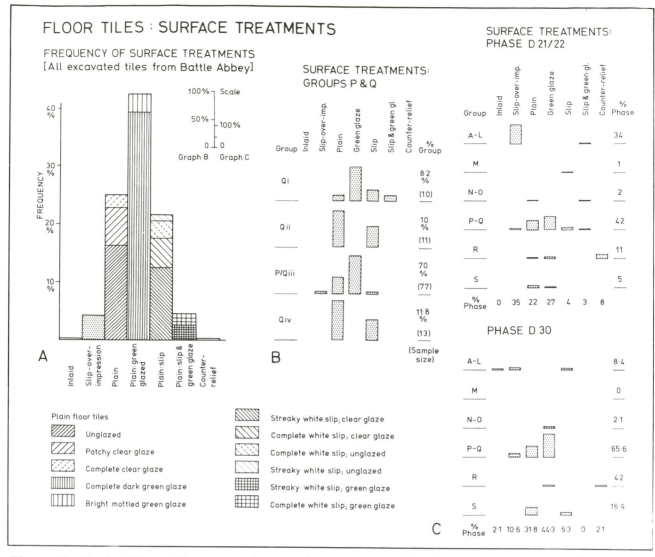

Figure 22   Battle Abbey. Histograms showing the occurrence of surface treatments on medieval floor tiles from all phases [A]; in Groups P and Q [B]; and among Dissolution debris in the reredorter area [C].

extent subjective, but the dimensions and thicknesses of tiles in Groups C–G are sufficiently similar for these to have been laid together. Conclusive evidence that bevelled and straight-sided tiles sometimes formed part of the same panel, is provided by no. 17, one of the few tiles which retains most of the mortar into which it had been set. It can also be inferred from the cut triangular tiles in Groups C, E, F and G that at least some panels may have incorporated mosaic borders.

Only a combination of Groups P and Q provides a large enough sample to suggest ways in which the later tiles might have been arranged (Figure 22: Graph B). Tiles in Groups Qii and Qiv are either plain or slipped, which probably implies a red and yellow chequer pattern. There are few examples in these groups, but plain tiles outnumber the slipped type by a ratio of approximately 2:1 in both sizes. This could be merely coincidence, but there may have been borders or larger panels of plain tiles. Green-glazed tiles predominate in Groups Qi and Qiii, and although Qi is represented by only ten

examples, the proportion is similar to that for Group Qiii, based on a sample of 77 tiles. Decorated Group P tiles which are similar in size to Group Qiii account for a very small proportion of the total. Both plain and slipped tiles in this group were made in the same sizes as the green-glazed examples. Even when the plain and slipped types are taken together, however, the green ones again outnumber the others by a ratio of approximately 2:1. Green and red/yellow tiles may therefore have been laid in similar combinations to the red and yellow tiles of Groups Qii and Qiv. Group S plain tiles on the other hand are of similar thickness to the mosaic and counter-relief tiles in Group R, which suggests that these two groups were probably part of the same arrangement. The smaller tiles were no doubt used as borders, but there are insufficient examples from which to draw more specific conclusions.

Analysis of the ratio between different surface treatments on the late medieval plain tiles has been based upon all examples, irrespective of their location, but nearly all of these came from the reredorter. Plain, green and patterned tiles of Groups P and Q occur as roughly equal proportions both in the dump outside the reredorter (Phase D21/22) and within the drain itself (Phase D30), which provides useful corroborative evidence that these tiles are probably from the same floor (Figure 22: Graph C). Unless the debris was carted around the end of the building and dumped through the open arches on the south side of the drain – which seems improbable – the most likely source for these tiles would have been either on the first floor of the dormitory/reredorter or from somewhere reached via the intermediate latrines at the west end of the reredorter. Debris could have been thrown both outside the building and into the drain from either of these places, but a source on the first floor of the dormitory or reredorter seems probable.

Unlike the plain tiles which occur both outside the reredorter (Phase D21/22) and in the drain (Phase D30), there is a markedly higher proportion of decorated tiles in the former (Figure 22: Graph C). The origin of these tiles is uncertain (p. 81), but the fact that they predominate in the debris *outside* the building suggests that they may have come from elsewhere in the abbey, rather than from the dormitory.

A detailed table showing the quantity of each tile group represented in all phases has been deposited with the excavation records, but only the Period D deposits in the reredorter area provide a large enough sample for detailed analysis (Figure 22: Graph C). Patterned tiles which can be identified more easily than the plain types are somewhat over-represented in these statistics (p. 84), but there were considerably fewer tiles of any type from the chapter house than in the reredorter.

Inlaid or plain tiles in the same group, were found in both areas. Group C designs were confined to the reredorter, although plain tiles with similar dimensions were also found in the chapter house (Phases D24 and E35). A small number of tiles belonging to Groups D–H were also represented in both areas, and the isolated examples occurring in Phases D21/22 and D30 suggest that tiles from other parts of the abbey, as well as from the east range, were probably discarded here (Figure 22: Graph C).

There is little evidence for major structural alteration to the east range after the thirteenth-century re-building, and the late thirteenth- or fourteenth-century slip-decorated tiles cannot therefore be linked with identifiable building campaigns in this area. They may represent repair of existing floors, but, as has been noted, they are more likely to have come from elsewhere. The dormitory was almost certainly (? re-) tiled in the fifteenth century.

Production and Distribution

The thirteenth-century inlaid tiles found at Battle were definitely not made at the same place as contemporary types from Lewes, but similarities with tiles from Robertsbridge Abbey suggest that both Battle and Robertsbridge may have been supplied from the same, yet unknown, centre. The possibility of an itinerant tiler at this period cannot,

however, be ruled out until more local comparative material is available.

Affinities with wasters from Rye can be traced in the slip-decorated tiles of Groups C–G, but the evidence for actual manufacture at Rye is not always conclusive. Tiles in Groups C and D are slightly different in both size and fabric, and those in Group E have nail holes. These are not found on the decorated tiles from Rye, although there are two plain tiles made in this manner. Groups F and G provide the closest parallel with Rye in terms of fabric, but the only example of an identical stamp used on tiles from both Rye and Battle occurs with a nail hole at the latter but not at the former.

The tile in question from Rye was not published by Vidler, but even such a small fragment cannot be dismissed merely as a stray. Two alternative interpretations of this evidence arise: either tiles both with and without nail holes were manufactured at Rye; or the stamp used at Rye was also used at another centre where the tiles were trimmed around a template secured by nails. In either case, there is strong evidence to suggest the existence of a distinctive local enterprise which had adopted an unusual trait of manufacture, possibly derived from the Continent (p. 87).

Although over thirty two-colour designs have now been identified at Battle, patterns and sizes which are distinctive of the 'Lewes group' French imports are not represented. This is surprising because of the extensive coastal distribution in Sussex (p. 82), but their absence may be a significant indication of more easily accessible supplies in the vicinity. Another tile from Battle (Group H) does, however, seem to belong to a different series of French designs.

Evidence for the manufacture of floor tiles at Battle itself relies upon tantalisingly inconclusive information. There was certainly an abbey tilery, but the only indication that its output included decorated floor tiles comes from a single fragment found at Tower Hill Farm (p. 80). If this does, indeed, indicate local manufacture, then tiles with nail holes formed part of the repertoire, and the Group E designs show that there must have been links with Rye.

Unlike the more remote Wealden sites, Battle Abbey would have been well-situated for the purchase of late medieval plain tiles imported from the Low Countries, and the dimensions of at least one group are the same as tiles from Winchester which are almost certainly Flemish imports. The presence of nail holes on a large plain tile from Rye, however, casts doubt upon the significance of this method of manufacture which has hitherto been assumed to be a distinctive feature of the imported tiles. Re-excavation and more extensive investigation of the kilns at Rye would be of value not only to pottery studies, but also to the assessment of floor tile manufacture.

Roof Tiles and Roof Furniture

Roofing Materials at Battle Abbey
In the absence of medieval or post-Dissolution sur-

veys – such as that of Bradwell Priory (Mynard 1974, 37), which itemised the materials used on different roofs of the monastery – the evidence for medieval roofing materials usually has to be assembled from scattered documentary sources and from the archaeological record.

Parts of the twelfth-century church at Battle were roofed with lead (*Chronicle*, 131) and there was a lead roof on the Lady Chapel in 1509 (VCH Sussex 1937, 103 n.1). The south part of the church, however, was covered with shingles in 1410 and 1434 (VCH Sussex 1937, 103 n.1), and, although there are various late medieval references to lead, this may only have been used for guttering or for lining valleys (*Cellarers' Accounts*, 82).

Apart from the church, the less important claustral ranges were roofed with slates, tiles or shingles. The dormitory was roofed with shingles in 1364–6. 9,000 shingles were bought for 72s and the work continued on a large scale the following year (*Abbey Accounts* 1365, 6). The shingles had probably been substituted for tiles before the Dissolution but Walcott (1865–6, 167) asserts that part of a later shingled roof remained in 1811. Shingles, shingle nails, and other necessities for repairs within the monastery were accounted for in 1400 (*Cellarers' Accounts*, 95), and these documentary references leave little doubt that several of the monastic roofs at Battle will have left no trace in the archaeological record.

The first reference to the purchase of tiles – presumably clay roof tiles – occurs in 1275 when 2s 6d was paid to Martin Tiler's wife for 2,500 tiles (*Cellarers' Accounts*, 42). The fact that these were paid for suggests that they were not necessarily made at the abbey tilery, the first conclusive reference to which occurs in 1279 (p. 79). However, tiles are incorporated in the fabric of the thirteenth-century rebuilding which demonstrates that they must have been available before the earliest documentary reference. Tiles made in the late fourteenth and fifteenth century, and mentioned in the cellarers' accounts, were also probably used on the monastic buildings.

An indenture dated 1528 between John Young of Battle, tiler, and the abbot and convent of Battle provided for maintenance of the monastic buildings (ESRO: AMS 5789/15). All materials, including tiles and bricks, were to be provided by the abbey. John Young was to receive an annual wage of 26s 8d, together with food and drink, in return for which he would be responsible for 'tiling, lathing, daubing, underpinning and repairing' all the conventual buildings and certain other properties in Battle, 'for as long as the said John shall be able to tile and labour in the works abovesaid'. The contract demonstrates a continuing need for tiles to be used in repairs, but by this date the tilery does not seem to have been run directly by the abbey (p. 80).

Taking into account the archaeological evidence of slate and stone roof tiles (p. 67), the clay tiles from the excavation, which are ubiquitous in the thirteenth century and later phases, can only have formed part of a wide range of roofing materials used at the abbey. Nevertheless, well-stratified roof

tile debris provides a valuable horizon for establishing a relative chronology for destruction of the monastic buildings. The roof is usually one of the first parts of any decaying structure to suffer the ill-effects of either the weather or deliberate molestation, and concentrations of tile debris are therefore likely to mark specific stages of destruction.

Structural interpretation is hindered by the apparent conservatism of production over many centuries, and, even when a roof has been replaced, old tiles – particularly ridge tiles – may have been reused. The most that can therefore be expected from the archaeological record is the recognition of new types added to the existing stock through time. Despite these limitations, however, the excavations at Battle Abbey have furnished evidence for an unusual form of early roof tile; for apparent differences between tiles on the roof of the reredorter and those from elsewhere; and for probable re-roofing of the reredorter on at least one occasion before the Dissolution.

Classification and Comparison

Fabrics

The roof tile fabrics have been classified according to the same criteria as the pottery and floor tiles (p. 107; 82.). Different code letters, however, have been used to distinguish these from the pottery fabrics, and similarities to other ceramics have been noted where relevant.

Descriptions

Z. Flint/shell-tempered fabrics

Zi. Grey core and surfaces. Hard, harsh texture; rough fracture. Moderate medium/coarse sand temper with moderate coarse flint; sparse flecks of shell and sparse ironstone. (TF 75) *cf.* pottery Fabric Bii.

Y. Sand-tempered fabrics

Yi. Grey core with red or grey surfaces. Hard, very harsh texture; rough fracture. Abundant coarse sand temper with moderate very coarse grains up to 2mm. Sparse fragments of siltstone or sandstone up to 5 mm. (TF G; Sample 1013) *cf.* floor tile Group C.

Yii. Grey or red core and surfaces. Hard, harsh texture; rough fracture. Abundant medium/coarse sand temper. (TF J; Sample 1015).

Yiii. Pale grey core with dark grey surfaces. Hard, fairly smooth texture; rough fracture. Abundant medium/fine sand with sparse ironstone inclusions. (TF 1) *cf.* pottery Fabric Di.

Yiv. Buff-red or grey core with buff surfaces. Hard, fairly smooth texture; rough fracture. Moderate fine sand temper and moderate coarse ironstone inclusions; sometimes with sparse fragments of siltstone. (TF K; not thin-sectioned).

Yv. Red-brown core, with light brown surfaces. Hard, harsh texture; rough fracture. Abundant medium sand temper with sparse ironstone inclusions. (TF A; Sample 1007).

Yvi. Grey core, sometimes with red margins and grey surfaces. Hard, harsh texture; rough fracture. Moderate medium sand temper with sparse fragments of siltstone (TF C; Sample 1009).

Yvii. Red-pink core and surfaces. Hard, fairly harsh texture; rough fracture. Moderate medium sand temper with sparse fragments of ironstone. (TF D; Sample 1010).

Yviii. Red, sometimes grey, core and red surfaces. Hard,

harsh texture; rough fracture. Moderate medium sand temper with sparse ironstone inclusions up to 2 mm and fragments of ironstone up to 5 mm. (TF E; Sample 1011).
Yix. Red core and surfaces. Very hard, harsh texture; rough fracture. Moderate medium sand temper with sparse ironstone inclusions up to 2 mm (TF F; Sample 1012).
Yx. Deep red core; sometimes with grey surfaces. Very hard, harsh texture; fairly smooth fracture (vitrified). Moderate medium sand temper with moderate ironstone inclusions and sparse fragments of siltstone (TF B; Sample 1008).
Yxi. Red core and surfaces. Hard, harsh texture; rough fracture. Abundant medium sand temper. Dark 'metallic' glaze. (TF L; not thin-sectioned).
Yxii. Purple core and surfaces. Hard, smooth texture; rough fracture. Abundant medium/fine sand temper with moderate ironstone inclusions and sparse fragments of siltstone. (TF H; Sample 1014).

Dating and Comparison

Some fabrics are confined to roof furniture (Fabrics Zi, Yii and Yiii) and others occur only in the post-medieval phases (Fabrics Yxi and Yxii). Only the early Roman-type roof tiles (see below) are found in Fabric Yi, and the hard-fired types (Fabrics Yix and x) are not represented among the small group of tiles from Period A.

Several fabrics occur in the later phases of Period A, but significantly only tiles of Fabric Yi were found in the presumed foundation trench for the chapter house, dated c. 1100 (Phase A1). The fragments of nib or peg tiles in the chapter house graves (Phase A3) may be intrusive. The less well fired tiles (Fabric Yv) account for a slightly higher proportion of the total in Periods A-C than in the later centuries, and they do not occur at all in deposits assigned later than Phase E37.

Apart from one residual fragment (no. 20), the roof furniture is confined to Periods A–C, but the fabrics used for other tiles persist throughout the monastic and post-Dissolution phases. However, hard-fired tiles (Fabric Yix) with small square peg holes appear only in Phase D23 or later.

The fabric of tiles found at Battle can be distinguised by eye from those at Bayham Abbey (Streeten, 1983, 88), but only one of the louvers (Fabric Yiii) can be attributed to a specific source, at Rye. Fabrics Yv-x contain the same range of inclusions, and the grain size frequency of the quartz visible in thin-section is similar in each of these fabrics. Tiles in this group which occur at the same date are therefore probably from the same kiln, and the presence or absence of siltstone in the fabrics is unlikely to be distinctive of different sources. It cannot, however, be assumed that post-Dissolution tiles were manufactured at the same place as those used on the monastic buildings.

'Roman-type' Roof Tiles (Figure 23)

Manufacture

Both flat, flanged *tegula* tiles and curved *imbrex* tiles were made in the same distinctive fabric (Yi). Most have a partial clear or sometimes green glaze which distinguishes them from their Roman prototypes. The *tegulae* were apparently moulded on a sanded base, and one of the *imbrices* is slightly tapered (Thompson 1978, 205).
1. *Tegula*. Partial clear glaze.
Fabric Yi. Phase A2.
2. *Tegula*. Splashes of green glaze.
Fabric Yi. Phase A2.

Dating and Comparison

The examples from Battle belong to a class of tile which

was first recognised at Southampton (Platt and Coleman-Smith 1975, 2, 185–90; Thompson 1978), and which is now represented among finds from London (Armitage et. al. 1981). Similar tiles are also known from Reading Abbey (A. Vince, pers. comm.) and they have been identified among wasters from the early phase of Scarborough ware production (P. and N. Farmer, pers. comm.). Other medieval tiles from sites with Roman occupation may not have been distinguished from earlier types, but the limited evidence available so far suggests that this method of tiling was confined to towns and monastic establishments in the middle ages.

An interesting feature of the Southampton tiles is that the use of green glaze within an albeit small sample of fragments, appears to be confined to the *imbrices*. A similar pattern recognised at Battle shows that this type of roof may have had the appearance of being dissected by vertical green 'lines' against a plain red or clear-glazed background.

The tiles from Southampton have been dated provisionally to the late twelfth century, and a similar date is suggested for those from London and Scarborough. The occurrence of this type at Battle in the presumed foundation trench of the chapter house (Phase A2), however, suggests that they were in use as early as c. 1100. In view of the implications for dating the introduction of this type of roof tile, however, it should be emphasised that these examples do not come from a sealed deposit. Fragments from Phase B7 are either residual or they may come from buildings replaced by the new range. The fabric of the Battle tiles is different from those at Southampton, but the similarity between the early roof tiles and the later floor tiles of Group C suggests that the same raw materials may have been used at different periods.

Nib Tiles (Figure 23)

Manufacture

The characteristic rough surfaces of the flat roof tiles indicate that they were made in a sanded mould, and there are usually prominent marks on the other side of the tile where the clay has been scraped to a uniform thickness. A nail mark on one example (no. 5), however, suggests that some roof tiles were made in the same way as certain floor tiles which are assumed to have been trimmed around a template (p. 82). The term 'nail mark' has been adopted here to avoid potential confusion between the identical 'nail holes' on floor tiles (p. 87) and the larger 'peg hole(s)' in a roof tile.

The nibs occur in a variety of different shapes and sizes, but they are normally formed on the smoother side of the tile. The most common medieval type of nib at Battle is hand made and pulled up from the edge of the tile, usually with a finger streak at the base of the nib. The method of manufacture must have been similar to that described in an eighteenth-century French handbook which shows that the tile-maker pressed the clay into a mould which had a gap in one edge. This left a small projecting piece of clay which could be pulled up to form the nib (Lloyd 1934, 16).

Knife-trimmed nibs are more common on the post-medieval products, but a distinctive type fixed to the sanded surface of the tile (no. 7) was used at Battle before the mid-thirteenth century. Unlike the other types, the smooth (as opposed to sanded) surface of these tiles would have been exposed when they were in position on a roof. The extent of the knife trimming varies considerably, but knife-trimmed nibs seldom account for more than 10% of the tiles in any phase. A comprehensive typology used for classification has been listed in the excavation records.

Most of the nib tiles used on the monastic buildings had both a nib and a hole, but there are a few examples with a

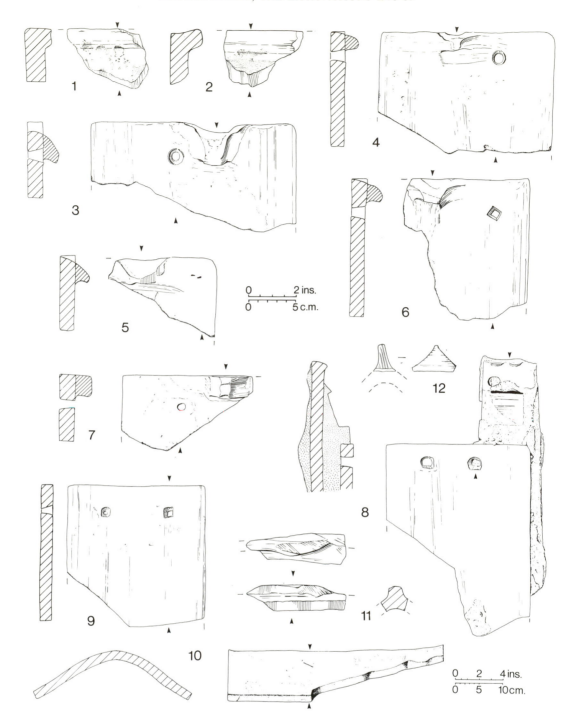

Figure 23   Battle Abbey. Medieval roof tiles. 1–9 and 11–12 ($\frac{1}{4}$); 10 ($\frac{1}{8}$).

central nib and no holes. One tile (Phase D21) had two nibs. The holes and nibs are usually placed close together (Figure 25: Graph F; measured centre to centre), and both round and square holes occur on either the right- or left-hand side of the nib (viewed from beneath). The earlier tiles are larger than the later types, and the size of the excavated ones (Phase B7) accords well with the width of contemporary tiles used for the fireplaces in the rere-dorter and in the 'novices room' beneath the dormitory (Figure 25: Graph B). There are few complete examples, but a tile built into the buttress at the north-east corner of the reredorter measures 305 x 210 x 14 mm thick.
3.   Nib tile, with round peg hole. Similar width to a tile built into the mid-thirteenth century reredorter. Fabric Yviii. Phase C14.

4.   Nib tile, with finger streak at the base of the nib, and with a round peg hole. Fabric Yviii. Phase C14.
5.   Nib tile, with finger streak at the base of the nib, and with two nail marks at the corner of the tile. Fabric Yv. Phase B7.
6.   Nib tile, with square peg hole. Fabric Yviii. Phase D21.
7.   Nib tile. Knife-trimmed nib applied to the sanded surface of the tile. Fabric Yviii. Phase B7.

Dating and Comparison
Nib tiles are now firmly established as a thirteenth-century type. They were used on a building demolished *c.* 1270 at Bishops Waltham, Hants. (Wilson and Hurst 1962–3, 319), and kiln debris including nibbed tiles was found in

make-up beneath the east range of the Dominican Priory at Chelmsford, Essex, apparently built in the second half of the thirteenth century (Drury 1977, 90). Further afield, nib tiles were found in the fill of the camera in Area 10 at Wharram Percy, N. Yorks., which was demolished *c.* 1250 (Thorn 1979, 66). Stratified examples from mid-thirteenth-century contexts at Battle, however, are the earliest so far recorded from East Sussex (Martin 1978, 34–42), and the evidence confirms that this type of tile was probably made at least as early as the second quarter of the thirteenth century.

Medieval tiles with a hand-made nib and peg hole are known from other local monastic sites at Bayham Abbey (Streeten 1983, 89) and Hastings Priory (Martin 1973, 40), and similar types occur on the roof of the surviving buildings at Robertsbridge Abbey. However, the tiles from a sealed deposit at Michelham Priory, dated *c.* 1300–1325, did not apparently include nibbed types (Barton and Holden 1967, 9). A few tiles with knife-trimmed nibs occur in the mid-thirteenth century at Battle, but up to 99% of the nibs among a large sample representing debris from the roof of the dormitory and reredorter (Phase D21/22) were formed by hand.

Peg Tiles (Figure 23)

Manufacture

Peg tiles have the same smooth and sanded surfaces as the nibbed types. The holes were made with a blunt, sometimes slightly tapering, round or square stick. Square holes are usually set diagonally, and, although small square ones (less than 10 mm) are found on some medieval tiles, these are usually distinctive of the later types (no. 9).

Like the nibbed tiles, holes on the few thirteenth- or fourteenth-century peg tiles tend to be placed closer together than on examples from the Dissolution debris (Figure 25: Graph G). The later peg tiles are also smaller, and the most common widths approximate to the standard 6¼ in. (159 mm) laid down in 1477 (Celoria and West 1967, 218; Figure 25: Graph B).

8. Peg tiles set in mortar with impression of wooden lath, viewed from beneath. (See p. 100 for discussion of methods of fixing tiles). Fabric Yviii. Phase E36.
9. Peg tile. Fabric Yix. Phase D23.

Dating and Comparison

The evidence from Battle confirms the impression formed elsewhere that medieval peg tiles are contemporary with the nibbed types (Drury 1977, 90). They occur in small quantities in Periods B and C, but are more common in Period D, which presumably reflects renewal of certain roofs before the Dissolution (p. 99–100). The smaller peg tiles at Winchelsea are ascribed to the fifteenth century (Martin and King 1975, 137).

Peg tiles used as packing in the foundations of Building Y have widely spaced holes and are of similar width to the most common sizes found amongst post-Dissolution debris in this area (Phase D24–28). Even these, however, are wider than the estimated dimension of a tile with square holes found during excavations on the presumed site of the monastic tilery at Tower Hill Farm, Battle (Battle Museum). The width of *c.* 140–145 mm is considerably narrower than the majority of medieval roof tiles from the abbey, and the form suggests that this may be a post-medieval tile.

Ridge Tiles (Figure 23)

Most of the ridge tiles are plain (*i.e.* without decorated crests) and these are in the same fabrics as the flat roof tiles. Two decorated examples, however, are similar to the

chimney pot (no. 16), and may therefore be from the same source. A crenellated fragment was found among wasters at Rye (Barton 1979, 254, no. 3); two crested tiles remain on the roof of the Court Hall at Winchelsea; and a crest with simple undercut band, similar to no. 11 from Battle, is reported from Hastings Priory (Martin 1973, 40–1, no. 11). Decorated ridge tiles are not common in East Sussex, where plain types predominate (Barton 1979, 63), and differences between the fabrics of the plain tiles and the decorated ridge tiles at Battle suggest that the crested types may belong to a specialist output.

10. Plain curved tile. Possibly used as a ridge tile on a low-pitched roof but this could be a half-round hip tile. Fabric Yviii. Phase D21.
11. Ridge tile with simple 'wavy' crest. Fabric Yiv. Phase B7.
12. Ridge tile with triangular crest. Fabric Yiv. Phase C12.

Hip or valley tiles

In the absence of the distinctive fixing holes for a hip tile or the plain head of a valley tile, curved tapering tiles are often assumed to be from a hipped roof. However, the sanded surface is usually concave, and, if laid consistently with the flat tiles, these would form a valley rather than a hip. References to 'guttertile' in the Statute of 1477 (Celoria and West 1967, 219) and elsewhere (Salzman 1952, 232) suggest that tiles, as opposed to lead, would sometimes be used to line valleys.

No complete examples with or without peg holes have been found at Battle, but tapering tiles are represented in both the chapter house and reredorter areas. It is difficult to suggest a function for those found outside the north-west corner of the reredorter (Phase D21/22), because there was certainly no valley at this point, and the roof is unlikely to have been hipped. If there was a pentice outside the 'novices room' and the ground-floor doorway at the north-west corner of the reredorter, then they may have come from there. It is possible that some of the later ancilliary structures may have been hipped, but the surviving gable at the south end of the dormitory is likely to be typical of the other claustral ranges, in which case there would have been no need for hip tiles on the principal buildings.

Roof Furniture (Figure 24)

Apart from no. 14 which is almost certainly from the roof of the reredorter, none of the roof furniture can be attributed to specific buildings. Zoomorphic finials, probably of wood (Dunning 1960), are shown on the well-known twelfth-century drawing of the reredorter at Christ-church Priory, Canterbury (Willis 1869, pl. 1 parts 1 and 2). It is tempting to speculate that no. 13 is an early anthropormorphic equivalent in pottery, from the demolished Norman reredorter at Battle. The louver (no. 14) and chimney pot (no. 16) from the chapter house area were both discarded before the Dissolution, and they are unlikely to have come from that part of the east range. They may, however, be from other buildings east of the chapter house.

13. Anthropomorphic finial (?). Fabric Zi. Phase A5. The decoration is similar to thirteenth-century finials illustrated by Dunning (1961, 79), but, because of its context, this specimen is probably earlier, possibly late twelfth or early thirteenth century. The form cannot be reconstructed in detail but the curvature behind the mask suggests that this was from the rounded top of a hollow finial (Dunning 1961, 79, fig 5.1, no. 5).
14. Knob finial from louver (?). Fabric Yiii. Phase D21. Solid knob finials attached to ridge tiles are represented

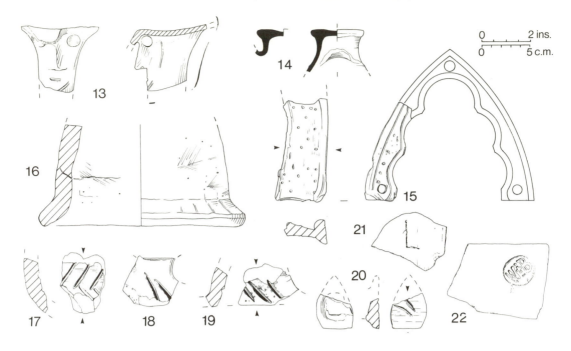

Figure 24   Battle Abbey. Medieval roof furniture and post-medieval roof tiles ($\frac{1}{4}$).

among the wasters from Rye (Vidler 1933, pl. x, B; Barton 1979, 254), but this example is hollow and has traces of an aperture on one side. It could have come from the top of a louver, but it is more likely to be an unusual type from the crest of a baffle plate, as illustrated in the reconstruction of a louver from the kilns at Nash Hill, Lacock, Wilts (Dunning 1974, 129). The absence of soot blackening would be consistent with use as a ventilator in the reredorter, and the fabric is similar to pottery attributed to the Rye kilns.

15.   Baffle plate from louver. White slip on the interior and on the face of the canopy; external green glaze on the sides. Fabric Yiv. Phase C12. Apertures in the sides of a louver usually had simple 'baffle plates' at the top of the opening as shown by the fine example from St Thomas Street, Winchester (Dunning 1972, pl. lxxiv). When the canopy extended down the sides of the aperture, the edges were sometimes thumb-pressed (Dunning 1968, fig. 3), but the white slip and 'architectural' treatment on the louver from Battle is unusual. Date: late thirteenth or probably fourteenth century.

16.   Chimney pot. Fabric Yiv. Phase C17.
Conical chimney pots are frequent finds in Sussex, but the fabric of this example is finer than the early flint-tempered types (Dunning 1961, 82). There would have been holes in the side and probably in the top as well, but none is visible on the surviving fragment. The base was added after the top half of the pot had been thrown.

Miscellaneous
17–19.   Fragments possibly from a louver. Fabric Yii. Phase A2. All three fragments are probably from the same fitting. Nos. 18 and 19 have the smoothed edges of an aperture(?), and, both are soot blackened on the 'interior'. These are therefore unlikely to be pieces of an elaborate ridge tile, but they have defied attempts at reconstruction. If they are indeed fragments from a louver, then this would be a very early example.

20.   Fragment, similar to nos. 17–19. Fabric Yii. Phase D24.

21.   Ridge (?) tile with incised 'L' scratched after firing. Fabric Yviii. Phase E47.

22.   Roof tile stamped 'W:B'. Presumably a local maker's mark. Fabric Yviii. Phase E47.
Not illustrated. Tiles with paw prints of a medium-sized dog. Fabric Yviii. Phases C12 and C14.
Another fragment from a thick unglazed tile has a cat's paw print (Phase D21), but this may be a floor tile. It is normally assumed that animal paw marks were made while the tiles were laid out to dry before firing. If so, some of the products must have been spread on the ground rather than in racks where they would have been out of the reach of an animal.

Discussion and Conclusions

Roof Tiles and the Monastic Buildings
Roof tiles made by more than one craftsman and fired on different occasions are likely to have been kept in stock for several months, and variation is therefore to be expected even among contemporary tiles laid on the same roof. Differences in size and the traits of manufacture, however, are sufficient to detect changes in certain phases. Large or significant groups have therefore been selected for analysis, but the size of the samples has been determined by practical rather than statistical considerations. There are few complete tiles, and even the width can be measured on only a proportion of the fragments. Some statistics such as the ratio of nibs to holes are based upon samples of several hundred fragments, but others rely upon less than 50 examples. Percentages have only been calculated for samples of twenty or more, and actual numbers are shown on Figure 25 where there are fewer than twenty fragments.

Tile thicknesses show little variation between Periods B, C and D, but the thinner types are

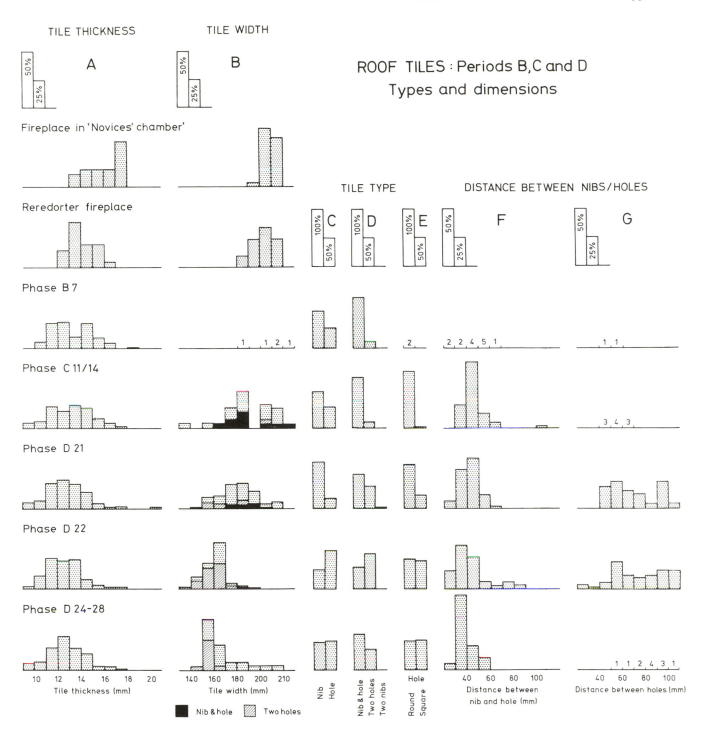

Figure 25   Battle Abbey. Histograms showing the dimensions and other characteristics of medieval and later roof tiles in selected phases.

slightly more numerous in the later phases (Figure 25: Graph A). Broad tiles, however, are distinctive of the mid-thirteenth century, and the width of the few examples from construction levels in the reredorter area (Phase B7) is consistent with a sample of measured tiles in contemporary fireplaces within the reredorter and east range (Figure 25: Graph B). Those fragments on which the width can be measured at the top of the tile show that 'nib and hole' types predominate both in Phase B7, and in the later

medieval make-up outside the reredorter (Phase C11/14; Figure 25: Graph B). Only in Phase D24–28 is there a reversal of the ratio when *all* nibs and holes are counted instead of just the near-complete tiles. The latter provides a more reliable index of the proportions of each type, but the low survival of complete tiles does not always provide a large enough sample for analysis (Figure 25: Graphs C and D).

Narrow tiles occur in larger quantities among the

later debris (Period D) and most of the identifiable fragments have two peg holes rather than a nib and a hole (Figure 25: Graph B). It appears, therefore, that a new type of tile had replaced some of the earlier ones by this period, but there is a marked contrast between Phases D21 and D22. The lower level of tile debris outside the reredorter (Phase D21) ends abruptly with the east end of the building (Figure 11), and almost certainly represents destruction of the monastic roof. The range of tile sizes is similar to phase C11/14, and the debris includes several 'nib and hole' types. Some of the tiles, however, are narrower than those associated with the thirteenth-century rebuilding (Figure 25: Graph B). The implication must be that the reredorter was re-roofed during the monastic period, and that some of the larger tiles were replaced by smaller ones with two peg holes.

The methods of fixing the nibbed and peg tiles on the same roof would have been different, but not incompatible. It can be inferred from the position of the holes that the nib tiles would usually have been secured by a large-headed nail driven into the lath underneath. Occasional instances where the hole has not been punched right through the tile indicate that nailing was not universal, and this may indicate that, in common with modern practice, only every fourth course or so was fixed to the lath. Mortar was sometimes used for fixing the tail of a tile. Tiles with two peg holes may also have been nailed, but, by post-medieval analogy, wooden pegs are more likely to have been inserted and hooked over the lath like a nib. It would be normal only to use one peg for each tile, the two holes allowing flexibility for the tiler to insert his pegs to either right or left of the intervening rafters. Two fragments set in mortar with the impression of a lath illustrate the arrangement (no. 8), but these are from final destruction of the reredorter (Phase E36) and, although they are probably from the late medieval roof, they may represent a later repair. Moreover, the extent of the mortar and the low pitch of the tiles implied by the angle of the lath impression suggests that this fragment probably comes from an awkward position on the roof and does not therefore set a standard for the roof as a whole. It is difficult to date renewal of the reredorter roof with precision, but the tile fragments from Phase C11/14 may represent construction debris, and the addition of a rainwater drainage system could well have been accompanied by repairs to the roof.

The assemblage of tiles from Phase D22 is quite different. Despite documentary evidence for shingles on the dormitory roof in the fourteenth century, however, the concentration of tile debris outside the north-west corner of the reredorter probably came from stripping of the dormitory roof after the Dissolution. The shingles had probably been replaced by tiles sometime in the fifteenth century. Material from Phase D22 includes artifacts which were apparently discarded at the Dissolution, and, unless the context is a mixed one, the roof tiles are therefore unlikely to have come from a later roof in this area. The only remaining possibility that these tiles were brought from elsewhere in the abbey at, or slightly after, the Dissolution seems unlikely.

By implication, this shows that other tiled roofs were also renewed, probably during the monastic occupation, because the contrast between tiles from Phase D22 and those attributed to Period B is even greater than compared with Phase D21 (Figure 25: Graph B). Indeed, the range of tile sizes is more akin to debris associated with the post-Dissolution buildings east of the parlour, but these may have incorporated re-used materials.

Statistical analysis has provided the basis for general conclusions about the nature and extent of re-roofing before the Dissolution. The methods require a rigid policy for collection of the data, and the statistical significance of criteria by which different types of tile can be identified has not yet been assessed. Meaningful results are only likely to be obtained from large-scale excavations, but this approach could undoubtedly be applied elsewhere, and when comparative information is available it will be possible to evaluate the different methods of sampling.

Production and Distribution
The monastic tilery at Battle is known from documentary sources to have been in operation at least by the last quarter of the thirteenth century. Tiles used on the earlier thirteenth-century buildings would no doubt have been manufactured nearby as well, and there is evidence that ceramic roof tiles were probably used at Battle before c. 1100. Medieval tiles found at the abbey are different from the material which came from excavations on the presumed site of the tile kiln, and the precise location of the tilery therefore remains in doubt.

The nib tiles belong to a widespread tradition of manufacture, but, like the decorated floor tiles, the example with nail marks is most unusual. Some of the roof tiles and floor tiles may have been obtained from a common source, but the roof furniture apparently came from elsewhere, and at least one of the fabrics can be attributed to the kilns at Rye. Another louver from the Bodiam moated homestead has been identified as a Rye product, and these potters seem to have met local requirements for roof furniture as well as coarsewares within a radius of at least 18 km (11 miles) from Rye.

Brick
Introduction
Brick occurs in contexts attributed to the thirteenth century and later, but pre-Dissolution brickwork only survives *in situ* in one of the drains east of the chapter house. Material derived from the early phases may have been imported, but significant quantities of locally-produced brick were found among the Dissolution debris in the reredorter area.

Classification and Comparison
Method of Classification
Fragments of brick with at least one measurable dimension were retained for analysis. Smaller pieces were also collected from significant early contexts.

The assemblage has been divided principally according to fabric using the same criteria as those for the pottery and floor tiles (p. 107; 82). All the fragments have been measured, and, where possible, the range of sizes has been indicated for each type. Details of this analysis are included in the archive. None of the bricks described in this report is machine-moulded; all were made by hand.

Type 1

Fabric Brown-red core and surfaces. Fairly hard, harsh texture; rough, slightly laminated fracture. Moderate inclusions of red iron ore; little sand visible to the naked eye; groundmass of fine quartz grains seen in thin-section. (TFa; Sample 1052).
Size No complete dimensions.
Comparison Although the size of these bricks is not known, they are definitely thicker than the thickest floor tiles (Group S). The reddish colour, as opposed to the buff and pink tones of the imported Flemish bricks, suggests that these may have been produced locally. Even if they are imports, their occurrence in Phase B7 places them among the earliest examples of brick in Sussex (p. 81).

Type 2

Fabric Mottled red-pink core and surfaces; Hard, harsh texture; rough fracture. Fairly fine sand; dark red and yellow-buff grog(?) inclusions. (TFg; not thin-sectioned).
Size 239–246 mm (*c*. $9\frac{1}{2}$ in) × 117–120 mm (*c*. $4\frac{3}{4}$) × 51 mm (*c*. 2 in)
Comparison The type occurs only on the bottom of the late medieval drain associated with the construction of Building X (*supra* p. 38, 41; Figure 7). The bricks used here do not necessarily represent a repair, and the narrow thickness would be consistent with a fifteenth- or early sixteenth-century date. The fabric, which includes pieces of buff-coloured (?) grog (similar to Type 3), suggests that these may be imported bricks.

Type 3

Fabric Yellow-buff core and surfaces. Fairly soft, smooth texture; rough fracture. Fine sand. Irregular lines scored on both the upper and lower surfaces of one fragment. (TFg; not thin sectioned).
Size *c*. 32 mm ($1\frac{1}{4}$ in) thick.
Comparison The thickness of only one of the two fragments found at Battle can be measured, and it is narrower than comparable Flemish imports from Bodiam and from Tower Hill Farm, Battle (Battle Museum). In view of the thickness and late context (Phases E36 and E42), there remains a remote possibility that these are post-medieval floor tiles. The distinctive fabric, however, leaves little doubt that this a medieval type from the Low Countries. Similar bricks have been dated to between the fourteenth and sixteenth/seventeenth centuries, and the examples from Battle are therefore residual.

Type 4

Fabric Red core and surfaces. Fairly hard, harsh texture; rough fracture. Moderate sand; sparse fragments of siltstone or sandstone (TFd; not thin-sectioned).
Size i 30–36 mm (*c*. $1\frac{1}{4}$–$1\frac{1}{2}$ in) thick
Size ii 107–117 mm (*c*. $4\frac{1}{4}$–$4\frac{5}{8}$ in) × 48–57 mm ($1\frac{7}{8}$–$2\frac{1}{4}$ in)
Size iii *c*. 69 mm (*c*. $2\frac{3}{4}$ in) thick
Dimensions of these bricks have been grouped on the basis of thickness alone. The only two fragments on which the

width survives are similar to sizes ii and v of Type 5.
Comparison Type 4 bricks occur among the Dissolution debris in the reredorter area, and the dimensions of sizes i(?) and ii are similar to late fifteenth/early sixteenth-century bricks in south east England (Lloyd 1925, 89). Size iii occurs only in Phase E47 and is probably eighteenth century or later (*cf*. Finchcocks, Goudhurst, dated *c*. 1725).

Type 5

Fabric Similar colour, texture and composition to Type 4, but with dark (?ironstone) inclusions (TFf; not thin-sectioned).
Size i 85–95mm ($3\frac{3}{8}$–$4\frac{3}{4}$ in) x 50–56 mm (*c*. 2–$2\frac{1}{4}$ in)
Size ii 97–107 mm (*c*. $3\frac{7}{8}$–$4\frac{1}{4}$ in) x 50–57 mm (*c*. 2–$2\frac{1}{4}$ in). Exceptional examples: 45 mm and 47 mm thick. Surviving lengths: 223 mm ($8\frac{3}{4}$ in) and 240 mm ($9\frac{1}{2}$ in)
Size iii 100–105 mm (*c*. $3\frac{7}{8}$–$4\frac{1}{4}$ in) x 60–65 mm (*c*. $2\frac{7}{8}$–$2\frac{5}{8}$)
Size iv 110–114 mm (*c*. 4–$4\frac{1}{2}$ in) x 54–60 mm (*c*. $2\frac{1}{8}$–$2\frac{3}{8}$ in). Exceptional examples. 44 mm; 50 mm; and 63 mm thick.
Size v 117–120 mm (*c*. $4\frac{5}{8}$–$4\frac{3}{4}$ in) x 54–62 mm (*c*. $2\frac{1}{8}$–$2\frac{1}{2}$ in)
Comparison These bricks are by far the most numerous type in Dissolution and later contexts, although intrusive fragments do occur in earlier phases. The only complete examples (size ii) come from Phase E38, but the dimensions are similar to those in sixteenth-century brickwork at Rolvenden, Kent (Lloyd 1925, 89). There is little difference in size between bricks from Period D and those from Period E. However, a considerably higher proportion of the fragments in Period E have been fired to a deeper purple colour, and, whereas glazed brick is virtually unrepresented among the Dissolution debris, it is more common in the later phases of Period D and in Period E.

Type 6

Fabric Red-pink core and surfaces. Hard, harsh texture; rough fracture fine sand; streaks of yellow clay; moderate inclusions of ironstone. (TFe; not thin-sectioned).
Size 102–114 mm (*c*. 4–$4\frac{1}{2}$ in) x 54–64 mm (*c*. $2\frac{1}{8}$–$2\frac{1}{2}$ in). Surviving fragments form an even scatter of dimensions within this range of sizes, with no obvious standardization.
Comparison Bricks from elsewhere in the Weald contain distinctive streaks of light coloured clay, and similar fabrics have been noted among the floor tiles (Group N). The occurrence of this type in Dissolution and later phases at Battle Abbey follows a similar pattern to Type 5, although there are few examples.

Type 7

Fabric Bright orange-red core and surfaces. Fairly soft, smooth texture; rough fracture. Fine sand; sparse inclusions of ironstone; moderate mica. (TFc; not thin-sectioned).
Size *c*. 67 mm (*c*. $2\frac{5}{8}$ in) thick.
Comparison There is only one example of this type in Phase E39.

Discussion and Conclusions

Brick may have been used as early as the thirteenth century, and it was certainly available in reasonable quantities at Battle before the Dissolution. Most of the fragments found among the Dissolution debris probably date from the early sixteenth century; and the use of over-fired bricks to form a pattern of 'blue headers' is known on fifteenth-century buildings elsewhere in the region (*cf*. Farnham Castle, 1470–5).

A notable feature of the bricks found at Battle Abbey is the increasing proportion of over-fired and glazed types in the later phases of Period D and in Period E. Only 9% of the fragments from Phases D21/22 and D30 in the reredorter area were glazed, whereas glazed brick accounts for between 58% and 60% of the material attributed to later phases.

There is no recognisably sixteenth-century brick-work in the surviving masonry of the east range. Although there may have been brick partitions which have disappeared, the bricks from the Dis-solution debris in the reredorter area were probably dumped from elsewhere. Some of the fragments from later phases are probably residual, but the differences in manufacture noted above imply that much of this material is derived from post-medieval structures and later alterations to the former monas-tic buildings.

Finds and Records

Like the pottery, the storage system for the ceramic building materials has been designed to enable the retrieval of either type samples or stratified groups. The finds and associated records have been depo-sited in the custody of the Historic Buildings and Monuments Commission, and the thin-sections have been retained in the Department of Archaeology, University of Southampton.

Finds include a fabric type series related to the thin sections; illustrated items; and other fragments of brick and tile stored by context.

The records comprise a phasing summary with context numbers; a concordance of 'interim' and 'publication' tile numbers; and a detailed classifica-tion of the floor tiles, roof tiles and brick, with numerical codes related to sets of data summary sheets.

Acknowledgements

Thanks are due to the same group of volunteers who worked on the pottery (p. 126) for their dedication to the routine task of processing the ceramic building materials. Mrs V. Coad assisted with supervision of the work, and a debt of gratitude is owed for the care with which she has prepared drawings of the finds to accompany this report. Dr J. Hare provided all the phasing information, and has generously made avail-able results of his research into the original documentary sources. Thanks are also due to Jennie Coy (DOE Faunal Remains Project, Southampton University) for identifying the animal paw marks on the tiles. Permission to publish drawings of tiles in Barbican House Museum, Lewes and in Battle Museum is gratefully acknowledged. Messrs. E.W. Holden and D. Martin have generously contributed constructive comments on an earlier draft of this report.

Chapter VII

Pottery

by Anthony D.F. Streeten

Introduction

The pottery from Battle Abbey provides important evidence for the dating of local wares, and the ceramics themselves have helped to establish a chronology for some of the late medieval alterations and subsequent stages of destruction at the abbey. Furthermore, the identification of kiln sources offers an insight into the organisation of medieval and later pottery manufacture and marketing in the region. Significant variations in the range of vessels represented at different periods can also be detected, and specific activities such as distilling have been inferred from certain unusual forms.

Successive alterations to the medieval and later ground levels have provided a valuable series of stratified archaeological deposits to which the ceramic sequence can be related. Thus, an accumulation of up to 1.0 m on the north side of the reredorter represents both occupation debris and deliberate make-up during the three centuries or so following construction of the building in the mid-thirteenth century.

The largest group of pottery was found in rubbish dumps outside the reredorter and contained a wide range of objects discarded at, or shortly after, the Dissolution. Similar, yet less productive layers were investigated in the chapter house. Earlier levels in both areas have provided valuable dating evidence for certain types of pottery. The later history of the site is not only represented by scattered sherds from the demolition rubble, but there is also an interesting group of post-medieval pottery from loam inside the demolished chapter house, which was at least partly sealed by an early nineteenth-century clay yard.

Taking the stratified assemblage as a whole, most of the vessels were discarded during Periods D and E, that is after the Dissolution in 1538 (Figure 36):

	weight	sherd count
Period A	1%	2%
Period B	2%	4%
Period C	4%	5%
Period D	67%	69%
Period E	25%	20%

Local Kilns and Markets

Over a century of antiquarian and archaeological interest in local pottery manufacture has provided evidence for no less than ten kilns dated to before *c.* 1600 within a radius of 30 km (19 miles) from Battle

(Figure 26). Of these, four kilns are within 10 km (6 miles) of the abbey, and there were also several later potteries in the area. Many of the marketed vessels found at Battle Abbey are known to have come from these nearby kilns.

Abbot's Wood, Upper Dicker, East Sussex TQ 564 074
Wasters (Barton 1979, 182–4). Finds deposited with Forestry Commission; sample sherds at Worthing Museum. Date: probably thirteenth century.

Boreham Street, East Sussex TQ 669 114
Kiln, excavated 1971–2 (not yet published; Barton 1979, 156). Selected finds deposited at Barbican House Museum, Lewes. Date: early sixteenth century.

Broadland Wood, Brede, East Sussex TQ 837 191
Clay pits and wasters (Austen 1946, 94–5). Finds deposited at Hastings Museum. Date: thirteenth/fourteenth century.

17 Acre Field, Brede, East Sussex
Possible wasters (A. Scott, pers. comm.) Date: probably fifteenth century.

Hareplain, Biddenden, Kent TQ 831 394 Kiln (Kelly 1972). Finds deposited at Maidstone Museum. Date: late fifteenth/early sixteenth century.

Bohemia, Hastings, East Sussex TQ 811 049 and 806 103
Wasters (including tiles) and kilns (Lower 1859; Ross 1860; Barton 1979, 184–90). Finds deposited at Hastings Museum. Date: probably fourteenth century.

Lower Parrock, Hartfield, East Sussex TQ 456 357
Kiln (Freke 1979). Finds deposited at Barbican House Museum, Lewes. Date: early sixteenth century.

Ringmer, East Sussex TQ 44 12
Wasters and kilns over a wide area (Legge 1902, 81; Martin 1902; Barton 1979, 180–2; Hadfield 1981). Finds deposited at Barbican House Museum, Lewes. Date: thirteenth/fourteenth century (archaeological evidence) extending to early sixteenth century (documentary sources).

Spittal Field, Rye, East Sussex TQ 921 210
Pottery kilns and wasters, including roof tiles and floor tiles (Vidler 1932; 1933; 1936; Barton 1979, 191–254). Finds originally housed in the Ypres Tower Museum, Rye now transferred to Barbican House Museum, Lewes (1981). Other vessels deposited at Hastings Museum and Winchelsea Museum. Date: late thirteenth(?) to fifteenth century.

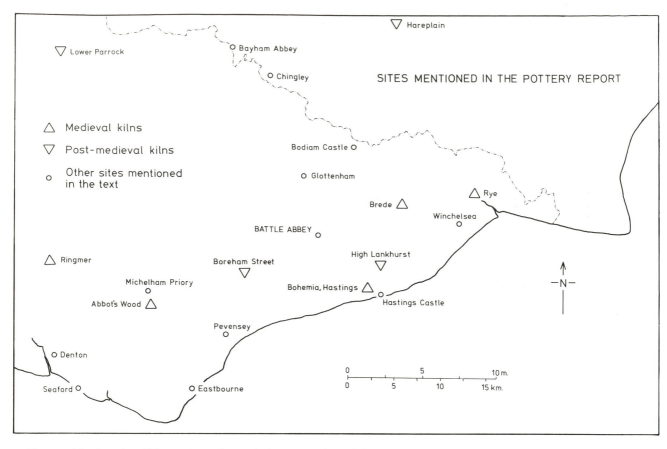

Figure 26   Battle Abbey. Location of sites mentioned in the pottery report.

High Lankhurst, Westfield, East Sussex TQ 818 135
Kiln excavated 1978–9 (not yet published; Cherry 1979, 281). Finds currently in possession of Hastings Area Archaeological Group (1979). Date: probably late sixteenth century.

There is no conclusive documentary evidence for other medieval pottery kilns in the vicinity of Battle, but personal and place-names may indicate the existence of potteries for which archaeological evidence has not yet been discovered. Among numerous examples, the place-name 'Crockers' at Northiam was probably associated with Hamo de Creueker who is recorded in the thirteenth century (Mawer and Stenton 1969, 524) rather than with a potter. Both personal and place-names at Pevensey, however, indicate that the town had its own potter (Dulley 1967, 219–20). The evidence, which is not always conclusive, has been discussed more fully elsewhere (Streeten 1980; 1981), but there can be little doubt that other yet unknown potters in the area may have sold their wares to the monastic community at Battle.

Supplies for the abbey were obtained from several different ports and markets, often some distance away. The fourteenth century cellarers' accounts for example show that wine was brought from as far afield as London, Canterbury and Sandwich, as well as from the local ports of Hastings, Rye and Winchelsea (*Cellarers' Accounts*, 65–6; 79). How-

ever, goods were normally purchased in the town (Searle 1974, 352), and household utensils such as pottery would likewise probably have been obtained locally. A market at Battle was authorised by William the Conqueror (*Chronicle*, 84), and by the thirteenth or fourteenth century this would have been one of the three nearest markets for the potters working at both Hastings and Brede (Streeten 1981, fig. 22.3). It is therefore unfortunate that the only two references in the cellarers' accounts to the purchase of earthenware, as opposed to metal or wooden vessels, in 1306–7 and 1464–5, do not indicate where they were bought (*Cellarers' Accounts*, 48 and 140). Potters would undoubtedly have attended local markets, but specific orders may have been obtained direct from the kiln, and it seems probable that imported wares would have been kept in stock at the nearby ports.

Ceramic Sequence
The stratigraphic sequence has been divided into five periods based upon the structural history of the monastic buildings. Each period includes several phases which form the basis for quantification of the pottery (Figures 36–38). Published vessels (Figures 29–35) have been assigned to these phases and can therefore be linked with the historical sequence. Both the date range and the quantity of pottery attributed to different phases varies considerably: some represent short-lived building activities; others

cover longer periods of occupation; and some of the most interesting deposits contain objects which were probably dumped within a short space of time but which may have been in use for many decades beforehand. Unfortunately, therefore, the absolute chronology remains ill defined during some of the most significant periods for ceramic history, in particular during the fifteenth and late sixteenth centuries.

Period A: Norman: Before the Thirteenth-Century Rebuilding

An important dated group of pottery comprises the small collection of flint-/shell– tempered sherds from the presumed foundation trench of the chapter house, which was probably completed by c. 1100 (p. 23). Evidence from other early contexts was less instructive because several of the chapter house graves had been disturbed, and there was no pottery from the make-up beneath Building Z. Drainage gullies in the reredorter area, however, did contain pottery which must be earlier than the thirteenth-century rebuilding, although, in the absence of clearly-defined construction debris, it has proved difficult to distinguish between material deposited before or during the building activity. Only finds from the primary silt of the drainage gullies or from immediately above the natural surface have therefore been attributed to Phase A5.

Period B: The Great Rebuilding: Thirteenth Century

Pottery was not recovered from limited investigation of the foundation trench for the dormitory at the north-west corner of the reredorter, but finds from make-up associated with the porch, which is contemporary with the rest of the range (p. 30), have provided important evidence for the dating of vessels attributed to the Rye kilns (p. 112). Construction of the reredorter would have entailed filling the earlier gullies at the east end of the new building, and a considerable depth of make-up was also added inside the reredorter. Although these deposits may have contained residual material they are definitely earlier than the mid-thirteenth century (p. 34). None of the finds from the area south of the reredorter was stratigraphically associated with the thirteenth-century rebuilding, and although some of the medieval layers may have originated during this period, they could not be distinguished satisfactorily from later occupation.

Period C: The Later Middle Ages

The addition of an extensive drainage system involved raising the ground level on the north and east sides of the reredorter. It is difficult to distinguish between the deliberate make-up (Phase C14), which contains a wide range of pottery fabrics, and any earlier occupation layers which may have been sealed beneath it (Phase C11). A sherd of Tudor Green ware in the make-up suggests that the alterations are no earlier than c. 1400 (p. 112); yet the deposit does not contain material which is later than the mid-fifteenth century. The presence of a marble shaft fragment possibly placed here after remodell-

ing of the cloisters offers circumstantial evidence for a date c. 1420. Only a few sherds were associated with other late medieval alterations.

Period D: The Dissolution and After. Sixteenth and Seventeenth Centuries

Debris was discarded at, or shortly after, the Dissolution in the area outside the reredorter (Phase D21/22) and within the reredorter drain itself (Phase D30). Whatever the precise date of this operation, finds from these deposits are likely to reflect the range of utensils which had been used during the final years of monastic occupation. Diverse dates, however, are represented among associated coins from the reredorter (p. 182). Dumps outside the reredorter were at least partly sealed by roof tile debris from initial decay of the buildings, and some finds were associated with primary destruction debris from the church and chapter house (Phase D20). Other phases within this period are associated with post-Dissolution activities. Some groups, such as the loam on the ground floor of the reredorter, contain finds which are indistinguishable from the Dissolution debris, but layers which were sealed by later masonry rubble rather than debris from initial decay of the buildings may be contaminated by later material.

In contrast to the Dissolution dumps which include a wide range of what are presumably residual sherds of the thirteenth to fourteenth century, these types are poorly represented among the layers inside the chapter house (Phase D23). A jetton from here is considered to have been in circulation c. 1600 (p. 179, no 28), and many of the pottery forms are typical of the late sixteenth and early seventeenth centuries. Odd fragments from later vessels were probably discarded before the early nineteenth-century clay yard was laid over these deposits.

Ceramics from Period D must therefore be divided into three separate groups (Figure 36):

i Dissolution debris in the reredorter area. (Phases D21 and 22).
ii Early post-medieval deposits containing pottery associated both with monastic occupation and with post-Dissolution activities (Phases D20 and D24–34).
iii Late sixteenth/early seventeenth century and later wares from inside the chapter house (Phase D23).

Period E: The Second Phase of Destruction and Afterwards. Eighteenth to Twentieth Centuries

Post-medieval deposits contain a wide range of residual sherds together with types which, with the exception of Phase D23, occur for the first time in this period. The reredorter was probably destroyed before c. 1720 (p. 45) and this area was reoccupied for stables in the late eighteenth century (p. 46). The early nineteenth-century clay yard provides a useful archaeological horizon for deposits both inside and outside the former chapter house, but even the recent garden soil above the clay contained some medieval sherds.

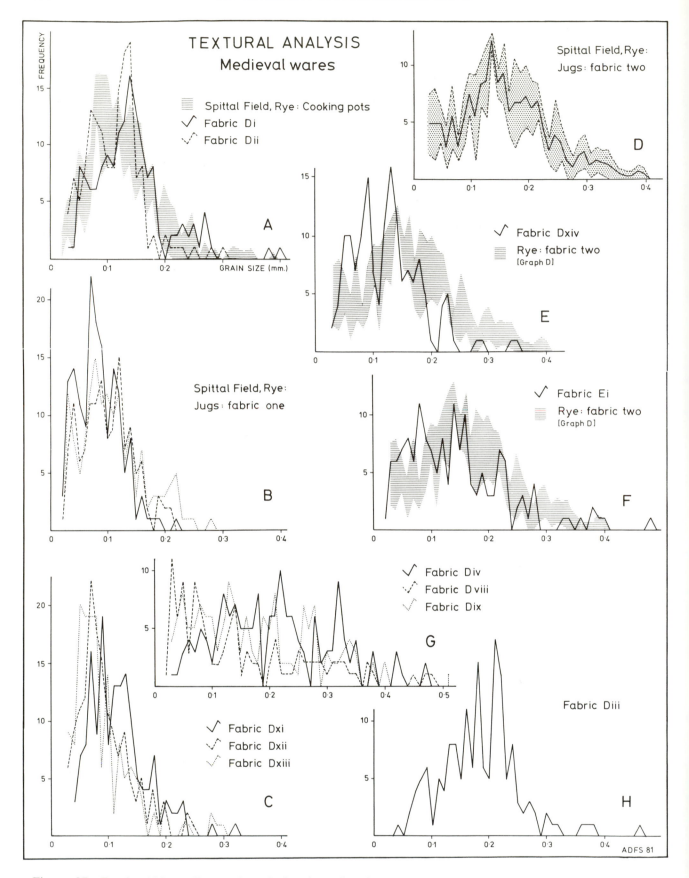

Figure 27   Battle Abbey. Textural analysis of medieval pottery.

Classification and Comparison

Method of Classification and Quantification

The pottery fabrics have been grouped according to their composition, texture and colour, and the descriptions follow conventions recommended by Peacock (1977). Thin-sections of the earthenwares have been prepared from type sherds (TF numbers), and sample numbers relate to a reference collection of microscope slides compiled by the author and deposited at Southampton University.

In the interests of speed and economy, the pottery was sorted by a small group of volunteers who had been given basic instruction in the techniques of identification. Uniformity has been maintained by reference to the type sherds, and identifications were checked as far as possible by the writer while the sorting was in progress. This proved to be a quick and efficient method of processing and recording a large number of sherds, but it was sometimes difficult to classify the hard-fired late medieval earthenwares.

Quantification has been based upon both body sherds and rim sherds because some phases comprise only small groups of pottery. Simple measures of weight and sherd count have therefore been adopted in preference to more sophisticated 'vessel equivalents' (Orton 1975, 31), but an estimated minimum number of vessels has been calculated for each phase and fabric. These figures are derived from an assessment of all sherds within each context. Apart from obvious joins, however, it was not possible to take account of different pieces from the same vessel which might have been found on different parts of the site.

Illustrated forms have been confined to unusual or near-complete vessels, and to items which assist with the dating of a particular fabric. Descriptive catalogue entries include only those features which are not visible on the drawing, and both the provenance and approximate date are indicated by the phase code. Most of the vessels which could be reconstructed were found among the Dissolution debris (Period D).

Textural Analysis

Sand-tempered ceramics can seldom be attributed reliably by eye to a specific kiln, unless either the form or decoration of the vessels is particularly distinctive. However, a technique of thin-section characterisation, which is based upon principles applied originally by Peacock (1971) to Romano-British pottery, has been developed in order to differentiate between the products of known medieval kilns in south-east England. Despite the absence of diagnostic mineral inclusions in locally-produced ceramics from an area of sedimentary geology, tests have shown that the size of the quartz grains in different pottery fabrics found in such areas varies sufficiently for marketed vessels to be attributed to their source by comparing the grain size frequency visible in thin-sections prepared from kiln wasters (Streeten 1982).

The samples from Battle have been compared with wasters from known kilns and with other marketed vessels from elsewhere, by rapid visual sorting of the slides under a petrological microscope. The fabrics have been grouped using sketches prepared from projected plain-light images of the thin-sections, and more sophisticated sampling has been undertaken in order to confirm the important identifications. In principle the method of detailed analysis relies upon comparison of graphs showing the grain size frequency curves derived from a standard sample of measured quartz grains in the thin sections. Results obtained from five different wasters found at each kiln have been combined using the mean ± one standard deviation for each size group, in order to define the variations among products of the same kiln. Marketed vessels can then be identified by comparing the profile of the frequency curve produced by the type sherds from Battle with the range of grain sizes found in wasters from local kilns (Figures 27 and 28). This method of analysis is not intended as a substitute for classification according to ceramic traits which are visible to the naked eye, but it does provide an objective means of comparing fabrics.

Thin sections from many of the medieval kilns in Sussex can be distinguished one from another quite easily (Streeten 1980, figure 38). Samples from the Rye kilns, however, show that jugs were sometimes manufactured in different fabrics at the same centre, presumably using different raw materials. The quartz grains in wasters of fabric 'one' (Figure 27: Graph B) are finer than those in fabric 'two' (Figure 27: Graph D). A similar pattern is repeated among the floor tiles made at Rye (p. 84), and marketed jugs in both fabrics have been identified at Battle (Figure 27: Graphs C and E).

The graph derived from sample cooking pot sherds from Rye is akin to that of jugs in fabric 'one', but with a few slightly coarser grains (Figure 27: Graphs A and B). Interestingly, the grain size frequency in the culinary wares is virtually indistinguishable from the grey coarsewares manufactured at Brede some 10 km (6 miles) upstream from Rye (Streeten 1980, fig. 38). Similar alluvial sands may have been used by these two industries. The Brede potters may also have transported their wares by water to the market at Rye (Streeten 1981, 333), and in this instance it is therefore unlikely that fabric analysis alone will provide sufficient evidence for interpreting the organisation of pottery distribution around the Brede kilns.

Thin section analysis not only provides a means of identification, but it is also possible to estimate the number of different sources represented in an excavated ceramic assemblage. At least four of the medieval fabrics found at Battle are sufficiently similar to be from the same kiln, and it is clear that the output of this, as yet unknown, industry included both grey coarsewares and sand tempered jugs (Figure 27: Graph G).

Medieval and Later Pottery

A. Flint-tempered Wares

Fabrics

Ai Grey core with brown surfaces. Hard, harsh texture;

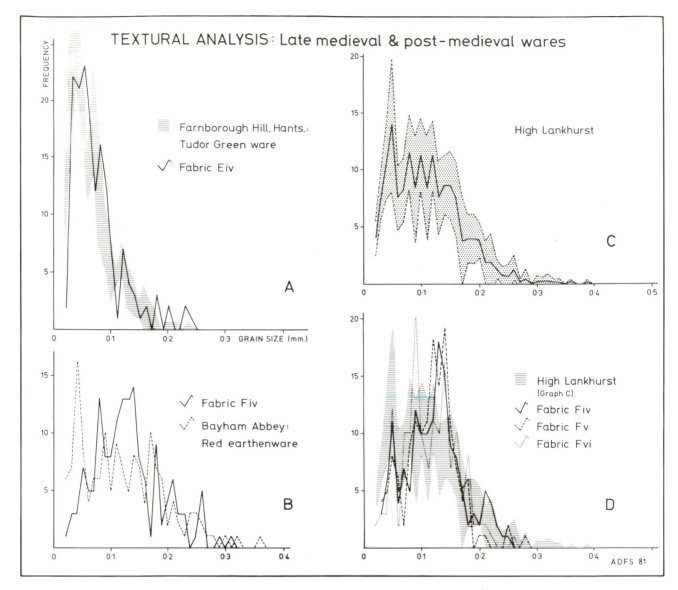

Figure 28   Battle Abbey. Textural analysis of late medieval and post-medieval pottery.

rough fracture. Moderate medium sand temper, with sparse fragments of coarse flint. (TF 71; Sample 1057).

Aii Pale grey core and surfaces. Hard, harsh texture; rough fracture. Moderate medium sand temper with abundant medium/coarse flint and sparse ironstone. (TF 42; Sample 998).

Aiii Grey core with red-brown surfaces. Fairly soft harsh texture; hackly fracture. Sparse medium sand temper with abundant coarse white flint and moderate ironstone. Probably Abbot's Wood kiln. (TF 38; Sample 994).

Aiv Grey core with red or red-brown surfaces. Hard, harsh texture; rough fracture. Moderate medium sand temper with moderate medium flint and sparse coarse flint; abundant ironstone and sparse fragments of sandstone visible in thin-section. Partial clear or pale green glaze on jugs. (TF 9; Sample 966).

Av Pale grey core with buff surfaces. Hard, fairly smooth texture; rough fracture. Abundant fine sand temper with sparse medium flint and abundant fine mica visible on surfaces. Partial green glaze on skillet. (TF 45; Sample 1001).

Forms and Manufacture (Figure 29)

Vessels in Fabric Ai are probably hand made; others are wheel thrown. The coarse flint-tempered fabrics were used principally for cooking pots and skillets, but jugs occur in Fabric Aiv, and there is a spouted pitcher in Fabric Aiii.

1. ?Cooking pot. Sherd with rouletted decoration. Fabric Ai. Phase B7.
2. Spouted pitcher. Fabric Aiii. Phase C14.
3. Cooking pot. Irregular lines on the exterior show where the rim (?hand-made) has been attached to the body. Small splash of glaze on interior of the rim. Fabric Aiv. Phase B7.
4. Tripod vessel. Applied thumb-strip decoration, possibly festooned around the body. Internal stabbing above applied foot. Internal pale green glaze. Fabric Av. Phase C14.

Dating and Comparison

The rouletted sherd (no. 1) is probably residual in Period B and dates from the twelfth century or earlier. All these wares occur in Periods A or B, apart from Fabric Av which appears for the first time in Phase C14. The evidence from Battle therefore confirms previous suspicions that flint-tempered fabrics persisted after *c.* 1300 in East Sussex (Barton 1979, 7).

Flint gritting is largely confined to southern areas of the county, and, although isolated flint-tempered sherds are known from the Weald, none of the pottery from Bayham Abbey contained flint. Unlike some sherds from Glottenham (Martin n.d.; Sample 189) which have little or no sand, all the flint-tempered fabrics at Battle contain at least some quartz. Thin-sections prepared from Fabrics Ai and Aii show a similar range of quartz grain sizes which may indicate that these vessels are from the same unknown source. Both the colour and texture of Fabric Aiii is almost identical to wasters found in Abbot's Wood, Upper Dicker, and similar wares have been reported from Hastings (Rudling 1976, 172, no. 64). The possibility that other centres were producing similar wares cannot be ruled out, but, if this identification is correct, then the occurrence of Fabric Aiii before the great thirteenth-century rebuilding at Battle may help to define the date range of the Abbot's Wood kilns.

Flint-tempered wares like Fabric Aiv have been found at Glottenham, but the range of quartz grain sizes is not precisely the same. Closer comparisons can be made with the flint-tempered wasters at Ringmer which are thought to have reached at least as far east as Michelham Priory (Streeten forthcoming a). The Battle fabric does not contain quite such a prominent groundmass of fine quartz as the Ringmer wasters but this identification remains probable. If it is correct, then the dating evidence from Battle confirms the early origin of the industry suggested by excavations at Ringmer (Hadfield 1981, 105).

The very sparse flint of Fabric Av, which is later than other types in this group, is similar to a vessel from Michelham Priory (Sample 365).

B. Flint-/shell-tempered wares
Fabrics
Bi Grey core, sometimes with red-brown margins, and grey or black surfaces. Hard, fairly smooth texture; rough fracture. Moderate fine sand temper with moderate coarse flint, sparse shell and ironstone. (TF 4; Sample 961).
Bii Grey core and surfaces. Hard, harsh texture; rough fracture. Moderate medium/coarse sand temper with moderate coarse flint; sparse flecks of shell and sparse ironstone. (TF 75; Sample 1060).
Biii Grey core with brown or red-brown surfaces. Hard, harsh texture; rough fracture. Abundant medium sand temper with moderate medium/fine flint and moderate specks of shell. Partial clear or green glaze on some sherds. Possibly Ringmer kilns. (TF 7; Sample 964).
Biv Grey core with dark grey or black surfaces. Fairly hard, slightly harsh texture; rough fracture. Moderate medium sand temper with moderate/sparse medium flint and occasional flecks of very fine shell. (TF 3; Sample 960).

Forms and Manufacture (Figure 29)
Some vessels are probably hand made, and the wide range of surface colours suggests that they were fired in clamp kilns. Most of the sherds are from culinary wares, but there is one jug in Fabric Biv. Decoration is confined to combing, and to thumbed strips on the cooking pots.
5. Cooking pot. Buff-coloured internal surface; mottled grey to red-pink exterior. Fabric Biii. Phase A2.
6. Bowl. Patchy external green and clear glaze. Fabric Biii. Phase D21.

Dating and Comparison
All of these fabrics occur at least as early as Periods A and B, and the well-stratified context before *c.* 1100 for no. 5 (Phase A2) is particularly useful for dating this simple form of cooking pot rim. Fabric Biv which is dominant in the same phase is similar to the published description of a twelfth-century cooking pot from Hastings Castle (Moore 1974, 167, no. 11), but, like the flint-tempered wares, other sub-types may have persisted well into the thirteenth century or later.

The combination of flint and shell temper may indicate the use of beach sand in some fabrics (Dulley 1967, 219–20). Many of the vessels from Michelham Priory have 'flint and calcite' temper (Barton and Holden 1967, 9), and similar inclusions have been recognised at sites nearer the coast. Fabric Biii is comparable in thin-section with some of the Michelham wares (Sample 474), and with another type from Denton (O'Shea 1979, 239; Sample 581). There is less quartz in the flint-/shell-tempered wares from Bramble Bottom, Eastbourne (Musson 1955, 162–6; Sample 556), and from Seaford (Freke 1977–8, 213, table 3; Sample 566), but the range of grain sizes in all of these fabrics is similar to the sand grains in wasters from Ringmer.

Specks of calcite are seldom to be seen in sherds found at kiln sites in Ringmer, but a few fragments from Norlington Lane (fieldwork by Mr C.E. Knight-Farr; Sample 591) do contain these characteristic white inclusions. The source of the Battle vessels cannot therefore be identified conclusively, but the affinities of Fabric Biii with finds from near the River Ouse suggests an origin in the region west of the abbey.

C. Shell-/sand-tempered wares
Fabrics
Ci Grey core with dark grey or black surfaces. Hard, fairly smooth texture; rough or hackly fracture. Moderate fine sand temper with abundant coarse shell. One sherd has traces of an internal white slip. Possibly Rye kilns. (TF 6; Sample 963).
Cii Grey core with grey or dark grey surfaces. Hard, harsh texture; rough fracture. Abundant medium/coarse sand temper with sparse coarse shell. (TF 5; Sample 962).

Forms and Manufacture (Figure 29)
Wheel-made vessels include both cooking pots and jugs, and there is a skillet in Fabric Ci. Decoration on the jugs includes stabbed and slashed handles, and combing. Some of the cooking pots have applied thumbed strips.
7. Cooking pot. Fabric Ci. Phase D24.
8. Jug. Fabric Cii. Phase C14.
9. Jug. Fabric Cii. Phase C14.

Dating and Comparison
Both fabrics occur in Phase A5 and in Period B, but they are more common in Period C, where flat-flanged cooking pot rims predominate. There is no conclusive evidence therefore that these shell-tempered wares were in use before the early thirteenth century.

Shelly wares are found extensively in Kent, Surrey and parts of Sussex, but they are less common in coastal regions of the county. Some of the coarsewares from Spittal Field, Rye have plate-like voids left by dissolved or burnt-out particles of shell, and the range of quartz grain sizes visible in thin-sections prepared from Fabric Ci compares closely with the Rye wasters. The Brede potters who used similar sands do not appear to have made shell-tempered wares.

Fabric Cii is coarser than the wasters found at Rye, and

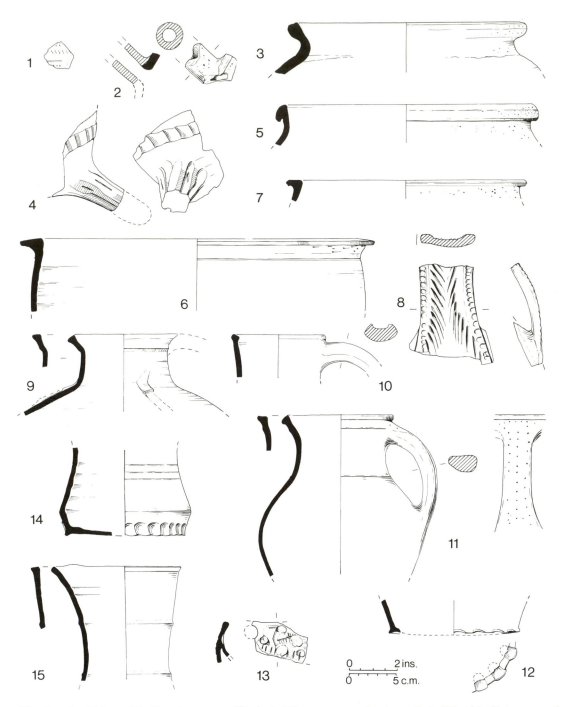

Figure 29　Battle Abbey. Medieval pottery ($\frac{1}{4}$). 1–4: Flint-tempered wares; 5–6: Flint/shell-tempered wares; 7–9: Shell/sand-tempered wares; 11–15: Sand-tempered wares.

it is superficially similar to the grey wares from Bayham Abbey (Streeten 1983, 92, fabric Ai; Sample 395). This fabric cannot, however, be matched with any of the local kiln products, but it may belong with another group of wares which includes both oxidised and reduced vessels (see below).

D.　Sand-tempered Wares
Reduced (Grey) Fabrics

Di　Pale grey core with dark grey surfaces. Hard, fairly smooth texture; rough fracture. Abundant medium/fine sand with sparse fragments of ironstone. Probably Rye kilns. (TF 1; Sample 958).

Dii　Pale grey core with black surfaces. Hard, smooth texture; rough fracture. Abundant fine sand with sparse fragments of ironstone. Traces of green glaze on some sherds. Probably Rye kilns. (TF 2; Sample 959).

Diii　Pale grey core with buff surfaces. Hard, harsh texture; rough fracture. Abundant medium/coarse sand. Jugs have partial green glaze. (TF 33; Sample 988).

Div　Pale grey core with buff surfaces. Hard, harsh texture; rough fracture. Abundant medium/coarse sand. Some jugs have white slip decoration and green or clear glazes. (TF10; Sample 967).

Dv　Pale grey core and surfaces. Very hard smooth texture; rough fracture. Moderate very fine sand temper. External green glaze and partial internal green glaze. (TF 72; Sample 1058).

Dvi　Pale grey core with pale buff margins and surfaces. Very hard, smooth texture; fairly smooth fracture. Moderate medium sand temper with abundant iron ore. (TF 73; not thin-sectioned).

Dvii Pale grey core with pale buff margins and surfaces. Hard, fairly smooth texture; rough fracture. Abundant fine sand temper. Green glaze. (TF 43; Sample 999).

Forms and Manufacture (Figure 29)

All vessels are wheel-thrown, and the repertoire of unglazed wares (Fabrics Di and Dii) includes jugs with incised decoration; stabbed and slashed handles; and thumbed bases, as well as cooking pots with flanged rims and applied thumbed strips. A jug in Fabric Div has applied pellets of red and white clay under a green glaze, and there is an oval dish in Fabric Dv.

10. Jug. Fabric Di. Phase D28.
11. Jug. Fabric Di. Phase D21.
12. Jug. Base thumbed from underneath. Fabric Dii. Phase D21.
13. ?Jug. Decoration applied to rim of ?jug, possibly representing a bearded face with applied pellets of red (stippled) and white clay. Hole and scar indicates probable broken spout. Fabric Div. Phase C14.
14. Jug. Patchy pale green and clear external glaze. Fabric Dvii. Phase E36.

Dating and Comparison

Examples of these fabrics, apart from Dvi, occur in Phase B7, and some reduced sand-tempered wares are represented in Period A. The form and decoration of the jugs is typical of the thirteenth to fourteenth century, but plainer forms such as no. 11 are probably fifteenth century.

Textural analysis confirms that Fabrics Di and Dii come from Rye, (Figure 27: Graph A). Output of the Rye kilns is not thought to have commenced much before *c.* 1300, but two sherds in these fabrics occur at Battle in contexts which are unlikely to be later than the mid-thirteenth century (Phases A5 and B7). The possibility that earlier wares made from similar raw materials were produced at another kiln cannot be ruled out, but oxidised glazed wares attributed to the Rye potters also occur in deposits associated with the thirteenth-century rebuilding (see below). Production may therefore have started by this time, and the longevity of these common fabrics is demonstrated by the apparent fifteenth-century form of no. 11.

Fabric Diii, with its distinctive buff surfaces, occurs in several of the early phases within Periods A and B, although it may be intrusive in Phase A2. Textural analysis demonstrates that these vessels do not come from Rye (Figure 27: Graph H), and, although the source is not known, buff wares are represented among wasters from the thirteenth-century kiln at Streat some 10 km (6 miles) north-west of Lewes (excavated in 1981 by Mr C. Ainsworth).

The source of the other reduced sand-tempered wares has not been identified, but Fabric Div is paralleled at Bayham Abbey (Streeten 1983, 92, fabric Bvi). It may be from the same centre as some oxidised sandy wares and one of the shell-tempered fabrics found at Battle (Figure 27: Graph G; see below).

Oxidised (Red) Fabrics

Dviii Pale grey core with red surfaces. Hard, harsh texture; rough fracture. Abundant medium/coarse sand temper with sparse very coarse grains and moderate ironstone. Partial pale green or clear glaze. (TF 47; Sample 1003).

Dix Red surfaces, sometimes with pale grey core. Hard, harsh texture; rough fracture. Abundant medium/coarse sand temper with sparse fragments of ironstone and siltstone. Partial pale green or clear glaze. (TF 34; Sample 990).

Dx Grey core with red surfaces. Hard, harsh texture, with badly spalled surfaces; rough fracture. Abundant coarse sand temper. Partial clear or green glaze. Possibly Ringmer kilns. (TF 16; Sample 973).

Dxi Red core and surfaces, sometimes with indistinct pale grey core. Hard, fairly smooth texture; rough fracture. Abundant medium/fine sand temper. Partial green or clear glaze sometimes with internal white slip. Rye kilns. (TF 8; Sample 965).

Dxii Red core and surfaces. Hard, smooth texture; rough fracture. Abundant fine sand temper with moderate red iron ore. Partial dark green or clear glaze, sometimes with internal white slip. Rye kilns. (TF 46; Sample 1002).

Dxiii Red core and surfaces, sometimes with pale grey core. Hard, smooth texture; rough fracture. Abundant fine sand temper, with sparse medium grains and moderate red iron ore. Partial green glaze. Rye kilns. (TF 44; Sample 1000).

Dxiv Pale grey core with pink surfaces. Very hard, fairly smooth texture; rough fracture. Abundant fine sand temper. Partial (sometimes complete) external green glaze. Rye kilns. (TF 69; Sample 1055).

Dxv Pink core and surfaces; sometimes with indistinct pale grey core. Hard, fairly smooth texture; rough fracture. Moderate fine sand temper. Mottled clear/green external glaze. (TF 65; Sample 1006).

Dxvi Red core with brown surfaces. Hard, harsh texture; rough fracture. Abundant medium sand temper with sparse iron ore. External green glaze. (TF 48; Sample 1004).

Dxvii Grey or pink core with brown surfaces. Hard, fairly smooth texture; rough fracture. Moderate medium sand temper with moderate red iron ore. Partial external green glaze sometimes with white slip decoration. (TF 18; Sample 975).

Forms and Manufacture (Figures 29 and 30)

Most of the identifiable sherds are from jugs, but skillets occur in Fabrics Dxii-Dxiv, and a vessel in Fabric Dx has an internally flanged rim. The jugs have a wide range of combed, incised and thumbed decoration, but repoussé 'raspberry' stamps and leaf ornaments, which are distinctive of the Rye wares, are confined to Fabrics Dxi and Dxii. Some vessels in Fabric Dxvii are knife-trimmed around the base, and others have white-painted decoration.

15. Jug. Thin internal white slip around rim. External pale green glaze. Fabric Dxi. Phase D31.
16. Jug. Patchy green glaze on exterior and at base of interior. Fabric Dxi. Phase D26.
17. Jug. Stabbed handle. Internal white slip. Patchy pale green external glaze. Fabric Dxii. Phase D21.
18. Jug. Mottled green glaze on exterior and at base of interior. Fabric Dxiv. Phase C14.
19. Cooking pot. Fabric Dxvii. Phase D21.
20. Cooking pot. Fabric Dxvii. Phase D21.

Dating and Comparison

None of the oxidised sand-tempered fabrics can be dated conclusively to before the early thirteenth century. One intrusive sherd (Fabric Dix) came from the disturbed chapter house graves (Phase A3), and other types attributed to Period A were recovered from levels in the reredorter area which could have remained exposed until the great thirteenth-century rebuilding (Phase A5). The less common earthenware fabrics (Dxv-xvii) appear for the first time in Phase C14.

The coarser wares (Fabrics Dviii-x) are superficially

similar to oxidised wasters found at Ringmer, but the quartz groundmass, which is distinctive in thin-sections of the Ringmer wares, only occurs in Fabric Dx. Textural analysis shows that Fabrics Dviii and Dix probably come from the same unknown source as the shell-tempered ware (Fabric Cii) and one of the reduced sandy fabrics (Div) (Figure 27: Graph G).

It is possible that this group represents a coarser type which has not been recognised so far among products of the Rye kilns, but analysis has shown that these fabrics are quite different from the known variants (Figure 27). Fabrics Dxi-xiv, however, definitely do come from Rye. The range of quartz grain sizes in all four of these types can be matched with either fabric 'one' or fabric 'two' at Rye (Figure 27: Graphs B–E). Sherds attributed to the Rye kilns are securely stratified in mid-thirteenth-century contexts at Battle, and one piece (Fabric Dxii) appears in Phase A5. Fragments from the area east of the dormitory (Phase B8) could be later, but other vessels are represented not only in the make-up which is contemporary with the reredorter (Phase B7), but also in the built-up ground associated with construction of the parlour porch (Phase B6). In view of the importance of these stratified finds, fabric identifications have been checked carefully by direct (macroscopic) comparison with the wasters from Rye. Even the sherd from Phase A5 stands up to careful scrutiny, and the form of the solid skillet handle from Phase B8 can be paralleled among the wasters (Barton 1979, 249; 251). Thumbed bases such as that from Phase B6 are not well represented at Rye, although they do occur (Barton 1979, 240, no. 6). It therefore appears that the output of these kilns may have commenced somewhat earlier than has been supposed hitherto. Barton (1979, 219) places the origins of the Rye industry 'no earlier than about AD 1300', but the diverse dates of pottery associated with the kilns demonstrates that the vesels recovered by Vidler may not be fully representative of this long-lived industry. The fabric of stratified sherds from Battle shows that at least part of the repertoire, if not the full range of forms, must have been established at least 50 years earlier than c. 1300.

The source of the other minor sand-tempered wares has not been identified, but Fabric Dxv is almost certainly non-local. The pink colour is similar to Scarborough ware (Farmer 1979, 28–31), but neither the range of inclusions nor the grain-size distribution visible in thin section is the same.

Sand-tempered wares persist throughout the medieval phases, and the oxidised jugs, like the reduced examples, are typical of the thirteenth/fourteenth century. Typologically no. 18 would be ascribed to the fourteenth century, but a strikingly similar form is shown on the decorated initial from a page in the account rolls for the Bailiwick of South Malling (near Lewes), dated 1445–6 (Legge 1902, 77). Dating from contemporary illustrations is hazardous, but this document, combined with circumstantial evidence for the date of the make-up in which the jug from Battle was found (p. 37), demonstrates that vessels of this shape remained in use during the first half of the fifteenth century.

The distinction between these fine sandy wares and the later hard-fired earthenwares is sometimes difficult to define with precision. White-painted decoration such as that represented in Fabric Dxvii has been dated independently to the second half of the fifteenth century in West Sussex, and the innovation of knife-trimming around the base of the vessels is also a late medieval innovation (Barton 1963, 31). Coarser fabrics, however, would have continued alongside the finer earthenwares, and the lid-seating on the rim of a vessel in Fabric Dx is similar to

types from Bodiam Castle which can have been discarded no earlier than c. 1386 (Myres 1935, 223).

E. English White Wares
Fabrics
Ei Off-white core and surfaces. Hard, harsh texture; rough fracture. Abundant medium sand temper. Partial green glaze. Possibly Rye kilns. (TF 31; Sample 989).
Eii Off-white core and surfaces. Hard, smooth texture; rough fracture. Moderate fine sand temper. Partial green glaze. Farnborough Hill kilns. (TF 11; Sample 968).
Eiii Same as fabric Eii, but with yellow glaze. (TF 14; Sample 971).
Eiv 'Tudor Green' ware. Farnborough Hill kilns. (TF 12; Sample 969).
Ev White core with faint traces of pink; off-white surfaces. Hard, very smooth texture; rough fracture. Sparse fine sand temper with sparse flecks of red iron ore. Yellow or green glaze. Probably High Lankhurst kiln. (TF 26; Sample 984).

Forms and Manufacture (Figure 30)
Identifiable sherds of the coarser sand-tempered white fabric (Ei) are confined to jugs, and a typical biconical profile has been reconstructed (no. 21). Other white wares are finer, and include the very thin-walled Tudor Green types (Fabric Eiv: Holling 1977, 62) as well as vessels with a slightly thicker body (Fabric Eii). Most have a characteristic lustrous green glaze, but there is a small group of yellow-glazed sherds (Fabric Eiii). Insufficient examples of the later white wares (Fabric Ev) were found to define the range of forms.
21. Jug. Bib of mottled green glaze on the shoulder, opposite the handle. Fabric Ei. Phase D21.
22. Jug. Bright green glaze on exterior and around inside of rim. Fabric Eii. Phase D22.
23. Dish. Knife-trimmed base. Internal pale green glaze. Fabric Eii. Phase D23.
24. Jug. Shiny clear (yellow) glaze on interior and exterior of rim. Fabric Eiii. Phase D22.
25. Jug. External lustrous mottled green glaze. Fabric Eiv. Phase D22.
26. Jug. Fabric Eiv. Phase D22.
27. Lobed cup. Fabric Eiv. Phase E42.

Dating and Comparison
White wares do not occur before Period C, and the yellow-glazed types (Fabric Eiii) appear for the first time among the Dissolution debris (Phase D21/22). Isolated sherds of post-medieval white ware were found in later sixteenth- or seventeenth-century contexts (Phases D23 and D26) and in Period E.

'Tudor Green' forms have been dated as early as the second quarter of the fifteenth century at several sites, and the type is thought to have been introduced c. 1400 (Moorhouse 1979, 54; 59). A sherd from Phase C14 at Battle therefore offers a *terminus post quem* for construction of the new drainage system on the north side of the reredorter, and also helps to date some of the associated coarsewares found in the same deposit.

Biconical jugs such as no. 21 were found at Bodiam Castle (Myres 1935, 22, fig. 3), and the form is conventionally ascribed to the fifteenth century. The colour and texture of Fabric Ei is superficially similar to wasters from the Cheam kilns in Surrey (Marshall 1924; Orton 1982), but a small number of off-white wares are also represented among the material from Rye. Pottery manufacture at Rye probably continued into the early fifteenth century (Barton 1979, 218–22), and textual analysis of the coarser

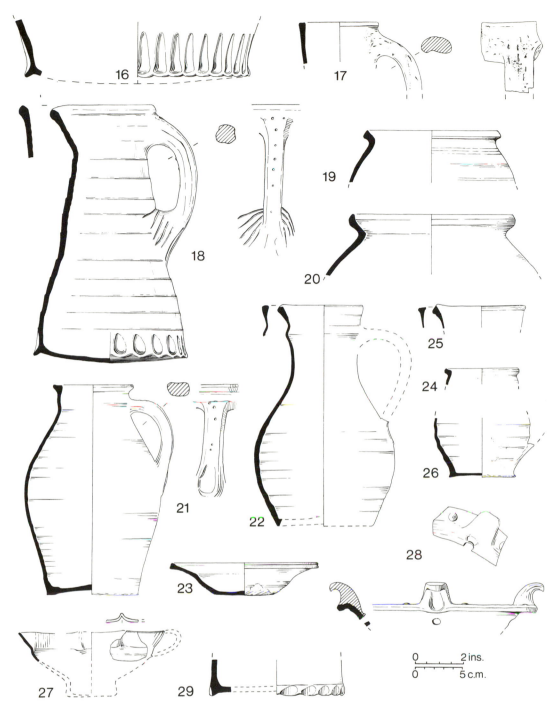

Figure 30   Battle Abbey. Medieval and later pottery ($\frac{1}{4}$). 16–20: Sand-tempered wares; 21–27: English white wares; 28–29: Hard-fired earthenwares.

white wares found at Battle suggests that they are more likely to be products of this local kiln, rather than from Surrey (Figure 27: Graph F).

It is difficult to distinguish some of the finer English white wares from French imports, and even the grain-size frequency visible in thin-section shows little difference. Textural analysis, however, confirms that both the Tudor Green wares (Fabric Eiv) and the thicker-walled vessels (Fabric Eii) are products of the Farnborough Hill kilns on the Hampshire/Surrey border (Holling 1971, 61; fig. 28 Graph A). The later sixteenth-century output of these kilns is also represented by the small dish (no. 23) which is typical of this period (Holling 1971, 73, fig. 2, no. A1).

Yellow glazes are not common among the wasters from Farnborough Hill (Holling 1977, 63) and significantly a thin-section of Fabric Eiii at Battle is different from the green glazed wares. The source of this type therefore remains unknown.

The fabric of the post-medieval white wares (Fabric Ev) is also different from the Surrey types. White clay was used by the local late-sixteenth-century potters at High Lankhurst, Westfield, but wasters from this kiln are virtually untempered (Sample 480). The Battle fabric does contain quartz, but the range of grain sizes is similar to some of the High Lankhurst red wares, and this is almost certainly a local rather than a 'Surrey' type.

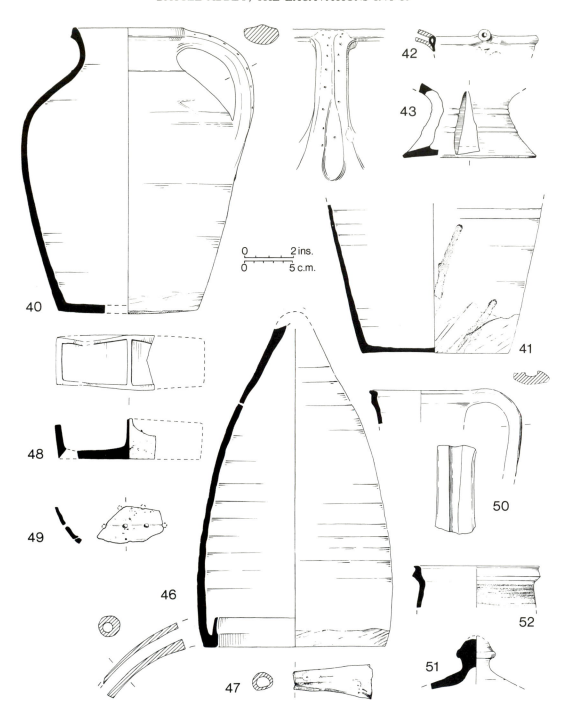

Figure 31   Battle Abbey. Late medieval/early post-medieval pottery ($\frac{1}{4}$). 30–39: Hard-fired earthenwares.

F. Hard-fired Earthenwares
Fabrics
Fi Pale grey core with brown surfaces. Hard, harsh texture; rough fracture. Abundant medium/coarse sand temper. Partial green glaze. (TF 67; Sample 1053).
Fii Buff core and surfaces. Hard, fairly smooth texture; rough fracture. Abundant fine sand temper. (TF 35; Sample 991).
Fiii Red core with dark grey or black surfaces. Hard, harsh texture; rough fracture. Abundant medium sand temper. Partial green or clear glaze. (TF 15; Sample 972).
Fiv Red or sometimes pale grey core with red or red-brown surfaces. Hard, harsh texture; rough fracture.

Abundant medium sand temper with moderate pellets of red iron ore. Partial clear or green glaze. Some later types probably High Lankhurst kiln. (TF 21; Samples 978–979).
Fv Pale grey core with red-brown surfaces. Fairly hard, harsh texture, sometimes with pitted surfaces. Moderate medium/fine sand temper with sparse pellets of red iron ore. Partial yellow-green or clear glaze. High Lankhurst kiln. (TF 24; Sample 982).
Fvi Pale grey core with red-pink surfaces. Hard, fairly smooth texture; rough fracture. Moderate fine sand temper with very sparse pellets of red iron ore. Partial green or clear glaze. (TF 49; Sample 1005).
Fvii Red core with dark grey-brown surfaces and mar-

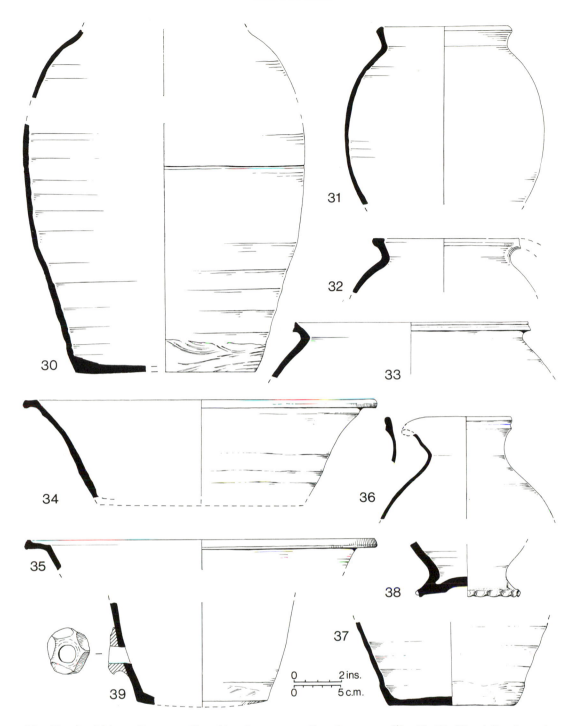

Figure 32 Battle Abbey. Late medieval/early post-medieval pottery ($\frac{1}{4}$). 40–51: Hard-fired earthenwares.

gins. Very hard, smooth texture; fairly smooth fracture (near-stoneware). Sparse fine sand temper. Partial colourless glaze. (TF 20; Sample 977).

Fviii Red core with 'metallic' sheen on surfaces. Hard, fairly smooth texture; rough fracture. Moderate fine sand temper. Partial (sometimes complete) green or clear glaze. (TF 28; Sample 985).

Fix Red core and surfaces. Hard, smooth texture; rough fracture. Abundant very fine sand temper. Complete lustrous brown glaze with 'metallic' sheen. (TF 25; Sample 983).

Fx Intermittent pale grey core with red-brown margins and dark grey external surface. Hard, fairly smooth tex-

ture; rough fracture. Abundant very fine sand temper with moderate pellets of red iron ore. Partial green or clear glaze. (TF 17; Sample 974).

Fxi Grey core with red margins and brown surfaces. Hard, fairly smooth texture; rough fracture. Fine sand temper with sparse medium/coarse quartz grains. Internal green glaze with white-painted external decoration. Graffham kilns. (TF 19; Sample 976).

Fxii Pink core and surfaces. Hard, smooth texture; rough fracture. Moderate very fine sand temper and streaks of pale coloured clay. Partial (sometimes complete) green or clear glaze. (TF 29; Sample 987).

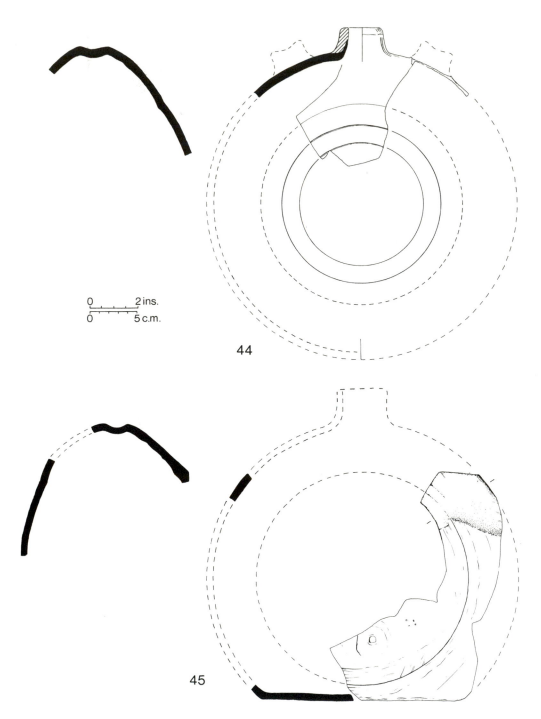

Figure 33   Battle Abbey. Hard-fired earthenware costrels ($\frac{1}{4}$).

Probable imports; source uncertain.

Fxiii   Red-pink core and surfaces. Hard, very smooth, 'soapy' texture; fairly smooth fracture. Moderate very fine sand temper. Partial internal clear glaze. (TF 22; Sample 980).

Fxiv   Purple-pink core and surfaces. Hard, fairly smooth texture; rough fracture. Moderate fine sand temper, and distinctive white specks showing in the fracture. Abundant mica visible in thin-section. Complete external green glaze. (TF 36; Sample 992).

Forms and Manufacture (Figures 30–34)

The range of forms and fabrics reflects the transition from late medieval to post-medieval ceramics. Streaky surface colours on some vessels are probably distinctive of a particular method of firing, and some of the very hard fabrics have been fired to high temperatures. Knife-trimming is common.

'Medieval' forms such as the jug with frilled pedestal base (no. 38) persist in these finer fabrics, and many of the jug handles are pricked in the medieval manner. Thumbing at the base of jug or bunghole-pitcher handles is more common among the later types than in the medieval wares, but decoration is both simple and sparse. Cooking pots and deep pans occur fairly frequently, but several entirely

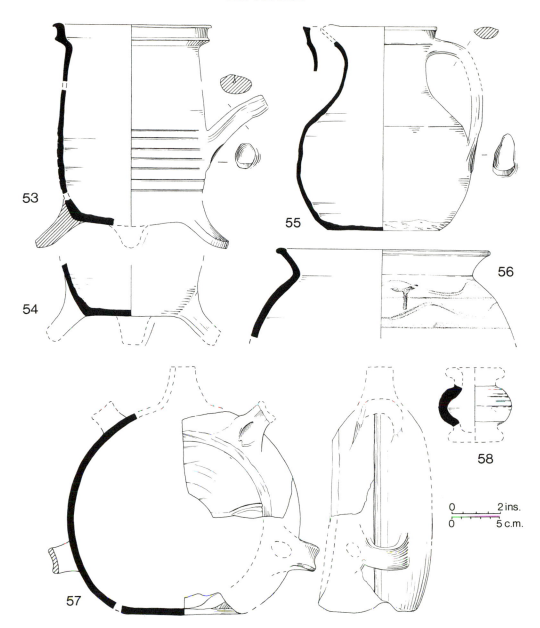

Figure 34   Battle Abbey. Late medieval and post-medieval pottery ($\frac{1}{4}$). 53–56: Hard-fired earthenwares; 57–58: probable imported earthenwares.

new forms appear for the first time in these fabrics. Chafing dishes occur in Fabrics Fi and Fiv, and the Dissolution debris outside the reredorter included large earthenware costrels (nos. 44 and 45). 'Industrial' ceramics such as the alembic (no. 46), the perforated vessel (no. 49), and possibly the divided dish (no. 48) imply that, by the early sixteenth century, local potters were also able to meet specialised requirements. Pipkins, however, have only been recognised in the later phases of Period D and in Period E.

28.   Chafing dish. Patchy internal green glaze. Repoussé decoration on rim. Fabric Fi. Phase D22.

29.   Jug. Traces of lime(?) encrustation on interior. Fabric Fiii. Phase D22.

30.   Cistern (?). Knife-trimmed base. Patches of clear glaze on underside of base. Fabric Fiii. Phase D24.

31.   Cooking pot. Fabric Fiv. Phase D24.

32.   Handled cooking pot. Scar on rim indicates that there was at least one and probably two handles. Fabric Fiv. Phase D22.

33.   Cooking pot. Fabric Fiv. Phase D22.

34.   Deep pan. Fabric Fiv. Phase D22.

35.   Bowl. Fabric Fiv. Phase D22.

36.   Jug. Fabric Fiv. Phase D30.

37.   Base of ?jug. Knife-trimmed base. Splashes of clear glaze on bottom. Fabric Fiv. Phase D30.

38.   Jug. Fabric Fiv. Phase D22.

39.   Bunghole pitcher. Fabric Fiv. Phase D22.

40.   Jug. Fabric Fiv. Phase D22.

41.   Cistern(?). Knife-trimmed around base. Patches of clear/pale green glaze on base. Trickles of glaze down the side of the vessel show that it was fired upside-down in the kiln. Fabric Fiv. Phase D22.

42.   Rim and spout of puzzle jug. Applied hand-made spout. Speckled clear and pale green glaze. Fabric Fiv. Phase D21.

43.   Base of chafing dish. Knife-cut hole and knife-trimmed on bottom. Sparse splashes of clear glaze. Fabric Fiv. Phase D21.

44.   Costrel. Applied spout luted on after two halves of

the vessel had been joined around the girth. Fabric Fiv. Phase D21.

45.   Costrel. Flat side and base. Patchy external glaze. Hole pierced through body with the scar of a presumed spout near the base of the vessel. Fabric Fiv. Phase D22.

46.   Alembic. Patchy clear internal and external glaze. Knife-trimmed base. Pierced (not rolled) spout, with knife-trimming at the end and on the sides of the spout. Fabric Fiv. Phase D22.

47.   Spout, probably from an alembic. Hand-made cylinder of clay with signs of knife-trimming on interior and at the end of the spout. Splashes of clear glaze. Fabric Fiv. Phase E35.

48.   Divided dish. Possibly a cruet or for an 'industrial' purpose. Moulded base and sides with sanded surfaces. Knife-trimmed on top and inside. Two prominent finger prints on the bottom of the interior. Fabric Fiv. Phase E35.

49.   'Industrial' vessel(?). Splashes of clear glaze on exterior. Small holes pierced before firing; spalled internal surface indicates that larger holes were drilled after firing. Function uncertain. Fabric Fiv. Phase D21.

50.   Jug. Deep and slightly tapering thumbed groove on the handle. This treatment is a distinctive feature of wasters from the High Lankhurst kiln. Fabric Fiv. Phase D23.

51.   Lid. Patchy pale green internal and external glaze. Fabric Fv. Phase E42.

52.   Jug. Dark green internal glaze. Band of white slip on exterior of neck. Fabric Fvi. Phase D23.

53.   Pipkin. Lustrous metallic internal glaze. Metallic sheen on external surfaces. Fabric Fviii. Phase D23.

54.   Pipkin. Internal metallic brown glaze. Slight soot-blackening on exterior. Fabric Fviii. Phase E42.

55.   Jug. Prominent throwing rings on base. Knife-trimmed around exterior of base. Fabric Fx. Phase D24.

56.   Cooking pot. External white-painted decoration. Green-glazed interior. Fabric Fxi. Phase E49.

Probable imports; source uncertain

57.   Costrel. Thrown in two halves and luted together around the girth. Base flattened *after* joining the two halves of the vessel(?). Extensive knife-trimming. Fabric Fxiii. Phase D22.

58.   Jar, possibly for mercury (R.G. Thompson, pers. comm.). Fabric Fxiv. Phase D22.

Dating and Comparison

It is not possible to make precise distinctions between late medieval and post-medieval vessels when there is only a small sample of sherds, and the identification of at least two of these fabrics in Period C illustrates the difficulties of classification. Thin-sections show that none of the hard-fired earthenwares appears to have been manufactured at the same centre as the earlier types, and these earthenwares, which are predominantly unglazed, occur for the first time in large quantities among the Dissolution debris in the reredorter area (Phases D21/22 and D30). The simple shapes of the cooking pots, bowls, jugs and pitchers are typical of the early sixteenth century (Figures 31 and 32) and can be paralleled among wasters from kilns of this period at Lower Parrock, Hartfield (Freke 1979) and at Kingston upon Thames (Nelson 1981). However, the pulled feet which are so common on vessels found in the London area are not represented in Sussex. At Battle, the proportion of the main fabric (Div) is significantly less in the later phases of Periods D and E (eg Phase D23), and output of these wares was probably confined to the late fifteenth and early sixteenth centuries.

Isolated sherds with a 'metallic' brown glaze also occur among the Dissolution debris, but they are more common in the later phases. This fabric would have continued into the later period, and the pipkin (no. 53) from Phase D23 is typical of the late sixteenth or early seventeenth century.

Superficially similar hard-fired earthenwares were manufactured both locally and on the continent, particularly in the Low Countries, during the early post-medieval period, and some of the vessels attributed to this group at Battle may in fact be imports. Stylistic influences introduced by migrant potters, however, make positive identification difficult. The two coarser fabrics (Fi and Fii) are similar, although not identical, to the hard-fired late medieval wares (Fabrics Dxvi and Dxvii). The principal group of red earthenwares (Fabric Fiv), and associated vessels with dark surfaces (Fabric Fiii), is similar to the predominant fabric found in a roughly contemporary assemblage at Bayham Abbey (Streeten 1983, 93, fabric Diii). Textural analysis, however, shows that the monastic communities at Bayham Abbey and Battle Abbey probably patronised different workshops during the early years of the sixteenth century, even though the two houses are only 22 km (14 m) apart as the crow flies (Figure 28: Graph B).

Certain vessels which occur in later contexts at Battle are indistinguishable, to the naked eye, from those found among the Dissolution debris, but the tapering thumbed groove on the handle of one jug or pitcher (no. 50) is identical to wasters from the High Lankhurst kiln. Thus, Fabric Fv with a distinctive yellow-green glaze, and Fabric Fvi are almost certainly products of that kiln (Figure 28: Graphs C and D). A small group of sherds with white-painted decoration occurs in Period E, and the same fabric is represented among the Dissolution debris (Phase D22). This distinctive type has been attributed to the Graffham kilns in West Sussex (Streeten 1980, 113, fig. 40).

Fabrics Fvii-viii and Fix-x represent two sources, but none of the other types can be attributed to a specific kiln. The very smooth earthenware (Fabric Fxiii) is similar to the texture of imported Martincamp Type 1 flasks (Hurst 1977a, 156–7), which have been identified at Camber Castle, but the form of the costrel in this fabric can be paralleled among English wares in a group of early sixteenth-century wasters from Woolwich (Pryor and Blockley 1978, 48, no. 25). Vessels which are similar to the small mercury jar(?) (no. 58) have been found in London and Southampton as well as in St Giles' Churchyard, Winchelsea (Winchelsea Museum); at Bayham Abbey (Streeten 1983, 103, fig. 43, no. 52); and at Canterbury (Macpherson-Grant 1978, 189, fig. 23, no. 63). Thin-sections of these wares contain abundant mica but there are no diagnostic inclusions. A possible Mediterranean source has been suggested by Mr R.G. Thompson (pers. comm.).

G. Medieval and Later Imported Earthenwares

Fabrics

Gi   White core and surfaces. Hard, fairly smooth texture; rough fracture. Moderate fine sand temper. Red-painted decoration. Probably French. (TF 68; Sample 1054).

Gii   Saintonge polychrome ware (TF 74; not thin-sectioned).

Giii   Off-white core and surfaces. Hard, very smooth texture; rough fracture. Moderate fine quartz sometimes with sparse pellets of red iron ore. External green glaze. French. (TF 13; Sample 970).

Giv   Red-pink core and surfaces. Hard harsh texture; rough fracture. Abundant fine sand temper with common plates of mica visible on the surface. Inclusions of granitic origin seen in thin-section. (TF 41; Sample 997).

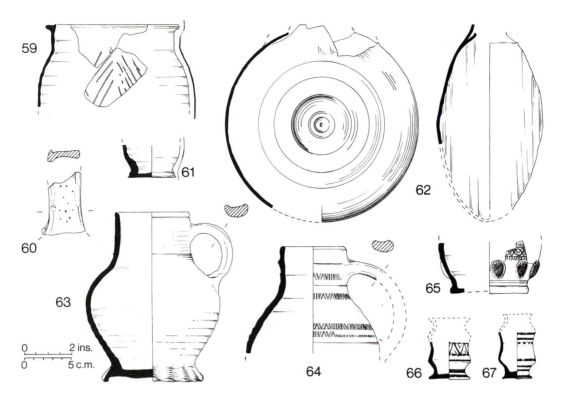

Figure 35 Battle Abbey. Medieval and post-medieval pottery (¼). 59–61: French white wares; 62–65: German stonewares; 66–67: English tin-glazed earthenwares.

Gv Pinkish core. Hard texture; rough fracture. Abundant medium sand temper. Thick and lustrous turquoise glaze with white slip decoration. E. Mediterranean (R.G. Thompson, pers. comm.). (TF 77; not thin-sectioned).

Forms and Manufacture (Figure 35)
In most cases the imported earthenwares are represented by a single sherd, but the distinctive shape of the handle in Fabric Giii confirms a French origin for this vessel.
59. Jug. Red slip with incised sgraffito decoration and clear glaze. Fabric Giii. Phase D22.
60. Jug handle. Mottled green glaze. Fabric Giii. Phase D26.

Dating and Comparison
A red-painted sherd (Fabric Gi) occurs in Phase D22 where it is almost certainly residual. The whiteness of the fabric and the character of the decoration suggest that this is an import from northern France (Dunning 1945).

Saintonge polychrome (Fabric Gii) is present in Phase C14, but these jugs are confined to a restricted date range *c.* 1300, and the sherds must therefore be residual. Plain French white wares have been distinguished from the fine English fabrics by their very smooth, soapy texture. White wares may have been imported from south-west France from the early thirteenth century, and plain green glazed types continued to reach Britain until the sixteenth century (Hurst 1974, 224). Isolated sherds occur at Battle in Periods C and D, but the precise dating of small sherds is impractical. Incised decoration similar to no. 59 can be paralleled on certain northern French wares (Platt and Coleman-Smith 1975, 132, no. 980).

Like the south-west French pottery, Iberian micaceous red wares were imported from the thirteenth century onwards (Hurst 1977b, 96). These vessels are found extensively in early sixteenth century contexts, and the type occurs among Dissolution debris at Battle (Phase D21/22). Costrels were probably made at several different centres in Spain and Portugal, and, although the sample from Battle contains inclusions of granitic origin like those recorded by Vince (1982, 138–40) in sherds from London, the quartz is finer than in comparable finds from Camber Castle (Sample 1038). A pilot study by Miss R. Tomber at Southampton University has shown that there is considerable variation among thin-sections prepared from Iberian micaceous wares, and specific sources are unlikely to be identified until more material from the probable areas of origin has been studied petrologically.

H. Imported stonewares
Fabrics
Hi Pale grey core with brown surfaces. Very hard, smooth texture; smooth fracture. Probably Martincamp-type stoneware. (TF 37; Sample 993).
Hii Buff core and surfaces with brown iron wash. Very hard, smooth texture. Langerwehe stoneware. (TF 64).
Hiii Cream-buff core and surfaces. Very hard, smooth texture. Siegburg stoneware. (TF 32).
Hiv Pale grey core and external surface; grey-brown interior. Very hard, shiny external surface. Raeren stoneware. (TF 55).
Hv Pale grey core with grey-brown or light brown surfaces. Very hard, smooth texture; shiny external surface. Raeren stoneware. (TF 56).
Hvi Grey core with light brown surfaces. Very hard, smooth texture with shiny surfaces. Langerwehe/Raeren stoneware. (TF 57).
Hvii Grey core and internal surface, mottled light brown exterior. Very hard, fairly smooth texture. Cologne/Frechen stoneware. (TF 58).
Hviii Pale grey core and internal surface; cobalt blue-glazed exterior. Westerwald stoneware. (TF 54).

Forms and Manufacture (Figure 35)

It is not possible to reconstruct the forms of either the Martincamp ware (Fabric Hi) or the rilled jugs in Langerwehe stoneware (Fabric Hii), but the Siegburg ware (Fabric Hiii) includes both jugs with flared rims and a costrel (no. 62). Raeren forms (Fabric Hiv-vi) are confined to the typical squat tankards with frilled bases (no. 63), but rouletting occurs on the shoulder of a Langerwehe/Raeren vessel (no. 64): The Cologne/Frechen wares (Fabric Hvii) are distinguished by ringed, as opposed to frilled, bases and one vessel has characteristic relief decoration (no. 65). Westerwald stonewares (Fabric Hviii) have the typical blue glaze and applied medallions.

61. Jug. Probably Fabric Hiii. Phase D22.
62. Costrel. The absence of handles indicates that this vessel would have been suspended from its cladding. Part of the wicker container for a similar costrel was found in the wreck of the Mary Rose. Fabric Hiii. Phase D22.
63. Tankard. Fabric Hiv. Phase D30.
64. Jug. Rouletted decoration. Traces of lime(?) encrustation on the interior. Fabric Hvi. Phase D22.
65. Jug or tankard. Fabric Hvii. Phase E37.

Dating and Comparison

Martincamp, Langerwehe, Siegburg and Raeren stonewares were all found among the Dissolution debris (Phase D21/22). A stoneware industry was established at Raeren during the fifteenth century but the principal output dates from the early sixteenth century (Gaskell Brown 1979, 36). The tankards are typical of this period, and the jug with rouletted decoration (no. 64) is possibly from Langerwehe (Platt and Coleman-Smith 1975, 161, no. 1214).

Frechen stonewares generally belong to the second half of the sixteenth century or later, and, significantly, these are absent from the Dissolution debris. The vessel with applied stamped decoration (no. 65) is probably from Cologne (Platt and Coleman-Smith 1975, 162, no. 1213). Production of Westerwald stoneware commenced in the sixteenth century but most of the imported vessels found in England are of seventeenth- or eighteenth-century date (Gaskell Brown 1979, 38). This fabric occurs in the later fill of the chapter house (Phase D23) and in Period E.

J. English stonewares

Fabrics

Ji Grey core and internal surface; mottled dark brown exterior. Very hard, fairly smooth texture. Fulham stoneware(?). (TF 59).
Jii Pale grey core with light orange-brown surfaces. Very hard, slightly harsh texture. (TF 62).
Jiii Pale grey core and surfaces. Very hard, fairly smooth texture. (TF 60).
Jiv Grey core with grey or brown surfaces. Very hard, very smooth texture. (TF 61).

Forms and Manufacture

None of the vessels could be reconstructed, but sherds in Fabric Ji are probably from 'Bellarmine' jugs; those in Fabrics Jii and Jiii may be from tankards; and Fabric Jiv is typical of more recent mineral water bottles.

Dating and Comparison

Fabric Ji is similar to Fulham stoneware and it occurs both in Phase D23 and in Period E. Other types are confined to Period E.

K. Post-medieval English earthenwares

Fabrics

Ki Red core and surfaces. Hard, smooth texture; fairly smooth fracture. Sparse very fine sand temper. Clear

(brown) glaze with flecks of iron; sometimes with white slip decoration. Sussex ware. (TF 23; Sample 981).
Kii Red-pink core and surfaces. Hard, smooth texture; rough fracture. Moderate fine sand temper. Clear (light brown) glaze; thick white slip decoration. 'Metropolitan slipware'. (TF 70; Sample 1056).
Kiii Off-white, slightly pink core and surfaces. Hard, smooth texture; rough fracture. Abundant medium/fine sand temper. Thin red slip with thicker white slip on top. Staffordshire-type combed ware. (TF 27; Sample 986).
Kiv Red core with grey surfaces and margins. Hard, fairly smooth texture; rough fracture. Moderate medium/fine sand temper. Dark 'metallic' glaze. (TF 40; Sample 996).
Kv Brown core and surfaces. Very hard, smooth texture; rough fracture. Moderate medium sand temper with sparse very coarse inclusions of ironstone. White slip and brown glaze. (TF 63; not thin-sectioned).
Kvi Smooth red earthenware. Flower pot. (TF 39; Sample 995).

Forms and Manufacture

Fine brown-glazed earthenwares (Fabric Ki) include cooking pots, jugs, pans and bowls. Some sherds from Staffordshire-type combed ware dishes (Fabric Kiii) have finger-pressed rims. A pipkin and large pans(?) are represented in Fabric Div, and some flower pots (Fabric Dvi) have stamped decoration.

Dating and Comparison

Dated examples of early eighteenth-century Sussex ware are recorded (Baines 1980, 11–12), but most of these wares belong to the late eighteenth or nineteenth centuries. Similar glazes appear on vessels in the later phases of Period D, but the typical 'Sussex' types are confined to Period E.

Thin-sections demonstrate the contrast between the local eighteenth-century wares (Fabric Ki), and the earlier 'Metropolitan slipware' (Fabric Kii). This was manufactured at Harlow, Essex (Newton and Bibbings 1960, 370–6) and elsewhere, and there are many dated examples from the early seventeenth century. Only one sherd of this ware occurs in Phase E38. Staffordshire-type combed wares and other post-medieval types are also confined to recent phases in Period E.

L. Tin-glazed earthenwares (Figure 35)

The tin-glazed wares are either plain (Fabric Li: TF 30) or decorated with blue (Fabric Lii: TF 50), or blue and yellow, patterns (Fabric Liii: TF 51). Two small ointment pots (nos. 66 and 67) are probably early seventeenth-century Southwark products (Lipski 1970, 73; Dawson 1976), but other types are later. Most are English wares, but one sherd which was firmly stratified among the Dissolution debris (Phase D22) is probably an import from the Low Countries.

66. Ointment pot. Blue linear decoration. Purple lattice pattern. Phase D23.
67. Blue pattern with yellow V-shaped over-painting. Phase D23.

M. China

Plain white (Fabric Mi: TF 52); transfer-printed (Fabric Mii: TF 53); and other types (Fabric Miii: TF 76) occur in Period E.

Discussion and Conclusions

Trends within the Ceramic Sequence

Quantification of the fabrics not only provides valu-

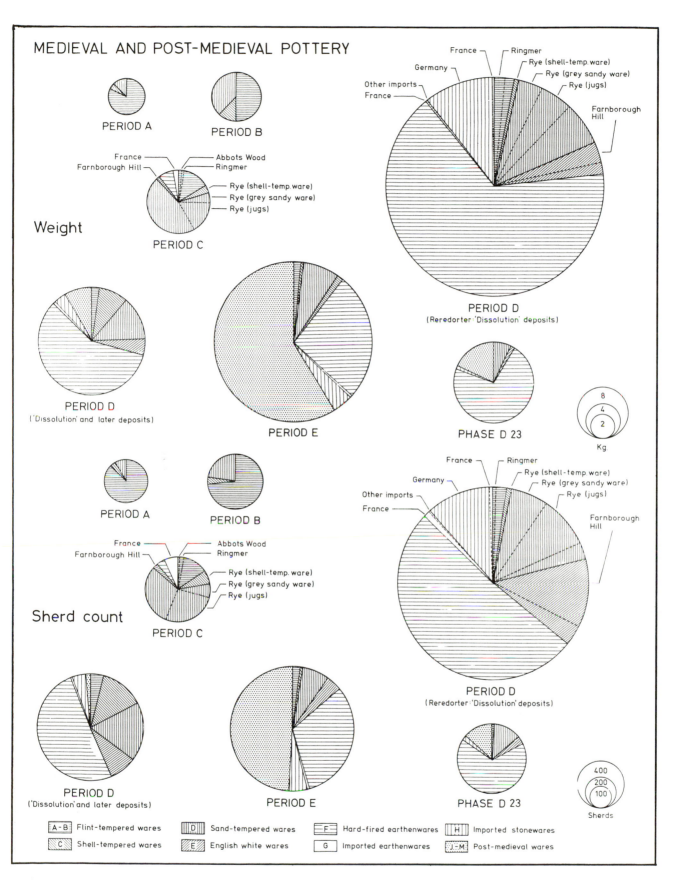

Figure 36   Battle Abbey. Proportional circles showing the relative quantity of pottery discarded at each period. The circles are divided according to the principal fabric groups, and probable kiln sources have been indicated for Period C and the Dissolution debris of Period D. Quantification is by weight [A] and sherd count [B].

able evidence for dating specific types (p. 108–120), but it also illustrates the more general trends within the ceramic sequence. Figure 36 shows the relative quantity of pottery discarded at each period, and on Figure 37 pottery attributed to the various fabric groups, is expressed as a percentage of all sherds in each phase. Thus each vertical column adds up to 100%, and the changing proportion of the fabrics through time is shown by the relative height of the histograms in the horizontal rows. Results using both weight and sherd count are generally consistent, but an estimate of the minimum number of vessels has been included on Figure 37 to indicate where the evidence is based upon small samples.

Flint-/ shell-tempered wares are dominant up to the mid-thirteenth century (Periods A and B), but the proportion of these types declines with the emergence of sand-tempered wares. There can be little doubt, however, that the deliberate make-up in Phase C14 contains a high proportion of abraded residual material.

Hard-fired earthenwares are dominant among the Dissolution debris (Phases D20; D21/22; D30), but residual medieval wares are still represented at this period. The circumstances under which the material was discarded are not fully understood, but medieval sand-tempered fabrics account for as much as 15% (weight: Phase D21/22 and D30) of the pottery which is presumed to have been thrown out in the reredorter area shortly after 1538 (Figure 36). Some abraded sherds may have come from the medieval ground surface, but ceramics found in the reredorter at Bayham Abbey, which are presumed to have been dumped deliberately when the house was dissolved in 1525, also included some 18% of medieval wares. Dumps such as these may therefore provide valuable evidence for assessing the life-span of coarsewares used by a monastic community. The proportion of the individual fabrics from Phase D21/22 at Battle has therefore been plotted for comparison with the pottery from Bayham, which was probably discarded a decade or so earlier (Figure 38; Streeten 1983, fig. 44). Both assemblages attest the persistence of medieval wares alongside vessels from several different sixteenth-century potteries. The presence of residual wares in less clearly defined archaeological contexts at Battle is not so surprising, and the disturbance of medieval levels or the small size of the sample would account for an abnormally high proportion of sand-tempered wares in the later phases of Period D.

Imports do not feature prominently at any period, but the early sixteenth-century Raeren stonewares are well represented among the Dissolution debris. The pattern of residual sherds in later phases is similar to that of the contemporary hard-fired earthenwares. The extent of post-Dissolution activity is conveniently illustrated by the proportion of later fabrics, such as the brown-glazed 'Sussex' earthenwares, compared with earlier types. In some cases there is little later pottery (Phases E35 and E37/39), but in others the quantity of post-medieval wares is considerable (Phases E36; E38 and E40–47).

Distribution and Marketing
Several fabrics have been attributed to specific local kilns on the basis of detailed fabric analysis (p. 107) but the quantities from each source can only be assessed by visual comparison with the type sherds. This is inevitably less precise than thin-section analysis, and some coarsewares such as the probable Abbot's Wood ware have been found in contents which are appreciably earlier than the date conventionally ascribed to these kilns. In the case of the Ringmer fabrics, however, the evidence accords with the early origin of the industry suggested by radiocarbon dates from the kiln sites (Hadfield 1981, 105). The identification of marketed products on the basis of their fabric alone is hazardous, but, in the absence of extensive excavation and absolute dating of the kilns, fabric analysis of marketed wares from securely stratified contexts may help to define the date range of particular industries. This principle has been used successfully to suggest an early origin for pottery manufacture in the Tyler Hill area near Canterbury (Streeten forthcoming b). It may be possible, once more corroborative evidence is available, as in the case of Ringmer, to demonstrate that production at some of the Sussex kiln sites commenced earlier than has been supposed previously. Fine wares from Rye, for example, have been recognised in contexts at Battle which must be earlier than the mid-thirteenth century. Some of these vessels are therefore earlier than the stylistic evidence from the wasters would suggest. With a few exceptions, however, the source of the pottery in Periods A and B cannot be identified with certainty.

In view of these difficulties, Figure 36 only shows probable sources of the pottery attributed to Period C and to the Dissolution debris in the reredorter area. The sizes of the circles, calculated by both weight and sherd count, are proportional to the total quantity of pottery assigned to the various phases, and no attempt has been made to exclude residual wares. Thus, although products of the Rye kilns account for some 5% of the pottery discarded at the Dissolution, this does not necessarily represent contemporary output; indeed, most of the German stonewares in Period E are residual.

This method of presenting the data highlights the nature of the Period D deposits because only at this time was pottery being dumped deliberately. The wares from Dissolution debris in the reredorter area represent a variety of different sources ranging from local earthenwares to the fragment of an East Mediterranean vessel. Imports account for 2% of the total in Period C, but the influx of German stonewares increases the proportion to 10% in the early phases of Period D (weight: Phase D21/22 and D30). At Camber Castle, on the other hand, German stonewares comprised 33% of the pottery from the north bastion which was filled with shingle *c.* 1570 (Wilson and Hurst 1964, 259–60). This reflects both the different dates of the assemblages and perhaps the contrasting demand for mass-produced drinking vessels used by a garrison compared with a monastic community.

Medieval Rye jugs were traded over considerable

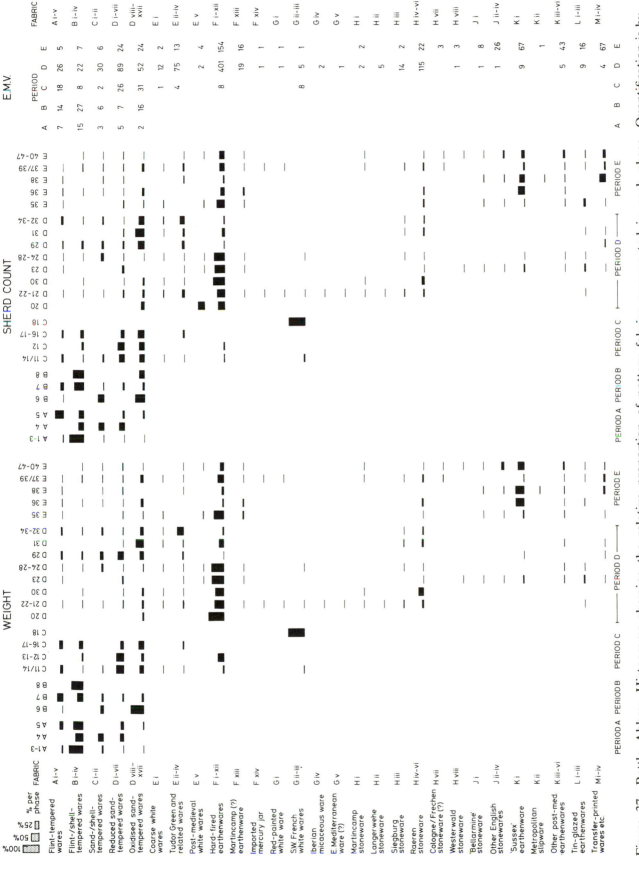

Figure 37   Battle Abbey. Histograms showing the relative proportion of pottery fabrics represented in each phase. Quantification is by weight and sherd count, and the size of the sample is indicated by the estimated minimum number of vessels (EMV).

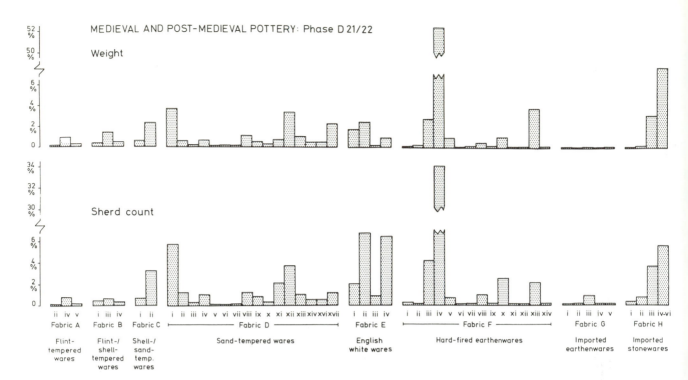

Figure 38   Battle Abbey. Histograms showing the proportion of each pottery fabric represented among the Dissolution debris outside the reredorter (Phase D21/22). Quantification is by weight and sherd count.

distances (Barton 1979, 232), and the identification of marketed coarsewares at Battle demonstrates that these potters also served local needs. It is possible that some vessels were in fact made at Brede (p. 107), but Rye wares certainly account for the highest proportion of identifiable medieval types. The large number of sherds attributed to another, albeit unknown, source may indicate local manufacture, but it is possible, although unlikely, that these fabrics are also from Rye.

There is evidence for competition with the potters' products from further afield at Abbot's Wood and Ringmer and if these identifications are correct, then Battle represents the eastern limit of the known Ringmer distribution.

The multiplicity of local sources in the medieval period, is also matched by a wide variety of later fabrics, but hard-fired earthenwares are predominant in the Dissolution debris (Figures 36–38). Similarity with the fabrics at Bayham Abbey probably indicates local manufacture, but some vessels may be Dutch imports. It is surprising that products of the Boreham Street kiln which were well-represented at Michelham Priory have not been recognised at Battle, but this reinforces the impression that minor early post-medieval potteries in East Sussex served very restricted markets (Streeten 1981, 342).

Later sixteenth-century products of the High Lankhurst kiln occur in small quantities at Battle, and similar fabrics were also found among the Dissolution debris. Like the medieval wares in Periods A and B, the source of these vessels cannot be identified with certainly, but earlier potters may

have used similar raw materials to those from which later vessels were made at High Lankhurst.

In addition to the local English earthenwares, fine white wares from Surrey reached Battle during the fifteenth and early sixteenth centuries. The thin-walled vessels are both light and liable to be broken into small fragments. Simple measures of weight and sherd count do not therefore provide a reliable indication of the quantities (Figures 36 and 37). Battle is one of numerous sites where these wares have been found at some distance from the centre of production, suggesting a sophisticated system of marketing for Tudor Green ware. Unlike at Bayham Abbey, however, products of the Cheam kilns do not appear to have reached as far as Battle. Forms and fabrics which are very similar to Cheam white wares are represented, but textural analysis shows that they are more likely to come from Rye than from Surrey. In the light of this evidence, the suggested identification of Cheam vessels at Bodiam Castle may require reappraisal (Myres 1935, 229; Orton 1982, fig. 26).

Few of the kilns which have been identified in East Sussex have been investigated and published thoroughly. Definitive identification of marketed vessels must therefore await further excavation at production centres, and there are many aspects of both dating and distribution which would repay further work at Rye.

Vessels and their Function
The range of forms represented in each phase reflects the general trends observed from study of the fabrics. The medieval repertoire is largely con-

MEDIEVAL AND POST-MEDIEVAL POTTERY: Vessel types

VESSEL TYPE	A1-3	A4	A5	B6	B7	B8	C11/14	C12-13	C16-17	C18	D20	D21-22	D30	D23	D24	D29	D31	D32-34	E35	E36	E38	E37/39	E40-47
	PERIOD A			PERIOD B			PERIOD C				PERIOD D								PERIOD E				
Cooking pot	●	●	–	–	●	●	●	●	●	–	–	●	●	●	●	–	–	–	●	–	–	●	●
Skillet	–	–	–	–	–	–	●	●	–	–	–	–	–	–	–	–	–	–	–	–	–	–	–
Tripod cooking vessel	–	–	–	–	–	–	●	–	–	–	–	–	–	–	–	–	–	–	–	–	–	–	–
Pipkin	–	–	–	–	–	–	–	–	–	–	–	–	–	●	–	–	–	–	–	–	–	–	●
Lid	–	–	–	–	–	–	–	–	–	–	–	–	–	–	●	–	–	–	–	–	–	–	●
Dish/bowl	–	–	–	–	–	–	–	–	–	–	–	●	●	●	–	●	–	●	●	–	–	–	●
Deep pan	–	–	–	–	–	–	–	–	–	–	–	●	–	–	–	–	–	–	–	–	–	–	●
Spouted pitcher	–	–	–	–	–	–	●	–	–	–	–	–	–	–	–	–	–	–	–	–	–	–	–
Bunghole pitcher	–	–	–	–	–	–	–	–	–	–	–	●	–	–	–	–	–	–	–	–	–	–	–
Earthenware jug	●	●	–	–	●	–	●	–	●	–	●	●	●	●	–	–	–	–	●	●	●	●	●
English white ware jug	–	–	–	–	–	–	●	–	–	–	–	●	●	–	●	●	●	–	–	–	–	–	–
Imported white ware jug	–	–	–	–	–	–	●	–	–	–	–	●	–	–	–	–	–	–	–	–	–	–	–
Imported stoneware jug	–	–	–	–	–	–	–	–	–	–	–	●	–	●	–	–	–	–	–	–	–	●	–
Stoneware tankard	–	–	–	–	–	–	–	–	–	–	–	●	●	●	–	–	●	–	–	–	–	–	●
Puzzle jug	–	–	–	–	–	–	–	–	–	–	–	●	–	–	–	–	–	–	–	–	–	–	–
Earthenware costrel	–	–	–	–	–	–	–	–	–	–	–	●	–	–	–	–	–	–	–	–	–	–	–
Stoneware costrel	–	–	–	–	–	–	–	–	–	–	–	●	–	–	–	–	●	–	–	–	–	–	–
Lobed cup	–	–	–	–	–	–	–	–	–	–	–	●	–	–	–	–	–	–	–	–	–	–	●
Chafing dish	–	–	–	–	–	–	–	–	–	–	–	●	–	–	–	–	–	–	–	–	–	–	–
Distilling apparatus	–	–	–	–	–	–	–	–	–	–	–	●	–	–	●	–	–	–	●	–	–	–	–
Divided dish	–	–	–	–	–	–	–	–	–	–	–	●	–	●	●	–	–	–	–	–	–	–	–
Other 'industrial' vessels	–	–	–	–	–	–	–	–	–	–	–	●	–	–	–	–	–	–	–	–	–	–	–
Tin-glazed drug jar	–	–	–	–	–	–	–	–	–	–	–	–	–	●	–	–	–	–	–	–	–	–	–
Tin-glazed dish	–	–	–	–	–	–	–	–	–	–	–	–	–	–	–	–	–	–	●	–	–	–	–
Stoneware bottle	–	–	–	–	–	–	–	–	–	–	–	–	–	–	–	–	–	–	–	–	–	–	●

Figure 39 Battle Abbey. Chart showing the occurrence of identifiable ceramic vessel types in each phase.

fined to cooking utensils and jugs, but the later hard-fired earthenwares include a variety of new forms (Phase D21/22). Figure 39 shows the occurrence of vessel types in each phase. Some forms could be identified from a single distinctive sherd, but identification of others is based upon larger rim fragments. No attempt has therefore been made to assess the number of vessels represented, but residual medieval wares have been excluded from Periods D and E.

Vessels such as the Saintonge polychrome jug or the fine green-glazed jugs from Rye would doubtless have served as table wares. Likewise it is known from contemporary illustrations that the early sixteenth-century Raeren stoneware tankards were used for drinking. Costrels would probably have been used by travellers, although the association with distilling apparatus should be noted (see below). Vessels which are assumed to be for the preparation or storage of food and drink predominate even among the large group of pottery discarded at the Dissolution and this may suggest that at least some of the material was derived from one of the monastic kitchens.

This assemblage also includes distilling apparatus, and what may be other 'industrial' vessels. Distillation would have been required in medicinal preparations, but this apparatus could also have been used for distilling alcohol or even in the practice of alchemy (Greenaway 1972, 83–88). A small jar, probably for mercury, was found in the same deposit (Phase D22) as the distilling apparatus, and a similar association has been noted at Bayham Abbey (Streeten 1983, 103, fig. 43, nos. 52 and 53). As at Battle, finds from Selborne Priory, Hants also included a pottery costrel or flask in a group of ceramics containing vessels which were probably associated with distilling (Moorhouse 1972, 98–101). Indeed, Battle may now be added to the growing list of sites where distilling apparatus has been found near the reredorter. Unfortunately, however, there is no clear indication from which part of the abbey the debris was derived. An origin somewhere in the east range or the infirmary would be logical but such a large number and variety of vessels as those found at Battle must surely have come from several different rooms.

Some of the fine post-Dissolution wares such as the Westerwald stoneware were probably discarded as rubbish from residential accommodation in the west range, but the deep pans and bowls of Sussex earthenware could have been used in outbuildings attached to the former dormitory and reredorter.

Conclusion
The ceramics from Battle add significantly to know-

ledge of the local pottery industry before the Dissolution. The transition from medieval to later wares is well illustrated by the contrast between the early fifteenth-century material associated with the installation of rainwater drains, and the much wider range of vessels discarded at or shortly after the Dissolution. There are few signs of continuity between the medieval and later traditions and what evidence there is for the location of post-medieval kilns suggests a change in the methods of marketing. In part this may reflect a wider trend which is appropriately documented in the town of Battle. In the later fifteenth century the declining weekly market was replaced by permanent shops in which a more diverse range of goods, perhaps including non-local ceramic table wares, could be kept in stock (Searle 1974, 365–6).

It is difficult, however, to make positive links between the precisely-dated documentary sources and the ill-defined archaeological sequence, because, despite the well-stratified contexts at Battle, there are difficulties in identifying contemporary types. Vessels may have remained in use for many decades and the extent of the residual material is clearly demonstrated in Period E. It is therefore ironical, although not surprising, that middens containing contemporary ceramics tend to be found on domestic sites where the independent dating evidence is poor, whereas the well-stratified medieval make-up levels at monastic sites such as Battle contain a high proportion of residual types, yet little contemporary rubbish.

Finds and Records
The groups of pottery from Battle Abbey are likely to be required for future comparison with other finds from the area, and the storage system has therefore been designed to enable the retrieval of either fabric samples or stratified groups. The finds and associated records are in the custody of the Historic Buildings and Monuments Commission, and the thin-sections have been retained in the Department of Archaeology, University of Southampton.

Finds include a fabric type series related to the thin sections; illustrated vessels; and other pottery arranged according to fabric within contexts.

The records comprise a phasing summary with context numbers; a concordance of 'interim' and 'publication' vessel numbers; a concordance of type sherds, published fabric groups and sample numbers; sketches of the thin-sections; charts showing the proportion of all fabric sub-types occurring within each phase; fabric summary sheets, including munsell numbers, vessel types and contexts; phased data summaries; and pre-printed data sheets for each context, listing associated artifacts.

Acknowledgements
The necessity for rigorous evaluation of the ceramic sequence using precise analytical techniques places a considerable burden of responsibility upon the excavator and volunteers at all stages of processing the finds. The thankless task of phasing has been undertaken by the director of excavations, Dr J. Hare. A particular tribute is owed to those who have helped with sorting and recording the pottery: Miss F. Boyd, Mr D. Burton, Miss G. Chambers, Miss C. Chapple, Mrs E. Edwards, Mrs A. Furlong, Miss J. Humphrey, Miss N. Mattoch, Mr M. McCall, Miss S. Mumford, Miss A. Naylor, Miss C. Perry, and Miss A. Ridge.

The assistance of Mrs V. Coad with supervision of the finds processing was invaluable, and special thanks are recorded for her painstaking pottery drawings which accompany this report. Identifications have benefitted from discussion with Mr J. Hurst, Mr S. Moorhouse, Mr R. Thompson, Miss R. Tomber and with Mr J. Thorn to whom the writer is also indebted for his help in many ways.

Chapter VIII

The Window Glass

by Jill Kerr

Introduction

The finds of this material were mainly from the Dissolution and post-Dissolution layers. This destruction debris was found in direct association with the chapter house itself and in the reredorter area, and represents a considerable extension of our knowledge of the repertoire of geometric grisaille motifs in the thirteenth century. Both contexts and locations are consistent with the destruction and removal of the window glass for the extraction of the valuable leads. Only three pieces of glass in lead were found (the most complete is illustrated, No. 21) and these, with the tangled ends of leads ripped from the adjacent glass are further evidence of lead stripping. Few lead cames have survived and they form seven distinct types. These are catalogued in detail in Chapter X, but material relevant to the glass finds has been included here. The majority of the glass found in the build up for the late medieval drain construction in the reredorter area appears to provide evidence for a contemporary glazing programme. Apart from this group, the finds in medieval contexts are slight and somewhat disappointing in that they provide little evidence of any significance.

The information derived from the window glass is divided into two sections according to whether the location of the find was the chapter house or the reredorter. The typologies are defined within each section, and all the discernible design types are illustrated. Where possible comparisons are made with extant glazing and much use has been made of the Corpus Vitrearum archive for Kent, an area which includes the largest survival of geometric grisaille glazing of any county in Britain. A full account of all the excavated glass including drawings of all the surviving painted fragments has been deposited with the site records.

With very few exceptions, all the glass is extremely fragmentary and in very poor condition. The total quantity of painted finds would just fill a panel 60 cm square. Burial and saturation has rotted nearly all the material to opacity. Not many grozed edges have survived intact, and there are even fewer complete pieces. From the remains of the broken edges, it is possible to confirm that all this glass was smashed before burial, although owing to the unstable state of the material, much damage and crumbling has occurred as the inevitable result of retrieval. Consolidation of all the deteriorated glasses was an essential factor in preserving this fragile collection.

Method of Examination
1978–9 Recorded and examined after consolidation in the Ancient Monuments Conservation Laboratory.
1980 Recorded and examined during excavation on site. Re-examined after consolidation in the Laboratory.

The Chapter House Glass (figure 40)

The most important collection of material from this site is without doubt the geometric grisaille designs. These provide evidence for the type of glazing for the chapter house, and it is possible to speculate that it would have been similar in apperance to the glass of the same period and type at Salisbury (Knowles 1932, fig 8) and Lincoln (Westlake 1881, pl. lxxxii Morgan 1983, fig. C). The paint is applied in a bold, decisive and highly competant manner, and the overall effect of the designs would have been most impressive and of high quality. This type of glazing, of predominantly clear glass with bold black geometrically complex designs in paint and lead, perhaps punctuated by coloured pot metal glass, is entirely appropriate to chapter house glazing. It would have had the additional advantage of letting in a great deal of light, as the chapter house is located in the shadow of both the abbey church and the dormitory, and would have depended on its eastern windows as the major source of light unless there was also an upper clerestory in the west wall.

The dating of this type of glass is difficult to define with precision, as so little comparable material has survived *in situ* which can be firmly dated, and a chronology for the development of geometric grisaille designs has yet to be delineated – especially for the early period. On the basis of the highly developed characteristics of the Battle repertoire of designs, a mid- to late-thirteenth-century date is appropriate, which indicates that the chapter house glazing is unlikely to be coeval with the rebuilding of *c.* 1200 (*supra* p. 25–26).

Despite the fragmentary and deteriorated state of the pieces bearing geometric grisaille designs, it is quite clear from the heavily weathered exterior surfaces, where these have not been protected by the lead shadows, and from the extensive corrosion pits, that this glass was *in situ* until the Dissolution. Its appearance, like that of the extant glass of this type at Salisbury, Lincoln and York Minster (Five Sisters window), would have been much darkened and marred by this weathering and corrosion, and it is perhaps surprising that the abbey did not see fit to replace this glazing in a later period. Perhaps this is an indication of the competence of the thirteenth-century glaziers; the leads would have been sound and weatherproof up to the Dissolution, and probably presented the destroyers with technical problems in stripping the leads. It is likely that the small quantity of broken pieces of glass found both inside and outside the chapter house, as well a scattered around it, are evidence of the smashing out of the heavily fixed panels for removal to a more convenient place, perhaps sited in the reredorter area, for the stripping of the leads.

There is no definite evidence from the fragments for the existence of heraldic, figurative or narrative glass in the chapter house. Some pieces of very perished painted designs may have been drapery (see below p. 131) but unfortunately the condition of the paint and the scant survival does not permit either illustration or certainty. There are no pieces of inscription, heads, hands, background designs or architecture. The only physiognomies to survive are fragments of two grotesques. The colour survival is extremely poor. There are definitely some fragments of unpainted blue and flashed ruby and the less durable range of purples, greens, yellows, pinks and browns may be represented among the severely rotted fragments which were too tiny and deteriorated to permit analysis. None of the glass is still translucent.

For the later periods, it is possible that some small unpainted, thin fragments may be of fifteenth-century date. There are only about nine tiny fragments in this category, and all are extremely flat and uncorroded with a distinctive iridescence on both surfaces. Only two small fragments of a quarry design can be attributed with any certainty to the fifteenth century (No. 20). These are the only fragments with yellow stain in the entire collection.

Fitments
No ferramenta or tie bars were found in this area.

Thirteenth Century

Glass in Lead (Figure 40 No. 21)
794962 D24.
Two fragments of blue unpainted glass oblong strips, width 20 mm, are retained in leads. The lead is heavily soldered at one end and twisted to break at the other. Neither piece of glass is complete and both retain evidence of the cement attaching to the lead. All the edges in the leads are grozed and the breaks occurred before burial. The lead was cast and the flange is 5 mm wide. The glass is pitted on both the interior and exterior although the latter is more pronounced. Probably a coloured strip, thirteenth-century, perhaps associated with the geometric grisaille designs. The heavily soldered end may have

been the panel edge; it is clear that the leads on either side once held glass slightly thinner than the coloured glass.

Leads
802622 D24 Medieval cast lead. 4 mm glass space, 5 mm flange. Twisted. No cement attached. This is the only fragment of lead came found in this area, apart from the pieces associated with the glass above.

Geometric Grisaille with Crosshatched Backgrounds Border Design I (No. 1)
785922 D20, 785923 D24, 785924 D20, 785926 D24, 794962 D24.
Strip of quatrefoil flowers with a central circle; the petals defined with a crescent.

Variants of this design are found as frames to figures and narrative panels at Canterbury (Caviness 1981, figs. 170, 203, 206, 207, 272), and fragments were recently discovered at Bayham Abbey (Kerr, 1983 fig. 17: 45, 46). The Battle type is distinguished by the addition of the crescents within each petal and the extension of the side petals into the unpainted border to the crosshatched background strip. The lead lines would have overlapped the edges of the side petals reinforcing the linear strip design. All the glass is 3 mm thick and the width of the border, where the grozed edges survive, is 47 mm. Many small fragments of this design are extant including several tiny pieces found in the reredorter (see below). Unlike the coloured pot metal strips at Canterbury, this glass was originally white like that at Bayham. The tone of the paint, a dark red-brown, is identical to types A–D of geometric grisaille stiff leaf foliage sprays. The exterior condition, with deep corrosion pits, and the scale and bold style of painting is also identical to groups A–D which implies an association between the leaf forms and the flower border similar to the designs at Lincoln (Westlake 1881, pl. lxxxii Morgan 1983, Fig. C) and Salisbury (Knowles 1932. fig. 58).

Design Types A and B (Nos 2, 3)
785922 D20, 785923 D24, 785924 D20, 785925 D23, 785926 D24, 785931 D23, 794962 D24. Stiff leaf foliage spray designs with trefoil, cinquefoil and lobed terminals. Type A (No. 2). Several incomplete examples of this distinctive design survive although in all cases the base from which the foliage springs is lost. The original geometric shape appears to be the apex of a vesica. From an indeterminate lobed base the stem divides into three; the centre stem is straight terminating at the apex in a cinquefoil, the side stems curve to complete the form at the base of the cinquefoil in profile trefoils. Type B (No. 3). Again several incomplete examples of this design survive without the base of the foliage springing. The geometric shape is a half vesica. The stem follows the curved edge terminating in a profile ?cinquefoil; from the lower stem springs a spur terminating in a lobe, above it a longer spur terminating in a profile trefoil.

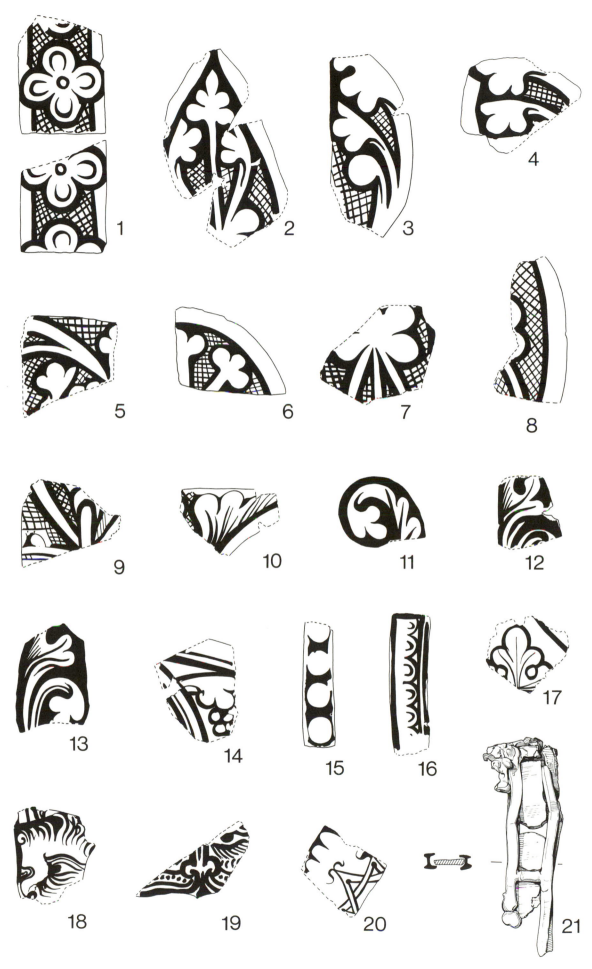

Figure 40 Battle Abbey. Window glass from chapter house ($\frac{1}{2}$)

Design Types C and D (Nos. 4, 5)
785922 D20, 785923 D24, 794962 D24.
Identical in scale of crosshatching, tone of paint and execution with types A and B. Unfortunately not enough of a single piece has survived to indicate the design relationships or to allow for reconstruction of the geometric shapes. Border type I and groups A–D are distinguished by the identical scale of the crosshatching, the red brown tone of the thick paint, the originally white glass 2–3 mm thick with identical heavy exterior weathering and corrosion pits, the occasional survival of distinctive 4–5 mm lead shadows, the same jagged grozing and the same method of defining the design with strong precise paint strokes, the edges of the shapes sharpened by removal of the paint before firing. None of these designs has any backpainting to reinforce the effect. It is notable that where the terminals connect with the stems a distinctive pointed spur articulates the join.

Design Type E (No. 6) 785922 D20.
A complete piece of a radiating frontal trefoil design within a curved border against a crosshatched background. The glass was originally clear white; unlike groups A–D it undulates, varying in thickness from 2–4 mm. The paint line is less flowing and more mechanical than the above groups from which it is further distinguished by the lack of a spur where the terminals relate to the stem. This could have been a corner point to a panel; the attenuation of the stems, which do not radiate to form a complete circular design if combined with similar shapes, is a curious feature.

Design Type F (Nos. 7 and 8)
785925 D23, 785926 D24, 794962 D24.
Incomplete examples of a multiple foil and stem design. The largest surviving pieces are illustrated. This also lacks the spur and the movement of the painting seen in types A–D. Type F has a quite distinctive white patina on the painted surface and the exterior is more densely corroded and weathered indicating a less durable glass than that of the above groups. There is a clear 2 mm lead shadow discernible on all the grozed edges. The paint is a strong red tone and stands proud of the surface. Unfortunately the highly brittle and friable nature of this glass has led to very incomplete survivals that are insufficient to permit reconstruction of the design.

Design Type G (No. 9)
785926 D24
Very few pieces of this design survive, and none are large enough to discern the original pattern. The paint surfaces are more perished with much loss of line, and the unpainted areas have the same type of white patina as group F. The exterior surface has quite a different appearance from all the other groupings; it is very flat with large blobs of corrosion. Different too is the distinctly brown toned paint and the method of application, which is extremely cursive, especially in the more imprecise crosshatching. The design is intriguingly incomplete and difficult to parallel or reconstruct.

Design Type H (No. 10)
785926 D24, 794962 D24
The association of crosshatching with more naturalistic veined leaf forms is a departure from the above groups. The fragment illustrated is the largest of many small scraps bearing veined leaf forms, none of which is of sufficient size to reconstruct a design. It is interesting to note that a relationship between naturalistic veined foliate and leaf forms and the more formal stiff leaf designs exists within the same panel at Salisbury. The condition of the glass is similar to type G, and the design is painted in a similar brown toned paint.

Design Type J.
785923 D24, 785925 D23, 785927 D20, 785942 D23, 794962 D24.
Large scale geometric grisaille fragments. The glass in this grouping is very fragmented and perished. Only pieces of stem and crosshatching have survived and none is complete enough to merit illustration. As none of the terminals is extant it is difficult to assign a type to this group, but the scale of the crosshatching, which is approximately three times larger than all the illustrated groups, is very striking. A similar jump in scale can also be seen at Bayham (Kerr, 1983 fig. 17: 42) where a considerable quantity of large scale crosshatched stiff leaved quarries were found. Perhaps these scant remains at Battle belonged to a similar type of design which is a definite Kent type surviving *in situ* at Great Mongeham, Westbere, Stockbury and Chillenden.

Geometric Grisaille Fragments with Crosshatching.
D20, D23, D24, E42
Many small fragments, too miniscule or deteriorated to attribute to a design grouping, were found in all these contexts. The scale of crosshatching is that of groups A–H. The exterior surfaces exhibited corrosion pits and weathering, and in many cases much of the painted surface had sloughed off. There are few grozed edges, and even fewer clean breaks as most of this fragmentary material has rotted and crumbled during burial.

Designs without Crosshatched Backgrounds
Design Type K (Nos. 11–13)
785922 D20, 785931 D23
Veined foliage designs set against a matt black background. The outline of these designs is picked out of a matt wash and the detailed veining painted on in very decisive flamboyant brush strokes. There is minimal exterior corrosion and the condition of the dark red toned paint is excellent. It is not possible to discern the original colour of the glass which may have been a coloured pot metal. This highly articulate and sophisticated design can be paralleled at Canterbury on a variety of coloured glasses (Caviness 1981, figs. 167, 171, 374), and a similar type was recently found at St Augustine's Abbey in the same City (Sherlock, forthcoming). In addition to the three fragments illustrated there are five more tiny pieces with no grozed edges surviving in a very perished condition. There are insufficient

extant examples to indicate the original function of this striking design.

Design Type L (No. 14)
794957 D24, 794968 D26
There are surprisingly only two surviving examples of fruiting stiff leaf in the entire collection. The unillustrated fragment is also 2 mm thick but has no grozed edges. It is very incomplete and bears part of a ribbed stem and four circles of fruit only. The paint on both is very dark red in tone and the exterior is slightly corroded. Both have devitrified to black but were originally white. This design was an important feature of the thirteenth-century geometric grisaille repertoire and existed alongside the crosshatched stiff leaf designs at the same period. There are many surviving examples in Kent, notably at Selling (Westlake 1894 I, pl. lvi e; II pl. lxxxii c.), Chartham (Westlake 1894 I, pl. lxxxix; II pl. lxxxii d.), Upper Hardres and Addisham. Several examples of this type of design were recently found at Bayham Abbey (Kerr, 1983 fig 16: 12, 13). It is unfortunate that the remains of this type at Battle are so slight and inadequate to establish the design function.
785922 D20, 785923 D24. This area produced several small fragments of extremely incomplete designs without crosshatched backgrounds which may belong to this group. It is interesting to note that none of the fragments of groups A–H have fruiting stiff leaf terminals.

Decorative Borders and Bosses associated with Geometric Grisaille Designs
The design types under this heading includes both plain and painted forms which can be seen in association with geometric grisaille glazing in extant contexts, notably at Lincoln and Salisbury. This does not preclude the possibility that the inclusion in the repertoire at Battle may have had a different decorative function. None of the forms is unusual and all are part of the decorative 'vocabulary' at the disposal of the thirteenth-century glazier.

Border Design II (No. 15) (for Border Design I, see above, p. 128)
Beading
This is an ubiquitous design found in all periods of glazing. These fragments, none of which survives complete, are all examples of very precise grozing, sometimes in very thick glass. The circles are picked out of a matt paint wash that varies in tone from red to brown to black. Not all the colours of the base glass can be determined apart from a few survivals of the white, blue and red range. None are still translucent.
785922 D20 white w.17 mm: 785923 D24 white w.17 mm; blue w.18–15 mm: 785925 D23 blue and white w. 15 mm: 785927 D20 colour not discernible w.17 mm: 785928 D23 white w.17 mm; 785931 D23 colour not discernible w.15 mm: 785933 D23 blue and colour not discernible w.17 mm: 794962 D24 red white and colour not discernible w.16–17 mm.

Border Design III (No. 16)
Crescents and Half-Circles
785922, D20
Only one example of this design has survived. It is painted on a base glass of which the colour is no longer discernible, in dark red toned paint. The lead lines would have obscured the edge painting which is probably to indicate the cut lines. The shape is slightly curved. Similar designs can be seen at Canterbury (Caviness 1981, figs 127, 169). Stanton Harcourt (Oxon.) (Westlake 1894 I, pl. lvi b), and Snodland (Kent).

Border Design IV
Unpainted Strips
The full range of colours is no doubt lost among the many deteriorated fragments in this category. Only white and red can be determined where the glass has not completely devitrified to black. The widths range from 17–19 mm and examples are found from D20, D23, D24, D30.

Quatrefoil
785922 D20 35 mm square,
One example only, now incomplete, of a quatrefoil design with a matt background and a central cross. The colour is no longer discernible, but similar bosses survive in various pot metals at Canterbury, Lincoln and Salisbury as decorative punctuation to geometric grisaille panels.

?Fleur-de-lis
785922 D20 incomplete, h. 45 mm w. 2 mm.
Painted on white glass with a matt background. Function as the quatrefoil.

Stiff Leaf Foliate Boss (No. 17)
794962 D24
Two fragments of this design survive, both incomplete. Reconstruction would indicate a square containing a formalised foliage design in the centre of four attached fleurs-de-lis. with central veining crossing at the middle. Extant examples of this design as the central boss to geometric grisaille can be seen at Lincoln, Salisbury and Kennington (Kent).

Small Painted Fragments
There remains the usual collection of tiny broken painted pieces that are too small to determine the design grouping. These exist in all contexts in varying amounts, but in some cases they are the only window glass finds: 785932, 794954, 794956, 794959, 794965, 794966. Phasing: D23, D24, D26, E35.

?Drapery
None of these pieces can be said with any certainty to be drapery, they could have been an ellision of stems or the remnants of lost designs. All are extremely small and very perished with considerable paint loss; none of the original colours have survived. 785922 D20: two pieces, no grozed edges, line painting in dark red, no backpainting. 785925 D23; one fragment of thick glass, 3 mm, surface very perished but examination under the microscope re-

vealed swirling line painting. Incomplete with no grozed edges.

The only piece that can be said to be drapery with any degree of confidence is a small fragment (No. 42) h. 22 mm w. 24 mm bearing a design of end folds picked out of a matt wash of brown paint and painted on with three thick and one thin brush stroke surviving; the paint is just visible to the naked eye but examination under the microscope revealed backpainting to emphasise the depths of the folds. This is part of 794970, E45 from the backfill of Brakspear's excavations, and unfortunately is not therefore necessarily associated with the chapter house. The piece is far too small for stylistic analysis but it could easily be thirteenth century in date.

A Grotesque Head (No. 18)
794955 D24

A grotesque head in profile, the nose distorted against the cut line, the eye facing left. The hair is jagged and resembles the mane of a lion. From the top of the head it is possible to discern the springing of a stem. Geometric grisaille designs springing from the head of a grotesque survive in York Minster chapter house vestibule and Merton College Chapel Oxford. In Kent, Chartham has grotesque masks from which foliage issues, and at Addisham there are similar grotesque lions comparable with the Battle fragment.

The paint stands proud of the glass and is a dull brown tone. There is no backpainting and the exterior is not corroded. The glass is completely opaque and the paint lines are difficult to discern. Microscopic examination reveals the glass to have been white.

This design is a unique survival at Battle. The style is decisively vigorous, and in its use of lines to emphasise the features is quite distinct from the subtle use of washes and line painting in all the Canterbury physiognomies.
Date: Thirteenth century.

A Cat Mask (No. 19)
785926 D24

A very striking design, painted on uncorroded translucent pale blue glass in thick matt grey paint. The paint is very unstable, and has flaked off in places, leaving a matt surface against the distinctive iridescent sheen of the unpainted area. No parallel has been found for this design, which is grozed along the mouth opening suggesting the associated leading of a congruent design on a different colour of glass. The frontal face suggests that it is unlikely to have been a Hellmouth and probably served a similar design function as the grotesque head above. (Westlake 1881, p. 29 pl. xii m)

Unpainted Fragments
These were found in association with painted pieces throughout the site but are especially notable in the following contexts: D20, D23, D24.

None of the original colours are discernible, very few grozed edges survive, all are fragmentary and have exterior weathering and corrosion pits. These remnants may represent the lost colour range of poorly durable potmetals.

Unpainted Shapes
Teardrop 100 mm x 70 mm 785922 D20. Reconstructed during conservation from a group of associated fragments. Originally white glass.
Square with a large and a small half circle cut from the top corners. 105 mm x 60 mm 785922 D20. Colour not discernible.
Square 60 mm x 40 mm 785926 D24. Colour not discernible.
Curved Strip 130 mm x 45 mm 785923 D24. Colour not discernible.
Triangle 794971 D20. Incomplete, one corner only survives. Originally white glass.
Circle? 40 mm x 17 mm 785933 D32. Incomplete, originally blue glass.
Interstice Design 45 mm x 50 mm 785929 D24. Two concave side edges terminating at the outer edge in a convex curve, at the inner in a straight edge one third of the length of the outer. Originally white glass.

These shapes probably originally came from an unpainted geometric window, the design carried by the leads. Similar fragments of this type of glazing were found at Bayham (Kerr 1983, 60), and are extant in Kent at Brabourne and Hastingleigh. Salisbury also has several examples, notably in the south transept (Westlake 1894 I, pl. lxxxv). All these examples are dated twelfth to early thirteenth century but there is no evidence that the form did not continue into the later thirteenth century. Perhaps a window of this type, which would let in more light than the geometric grisaille designs, was deemed suitable for the windows overshadowed by the south transept gable. Alternatively, it is quite possible that these geometric shapes were incorporated into the painted geometric grisaille designs.

Unpainted Coloured Glass
The survival rate for discernible coloured glasses is extremely low. However there are examples of flashed ruby among the fragments from 785922 D20 and blue glass in 785923 D24. Both colours are in exceedingly poor condition and no examples are still translucent.

Post-Thirteenth-Century Glass
Quarry Design (No. 20)
794962 D24, 794964 E42

Two fragments only survive, the most complete is illustrated. It is possible to reconstruct a quarry design of an eight pointed star defined by two intersecting four point forms. The edges of the quarry have a frame of small points and the points of the star are decorated with flourishes. The exterior is uncorroded with only slight weathering and the glass is still translucent in places. This type of quarry design is appropriate to a fifteenth-century date. There is a clear survival of yellow stain on the exterior for the design of the star.

Unpainted Glass
A group of very flat uncorroded unpainted glasses with a distinctive iridescent surface was found associated with medieval glass in D24 and E35.

No grozed edges had surved and all the glass has devitrified so that the colour can no longer be determined. It is possible that these glasses are post-Dissolution.

The Reredorter Glass (figure 41)
With few exceptions all the window glass from this area was found in Dissolution contexts. The scatter of fragmented and shattered glass throughout the reredorter does not fall into any precise pattern, and perhaps indicates an adjacent area being used for the dismantling of panels from all over the abbey in order to extract the valuable leads for re-use, and to smash the glass for frit. Most of the painted fragments and some of the unpainted pieces are thirteenth century; there are notably few painted remains that can be attributed with any certainty to the fourteenth century (Nos. 35–7, 41), and even less to the fifteenth.

Of the unpainted pieces there is a considerable quantity of late medieval unglazed fragments, perhaps evidence for reglazing of the abbey buildings. Survival of coloured glass is minimal, and the range is consistent with the early and late dates derived from the evidence of the painted pieces. There appears to have been a glazing gap in the fourteenth century here; at least the evidence for material of this date has not survived among the archaeological remains. It is interesting to note that there is a similar gap in the glazing programme in the extant glass at Canterbury.

Five of the design types defined from the chapter house context are represented among the fragments recovered from the reredorter; apart from these, it would be unwise to speculate on the original location of this material in the abbey buildings. Suffice it to say that it is highly unlikely that such an heterogeneous collection of painted and unpainted fragments would have been originally glazed into the reredorter.

Apart from one small legible piece of inscription (the letter S, No. 40) and three survivals of drapery painting (of which the most complete is illustrated, No. 42), there are unfortunately no survivals of any figures, iconographies or evidence of anything substantial in terms of design types for the thirteenth-century painted pieces apart from geometric grisaille. For the fourteenth century, the most important remains are those of an extremely interesting vine leaf design against a crosshatched background (Nos. 35–37). No precise parallels for this highly distinctive and sophisticated design have been found in England, and its origins may well be French. The only heraldic fragment to survive in the entire collection is also fourteenth century (No. 41); there are again no examples of narrative or figurative iconographies, or even backgrounds or architectures. This dearth of survivals of what are the most common features of fifteenth as well as fourteenth century window designs is even more notable for the fifteenth century

and later periods of glazing remains at Battle. The only fifteenth-century designs to survive are a collection of pitifully fragmented shatters of quarry designs, none of them sufficiently substantial to reconstruct the complete pattern.

Thirteenth Century

Glass in Lead (No. 21)
794918 D22 3 mm glass space 5 mm flange; lead cast. The leads are intact around a broken piece of unpainted ?originally white triangular glass one point of which is cut to about an intact half circle of ?originally pot metal glass. The leads are twisted and torn away; none appears to have been the panel edge. Above the shortest edge of the triangular piece the lead has been doubled by the addition of a soldered piece, perhaps an *in situ* repair. 794928 4 mm glass space, 5 mm flange; lead cast. An unpainted triangular piece of very perished glass, colour not discernible, enclosed by lead, the cement intact.

Lead
802559 D21 2.5 mm glass space, 4 mm flange; lead cast in two-piece mould, distinctive flash along the outer edge.

Fitments
No ferramenta or tie bars were found in this area.

Geometric Grisaille with Crosshatched Backgrounds
Design Type M (Nos. 22, 23)
785936 D30, 802056 D22
Border or edging strip design of stiff leaf trefoils, the outer leaves pointed, the centre rounded; veined within a double lined border against a cross hatched background.
785936 D30 (No. 22) is slightly larger in scale and is still glassy. Both have extensive exterior corrosion pits and are painted in characteristic red toned paint. The scale of the crosshatching and the precision of the application of the painted design is smaller in scale and more exact than the design types A–F found in the chapter house. Identical design types to Battle M are found at Salisbury (Westlake 1894 I, pl. lxxxiv fig. 1; Knowles 1932, fig 58), Bekesbourne, Lympne and Stodmarsh (Kent), and were recently excavated at Bayham (Kerr, 1983 Group F, fig. 17:32). The Battle type is distinguished by the three veins emanating from a single point.

Design Type N (Nos. 24, 25)
794922 E36 802059 D22
Palmette quarries from reticulated glazing. Extant examples of this type are common thirteenth-century geometric grisaille motifs and can be seen at Salisbury (Westlake 1894 I, pl. lxxv), Lincoln (Westlake 1894 I, pl. lxxxii), and in Kent at Molash, Stodmarsh, Chartham and Snodland (Westlake 1894 II, pl. xciii no. 16). Examples of identical designs were found at Bayham (Kerr, 1983 Group D: fig 17:34). The Battle type (No. 24) is interesting in that the grozed edge at the top cuts the palmette in half.

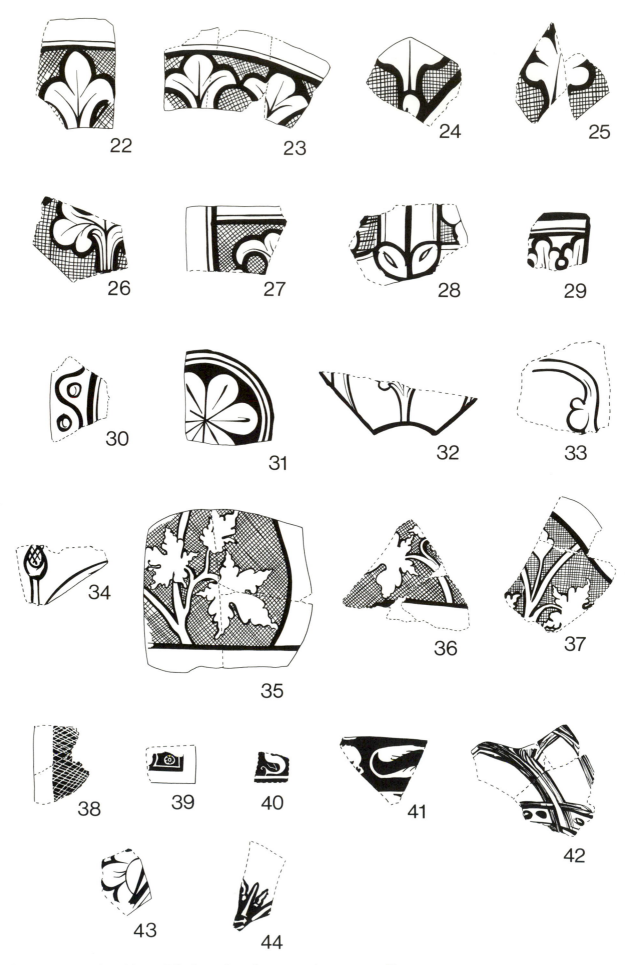

Figure 41   Battle Abbey. Window glass from reredorter area ($\frac{1}{2}$)

Design Type O (Nos. 26, 27)
794918 D22, 802095 C14
Veined stiff leaf quarries. Neither design is complete enough for accurate reconstruction. The circles of crosshatching formed by the outer touching point of the side and centre edge leaves is quite distinctive.

Design Type P (No. 28)
794918 D22
The paint line is comparatively cursive and imprecise. Although the fragment is extremely incomplete, sufficient survives to determine that no precise parallel for this distinctive design has been located.

Designs without Crosshatched Backgrounds
Design Type Q (Nos. 32, 33)
794917 C14 794918 D22, 802059 D22
Stiff leaf foliage trails against a plain background are a distinctive feature of thirteenth-century design repertoire. Outstanding examples of this design type are listed under design type L. A possible remnant of fruiting leaf, too incomplete to define with certainty, was found in 794917 C14.

Border Designs and Bosses associated with
Geometric Grisaille Glazing
Border Design V (No. 29)
Incomplete fragment of strip palmette without crosshatched background. Similar designs are plentiful in association with geometric grisaille and as decorative borders to panels. (Kerr, 1983 fig 17:39; Westlake 1894 I, pl. lxxxvi fig. 1–Salisbury; pl. lxiv fig. e–Canterbury; and Preston (Kent).

Border Design VI (No. 30)
785937 802095 C14, 802067 C14
Serpentine line between a row of circles within a line border. Small fragments of this design survive. There are two types: the illustrated example is less common and is painted on; the more frequently found design is picked out of a matt wash. Two fragments of the latter were found in 802095 C14 w. 25 mm. The condition of the glass is too perished to determine the original colour. Extant examples can be seen at Stanton Harcourt and Selling (Westlake 1894 I, pl. lvi).

Border Design VII (No. 38)
794918 D22, 802059 D22
Cursive crosshatching picked out of a matt wash. The glasses bearing this design are excessively fragile and perished. They are 3 mm thick. Such designs associated with geometric grisaille as a border to vesica can be seen at Selling (Kent).

Foliate Boss (No. 31)
794917 C14, 794922 E36
Sexfoil flower within two line border against a matt background. Colour no longer discernible. The illustrated example is interesting in that it is complete and the grozing of the right angle corner does not follow the geometric divisions of the design. The unillustrated example (h.16 mm w.26 mm) is a quarter circle bearing two half and one complete petals on what was originally pot yellow glass. Both designs are common as colour points in geometric grisaille contexts.

Design Fragments Identical to Chapter House Types

Border Type I Fragments in 802059 D22 and 794947 C14. Very perished.
Border Type II A fragment in 802070 C14
Design Type F 802063 D21, 802102 C14, 802092 D34 Very perished.
Design Type J 785940 D30, 785938 D30. Very perished.
Stiff Leaf Foliate Boss (No. 17) 794918 D22.
None of these survivals is of sufficient size or in a good enough state of preservation for illustration.

Inscription (No. 40)
802070 C14
The lower half of a letter S picked out of a matt black background. Very deteriorated. Similar to the epigraphy of the Canterbury Trinity Chapel clerestory (Caviness 1981, pl. 162). Another tiny fragment of similar type was found in the same context but the surface was too damaged to discern the letter form.

Unpainted Shapes
Squares and Strips: 794936 D30, 44 mm x 19 mm colour lost; 794929 E37, 35 mm x 30 mm, 46 mm x 35 mm colour lost; 794923 D22, w.17 mm white.
Curved: 794922 E36, w.16 mm colour lost; 802059 D22, 30 mm x 70 mm; 794954 D24, 85 mm x 35 mm colour lost.
Triangles: 802093 E39, 25 mm x 25 mm colour lost; 794928 D30, 73 mm x 92 mm white.

These designs probably served similar design functions to the unpainted shapes found in association with the chapter house. It is also possible that some may have been from domestic glazing. All these glasses are extensively weathered from having been *in situ* a considerable time before burial. They vary in thickness from 2.5 – 4 mm, and are all imprecisely grozed.

Painted Fragments
The reredorter area yielded a considerable quantity of very small fragments of painted glass in extremely perished condition. None of the surviving surface area retains sufficient quantities of paint to discern the design grouping and very few grozed edges survive. It is interesting to note that there was no discernible distinction whatsoever between the painted fragments from the medieval contexts associated with the construction of the drainage system in this area and the fragments from the Dissolution and later levels.

Crosshatched Geometric Grisaille Fragments were found in C11, C14, D21, D22, D30, D34, E36 and E47.
Fragments with Lines only were found in B7, C14, D21, D22, D30, E36, E37 and E47.

Fragment of Drapery (No. 42)
794918 D22
?Thirteenth or fourteenth century. Not enough has survived for stylistic analysis. One piece only bearing a decorative band of circles within a double line border, the remains of two folds. The paint line is rough, impressionistic, and imprecise to articulate the folds, emphasised by a light wash at the side of the lines and matt backpainting for depth. Nothing quite like this style of painting has been located. Decorative bands painted on the same glass as the drapery folds can be seen at Canterbury (Caviness 1981, figs. 127, 151, 155, 171, 199, 306, 308). The original colour of the glass is no longer discernible, and the cursive paint lines quite unlike the precise articulation of drapery at Canterbury. The glass is very perished and decayed and appears to have been a hem from a large scale figure. There is pitting on the exterior surface and the glass is 3–4 mm thick.

Fourteenth Century
Naturalistic Geometric Grisaille Design Type R (Nos. 35, 36, 37)
794918 D22, 794931 D24, 794950 D21, 802059 D22. An extremely unusual combination of naturalistic vine leaf and stem set against a crosshatched background. The exterior surface has no corrosion but burial has decayed the originally white glass opaque and caused the paint to rot and shale off. The paint is very red in tone and is applied with considerable skill. This is an extremely beautiful design for which no precise parallel has been found in England. Naturalistic vine trails without crosshatched backgrounds are not uncommon; complete windows with this type survive at Merton College Oxford and York Minster. Naturalistic foliage with crosshatched backgrounds are frequent survivals in Normandy (Lafond 1953, 317–57) and can also be seen in the hemicycle triforium at St Père, Chartres.

Heraldic Lion Passant Guardant (No. 41)
794945 D30
An incomplete fragment the top edge grozed. Possibly from a shield bearing the Arms of England. A similar type with the furred tail can be seen at Canterbury (Caviness 1981 fig 531). The paint surface is curiously corrugated and the design is picked out, with the hair lined painted in. The colour is no longer discernible and the exterior is uncorroded with no backpainting.

Fifteenth Century
Fragments of ?Quarry Designs
None of these is complete enough for reconstruction. Several incomplete examples of the type found associated with the chapter house (No. 20) were found in 794918 D22. 802056 E36 produced one cursively painted design (No. 34) with traces of yellow stain on the ?acorn. A ?wavy star cluster with traces of yellow stain is illustrated (No. 44), but is too incomplete to determine the design. In the same category are fragments found in the following phases: D22, D30 and E36.

Undefined Designs
Two unpainted fragments appear to have been cut as possible backgrounds to figures; both are incomplete, 2 mm thick, relatively uncorroded compared with the earlier pieces of thicker glasses. Neither retains its original colour. 794922 E36 may well have been white, it is a wavy edged rounded end apex of a larger piece. 802071 C14 has curved edges, is similar in condition and equally incomplete. Either piece could have been cut to fit the shape of a figure, neither is similar to the geometric shapes discussed above.

In addition to these unpainted fragments several small painted pieces with paint lines outlining designs that are too fragmented to reconstruct may belong with this period grouping. The tone of the paint is light brown; the glass is generally thin and there is evidence of tone washes. Two pieces found in 794930 D21 and 794940 D30 are possibly drapery and there are tiny pieces of a foliate background design from 802088 E38. The fragmentary remains of a design picked out of a matt wash (No. 39) is illustrated as the only survival of this type of design in the collection. The veined flower design (No. 43) has traces of yellow stain on the exterior surface and was found in 794951 E36. There are no fragments of architectures or figures.

Coloured Glass
It is not possible to date these scant survivals with any certainty. With few exceptions that may be fifteenth century, all are very perished and devitrified with signs of weathering. Burial has destroyed the poorly durable range of pinks purples and browns.

Flashed Ruby
794945 D30. One piece of 2 mm thick pale red still translucent, uncorroded and possibly fifteenth century. The surface has a matt patina. Unpainted.
794928 D30, 794952 unstratified. Very deteriorated and perished fragments with no grozed edges.
802074 D30. A shaped piece of ?background unpainted with one undulating grozed edge and a triangle piece.

Blue
794918 D22. A fragment of uncorroded iridescent translucent mid blue with a single paint line.
785940 D30, 802088 E38. These pieces are very pale blue and uncorroded with traces of what may be oxidised paint lines. Examination by microscope did not reveal enough of these to reconstruct any designs.
794922 E36, 794919 D31, 802059 D22. Very decayed fragments.

Murrey
794919 D31. One piece only, extremely decayed and opaque with shaled off surface.

Green
794919 D31, 794945 D30. Several small pieces of

dark green; both surfaces completely shaled off and iridescent.

Yellow
794919 D31. Extremely decayed and rotted fragment.
794940 D30. A translucent piece 2 mm thick with no exterior decay bearing the remnants of what could have been a foliage trail.
794922 E36. Foliate boss catalogued above p. 000 with fig. 31.

Unpainted Fragments
Unpainted fragments, some still slightly glassy and translucent with brown flecks in, mostly opaque and devitrified were scattered throughout this area in the following phases: C14, D21, D22, D30, D31, D33, E36 and E47. Again, microscopic examination revealed no difference between the fragments from the late-medieval drain construction areas and the Dissolution and post-Dissolution layers. This group is distinguished from the thirteenth-century glass by its thinness 2–3 mm, its lack of exterior weathering and heavy corrosion of the type prevalent on the earlier glass, and by the translucence of some of the fragments with the characteristic brown interior flecking. There were very few grozed edges and no lead shadows discernible. Some of the decayed glasses may represent the lost colour range of glass from this period.

Unglazed Fragments
An extremely interesting group of glassy shivers of shattered panes with no grozed edges, lead shadows, traces of paint or weathering was found in several contexts in association with smashed bulls and uncut edge pieces of crown glass. None of these fragments ever appear to have been glazed into windows or shaped, and probably represent workshop debris.

An unusual feature of these deposits was the accretion of gravel and slivers of shattered glass to the surface of the larger pieces by a cement-like substance which could be mortar debris. The majority of this glass appears to have been clear and poorly durable, and with the association of the mortar detritus may represent domestic glazing work.

Glass of this type with bulls and edge pieces was also found in significant quantities in D24, D31 and D34 (794952, 794927, 794954 and 802092).

Two notable heaps of glass debris were found in C14 under the site of two of the north-facing reredorter windows (794916, 794917). They were the very smashed type, with mortar debris and no evidence of having been glazed, described above. 794917, however, contained some extremely interesting fragments of thirteenth-century/early fourteenth-century painted designs with the characteristic exterior corrosion and weathering. These are catalogued above as Border Design V (No. 29), Foliate Boss (No. 31), and Design Type Q (No. 32). There were also some unpainted fragments of glass with exterior decay and lead shadow and twelve

small fragments of painted designs, too perished to determine the form. None of these painted designs is related to any of the chapter house designs, and there was only one tiny (15 mm x 13 mm) fragment bearing what could be perished crosshatching and a fruiting leaf. However, none of the original grozed edges had survived and the paint had deteriorated too much to illustrate the design. It is possible, in view of the scant survival of painted pieces of such a distinctive type from the chapter house glazing, that these two heaps are evidence of a late medieval reglazing elsewhere in the abbey. Again, none of these painted remnants could be construed as inscriptions, evidence for figures, architectures or heraldry.

Random samples of the devitrified rotted opaque glass with exterior corrosion and some of the flat uncorroded opaque glasses from both these heaps were subjected to X-Ray Fluorescent analysis which revealed the presence of red and blue glass. As small discards of milled leads were found in association with the glass in these heaps, this would appear to confirm the hypothesis that this material represents evidence of both destruction and construction glazing detritus discarded against the reredorter wall between the buttresses during the construction build-up for the drainage system in the late medieval period.

Post-Medieval Glass
Some distinctive fragments of flat, thin (2 mm) glass, with iridescent unpainted surfaces were found in 794948 D21, 794951 E36 and 802087 E38. There were also some characteristic flat fragments of poorly durable plain glazing. This group is likely to be sixteenth or seventeenth century.

Window Glass Finds from Medieval Contexts
B7
The glass fragments found in the thirteenth-century rebuilding of the reredorter range are very uninformative and extremely perished. They are merely a handful of tiny decayed, devitrified, opaque pieces with only two remnants of grozed edges and very few surfaces intact. Only two of these sad remnants have any traces of paint on them, and unfortunately neither is sufficient for the design to be discerned. The paint is now pale red, and the unpainted surface has iridesced. No colours could be distinguished under the microscope among any of these fragments, but one piece of completely rotted shaling glass which sugared to the touch, was a distinctive pale yellow. It is impossible to say whether this colour was a result of burial, or whether this was originally pot yellow. None of the intact surfaces appeared corroded, and on the two roughly grozed edges that survive, there was no lead shadow. Weathering of a very slight degree could be discerned on one or two fragments which was the only distinguishing characteristic that indicated these fragments are window glass rather than perished vessel glass. Where any edges that were not grozed survive intact, the glass was clearly shattered before burial.

C11 and C14

As it was not possible to make any clear distinction between the fragments phased in the C11 build up before the construction of the drains and those in the C14 construction of the drainage system in the late medieval period, these two groups are discussed together.

Throughout this drainage construction area were a significant quantity of fragments of the thirteenth-century cross hatched geometric grisaille designs. These included remnants of Design Type 0 (Nos. 26 and 27), veined stiff leaf quarries; Border Design VI (No. 30), serpentine lines between circles and borders: and from the chapter house repertoire, Border Type I (No. 1) the quatrefoil strip design; Border Type II (No. 15) beading, and Design Type F (Nos. 7 and 8) the multiple foil and stem design. The most interesting painted glass from this phase is the fragment of an inscription, the letter S (No. 40). All these types are catalogued in detail above (pp. 128–35). Also included above are the small fragments from this phase whose fragmentary state precludes categorisation within the design typologies; these small pieces are catalogued with the painted fragments and the unpainted fragments (both on p. 135). A complete record of all the glass with detailed measurements, drawings of the painted pieces and an account of all the contexts in which they were found has been deposited with the site records.

The thirteenth-century glass from this phase is recognisable where the interior surface retains the painted design or where the exterior surface has survived with the characteristic deep corrosion pits and weathering contracted while *in situ* for a considerable length of time. Some of the fragments can also be assigned to this group because where the grozed edges are intact a distinct lead shadow has protected the exterior surface. However, all the thirteenth-century glass from this area is found in association with late medieval glazing, including a quantity of discarded edge pieces from crown glass, bulls with pontil marks, and shattered fragments of clear unpainted glazing. Much of this glass is poorly durable and has laminated surfaces and may represent inexpensive domestic glazing. It is probable that this material, including the scatter of earlier glass incorporated with it, is evidence of late medieval destruction and construction glazing detritus. Its condition is physically similar to the two heaps catalogued above, p. 137, from the same context, and is notable for the variety and variability of its generally deteriorated state. This is entirely consistent with its being discarded in the construction debris of the late medieval drainage disturbance. Where the shattered edges survive it is clear that they were broken before burial, and it is interesting to note that there are no characteristics that distinguish the remains of window glass in this phase from those found in the dissolution layers.

C17

The rebuilding of the chapel in the south transept area yielded one small piece of painted glass and two tiny fragments of shaled off deteriorated clear glazing. The painted fragment is very small (19 mm x 18 mm), has one grozed edge, exterior corrosion and bears part of a crosshatched design. Unfortunately these scant remains are too fragmentary to provide any further information.

C19

Some small pieces of window glass were found in the late medieval remodelled entrance arrangements at the west end of the reredorter. These comprise tiny fragments of decayed glass that may once have been pot metal coloured glass; a fragment of perished glass with exterior corrosion, opaque with the laminations sheering off; some glassy white fragments with perished mortar accretions encrusted with gravel and shattered glass frit deposits; and finally, the only piece with paint surviving, a small sliver of what could be geometric grisaille, slightly corroded with two grozed edges and the cut lines painted. Its greatest width is 12 mm at the broken base. The survival of the design is too slight to discern, but it is interesting to note that burial in a somewhat drier context than the other excavated fragments of this type has caused the glass to decay with less severity.

Acknowledgements

The author is extremely grateful to Dr John Hare and Mr Anthony Streeten for indispensible assistance and exemplary patience in providing the answers to many questions in the compilation of this report. Dr Jane Geddes deserves the credit for first recognising the interest and importance of the chapter house glass, for drawing my attention to this material and arranging for me to join the 1980 excavation.

Thanks are due to Mrs Marjorie Hutchinson of the Ancient Monuments Laboratory for consolidating all the material and providing the facilities for the examination of the glass. I am also grateful to Dr Barry Knight for the analyses of the lead finds, and to Miss Justine Bayley for undertaking the X-Ray Fluorescent assays for coloured glass. Miss Judith Dobie of the Ancient Monuments Archaeological Drawing Office produced the illustrations.

My colleague, Mr Nigel Morgan, very generously made his unpublished Kent and Lincoln material available to me, and kindly discussed the developments in grisaille design. I am also much obliged to my colleagues in the French Corpus Vitrearum for assistance and advice, as well as to Dr Peter Newton, Mr David King and Mr David O'Connor of the British Corpus Vitrearum Medii Aevi.

Chapter IX

Vessel Glass

by R.J. Charleston

I. Mainly Green Utilitarian Glass, Mostly of Late Medieval or Sixteenth-Century Date

The vessel glass found at Battle Abbey agrees well enough with that from comparable monastic sites where there is an admixture of late-medieval with post-Dissolution material. Apart from a very few distinctive fragments which may with reasonable certainty be assigned to the thirteenth to fourteenth centuries (see p. 145 below), the great majority fall into three or four categories of utilitarian glassware which are common on conventual sites, as at Denny Abbey (Charleston 1980, 209, Nos. 1–9) or Bayham Abbey (Charleston 1983, 115, Nos. 3–32). Until well on into the seventeenth century, and sometimes later, these utilitarian glasses were made of un-purified green 'forest glass', the flux being potash and the green colour being produced by the iron-content of the sand used, usually from local sources. There seems little doubt that most, if not all, of this glass was drawn from the Wealden industry of Surrey/Sussex, some fifty miles away (Kenyon 1967, *passim*). It was a glass prone to decay, and much of this erstwhile green glass at Battle Abbey has turned black, sometimes becoming completely denatured, losing weight and being prone to crumble into dust. Where no note on the condition of the glass is given, it may be assumed that it is in an advanced state of decay.

Lamps (Figure 42, Nos. 1–9)
Lamps were found on the site in relative profusion (some two dozen examples). They all came from the reredorter area, most from the main Dissolution rubbish dump in the north-western corner of the excavations. They are readily recognizable by the stubs of their tapering thick-based stems, these stubs seldom exceeding some 50 mm. in height. They vary in basal diameter and thickness, and in the degree of their taper, some being relatively flat-based, others relatively conical. The pontil-mark on the base is nearly always clearly in evidence, and is usually from a ring-pontil. In two instances (794973 and 801916, not illustrated) this excrescence is almost all that is left to identify the lamp. No single lamp could be reconstructed to show the typical cup-topped form. In a few instances, however, the stubs were associ-ated with rim-fragments which may have belonged to them, but which were not sufficiently large or numerous to permit a reconstruction. The diameters indicated by these fragments, however, seem un-usually large, of the order of 170 mm., whereas at Bayham Abbey, where very numerous rim-fragments were preserved, the greatest diameter was some 140 mm. With such small fragments, however, exact measurement is difficult. The well-preserved sixteenth-century lamp at Northampton (Oakley and Hunter 1979, fig. 131, GL53) is about 130 mm. in diameter; the thirteenth-century example at Win-chester some 170 mm. (Harden 1970, fig. 4); an unpublished example from Woodperry, Oxon. has a portion of rim remaining, giving a diameter of some 130 mm. : it is apparently of twelfth-/fourteenth-century date.

Nearly all of the identified lamps came from Period D (D21, D22, D30 and D34) and from phases containing Dissolution rubbish. They should there-fore be seen as coming probably from the monastic period, when such lamps would have been used in considerable numbers.

It is not possible to use the Battle Abbey material as the basis for any scheme of typological develop-ment, but it may be supposed that those lamps made of almost totally denatured glass (a characteristic of glasses found in e.g. fourteenth-century contexts) would be earlier than those with only slight weather-ing on a greyish-green material.

1. Base-fragment of bluish-green glass with slight spotty brown weathering. D30 794988.
2. Base-fragment of originally green glass, now denatured and black. D22 794993.
3. Base-fragment of originally green glass, now denatured and black. D22 794993.
4. Base-fragment of originally green glass, now denatured and black. D22 794993.
5. Base-fragment of originally green glass, now denatured and black, with large pontil-mark. D22 801916.
6. Base-fragment of originally green glass, now denatured and black. D21 801923.
7. Base-fragment with large pontil-mark. D21 801938.
8. Rim-fragments, originally green glass, now den-atured and black. D22 794918.
9. Rim-fragments, originally green glass, now den-atured and black. C11 801932.

Urinals. (Figure 42, Nos. 10–21)
Urinal fragments are found on most medieval sites, particularly the characteristic convex base-fragments with pontil-mark projecting like a nipple on the rounded external surface (whereas in bottles it occu-pies the apex of the 'kick', sitting in a concavity).

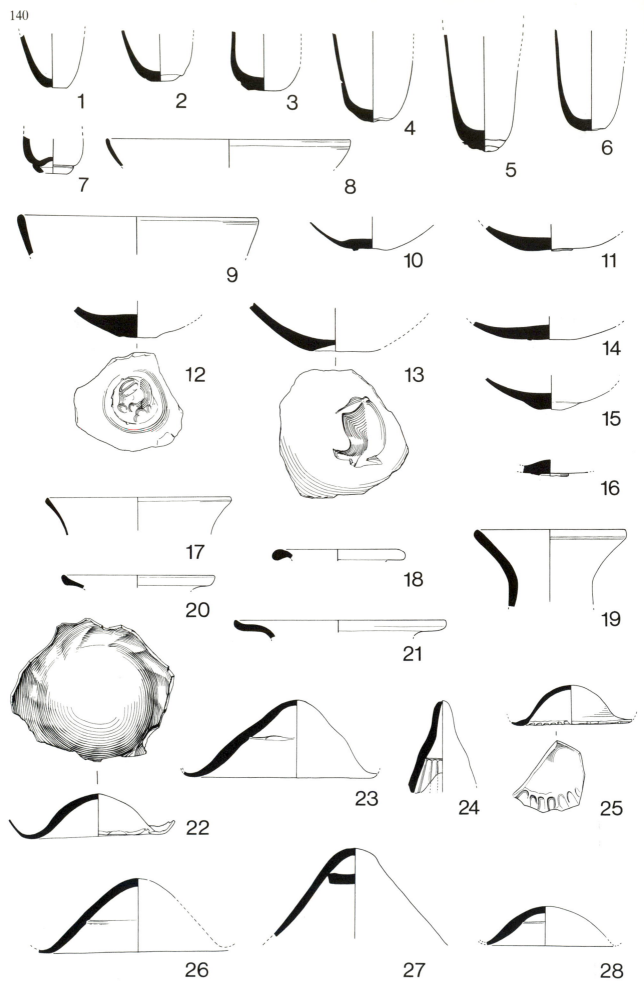

Figure 42   Battle Abbey. Vessel glass nos. 1–28 ($\frac{1}{2}$)

Two main shapes have hitherto been distinguished, one with spherical body, cylindrical neck and broad horizontal lip, the other with piriform body passing straight into a tapering neck terminating in the broad horizontal lip (Charleston 1981, 71–2). Evidence from Bayham Abbey, however, has forced a reconsideration of this simple division. There an exceptionally heavy base occurred with extensive fragments of a wide- but short-necked vessel with spreading lip made apparently in the same thick green glass : a second base-fragment seemed to match well with further neck-fragments of the same general character, giving a globular vessel with short neck and spreading, but not horizontal, rim (Charleston 1983, 113–5). This material has forced a reconsideration of the evidence for the shape and character of the medieval urinal, and in particular of the indications from the graphic sources. A number of contemporary illustrations show doctors holding vessels which do not fit in well with the two shapes of urinal already admitted to the canon. These painted, engraved and carved representations show a roughly bell-shaped vessel with spreading funnel-neck. Examples may be cited from Barrelet (1953, Pl. XXVII, A and B, miniatures of the fourteenth century); Amis (1968, figs. 4–5, fourteenth- and fifteenth-century miniatures, and 6, woodcut of 1484); Zigrosser (1955, Nos. 3, woodcut of 1500, 4, woodcut of 1516, 14, woodcut of 1532 and 34, woodcut of 1531); Thorpe (1961, Pl. XIVa, carving of c. 1300). These shapes are not wholly consistent with each other, and had hitherto been discounted by the present writer as probably unreliable evidence. All, however, have the broad outward-sloping mouth as opposed to the horizontal rim of the two already established types. The pictorial testimony is supported by further archaeological evidence. Excavations on the site of the old Carmelite Priory at Ipswich have produced (in company with pottery of the thirteenth/fourteenth century) two urinals with the characteristic base, the neck-fragments of one showing a fairly wide cylindrical neck with horizontal lip, but those of the other giving a spreading neck of the type under discussion.

A second notable feature of this third type of urinal is its thickness. Although the Bayham Abbey examples could not be completely reconstructed, it seems impossible that their walls could have become so abruptly thin that they could really have been used for uroscopy. This feature therefore raises the question whether perhaps some of these urinals were not used merely as chamber-pots and not for purposes of medical examination. An alternative name for a vessel of this kind in the medieval period was 'jordan' (Amis 1968, 6–9). Chaucer in the 'wordes of the Hoost to the Phisicien' writes:

I pray to God so save thy gentil cors,
And eek thyne urynals and thy jurdones

– a passage which perhaps suggests that although parallel in function the two types of vessel may not have been identical. The 'jordan' could apparently be made of clay (and would therefore be opaque), but a fifteenth-century text refers to a 'good thicke jordan of glass' (Amis loc. cit.). The thick glass urinal may therefore be a 'jordan' intended rather as a chamber-pot than designed specifically for uroscopy. It is evident, however, that the vessel with spreading neck was used for uroscopy, since it is shown being scrutinised by the physician : possibly it was made in varying thicknesses. The Battle Abbey excavations, which yielded nearly fifty base-fragments or urinals, produced some fourteen assemblages which could be reconstructed into the thick-walled neck-form already identified at Bayham Abbey.

The heavy incidence of urinals on monastic sites is perhaps to be expected. The fifteenth-century John Russels Boke of Nurture contains the instruction '. . .looke that ye have the bason for chambur and also the urnalle'. In a monastic setting, with the house of easement so close to the dorter, as at Battle, there was probably no call to provide close-stools; but the hygiene and decency of the monastery might well demand the provision of urinals on a considerable scale. The almoner's roll for 1402–3 at the Abbey of Durham records payment for '7 jordan' (Amis op. cit., n.15).

Although emphasis has been laid here on the third type of urinal, the characteristic horizontal lip (often with upturned rim) of the two other types of vessel is also well represented at Battle. Since this feature is also found on sixteenth/seventeenth-century sites (e.g. Charleston 1964, 150–1; Nonsuch fragments, unpublished, etc.), it may represent a refinement evolved in the late medieval period. At present, closely datable examples have not been identified in sufficient numbers to enable one to propose a morphological series with any confidence. At least one Battle Abbey neck-fragment (from D22) seems to come from a urinal of the relatively rare type with tapering conical neck and horizontal rim.

10.   Urinal-base of clear pale-green glass with light surface weathering, the thickness tapering sharply to .8 mm. or less. Clearly visible ring pontil-mark. D30 794982.

11.   Urinal-base of originally green glass, now black, accompanied by numerous thin curved fragments, perhaps from the body of the vessel. D.30 794988.

12.   Urinal-base with pronounced nipple-like pontil-mark. D22 794993.

13.   Urinal-base with large broken-away pontil-mark. D22 794993.

14.   Urinal-base with part of large ring pontil-mark. D22 801919.

15.   Urinal-base with pronounced nipple-like pontil-mark. D21 801925.

16.   Probably urinal-base of green glass denatured to black and very light in weight. C11 801932.

17.   Probably urinal-rim, clear pale-green glass with light surface weathering (see above. No. 10) D30 794982.

18.   Probably urinal-rim (see above, No. 11) D30 794988.

19. Probably urinal-rim C14 801939.
20. Urinal-rim, originally green glass, now black and denatured. E42 794963.
21. Urinal-rim, originally green glass, now black and denatured. D21 794989.

Bottles (Figures 42, 43, Nos. 22–34)
Not unnaturally, bottles of green glass are one of the most frequently found types of common glassware on medieval and sixteenth/seventeenth-century sites. Nor are very significant changes observable between early and late (see e.g. Hume 1957, 104 ff.; Charleston 1975, Nos. 1573–7; Hume 1956, figs. 3, 7.). Only one fragment at Battle Abbey seems to date from the thirteenth-century phase (B7–801933 not illustrated) a tallish kick (app. 20 mm.) with an estimated base-diameter of some 42 mm., showing clear traces of a ring-pontil. There is nothing to distinguish it from its late-medieval and later counterparts. The typical shape of these universally occurring bottles (some 35 bases were found) is normally a depressed-globular body with slight kick, a tapering neck and an out-turned funnel-mouth, often cut off slantwise at the rim. The base is often roughly finished and asymmetrical (see No. 23). Occasionally the bottle has been blown in a ribbed mould, imparting vertical ribbing to the body of the vessel; this sometimes shows mainly on the neck and base, having been flattened almost to invisibility on the body by subsequent working. Sometimes the ribbing is most clearly seen under the base, and two good examples of this occur at Battle (Nos. 24 and 25). A further refinement is when the vertically ribbed paraison is twisted spirally ('wrythen'). An example of this is the bottle neck No. 32. Occasionally smaller flasks have a deep conical 'kick' (e.g. No. 24 and 801928 – not illustrated), a feature which seems to be common on late-fifteenth-century glasses both in England and Germany (Rademacher 1933, Pls. 24 a–c, 26 a–b), but which certainly continued on into the first quarter of the sixteenth century or even later. A number of bottles show very clear traces of a ring-pontil, a feature also observable on the urinals and lamps at Battle. A striking instance of this is the large base No. 27. In general, the bottles at Battle run closely parallel to those at Bayham (Charleston 1983, Nos. 17–29). It is noteworthy that the Battle finds include no examples of the flattened flask with ribbing mould-blown on a second gather – a type probably inspired by German examples (Rademacher 1933, Pl. 8 c, e) – such as seem to characterize the second half of the sixteenth century in England (Hume 1956, fig. 12; c.f. Charleston 1983, 114).

For sixteenth/seventeenth-century vials, see below.
22. Bottle-base, clear pale-green glass with patchy brown weathering, showing mould-blown 'wrythen' ribbing (cf. No. 32). D30 794982.
23. Bottle-base, yellowish-colourless where translucent (See No. 29) D30 794983.
24. Bottle-base, originally green glass now black, with silvery surface weathering, showing mould-blown vertical ribbing. D22 794993.

25. Bottle-base, greenish-colourless glass with silvery weathering, showing mould-blown ribbing. D22 794993.
26. Base of large flask (four further fragments of the same type were found in this group). D22 794993.
27. Bottle-base, originally green glass now black and denatured, showing remains of large ring-pontil. D21 801925.
28. Bottle-base, originally green glass, now black, showing traces of wide circular pontil. D29 801943.
29. Bottle-neck (see No. 23). D30 794983.
30. Bottle-neck, originally green glass now black and denatured, with silvery weathering. D22 801916.
31. Bottle-rim. D22 801917.
32. Bottle-neck, originally green glass, now brown/black, showing mould-blown 'wrythen' ribbing (cf. No. 22). D22 801918.
33. Bottle-neck, originally green glass, almost completely denatured, now black and very light. D22 801919.
34. Bottle-rim fragment, with traces of mould-blown ribbing. C14 801924.

Distillation equipment. (Figure 43, Nos. 35–6)
An important sphere of activity for the indigenous English glass-industry was the manufacture of laboratory-equipment for distillation and alchemical investigation. Chaucer in the late fourteenth century, in the *Prologue* to the *Canon's Yeoman's Tale*, refers to:–

'. . .sondry vessels maad of erthe and glas,
Oure urynals and oure descensories,
Violes, crosletz, and sublymatories,
Cucurbites and alambikes eek.'

All these vessels (save the urinal and vial (flask), which might, however, be used *ad hoc* for chemical purposes) were destined for laboratory work, the descensory being a type of retort; the crosslet a crucible; the sublimatory an apparatus for producing a purified substance from a vaporised solid; a cucurbit the vessel which contained a liquid for distillation; the alembic the domed vessel which fitted over this and delivered the distillate through a tube into a flask-like 'receiver', for which function urinals and vials would serve well enough. Many fragments of glass apparatus of this kind have been found in English excavations (Charleston 1981, 72 and 85–7, figs. 29–30), and they have been more than usually frequent on monastic sites (Moorhouse 1972, 89 ff.). Unfortunately, none of the distinctive alembic fragments appear to have occurred at Battle, but a rim-fragment which may have come from the neck of a cucurbit, and another thick neck-fragment (Nos. 35–36, both from phase D22, may well have formed part of still-house or laboratory equipment. Other possible fragments within this group were 794994 and one rim-fragment from 794981 (not illustrated).

It is most likely that these pieces were made in the Weald, not far away. Some often-quoted lines from

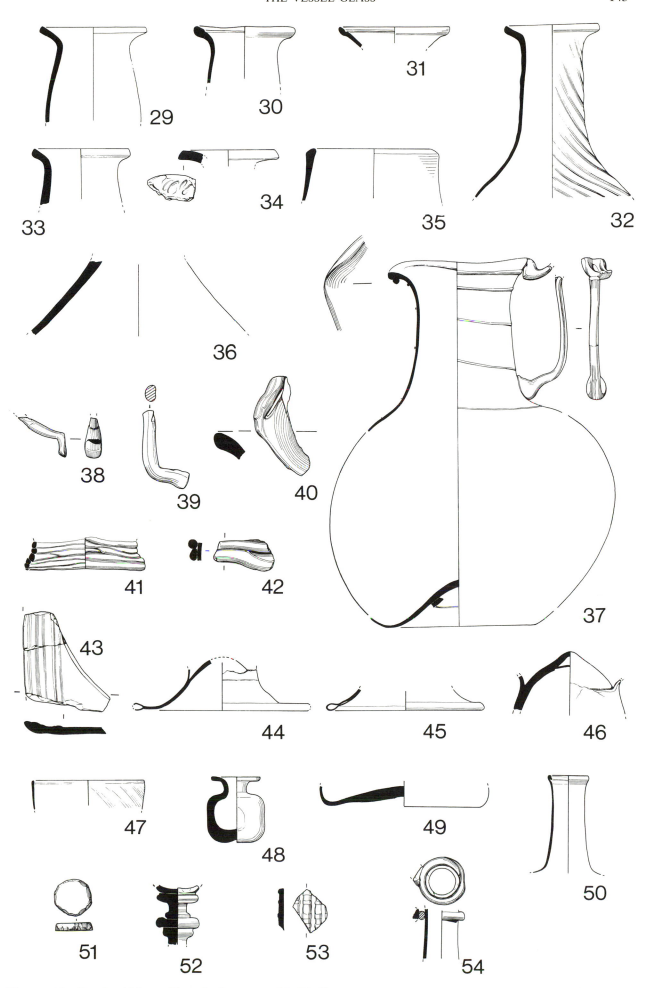

Figure 43 Battle Abbey. Vessel glass nos. 29–54 ($\frac{1}{2}$)

T. Charnock's *Breviary of Philosophy* (1557) throw light on the situation (*cit.* Thorpe 1929, 55):–

'As for glassmakers they be scant in the land
But one there is as I do understand
And in Sussex is now his habitacion,
At Chiddingfold he works of his occupacion,
To go to him it is necessary and meete
Or sende a servante that is discreete,
And desire him in most humble wise
To blow thee a glasse after thy devise:
It were worth many an Arme or a Legge
He could shape it like to an Egge;
To open and close as a haire,
If thou have such a one thou needst not feare.'

The meaning of 'egg' here is explained by a passage in Boyle's writings (1691): 'there was taken a great glass-bubble with a long neck, such as chemists are wont to call a philosophical egg' (*NED*). That equipment of this kind was in fact made in the Weald is demonstrated by finds made on the site of Knightons glasshouse, near Alfold, Surrey (Kenyon 1967, 208). This sixteenth-century site turned up fragments of alembics as well as of tapering necks probably belonging to cucurbits, or possibly receivers (Wood, 1982, 32–4; Charleston 1981, 72). Examples of alembics, cucurbits and receivers were found in fifteenth-century contexts at Selborne Priory and St. John's Priory, Pontefract (Moorhouse 1972, 89–104).

35. Rim-fragment, probably of a receiver originally green grass. D22 794993.
36. Neck-fragment, probably of a laboratory vessel, originally green glass D22 794993.

Jugs. (Figure 43, Nos. 37–40)
Fragments found in the post-Dissolution phase D28, permitted the reconstruction of a jug (No. 37) of more or less globular form, with pinched out lip, thin rod handle, and decoration in the form of a sparse self-coloured trail applied in widely spaced turns. The metal is a pale greenish-yellow with patchy black weathering. The fairly pronounced base 'kick' is asymmetrical and shows traces of a large and somewhat uneven pontil-mark.

The nearest analogy with this piece is a jug of pale-green glass decorated with an opaque-red trail, found in the High Street, Southampton, in a context of the first half of the fourteenth century (Charleston 1975, 216–7, No. 1489). The fragments of a second green-glass jug with applied opaque-red threading 'combed' into an arcaded pattern were found in a context of *c.* 1500 at Pevensey Castle (unpublished). Although the quality of the Southampton jug, taken in conjunction with its early date, has suggested that it might be an import (Charleston 1981, 69), opaque-red glass is known to have been made in the Weald (Kenyon 1967, 161), and was used to decorate locally made vessel-glass (fragments in Haslemere Museum and Victoria and Albert Museum). The thumb-rest of the Battle jug is missing, but the lower sticking-part of the handle lacks the decorative kink present on the Southampton jug and found also on the Pevensey jug, on a jug-neck of probably

fourteenth/fifteenth-century date in the Museum of London (Harden 1970, 107, fig. 19), and on a blue jug of thirteenth/fourteenth-century date found at Penhallam, Cornwall (Beresford 1974, 138–9, fig. 42, No. 35). This last-mentioned jug, however, had no pouring lip, no thread-decoration, and a base with pinched-out footrim. The analogy with the Pevensey jug seems on the whole the closest, and the proximity of the find-spots is suggestive.

Two fragmentary handles (Nos. 38 and 39) from post-medieval contexts may come from similar jugs, and a rim-fragment strengthened with a thread may be the pouring-lip of another (No. 40). The handle-fragment No. 38 is made, like the Penhallam jug, of blue glass.

37. Fragmentary jug, greenish-yellow glass with patchy black and allover silvery weathering, decorated with self-coloured trail. D28 794999.
38. Fragmentary handle, blue glass with brown encrusted weathering. D21 794978.
39. Fragmentary handle, originally green glass, now black, with slight patchy brown weathering. D30 794988.
40. Perhaps lip-fragment of a jug, originally green glass, now black, with (?) strengthening thread. C14 801930.

Fragments of uncertain date and character. (Figure 43, Nos. 41–3)
(i) Fragments of (?) feet made of coiled thread. In D22 were found two fragments (No. 41) on which some six thickish threads of glass were conjoined to give a rough cylinder, possibly the foot of a jug or large flask. This type of foot probably developed from the simple supporting ring formed of a single overlapping cordon of glass laid round the base of a vessel. In Germany it was progressively developed in the sixteenth century on the green prunted glasses coming under the general denomination of '*Nuppengläser*': it reached its furthest point of development during the seventeenth century in the tall conical foot of the '*Roemer*' (Rademacher 1933, Pls. 43, c; 45, c; 46, c, etc.) It was, however, occasionally used on other shapes, where it was more likely to assume the form of a cylindrical collar rather than a spreading conical foot-ring. An interesting example has of recent years been excavated at Göttingen, in the form of a globular handled jug with cylindrical neck and a ring-foot which spreads out below into a frill of pulled-out points in typically medieval fashion (Schütte 1976, fig. 7, No. 3; fig. 8). Unfortunately, the Göttingen glass was undated by context, but was considered to be 'late medieval' by the scholar who published it, a view borne out by its similarities to 'late medieval' salt-glazed stonewares. No instances of this technique seem so far to have been identified in England. Battle, however, produced what appears to be a second example (794992, not illustrated), this time in clear colourless glass with patchy black and iridescent weathering. The fragment appears originally to have been some four strands deep, and shows a diameter of approximately 65 mm. It may possibly fit into the category of colourless thirteenth/fourteenth-century glasses, but if so

this technique seems not to have been recorded hitherto in this class of glasses.

41. Cylindrical (?) foot-fragment made up of coiled thread, originally green glass with black weathering, almost totally denatured and light in weight. D22 794993.

(ii) A further fragment exhibiting thick threading, but this time applied to a curved surface, is difficult to interpret. The curvature suggests a large diameter, which makes it unlikely as a footrim.

42. Fragment with applied threading, originally green glass, now black, denatured and light in weight. D21 801921.

(iii) A flat fragment with pronounced ridges parallel to a straight edge (No. 43) is also difficult to identify. The ridges make it unlikely to be a window-pane, but no other use can be suggested.

43. Flat fragment with parallel ridges, originally green glass, now shiny black, denatured and light in weight. D22 794993.

II. Thirteenth/Fourteenth-Century Types

From phase C12 came the fragment of a handle in bright yellow glass (794995, not illustrated) of a type characteristic of some rare glasses of fourteenth-century date (Charleston 1981, 68).

III. Sixteenth/Seventeenth-Century Types

A few fragments of out-and-out sixteenth- and seventeenth-century glasses were found, particularly in the accumulation of rubbish inside the chapter house (D23).

Green Glass (Figure 43, Nos. 44–7)
(a) Fragments of Cylindrical Beakers.
From phase D23 were three fragments evidently from the same 'pushed-in' beaker-base (the whole glass being made from a single paraison), in pale green glass with patches of black encrustation and an overall film of iridescent weathering (No. 44). In the same context was a rim-fragment (No. 47), perhaps of the same beaker, and a footrim-fragment from another (No. 45), distinguished from the first by a different curvature and a more colour-free material. A substantial base of yet another beaker of this type (No. 46), of thicker glass than those already mentioned, was found in a later context. No examples of this type of beaker antedating 1550 have been identified, whereas they are very common in the second half of the sixteenth and well into the seventeenth century (Charleston 1981, 87–88; Hume 1962, 269–70; *id.* 1968, 259–61). It is tempting to suppose that this family of glasses owes its existence to the increasing Continental influence which made itself felt in English glass-making about the middle of the sixteenth century, culminating in Jean Carré's takeover bid in 1567 (Charleston 1981, 81–2).

44. Fragmentary beaker base, pale green glass with patchy black and iridescent weathering (see No. 47). D23

45. Fragment of a beaker base, greenish-colourless glass with iridescent silvery weathering and patches of black encrustation. D23

46. Fragmentary beaker base, pale green glass with patchy black and iridescent silvery weathering. E47

47. Rim-fragment (see No. 44), with faint oblique mould-blown ribbing. D23

(b) 'Apothecaries' Vials'
Almost certainly of sixteenth-century date, although unstratified, is an intact small squared-off vial (No. 48) with short neck, broad rim and slightly concave sides and base, the last with a small pontil-mark. A similarly squared-off small bottle with concave sides, but with height approximately double its width, was found intact on the Brookland Farm glasshouse-site, near Wisborough Green in Sussex, a site where pottery and other glass finds suggested a date in the second half of the sixteenth century (Kenyon 1967, 182–4, Pl. XVI, 2, 3). Comparable flasks found in London came from a context of about 1600 (Hume 1956, 99–100, fig. 4).

Of probably even later date is the base-fragment of a large cylindrical flask (No. 49) found in the accumulation of rubbish inside the chapter house (D23). Of markedly bluish-green metal, it has a large patch of black encrustation and an overall film of iridescent weathering. Below the slightly domed base is a small neat pontil-mark. This type of cylindrical 'apothecary's' flask seems to be a typical product of the seventeenth century, and even lingers on into the eighteenth century (Hume 1956, 102–3). Parallels may be cited from Newcastle (Ellison 1979, 173, No. 48a, with suggested date of *c.* 1650–1700) and Basing House, Hants. (Moorhouse 1971, 70, No. 60, probably before 1645). A flask neck made of exceptionally thin greenish-colourless glass with black encrustations and an overall film of iridescent weathering, was found in the same layer, and may be of comparable date (No. 50). The slightly projecting rim is curved back inwards on itself.

48. Vial, green glass, with slight iridescent weathering, perhaps mould-blown in square mould. unstrat. 794991.

49. Base-fragment of cylindrical flask, pale green glass with patchy black and iridescent silvery weathering. D23.

50. Neck-fragments of a flask, thin pale green glass with iridescent weathering. D23.

(c) Counter or Gaming-Piece(?)
This object (No. 51) from the reredorter drain is cut from a piece of flat (window) glass trimmed to a bevel, probably by 'grozing' round its outer edge. Two similar discs were found on the mainly sixteenth-century site of Knightons glasshouse, near Alfold, Surrey (see Kenyon 1967, 208; Wood 1982, 22–3).

51. Fragmentary (?) gaming-piece, pale green glass now black with patchy beige weathering, the edges grozed. C14 794984.

Colourless Glass. (Figure 43, Nos. 52–4)
A few fragments of colourless glass represent the Venetian or '*façon de Venise*' *cristallo* of the sixteenth-seventeenth centuries. Glass of this character was much imported, but also made in England.

(a)   Stemmed Drinking-Glass
From phase D23 came a stem-fragment of a beer- or wine-glass in greyish-colourless metal with an overall film of iridescent weathering (No. 52). The fragment shows the base of the bowl, joined by a solid capstan-like section to a wide solid button (or 'merese'), itself joined to the upper part of the stem proper, which was probably hollow blown. This exact formation is unusual, the more normal order being for the lower flange of the top capstan to be joined directly on to the hollow-blown stem proper (see e.g. Charleston 1979, figs. 1 and 3). A number of variants occur (see, e.g., Moorhouse 1971, fig. 27, Nos. 11–12, probably datable before 1645), but the most direct parallel is a fragmentary goblet found at Nonsuch Palace (Dent 1962, Pl. 17, b). This exceptional glass, found in a context suggesting a date before 1650, has the features mentioned leading into a hollow-blown inverted piriform stem. A variation occurs in another Nonsuch glass, of exceptional elegance, found in a post-1650 context. This has a depressed hollow-blown ribbed knop in place of the solid merese, a feature seen again in a saucer-bowled drinking-glass with lion-mask stem in the Corning Museum, New York (Mus. No. 58.3.180), a glass which would by most be unhesitatingly accepted as Venetian. Further fragments showing the same feature also occur at Nonsuch, a royal palace where certainly Venetian glass occurs and where one would expect to find the finest glasses available. A date in the first half of the seventeenth century would seem reasonable.

52.   Upper part of beer- or wine-glass stem, greyish-colourless 'cristallo'. A second fragment of colourless glass was found in the same context, but it is impossible to be sure whether it formed part of a wine-glass bowl, a bowl or a dish (not illustrated).

(b)   Beaker with 'Chequered Spiral Trail' Decoration
One tiny greyish-colourless fragment (No. 53), belonged to this class of cylindrical beakers decorated by means of a continuous spiral trail of glass applied to the body from the base upwards and then blown into a vertical ribbed mould to produce the 'chequered' effect (Tait 1967, 94–112). These glasses probably date from the late sixteenth to early seventeenth century.

53.   Wall-fragment of beaker with 'chequered spiral trail' decoration, greyish-colourless glass, with four vertical ribs and four turns of threading. D24 801946.

(c)   Bottle
From phase D23 came the neck-fragment of a (?) half-pint bottle, the neck strengthened by an applied overlapping thread (No. 54). This formation, more normally found in thick green bottles, also occurs on small flasks of quarter-bottle size, sometimes in pale-green and sometimes in colourless glass. An example of the former kind, probably a London find, is in the Victoria and Albert Museum; of the latter, an example has been found at Winchester (unpublished). The neck-ring of the Battle piece shows an attached fragment of glass which may have been the upper part of a handle. The flask may have been used as a cruet or small jug. Probably c. 1650.

54.   Neck-fragment of a (?) half-pint flask, colourless glass with overall iridescent weathering.

Chapter X

The Small Finds

by Jane Geddes

The items recorded and discussed in this catalogue are only a selection of the great quantity of objects found. It was neither practical nor economical to publish an exhaustive record. The criteria for selection varied for each substance. All the precious metal and almost all the bone, lead and jet were included. Of the copper alloy, examples of all the recognisable types of objects were chosen, omitting many tags, pins, plain buckles, bits of coiled wire, broken strips and off-cuts. Ironwork was the most severely pruned although at least one example of each type of object was selected. Thus all keys (minus a few fragments), tools, spurs and most horse furniture were included, while the great quantity of miscellaneous nails, bars and strips were omitted.

The majority of significant small finds occurred in D21 and D22, two Dissolution contexts. They covered a wide range of objects in household and monastic use. Writing implements and clothing accessories were particularly well represented. The significance of these collections is discussed separately below. The coins and some of the jettons found in these layers were of pre-sixteenth-century date suggesting they had been mislaid around the monastery some time before the Dissolution, and were eventually collected and dumped in this tip. The clothing items, while not so closely dateable, would tend to corroborate this. None of them are noticeably fashionable items of the 1530s and the majority are fifteenth-century types. However a few ecclesiastical objects, especially those made with precious metal and the copper alloy cross fragments were probably broken up at the Dissolution and were swept away with the rest of the household rubbish.

Gem Stone (Figure 44)
1. An oval, transparent and colourless stone cut as a 'hog's back' crystal, the underside of which is a shallow cabochon while the top consists of two convex faces which meet at a central ridge. All three faces have been well polished but the girdle has been left rough. From its specific gravity, refractive index and characteristic inclusions the stone can be identified as quartz, variety rock-crystal. Crystals of this form were often used in the early medieval period to decorate crosses and book-covers. D22 793442. Identification by *M.E. Hutchinson* (1982).

Jet (Figure 44)
1. Toggle. Bi-conical with irregularly grooved sides and three turned grooves at one end. Perforated. Possibly spacer for rosary. D22 801984.

2. Oval bead, possibly from rosary. D34 801985. 19 mm long. Not illustrated.
3. Oval bead fragment, similar to 2. D34 801986. Not illustrated.

Silver and Gold (Figure 44)
Decorative Fragments
Items Au 3, 4; Cu 41, 52, 86, 87, 88 are decorated with *vernis brun*. This is a technique used to darken copper described in the eleventh-century technical manual *De Diversis Artibus* (Hawthorne and Smith 1963, 147–8). The instructions are to draw flowers and animals on the sheet with an engraving tool and smear linseed oil on the surface with one's finger and a feather. The sheet is heated quite gently until the oil dries out, and then strongly until it ceases to smoke. If the colour is not dark enough the process should be repeated with more oil. The sheet is cooled in air, not water, the flowers scraped out with a sharp scraper and the cleared surfaces are then gilded. The amalgam will not adhere to the varnished areas. Although Au 3 could be Mosan, the other items are likely to be English, and indicate that the technique was known in England and remained in use from the twelfth to the late fifteenth century (see Cu 88 for chemical analysis of *vernis brun*).

1. Fragment of copper alloy with raised bands of gilded decoration. Pattern shows traces of interlacing tendrils.
D22 793198.
2. Fragment of copper alloy sheet fire gilded, with interlace pattern. All edges broken.
D22 793199.
3. Copper gilt plaque decorated with a bold Greek cross motif in *vernis brun*, and a plain margin. The outline of crosses is made with a graving tool. Rivet holes punched through from the front indicate its original manner of attachment. Later, nail holes were roughly punched through from the back, and one iron nail head still remains on the back. This indicates the plaque was reversed and probably used as a patch. This may account for its survival because the gold was not visible in its secondary attachment. (Also mentioned in *English Romanesque Art* 1984, 254). A similar bold cross pattern, combined with panels of other geometric motifs is found on the Mosan aquamanile in Vienna, made in the mid-twelfth century (Stuttgart 1977, Abb. 457, Cat. 651. In Vienna Kunsthistorisches Museum, Inv. 83).
D22 801968.
4. Copper gilt strip with running foliage scroll

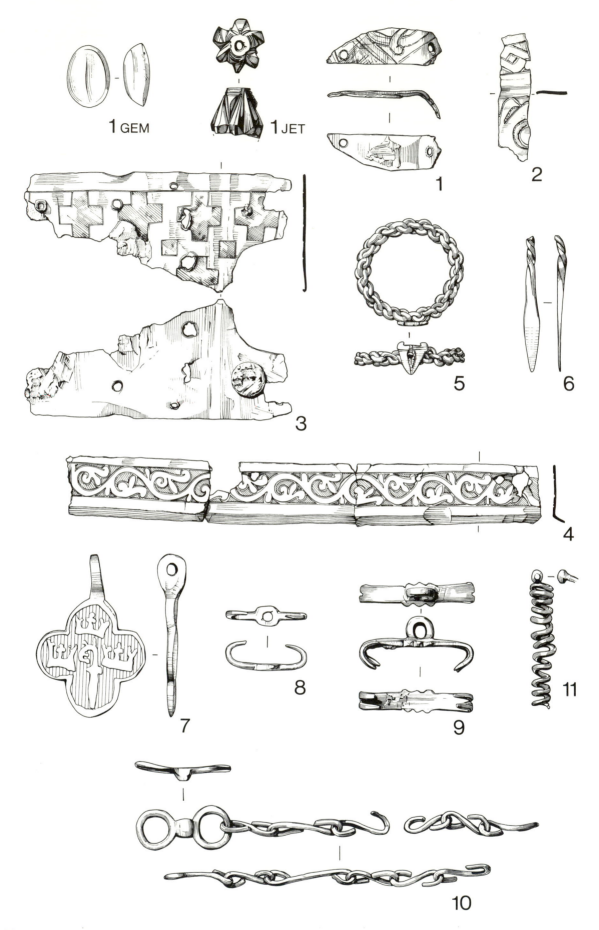

Figure 44   Battle Abbey. Gem stone, jet, silver and gold decorative fragments ($\frac{1}{2}$)

decoration in *vernis brun*, found folded in concertina fashion so that, as with 3 above, little precious metal was visible. After conservation it was apparent that the strip was originally folded all along one edge to fit, for instance, around the edge of a book cover. (Also mentioned in *English Romanesque Art* 1984, 254). Very similar borders are used in mid-twelfth-century English manuscript illumination, as in Victoria and Albert Museum MS 661, a psalter from Christchurch Canterbury, 1140 (Kaufmann 1975, 93).
D21 801969.

Personal Adornment
5.   Ring made of plaited silver wires, silver gilt shield or mitre with incised leaf and linear pattern soldered on. Unused rivet hole in centre of shield or mitre.
D21 793197.
6.   Pointed copper alloy implement with gilt spiral stem. Possibly part of a pendant manicure set (Platt 1976 no pagination, Gay 1887, 526).
D22 793200.
7.   Quatrefoil gilt bronze pendant, with translucent green enamel. The design has three crowns each with a trefoil on the central crest. Bottom quarter of design obscure, might have been a crozier.
D21 793202.
8.   Silver hooked fastening with central eyelet. Illustrated as belt decoration from Schloss Fredensborg 1500–25, by Fingerlin (1971, plate 409, cat. 126).
D21 793344.
9.   Gilt hooked fastening with central eyelet and bifurcated hooks at each end. Belt decoration as above.
D22 801970.
10.   Chain made with S links, irregular size, attached to double ring. Traces of gold on surface with mercury, indicating fire gilding. Probably for attaching some personal object to belt.
D21 802233.
11.   Coiled silver wire with a point at one end and soldered head at the other. Like a coiled pin. A similar object in Northampton, in copper alloy. (Williams, 1979, 253, Cu 26).
D21 801966.

Bone (Figures 45–47)
Handles
1.   Handle fragment. Bone sheet forming one side of handle, with tapered groove on inside centre for tang. Four irregularly spaced fixing holes, with one bone peg surviving. Edges rebated for insertion of metal strip. Upper surface scored with geometric patterns.
D22 793407.
2.   Tapered rectangular handle with circular hole for tang.
D22 793420.
3.   Fragment. Bone sheet forming one side of handle. Rectangular section, rivet holes, curved point at one end.
D22 793426. Not illustrated.

Writing Equipment
Among the rubbish deposited outside the reredorter at the Dissolution are a wide variety of objects connected with book production. There are certainly enough of them to show that the abbey was producing books until the end of the middle ages. No evidence has emerged to locate a specific room as a scriptorium and the monks probably used the equipment in several parts of the monastery: in 1501 there were desks in the dormitory (p. 00). David Brown has discussed the use of parchment prickers (Biddle forthcoming) and the following comments are based on Mr Brown's work. The prickers have a slender metal tip, and round knob at the other end. They are generally too short to be held comfortably like a pen, but the round knob is suitable for holding in the palm of the hand, and pressing into the parchment. The metal tips would make only a small neat hole, while the bone shoulder above would prevent the point from being inserted too far. A whole quire could be pricked through in one operation, as in the Aberdeen Bestiary (Aberdeen University Library MS 24). It is possible that the prickers with shouldered and 'hooded' terminations were used differently, but they may signify no more than the variations found on modern fountain pens. The function of the short pins (B 15), which appear to be normal prickers whittled down to a bone point without a metal tip, is not clear. Several objects similar to the long prickers have been found, for instance in London (Henig 1974, 198, nos 214–8) and Whitby (Peers and Radford, 1983, 71, nos 108–9), but their close connection with writing is established by the find in the old town school of Lubeck (Warneke 1912). Here one wooden pricker was found in association with books of wax tablets, inkwells and wooden bats for chastisement. The association at Battle of prickers and tablets in D22 is comparable. Prior to the eleventh century, lines on manuscripts were scored into the vellum, but thereafter the page was pricked out and lines ruled with lead or ink. Alexander Neckham, writing in the late twelfth century, mentioned a *punctorium* or pricker as an essential part of a scribe's equipment. (Gay 1887, I, 602). The whetstones with a groove for sharpening a point or tiny blade (p. 00), found in conjunction with the prickers, may also have been used with the latter.

Among the tiny fragments of wax tablet, B5 is perforated to accommodate a hinge, forming a diptych or polyptych. The tablets found in Lubeck ranged from single sheets to books of nine tablets hinged together. It is unlikely that the short pins (B15) would have been used as styli because they are too blunt, but the fragment Cu 100 may be part of a stylus. Also possibly connected with writing is the tau cross fragment (B21). The worn patches are not merely caused by being held like a walking stick or for processional purposes. The fragment looks as though it was used specifically for rubbing after it was broken. It could have been used to stretch out tight bindings, or for burnishing gold leaf. The lead pot (L8) which once contained cinnabar or mercuric sulphide is suitable for containing a small quantity of

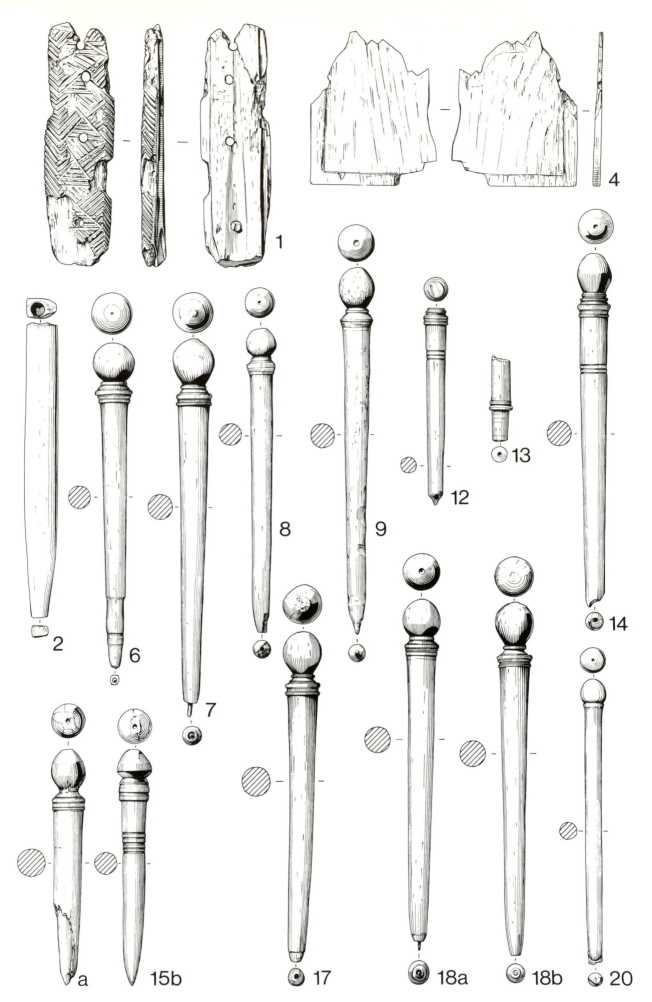

Figure 45   Battle Abbey. Bone objects nos. 1–20 ($\frac{1}{2}$)

paint for illuminating manuscripts. The seal matrix blank, if such it is, (Cu 64) has an unusual shank, unlike the normal concave hexagonal type. Lacking a device, it is either unfinished or was simply used for closing letters rather than attesting documents. The hooked book clasps (Cu 65, 66, 67, 69) would have been attached to straps on the book cover and served to hold the lively vellum or parchment pages together. They range in date from the fourteenth to sixteenth century but their form is not sufficiently elaborate to say if they are English or continental. The rosette studs Cu 53–55 could have been used as binding protector, four or more being attached to the front and back covers of a book (Hirst, Walsh and Wright 1983, 176–177, 204–205). The gem stone is likely to have come either from book-bindings, or from a decorated cross, as is the gilded strip (Au 4). Lastly, the spectacles (B27), a rare find from the middle ages, deserve mention, whether they were used for book work or not. They were found in a pre-Dissolution context.

4. Corner piece of tablet with raised margin. A complete tablet of similar thickness was found in a fifteenth to early sixteenth century context at Finsbury Circus (Museum of London acc no 10890). D22 793411. Another corner piece D22 793429, 7 mm wide 13 mm long. Not illustrated.

5. Fragment with two perforations for hinge. The tablet would have been part of a dyptych or polyptych as at Lubeck (Warnecke 1912). Not illustrated. D22 793412.

6. Turned shaft with spherical head, tip tapered in stages, with holes for insertion of copper alloy pins. Green metallic stain around holes. D22 793413 86 mm long.

7. Turned shaft with spherical head. Copper alloy pin inserted at end. D22 793414 102 mm long.

8. As above. D22 793415 98 mm long.

9. As above. Pin missing. D22 793416 82 mm long.

10. Fragment with spherical head, pointed end missing. D22 793417 54 mm long. Not illustrated.

11. Fragment. Moulded shaft, spherical and pointed ends missing. D22 793418 32 mm long. Not illustrated.

12. Fragment, head missing. Moulded shaft with nibbed tip and hole for insertion of pin. D22 793419 52 mm long.

13. Fragment, moulded shaft, with two ridges. Spherical and pointed ends missing. D22 793435.

14. Spherical knob and nibbed tip with hole for insertion of pin. D22 802013 96 mm long.

15A and B. Turned bone pins with spherical head, tapered shaft whittled to point. No hole for pin. These pins appear to be parchment prickers with their pointed ends adapted for a slightly different function. D22 802015A 802015B Both 65 mm long. 15B not illustrated.

16. Fragment, turned head and part of shaft. D22 802024 54 mm long. Not illustrated.

17. Turned tapered shaft, spherical head, hole at tip for insertion of pin. D22 802025.

18A and B. Turned tapered shaft with shouldered tip, spherical head. D22 802026A Pin *in situ*. 802026B Pin missing.

19. Fragment, head of parchment pricker. D22 802031 43 mm long. Not illustrated.

20. Pin with spherical head and metal tip. D21 793437.

Croziers

21. Fragment of tau cross. A full discussion of this valuable work of art has been published by Mr T.A. Heslop (1980). The piece was originally one shoulder of a double volute tau-cross forming the upper terminal of an ecclesiastical staff. Below the volute is an inscribed blank circle presumably designed to contain an appliqué panel of metal, crystal or mounted gems. The style of the acanthus foliage decoration and the use of beading suggests the ivory was carved in the first half of the twelfth century. The position of worn patches on the fragment would suggest it continued to be used for some secondary function after it broke, and may have ended up in the scriptorium as suggested above. D22 793408. (Also described in *English Romanesque Art* 1984, 193, and Geddes 1983, 90–95).

22. Turned moulded knop of crozier, A3 802033. This was the only significant personal find in the graves.

Gaming Pieces and Miscellaneous

23. Gaming piece. Pelleted decoration around sides was grooved horizontally on lathe, and vertical incisions were carved afterwards. Carved crenellated pattern on end. D22 793410.

24. Decorated turned pin. Shaft is shouldered at one end to form a slender tip. Resembles a cribbage peg. D22 793424.

25. Gaming die 6 mm cube. Not illustrated. D22 802014.

26. Pin, probably half finished. Roughly chamfered, oblong head, tapered shaft of circular cross section. Blunt tip. D22 793421.

27. Fragment of spectacle frame, with groove on inner curve for lens and tab for junction piece of adjacent frame. For similar more complete example see Rhodes (1980). C14 802023.

Musical Instrument Pegs

The following pegs for musical instruments were found. The analysis and discussion was kindly contributed by *Dr Graeme Lawson*.

28.	D21 812471	31.	E39 802018
29.	D21 812469	32.	D22 793431
30.	D21 812470	33.	D22 793422

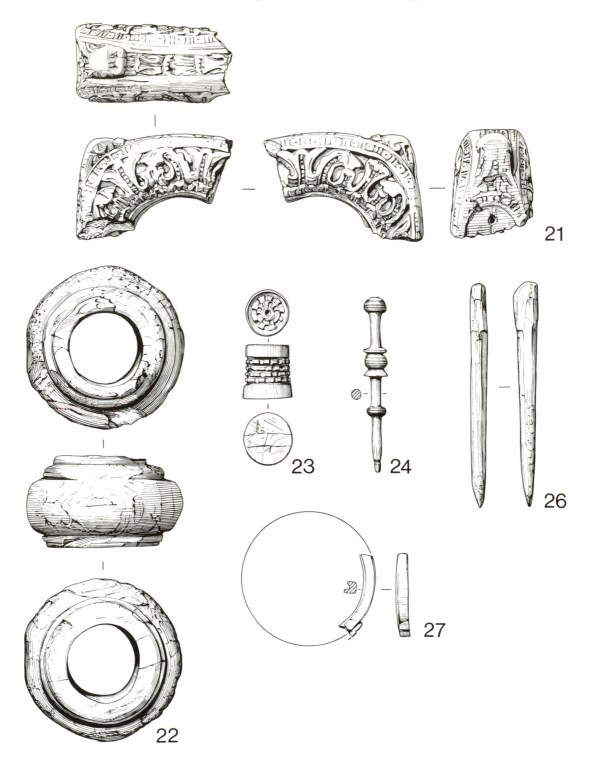

Figure 46   Battle Abbey. Bone objects nos. 21–27 ($\frac{1}{2}$)

34. D22 793427
35. D22 802012
36. D21 802022A
37. D21 802022B
38. D22 802034
39. D21 802028

Altogether twelve bone tuning-pegs, of which nine were whole, were recovered from the excavations. They range in length from 34 to 61 mm, which is usual for late medieval pegs, comparable variations occurring notably at St Aldates, Oxford (35 to 53 mm), Winchester (33 to 62 mm) and Bristol (42 to 64 mm). Like these other finds they fall into two basic categories: a short type (B) in which the strings were attached to perforations in their squared ends (no. 39) and a typically longer variety (A) in which attachment was achieved by means of perforations in their opposite, narrower ends (nos. 28–38).

The heads of all but one of the Battle sample appear to have had square cross-sections, probably cut initially by knife and then filed smooth. This square section is consistent with tuning by means of

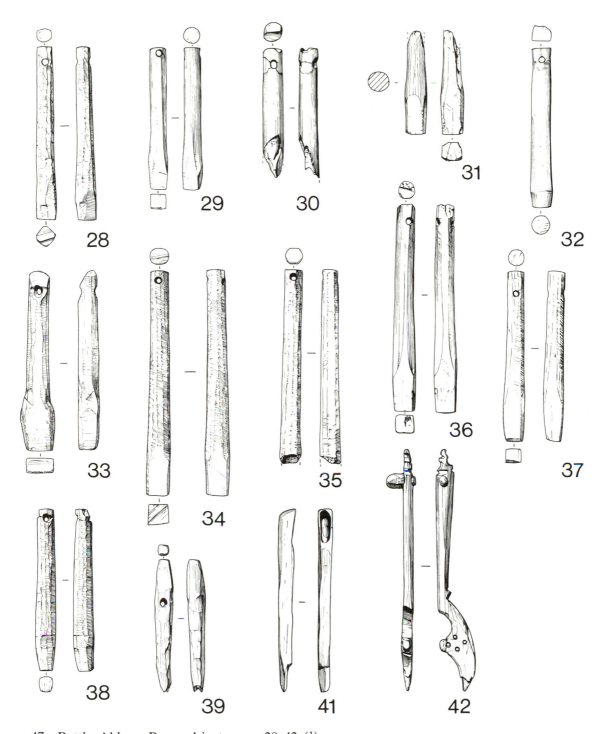

Figure 47 Battle Abbey. Bone objects nos. 28–42 ($\frac{1}{2}$)

socketed keys, which appear frequently in medieval manuscript illustrations of harps, and whose use is confirmed here by the sort of damage visible on the corners of nos. 28, 32 and 37. It is also consistent with a late medieval date, although slightly flatter, rectangular-section heads are also known from other sites of the same period. The one exception here however (no. 33) bears instead a rather broader handle for hand-tuning, a rare variety known previously in England from only a single find from York.

The shafts of most of the Battle pegs show signs of having been coarse-filed to shape, rasp-marks being particularly well preserved in nos. 28, 34 and 38. Only one has clearly not been rasped, again no. 33, which has been shaped purely by knife-strokes and is quite crude by comparison. The polished areas and microscopic annular scratches found superimposed upon the rasp-marks of four (30, 35, 36 and 38) are an interesting indication of usage, resulting from repeated twisting in their sockets. Four pegs (nos. 34, 35, 36 and 38) are tapered distinctly and evenly from shoulders to tips, while two others (nos. 29 and 33) are clearly not. This latter, parallel-sided form is not uncommon elsewhere, despite its reduced efficiency. Such pegs, although obviously less sophisticated, do nevertheless taper a little in the region of their shoulders, which is just sufficient to maintain adhesion when under tension.

All of the pegs found at Battle Abbey bear small perforations for the attachment of strings, which, though normal, is by no means universal. Two of the four pegs from Whitby, for example, had sawn slits instead, while the same has recently proved true of three from Montgomery Castle and one from Wallingstones, Herefordshire (Fry 1976; Lawson 1978; 1980, 225–6). With the exception of the perforation of no. 33, which is bi-conical with crudely rebated apertures (the latter another unusual feature), all the pegs here have finely drilled cylindrical bores of between 1.6 and 2.1 mm diameter.

Unfortunately, none of these perforations bears any marks that could be attributed with certainty to the wear and tear of stringing. This however might well indicate the use of soft, non-metallic stringing materials such as animal-gut or horse-hair (both of which are feasible propositions for the period in question) since it is clear from damage to the tuning-heads of nos. 28, 32 and 37, and the partial polishing and minute annular scratching on the shafts of nos. 30, 35, 36 and 38, that some at least have indeed seen use. Only one peg, no. 34, bears no visible trace of any usage whatever, and could perhaps represent an unused spare. There were however no other indications on the site of the presence of any instrument-making or bone-working workshop of the kind suggested recently by similarly unused finds from St. Aldates, Oxford (Durham 1978, 165–6).

The exact identity of the instruments with which these pegs might have been associated is at present still unclear, despite the increasing frequency with which others like them are now being recognised during excavations. A distinction between instruments using type A and type B pegs is of course likely from the suitability of type B pegs and the unsuitability of those of type A for instruments with box-like, rather than open, frames (eg various zithers, psalteries and most keyboard instruments). For type A pegs, in which perforations and tuning-heads lay at opposite ends, an open frame would have been essential. Suitable instruments in this respect would have been restricted to harps, lutes (including fiddles) and perhaps lyres at that time, although the likelihood of the last of these diminishes rapidly towards the end of the Middle Ages.

Among the type A pegs from Battle, the presence of a flat handle on no. 33 tends to rule out a harp-based interpretation for at least that one, which would probably have been more suitable for the wider spacing of simple fiddles such as the *rebec*. It is interesting in this connexion to note the close similarity between its length and that of its parallel in York, both of which are quite small compared with the rest of our Insular assemblage. Unfortunately, the remaining, square-headed pegs are more difficult to place. They do not, for example, cluster convincingly around any particular lengths, either within the Battle group or nationally, despite the breadth of

their variation (39–61 and 39–69 mm respectively). Nevertheless it seems hardly possible that our smallest Battle peg (no. 29) could have belonged to the same kind of instrument as the largest, almost twice its size (no. 34), and the same might equally be said of nos. 35 and 38 whose shaft-lengths (from shoulder to perforation) measure 48 and 24 mm. For the moment perhaps it may be sufficient to note that later medieval harp-necks were quite probably rather broad, for structural reasons. This would have demanded longer rather than shorter pegs, whereas simpler, fewer-stringed instruments of *rebec*/fiddle and related types often had comparatively thin flat peg-boards compatible with shorter varieties. The squared forms of the tuning-heads of the smallest of the Battle Abbey pegs need not preclude such an interpretation.

Cu 93 is possibly a sawn off part of a tuning key. See also slate inscribed with music stave p. 175.

Toilet Equipment
40.   Double sided comb with teeth wider on one side than the other. Upper surface curved, lower surface flat. Not illustrated.
D21 793436.
41.   Toilet implement with ear scoop at one end and pointed tooth pick at the other. See also Cu 77.
D22 793409.
42.   Fragment of toilet set. Reverse side flat, front side curved section. One end spatulate with open work decoration. Shaft ends in finial pierced by metal rivet. Possibly a cover or tooth pick from manicure set. Comparable implement with rivet holes at one end found in sixteenth-century context at St Michael's House, Southampton (Platt 1976, unpaginated; Gay 1887, 526).
D22 802027.

Lead (Figure 48)
Architectural Fragments
1A and B. Openwork vent covers, cast in delicate tracery patterns.
D22 802501A, 802501B.
2.   Cames by *Dr. B. Knight*, Ancient Monuments Laboratory.
Six different came profiles were identified amongst the large quantity of twisted and fragmentary window lead. The type examples are taken from the earliest phases in which they occur. The illustrations are idealised versions of the profiles – drawings of twisted fragments of came would not be informative. It must also be borne in mind that types A, B and C are made by hand, so that the measurements of each piece differ somewhat (Knight 1983, 49–51).

Type A, e.g. 802715, B7, was cast in a two-piece mould as described by Theophilus in Book II, Chapters 24–25. (Hawthorne and Smith 1963, 67–69). It has thick diamond-shaped flanges and a prominent casting flash along the outside edge.
Type B, e.g. 802490, D21
Type C, e.g. 802649, D21
These have been made from cast lead as type A by scraping off the casting flash. This process is described by Theophilus in the last paragraph of Book

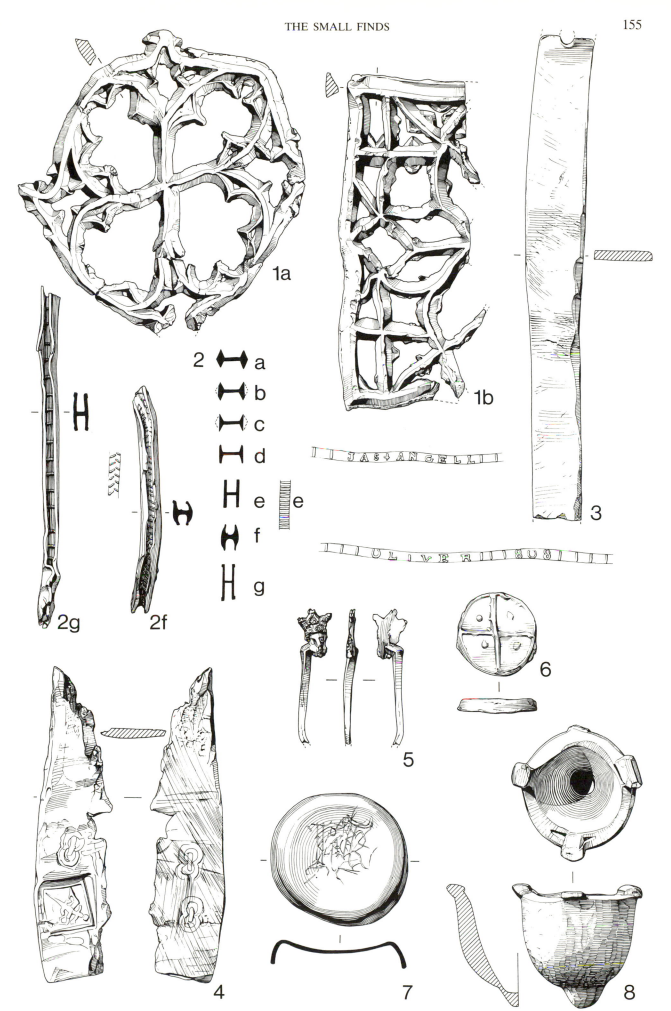

Figure 48 Battle Abbey. Lead objects ($\frac{1}{2}$)

II Chapter 26 (Hawthorne and Smith 1963, 70). The only difference is in the amount of lead which has been removed from the flange.

Type D, e.g. 802697, C14, probably milled in a toothless mill, almost square H section.

Type E, e.g. 802613, C16, milled in toothed mill, straight tooth marks about 1 mm apart.

Type F, e.g. 802657, E36, milled with V-edge tooth marks about 1.5 mm apart and semicircular flanges.

Type G, e.g. 802664, E39, milled with straight tooth marks about 5 mm apart, wide flanges. Inscribed in web OLIVER 1808. Other pieces have inscribed OLIVER 1760, and JAS+ANGELL: 802629, E42; 802717, E39.

Cast cames are the earliest technologically, and by far the largest amount of came is type A, followed by type D. Although most of the came fragments were found in the Dissolution layers D21 and D22, one example of type A was found in B7, a thirteenth-century context, and one example of type D was found in C14, an early fifteenth-century context. While the presence of cast came at an early date is not surprising, the presence of milled lead in the fifteenth century is interesting because the earliest documentary evidence for the lead mill is mid-sixteenth century (Knowles 1930, 133–139). It is not impossible, however, that a simple toothless mill operating rather like a mangle was invented before 1500, and that toothed rollers were introduced later to prevent the lead from slipping. Types E, F and G were made in toothed mills and are post-Dissolution in date, the latter two being eighteenth to nineteenth century. Only a few fragments of these types were found.

Qualitative X-ray fluorescence analysis was performed on uncleaned sections of came. This showed the presence of a small amount of copper (perhaps 1%) and minor quantities of tin and zinc. Silver and antimony were not present (less than 0.1%). This amount of copper would increase the resistance of the lead to fatigue cracking (Newton forthcoming), but it is hard to say whether it was added deliberately or not.

3. Perforated lead strips. The majority of these strips (24 out of 32) were found in D22 and the rest were scattered in later phases. Nearly all are broken at the perforation. Viollet-le-Duc (1864, 212) illustrates the thirteenth-century lead roof of Chartres cathedral, with the bottom of each sheet held in place by strips of this sort. The strip was hammered directly to battens and bent over the lower edge of the sheet to prevent the latter being raised by the wind. This method avoided perforating an exposed face of the lead sheet.
D22 802543.

Miscellaneous
4. Fragment with scored surface. One side stamped with two figures-of-eight motifs. Other side stamped with one figure-of-eight motif and square stamp showing sword with circular pommel and straight hilt passing through a crown with fleur-de-lis crests.
D22 802502.

5. Pilgrim badge with crowned head. Head cast in one piece with pin. Crown has three sets of two concentric circles on head band, two concentric circles on base of each point. Bulbous eyes under heavy brows, thick nose and lips. Very similar to pin found at Dowgate, London (Hugo 1859, pl IV, no. 7).
D22 802551.
6. Disc with raised long arm cross and pellet in each quadrant on one face. Reverse blank.
D22 802590.
7. Circular cap with down-turned lip. Inscription/ monogram scratched on surface IR?
D22 802644.
8. Pot with rounded bottom tapering to blunt point. Four lugs on lip, one broken. Pink colouring on interior with some streaks on exterior, in cinnabar (mercuric sulphide). Tested by Dr B. Knight, Ancient Monuments Laboratory.
D22 802681.

Copper Alloy (Figures 49–53)
Clothing
The majority of clothing accessories, both of precious metal and copper alloy, were found in D21 and D22. While it is not possible to date them with great precision, it appears they cover a fiarly wide time span from the thirteenth to sixteenth centuries. For example the brooches Cu 1–7, and chape Cu 30 are all *c.* 1200–1400, but the silver hook (precious metal 8), chape Cu 28 and clasp Cu 70 are all sixteenth century. This suggests that the earlier items had probably been discarded or lost for some while before they were swept up at the Dissolution. The eighteenth-century shoe buckles were found appropriately near the surface in the chapter house area (Cu 22, 23).

Brooches
Ring brooches like numbers 1–7 below are a thirteenth- to fourteenth-century type (LMMC, pl LXXVII, 275, nos 1 and 2; Williams 1979, no. Cu 3, 1250–1400).
1. Plain annular brooch with pin.
D21 793337. Not illustrated.
2. Plain annular brooch with pin.
D22 802237. Diameter 35 mm. Not illustrated.
3. Broken pin with two grooves on ridged shoulder, from annular brooch.
D21 793323A. Not illustrated.
4. Broken pin with four grooves on ridged shoulder, from annular brooch.
D21 793323B.
5. As above.
D22 802142 52 mm long. Not illustrated.
6. As above.
D22 793208. Not illustrated.
7. As above.
D22 785966 50 mm long. Not illustrated.
8. Acorn brooch, cast in one piece with two short pins on reverse.
E35 793394.
A similar example from City Road, London, date unknown, Museum of London A19100.

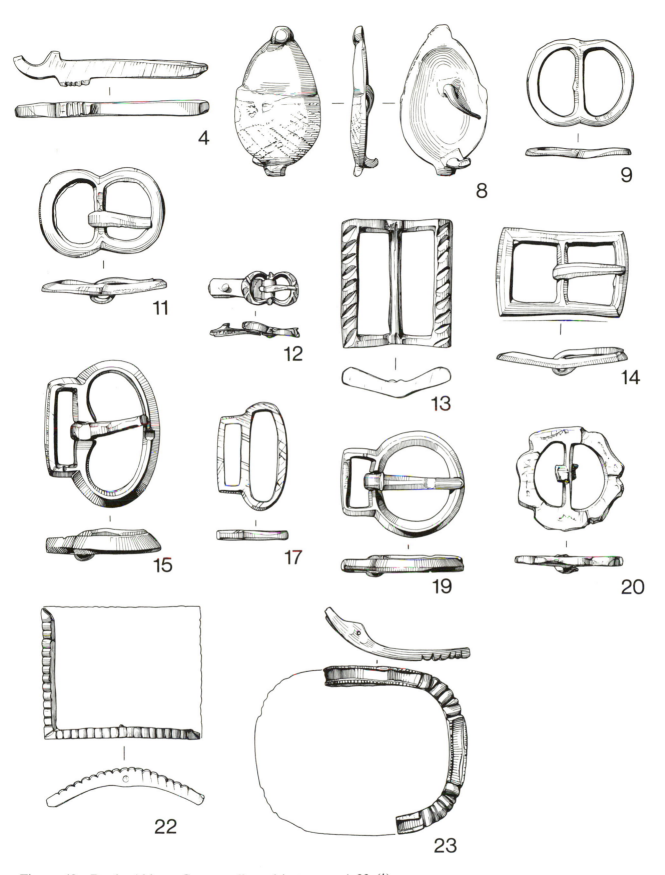

Figure 49   Battle Abbey. Copper alloy objects nos. 4–23 ($\frac{1}{2}$)

Buckles

9. Double loop buckle, figure-of-eight shaped, D Section.
D35 793392.
10. As above. Not illustrated.
D22 793223 22 mm long.
11. Double loop buckle as above.
D23 785970.
12. Double loop buckle with pin and attachment for strap.
D22 802239.
Double buckles of this type (9–12) were fashionable in the late fifteenth and sixteenth centuries. (LMMC, 278).
13. Rectangular double buckle with diagonal groove pattern on the edges.
D22 793214.
14. Plain rectangular double buckle.
D23 785982.
15. Oval buckle, single loop, quadrant section, seating for pin, slot for strap.
D22 802158.
16. Similar to above, loop rounder. Not illustrated.
D22 802143.
17. As above.
D21 785978.
18. Similar to above without seating for pin.
D22 793290A, 793290B. (Not illustrated.)
19. Circular buckle, triangular section, rectangular slot for strp, pin *in situ*.
D22 793312.
20. Circular buckle with central bar. Shaped like five petalled rose, iron pin.
D22 793287.
21. Larger version of above. Petals have slightly ribbed edges.
D22 793234. (Not illustrated).
22. Curved shoe buckle with ribbed surface. The whitish surface colour is tin plating on high zinc brass. Eighteenth century.
E47 801965.
23. Half of curved copper alloy shoe buckle. Eighteenth century.
E42 802614.

Strap Ends and Belt Chapes

24. Belt chape, forked type. Two flat sheets rivetted over forked spacer. Decorative finial broken. Fourteenth-century type.
(Fingerlin 1971 pl. 127, illus. 207, cat. 203; LMMC, plate LXXV, No 11 c. 979).
D22 793248.
25. Belt chape, fragment. Forekd spacer piece with decorative finial like 27 below.
D22 802151.
26. Belt chape, fragment. Forked spacer piece from circular chape, with acorn-derivative finial, like 28.
D36 802130. Not illustrated.
27. Belt chape. Two circular plates with open work motif at strap end and acorn derivative finial.
D21 793342.
28. Belt chape. Two circular sheets with oval perforation at strap end. Spacer has acorn finial. Similar

chape of forked type from Bassingbourne, now in British Museum, early sixteenth century. (Fingerlin 1971, p. 117, illus. 205, cat. 203). This type was current from the mid-fifteenth to sixteenth century.
D22 793216, 793217.
29. Oblong belt chape with central groove and undulating edge at strap end.
D22 793242. Not illustrated.
30. U-shaped chape with ornamental inner edge. Thirteenth to fourteenth century.
(LMMC, 280–84).
D22 793252.
31. Oblong belt chape, two plates rivetted together with open slit down the centre.
D22 793249. Not illustrated.
32. Copper alloy sheet with part of an incised pattern, cut down and reused as possible strap end. One edge cut with zig zag, one rivet hole.
D22 785965.
33. Strap end made from reused decorative copper alloy sheet. Incised foliage design offset and fragmentary. Reverse of sheet with hatched border.
D21 785976.
34. Part of strap end. Sheet curved at one end and fringe-like incisions at strap end. One rivet hole.
D22 793269. (Not illustrated).
35. Strap end made from reused decorative sheet. Single strip folded over and rivetted. Patterned fragment embossed and hatched.
D22 793309.
36. Strap end made from single folded sheet with one serrated edge, two rivet holes.
D21 802213 15 mm long. Not illustrated.
37. Hinged belt chape with terminal eyelets.
E39 802135.
38. Fragment as above.
D21 802223 Not illustrated.
39. Fragment as above.
D22 802191 Not illustrated.
40. Fragment as above.
D22 802190. Not illustrated.
Fifteenth century chapes tend to be small with a small ring for attaching a tassel or trinket at the tip. (LMMC, 268, plate LXXV, 13, probably fifteenth or sixteenth century; and Museum of London A2553, undated from Thames Street).
41. Narrow copper alloy strips cast in one piece with gap at one end, possibly for insertion of strap. Traces of foliage pattern in *vernis brun* arranged in triangular frames. Possibly late fifteenth-century belt chape, of long narrow type (LMMC, 268).
D22 793218.
42. Crudely folded sheet, possibly simple sword or dagger chape.
E42 785953.

Belt Stiffeners

43. Two plain rectangular sheets held by two rivets with central perforation. As used to stiffen belt hole on the statue of Moses by Claus Sluter, *c.* 1400. (Fingerlin, 1971 page 397, fig 452).
D22 793266. Not illustrated.
44. Jetton reused as belt stiffener. Plaque with central perforation and two iron rivets. The jetton is

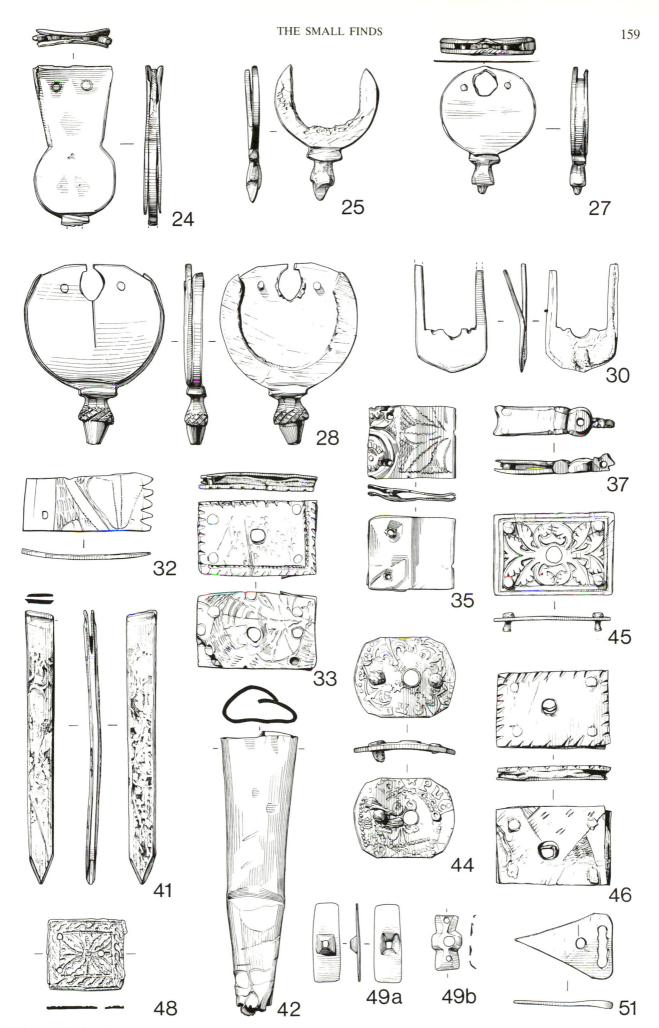

Figure 50   Battle Abbey. Copper alloy objects nos. 24–51 (½)

clipped off-centre. Jetton is fifteenth century, French, Ave Maria Gracia Plena, France modern/ cross Fleury type. See p. 181, no. 61. Identification by *Marion Archibald*.
D22 793289.
45. Plaque with four rivet holes and larger central perforation. Centre filled with incised foliage decoration edged by plain border.
D22 801973.
46. Two plaques with rivets in four corners holding leather. Front has scored edges. Central perforation.
D22 802155.
47. Two plain rectangular plaques complete with four rivets and leather between them. Central perforation.
D21 802248 28 mm long. Not illustrated.
48. Rectangular plaque with three rivet holes. One edge has two broken projections. Inside pattern of four petals surrounded by frame filled with wavy lines. Possibly belt plaque.
D24 793389.
49a. Back plate with one hole.
49b. Winged belt fitting, three rivet holes.
(Fingerlin 1971, 59, illus. 41, cat. 97. Gran Estergon, Kunst Museum, 1350–75).
D21 793325.
50. Rectangular belt stiffener with nicked edges and three holes.
D22 802176 16 mm long. Not illustrated.
51. Triangular fitment with rectangular and circular perforation.
E47 793383.
52. Pair of fragmentary sheets with two rivet holes. One sheet has zig-zag pattern in *vernis brun*.
D21 793381.

Studs
53. Perforated rosette stud.
E42 785955.
54. Six petalled domed stud.
D30 793368.
55. Six petalled domed stud with triangular incised pattern on petals.
D22 801976.
56. Fragment as above.
D21 802210 17 mm wide. Not illustrated.
57. Stud with central indent and raised spoke pattern.
D21 802246.
58. Two petalled rivet collars.
D22 802174.

Pins
59. Pin with looped end.
D22 793302.
60. Pin with moulded necking.
D22 793305.
61. Pin with moulded necking.
D22 802169.

Clothes Hook and Fasteners
62. Fastener with two hooks and decorative bone beads stained copper green at each end, held together by tightly bound wire. Compare Baart (1977, 154).
D22 802037.
63. Clothes hook made of three pieces of bent wire bound around the middle with narrower wire. Hook at each end.
D22 793297.
64. Bronze stud or button, comments by *T.A. Heslop*. The concentric circle design on the face was turned on a lathe, with the central pivot point remaining. The shank and face are cast in one piece but the shank has chisel marks on it suggesting that it has been altered to fit a smaller context than at first envisaged. Although it somewhat resembles a seal matrix found at Denny Abbey (Rigold 1977, no. 10) its face is slightly curved, not flat and it is turned, not cast.
D21 793311

Hooked Clasps
The exact function of these clasps is sometimes debatable. They are all hooks which are intended to be attached to straps. Some are recognizable as book closures, other are more likely to be for belts. The book clasps were examined by Howard Nixon, Librarian of Westminster Abbey.
65. Book clasp. Two strips rivetted together with traces of leather straps between them. Hook attached to upper strip. Arm has chamfered edges, strap ends splayed, undulating edge. Fourteenth to sixteenth century.
D22 793244.
66. Hooked book clasp, plain rectangular sheet on rear. Front has splayed scalloped edge on strap end and incised concentric circle decoration. 1450–1530.
D30 793371.
67. Hooked book clasp similar to above. Plain rectangular sheet on rear. Front has splayed scalloped strap end and scored X pattern on surface. Traces of gilding.
D30 793365.
68. Hooked clasp, plain sheet, strap end broken, hooked end shouldered and rounded. Two rivet holes and one large perforation behind hook.
D30 793359. Not illustrated.
69. Book clasp. Two rectangular sheets rivetted together. Front has two scored edges and trefoil open work design at strap end. 1450–1530.
D21 793339.
70. Hooked clasp with leather between two rectangular plates. Edges of top plate scored, ogee open work motif on strap end. Eyelet projects from face, compare Fingerlin (1971, 143, fig. 257, cat. 454, from Rouen 1550–1600; fig. 259, cat. 416, early 1600's). These two examples lack the projecting eyelet which could be for attaching a trinket or tassel. Compare Williams (1979, 149, Cu 11, with loop).
D22 802172.
71. Hooked clasp with leather between two rectangular plates. Edges of top plate serrated, surface stippled, eyelet projects from face.
D22 801972.

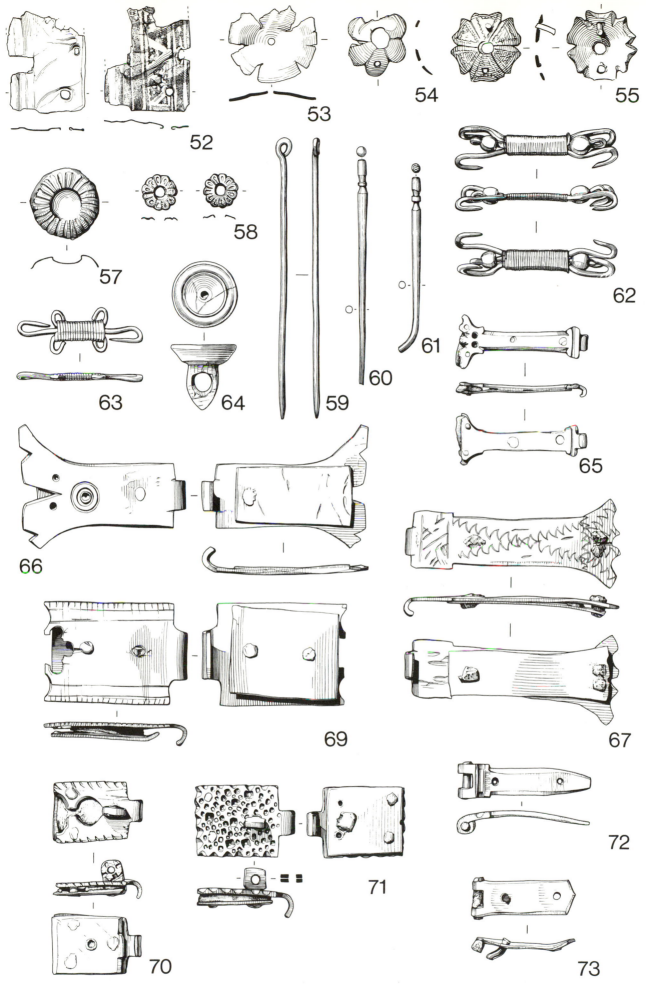

Figure 51   Battle Abbey. Copper alloy objects nos. 52–73 ($\frac{1}{2}$)

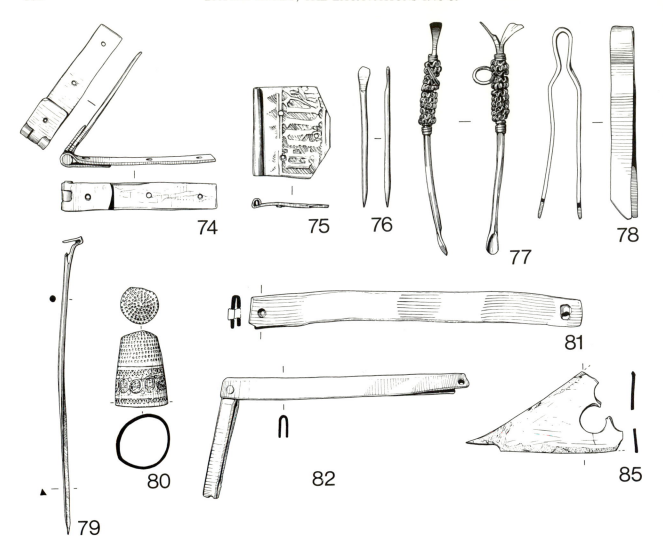

Figure 52   Battle Abbey. Copper alloy objects nos. 74–85 ($\frac{1}{2}$)

Hinges
72.   Hinge with pintle and two rivet holes.
D30 793372.
73.   Hinge with pintle and two rivet holes.
D30 793362.
74.   Double hinge with pintle, rivet holes along each arm. Possibly for diptych.
D21 793319.
75.   Reused copper sheet with inscription, possibly- . . .GOIE. . . . Curled over at one end, as housing for pintle.
D22 793294.

Toilet Implements
76.   Implement with ear scoop at one end and tooth pick at the other. See also Bone 38.
D22 793304.
77.   Implement with spatulate scoop at one end and two flat probes at the other. Knotted wire work on handle and ring for attachment to cord. For ears, teeth and nails. Sixteenth-century French example with figure on stem in Pichon (1897, 36, No. 207: Gay page 526. Also at Verulamium Museum no.

78.898 context unknown, with wire work on handle). D21 802225.
78.   Tweezers with flat blades made from flat copper strips.
D22 793316.

Sewing
79.   Needle for leather. The eye end is of circular section, point end triangular section.
D22 802178.
80.   Modern thimble with stippled top and sides, rosette border around bottom.
E42 785984.

Edging Strip
81.   Folded strip with perforation at each end.
D22 785967 19 mm long.
82.   Edging strip rivetted to form corner.
D21 785977.
83.   Two plain fragments of edging strips including one rivet.
D21 793320. Not illustrated.
84.   Edging strip.

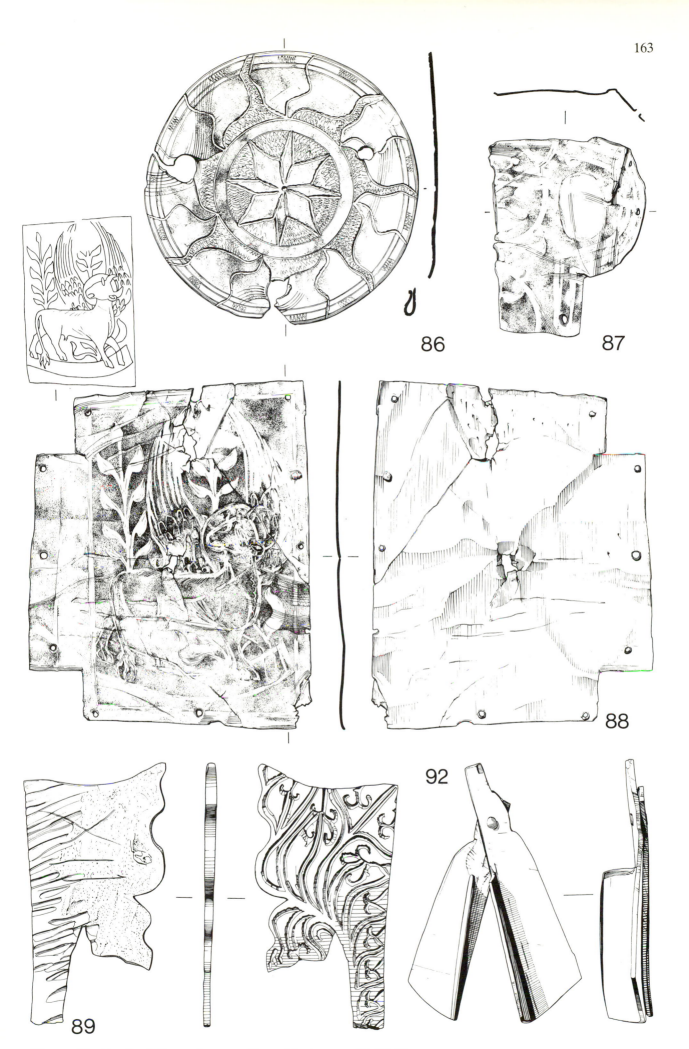

Figure 53 Battle Abbey. Copper alloy objects nos. 86–92 ($\frac{1}{2}$)

E39 785958. 40 mm long. Not illustrated.
Cu 81–84 possibly for framing sheets of horn, for example, on window of horn lantern (LMMC, 184, fig. 58, A1365).

Decorative Plaques
85.   Fragment of triangular sheet with central open work motif. Lead/tin solder around edges.
D22 793245.
86.   Flat disc with incised geometric decoration, *vernis brun*, and three rivet holes. Traces of leather behind one hole. Early sixteenth-century bridle boss with distinct convex section from the Thames, London has a similar bold geometric pattern. This one would have concealed either end of the mouth piece to a bridle. The Battle disc is flat and might therefore have fitted on the side of the head band on a bridle. (LMMC, 85, fig. 22).
D25 802177.
87.   Fragment from a cross arm, broken on three sides but semicircular end complete, with rivet holes. The decoration, in *vernis brun*, is barely decipherable but a double line border and some scrolls are visible. The sheet, attached to a piece of wood, could have formed a semi-circular enlargment in the centre of a cross arm. See also 88.
D34 802255.
88.   Sheet from right arm of a cross potent with rivet holes on all sides, flange on left side and decoration in *vernis brun*. The winged bull of St Luke stands on a banner from which grow trees or scrolls with asymmetrical leaves. The shape of the leaves suggests a date around 1300.
D21 793348.

Both 87 and 88 would have been attached to wooden crosses. All the altars at Battle Abbey would have required their own crucifixes and these, with their fairly humble materials would have come from a minor altar. Large numbers of copper plated crosses survive in Italy and Spain, (eg Zastrow, 1978).

A sample of black lacquer from 88 was analysed by *R. White* of the National Gallery: Gas chromatography showed surprisingly low levels of lipids for the size of sample examined. Lipids are material soluble in organic solvents, not in water. There was some indication of a drying material present and the palmitate/stearate ratio suggests there is a little linseed oil present. No diterpenoid or triterpenoid resins could be detected. Terpenes are constituents of plant oils and present in natural resins like rosen. These results are inconsistent with the presence of plant resins and waxes, but not inconsistent with the presence of linseed oil, although the quantity of compounds characteristic of linseed oil are rather small. However there has been little work on the analysis of true lacquers and, apart from shellac, it is difficult to find useful indicators for gas chromatography purposes.
89.   Fragment of monumental brass plaque incised with foliage pattern. XII scratched on reverse. Surface find east of trench N prior to excavation.
E47 793405.

Miscellaneous
90.   Coiled bent spring. Not illustrated.
D22 793273.
91.   As above.
D22 793256. 57 mm long. Not illustrated.
92.   Blades of candle snuffer. Horizontal blades overlap each other to trim wick when closed. Vertical blades then touch to snuff candle.
D22 793243.
93.   Polished fragment, turned moulding at one end, square tapered cross section, plain end sawn off and crushed. A possible musical function, as part of a turning key for a stringed instrument, cannot be ruled out, though Graeme Lawson reports that its lack of any facility for rigid attachment to a shaft or handle argue against this. Its bore is also larger than the heads of bone tuning pegs recovered from both this and other English medieval excavations.
D22 793263.
94.   Loop of polished bronze strip with cross hatched surface.
D34 802257.
95.   Links of mail, from armour.
D22 802192.
96.   Ring of thin twisted wire, too fragile for finger ring.
D21 793340.
97.   Very thin wire plaited into a rope.
D22 802154.
98.   Tapered bone finial with copper alloy wire necking and bone rib on one side of neck. Possibly part of knife handle.
D22 802148.
99.   Strip fragment with flat incised decoration. Broken along butt end.
D22 801975.
100.   Polished spike fragment, with tool marks on front and back. A similar complete object is identified as a stylus (?) in *English Romanesque Art* (no. 251 p. 251).
D21 793349.
101.   Plate rim fragment with incised decoration of concentric circles.
D21 793345.
102.   Unseamed tube with three rows of six perforations, one end bent backwards to form flange.
D21 793322.
103.   Strip with snipped edge and linear dot pattern.
D22 793301.
104.   Folded sheet strip with rivets and rivet holes.
D21 785975.
105.   Solid rod inserted into stopper and fixed by two iron rivets. Stopper has milled bottom and stippled marks on either side caused by being gripped in a vice. Modern, function unknown.
E47 785974.

The Waste Material
Excluded from the catalogue and illustrations was a miscellaneous collection of copper alloy wire fragments of various dimensions and off cuts from alloy sheet. It was not always possible to distinguish the latter from broken fragments of completed objects

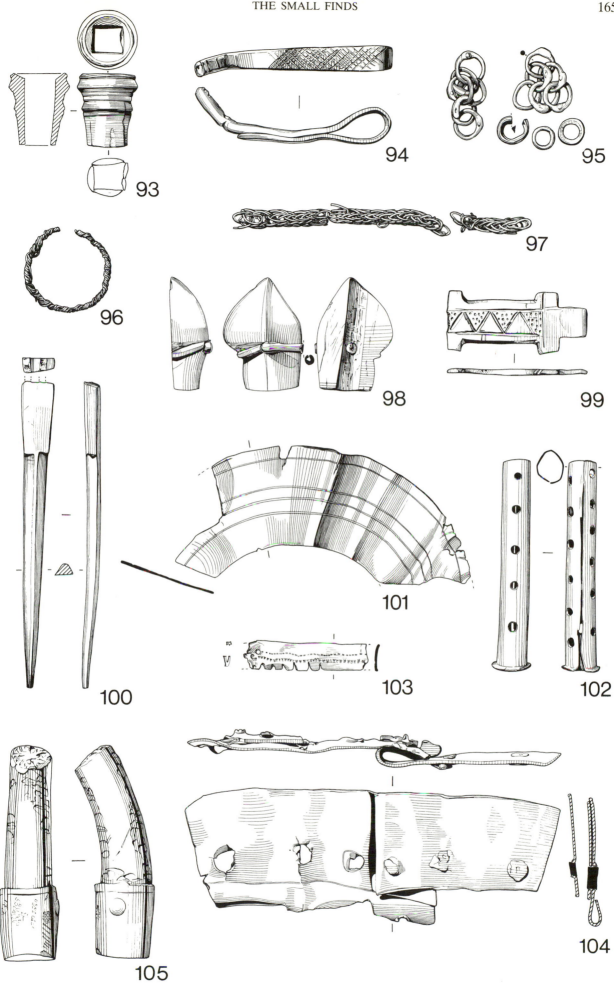

Figure 54   Battle Abbey. Copper alloy objects nos. 93–104 ($\frac{1}{2}$)

but many examples were clearly scraps of waste material, predominantly from D21 and D22. This suggests that there was a metal workshop somewhere in the area although no specific tools for copper working have survived. This may have existed in the monastic period or more likely at the Dissolution. In this connection it should be noted that some surviving objects were cut up and reused for a different purpose, notably Cu 32, 33, 44, 75 and also the gilt plaque Au 3. These modifications could have been made in an abbey workshop. Alternatively fragments could have been discarded at the Dissolution, when gem stones were cut out of the church plate and ecclesiastical objects were broken up.

Justine Bayley of the Ancient Monuments Laboratory examined some of the copper alloy to determine its composition. Her results are as follows: Cu 41, brass containing small amounts of lead and tin; Cu 94, brass with a little lead; Cu 101, gunmetal containing some lead, Cu 104, rivets of similar metal to sheet, low tin bronze (about 5% tin) with some lead, zinc, arsenic and silver (the last barely detectable); Cu 105, both parts have the same composition, brass with a little lead; 793226 (a bent rod, not in catalogue) brass with a little lead; 793256 (a spring, not in catalogue) brass with very little lead and less silver.

It would seem that the most popular alloy was a brass (copper and zinc) containing a small percentage of lead. This appears to have been used both for cast and wrought work. The spring (793256), as expected, contains less lead than the other objects because leaded alloys do not have the necessary resilient properties. The gunmetals contain both zinc and tin in significant amounts.

Iron (Figures 54–61)
All the iron has been X-rayed by the Ancient Monuments Laboratory. The X-ray negative numbers are:
Series A, 2924–2942, 2945–2948, 2952–2963;
Series B, 2886–2929, 2931–2950, 3043–3085.

Keys
The dating and typology used below are based on the London Museum Medieval Catalogue (LMMC)
1. Casket key, circular bow, solid shank, elaborate toothed bit. Compare LMMC (type IV, p. 138) fourteenth to fifteenth century.
D22 795080.
2. Casket key, solid circular bow with central perforation, solid shank, elaborate toothed bit. Fourteenth to fifteenth century as above.
D22 802346.
3. Key, oval bow, solid shank, elaborate toothed bit. Fourteenth to fifteenth century as above.
D22 795024.
4. Key, oval bow, solid shank, fourteenth to fifteenth century as above.
D30 795118.
5. Key, oval bow, projecting stem, wards perpendicular to stem. LMMC (type VIIA, p. 141, plate

XXXI, No. 43) fifteenth century.
D22 795084.
6. Key, oval bow, projecting stem, wards perpendicular to stem. LMMC (type VIIA, p. 141, illus. XXXI, 44, 48) fifteenth to sixteenth century.
D24 795258.
7. Key, kidney bow, projecting stem, wards surround central opening. LMMC (type VIIB, p. 141, illus. XXXI, No. 56) fifteenth to sixteenth century.
E35 795212.
8. Key, kidney bow, solid shaft, octagonal section changing to narrow or circular section with rounded knob on tip. LMMC (type VIIB, p. 138) fifteenth to sixteenth century.
E42 786083.
9. Key, kidney bow, stem narrow to projecting tip, wards surround central opening. LMMC (type VIIB, p. 141, illus. XXXI, No. 55) fifteenth to sixteenth century.
E35 802300.
10. Key, heart bow, projecting stem with knob on tip, wards surround central opening. LMMC (type VIIB, p. 141) fifteenth to sixteenth century.
F48 795293.
11. Casket key, kidney bow with point at bottom, central symmetrical turn piece. LMMC (type IX, p. 143) fourteenth to fifteenth century.
D23 786030.
12. Casket key, open work bow with three perforations and scrolled tinned, baluster shaft and delicate bit. LMMC (type IV, p. 138). Tri-lobed open work handles in use fifteenth to sixteenth century (d'Allemagne 1968, 73 and 91, but baluster shape more common in eighteenth century, plate 60, 61).
E35 802301.

Doors, Caskets and Window Fittings
13. Strap with two fleur-de-lis terminals. Casket binding. Compact fleur-de-lis terminals for instance, on corners of lock plate in Zouche Chapel, York Minster, dated by Dr John Fletcher, by dendrochronology on cupboard, to *c.* 1395–1410 (Fletcher and Tapper 1984, 123); also on casket (fourteenth to fifteenth century), d'Allemagne (1968, plate 393).
D22 795086.
14. Similar to above.
D22 802355. Not illustrated.
15. Similar to above.
D22 795014.
16. Iron strap with trifid lobed terminal.
D24 795257.
17. Iron strap with trifid terminal, less pronounced than above.
D24 795292.
18. Iron strap terminal with pointed lobe and petals. Rosette petals of this sort in Zouche Chapel, York Minster, *c.* 1400.
D22 795073.
19. Strap with lobed terminal.
E42 786008C.
20. Iron scroll with split curls, from casket.
D22 795013.
21. Plain complete strap hinge.
D22 802386. Not illustrated.

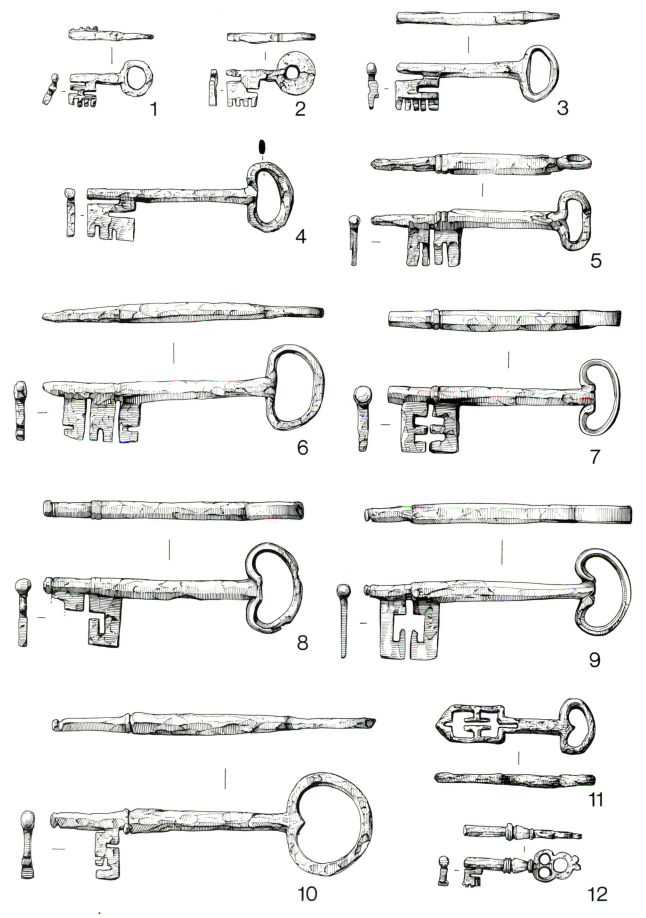

Figure 55 Battle Abbey. Iron objects nos. 1–12 ($\frac{1}{2}$)

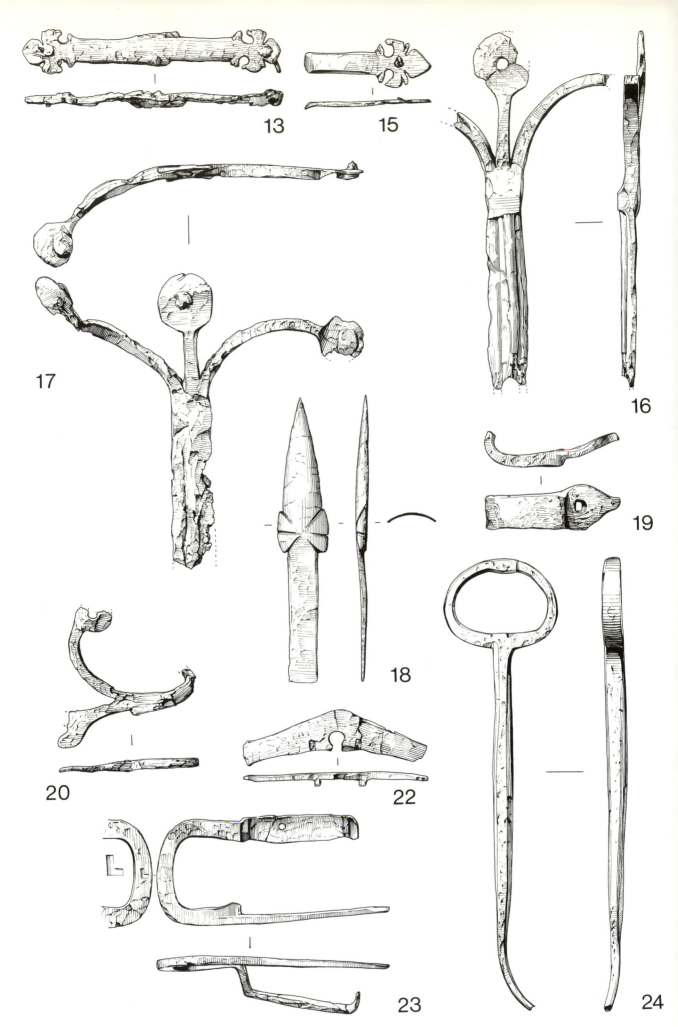

Figure 56 Battle Abbey. Iron objects nos. 13–24 ($\frac{1}{2}$)

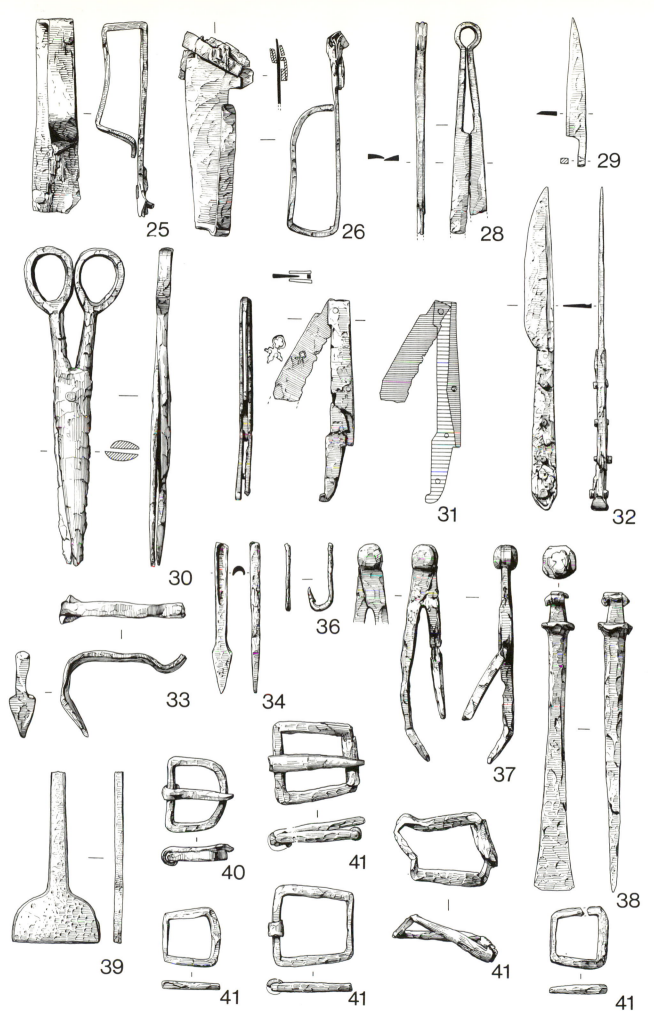

Figure 57   Battle Abbey. Iron objects nos. 25–41 ($\frac{1}{2}$)

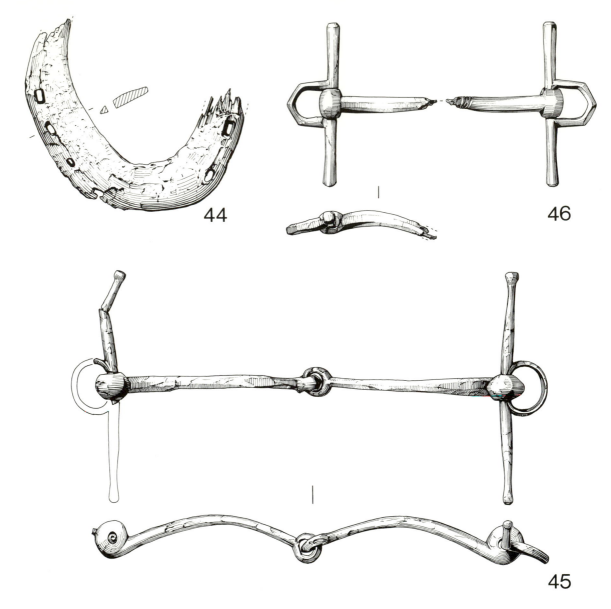

Figure 58   Battle Abbey. Iron objects nos. 44–46 ($\frac{1}{2}$)

Miscellaneous Fittings
22.   Elbow shaped piece with two attached tabs. Ward from lock.
D22 802346.
23.   Part of lock? Maker's mark depressed L shape.
D22 795094.
24.   Latch lifter, oval bow, solid tapered stem curved at tip. Also at Ardingly 1680–1730 (Bedwyn 1976, 63 no. 36).
D23 786001.
25.   Bent iron strip, shaped like delicate handle.
E42 785995.
26.   Bent iron strip with rivet for fastening at one end. Possibly window catch.
E42 795326.
27.   Iron bar, pointed at one end. Hooped around with rivet holes at the other end. Staple? Not illustrated.
D24 795244.

Cutting Tools
28.   Shears. Square shouldered blades, pronounced circular loop. LMMC (p. 153, type 1B, fig. 48 No. 19), sixteenth-century example from town ditch, New Broad Street, London.
D22 802345.
29.   Fragment of shears, square shouldered blade as above.
D21 795110.
30.   Scissors, oval handled, long tapered blades.
E35 795209.
31.   Hinged pocket knife with maker's mark of tulip on quatrefoil.
B7 802465.
32.   Knife with flat tang.
D22 795089.

Tools and Weapons
33.   Arrow head.
D22 795059.

34. Auger bit with curved cutting edge and flat pointed tang.
D23 786033.
35. Auger bit, flat blade with point. Not illustrated.
E42 786071.
36. Barbed fish hook. Not illustrated.
E36 786078.
37. Pair of dividers. Not illustrated.
E42 786011.
38. Chisel, rectangular flat blade tapering to circular section, tang square section and bearded i.e. compressed by hammering.
D27 786004.
39. Bolster, broad semi-circular blade, narrow shaft.
E42 786002.

Buckles
40. 'D' buckle with pin.
E35 795207.
41. Two sets of trapezoid buckles, three with maximum width 42 mm, one with pin; two 30 mm wide. Probably from harness.
E42 785999.
The following plain buckles were omitted from the catalogue for reasons of space: 795023, 802353, 802357, 802362, 802383, 802384, 802438.

Horse Furniture (Figures 58–61).
42. Horseshoe. Rectangular nail holes, calkins not visible. Not illustrated.
D30 795187.
43. Fragment of horseshoe with rectangular holes. Not illustrated.
D36 795158.
44. Fragment of horseshoe with rectangular nail holes.
E47 786066.
The following entries (nos. 45–54) and discussion of bridle harness and spurs were contributed by *Mrs B.M.A. Ellis*.

The bits and spurs are all probably associated with the stable which occupied the adjacent dormitory at the beginning of the nineteenth century. The snaffle bits 45 and 46 are of a simple type used over a very long period, from medieval times (LMMC, 80–81, fig. 19a, type c) until the eighteenth century when one was illustrated by Diderot in his *Encyclopédie* (Diderot, section Eperonnier, 1763, pl. III, fig. 7). The latter work also shows (pl. VI-X) curb bits with cheek pieces reminiscent of Battle Abbey 47.

The slender straight sided spurs 51, 52, 53, 54 are typical of the eighteenth century, when spurs were mainly small and functional as riding aids and rarely elaborately decorated as in the past. Spurs with curved sides such as 50, though less common than in the previous century, were still favoured by some eighteenth-century riders. Spur 50 has the unusual feature of one terminal larger than the other. A spur with curved sides very similar to 50 was found with a straight-sided spur of the same type as 53 and 54, together with eighteenth-century pottery at St Cross,

Oxford (Oxfordshire Department of Museum Services, Primary Record Number 6648). The Oxford spurs are iron and both have stud attachments for the leathers, while the curved sided spur has a buckle similar to that of Battle Abbey 54. 53 and 54 may be a pair but one cannot be certain of this as several similar pairs may have been in use at the same time.
45. Jointed snaffle bit with possible traces of non-ferrous plating. Mouth piece of two sections joined by loosely interlocked ring loops. Each section is a round bar evenly curved along its length and tapered to become most slender at the centre of the mouth. The outer ends of these sections swell into solid concave discs through which the cheek pieces pass, flanked by the ends of the slender D-shaped rein loops. One rein loop is now broken off with half of one cheekpiece. The complete cheekpiece is a very slender straight bar, rounded and tapered with swelling extremities. Mouthpiece width 225 mm. Cheekpiece bar length 122 mm.
E35 795285.
46. Fragment of a snaffle bit, with considerable traces of non-ferrous plating. Of the same type as 45, consisting of part of a slightly curved, round section mouthpiece broken towards the centre, rigidly attached to the middle of a straight cheek-piece bar of round section swelling a little at each end. The junction of mouth and cheek-piece is flanked by the sides of the rein loop, of D-section inside with four flat outer edges coming to a central point. Length of mouthpiece fragment 60 mm. Length of cheekpiece bar 86 mm.
E42 802304.
47. Horse's bit. Consisting of:
786008A Two sections of a three part jointed mouthpiece. The first section is a slender bar tightly covered by eleven rings, graduated with the largest in the centre of the group. The central section is an arched port which joined the flanking sections by simple D-shaped loops. A flat triangular pendant 'player', its end pierced with two small holes, hangs from a ring loop at the centre of the port. The ring loop is now rigid like a spade, but was probably originally loose. A small elaborately looped link is attached to the mouthpiece ring next to the port and may have been part of another pendant, now missing. The upper part of the broken cheekpiece swivels on the outer end of the mouthpiece with the broken end link of a chain attached to its extremity No. 786012 completes this cheekpiece which is similar to the second unbroken cheekpiece No. 786051. The latter is a straight cheekpiece with short, flat upper part pierced for a rivet and, at its broader extremity, with a rounded heart-shaped loop. Surface decoration of three incised lines. A D-shaped loop is opposite the bar on which swivels the third section of the mouthpiece: a slender bar which has lost its encircling rings. The lower part of the cheekpiece commences with a square hole below which is a vertical bar of triangular section, the bottom of which turns back into a double-curled loop, pierced horizontally on its rear edge with a round hole for the attachment which held the rein ring. 786007

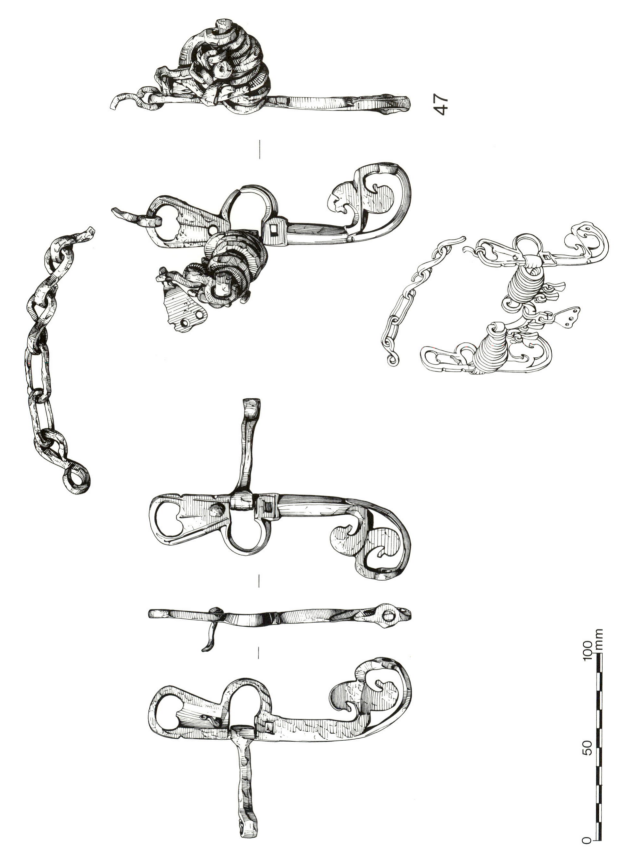

Figure 59   Battle Abbey. Iron object no. 47

Chain. Three figure–8 links twisted so that the opposite loops are at right angles to each other, next to two long oval links, beyond which is another, heavier, twisted figure–8 link. Measurements: Cheekpieces length 135 mm. Jointed mouthpiece width 150 mm, height of port 30 mm. Chain length 156 mm.
E42 786007, 786008A, 786012, 786051.

48.   One side of a curb bit. One long cheekpiece with a D-section bar gently curved along its length. A ring loop 25 mm diameter at the upper extremity. The lower extremity has a smaller ring through which is passed the base of a loose loop fitting, holding the thin pendant rein ring 30 mm, diameter. One section of a jointed mouthpiece swivels on to the cheekpiece; it is of round section, slightly curved along its length and tapered to about half thickness at the broken loop from which the rest of the mouthpiece is missing. Possible traces of non ferrous plating. Cheekpiece length 187 mm. Section of mouthpiece width 83 mm. Bits of this type appear in military paintings of the first half of the nineteenth century.
E35 795196.

49.   Curb chain from a horse's bit. Consisting of links forming a dense flat chain of the kind still used today. At one end of the chain is an elongated evenly curved attachment with a closed ring at one end and an open ring at the other. At the opposite end of the chain are two loose links. Length (extended) about 185 mm. (The chain has now solidified into a curve).
E42 795332.

50.   Rowel spur. The sides, of D-section, curve under the wearer's ankle. Figure–8 terminals, one larger than the other. There is a double moulding at the commencement of the short, slender neck. This is divided for most of the length by the rowel box which is slightly down-curved. Rowel pin and rowel missing. Length overall 120 mm. Length of neck 30 mm. Length of rowel box 25 mm. The difference in size of the terminals is unusual.
E42 786029.

51.   Rowel spur, with straight D-section tapered sides becoming very slender next to the one remaining evenly set figure–8 terminal. Terminal end of the other side missing. Short, straight neck projects slightly downward from the moulding behind the heel; the rowel box divides most of its length. Rowel pin remains but rowel gone. Length overall 110 mm. Length of neck 22 mm. Length of rowel box 19 mm.
E42 786000.

52.   Rowel spur, D-section straight sides, terminal end of one missing. The complete side tapered to become very slender next to the evenly set figure-8 terminal, which retains fragments of two attachments for the leathers. The commencement of the neck is moulded and encircled by an incised line. The slender rowel box divides most of the neck and although mainly straight, droops very slightly. Small star rowel of six sharp points. Length overall (excluding rowel) 110 mm. Length of neck 26 mm. Rowel diameter 23 mm.
E47 786003.

53.   Rowel spur, of slender proportions. Straight D-section sides tapered towards the small rectangular terminals which have double horizontal slots. One stud attachment for a leather. Short, fairly straight neck tapers to become very slender next to the unusual D-shaped rowel boss (one rowel boss is missing). Part of rowel pin remains, rowel missing. Length overall 116 mm. Length of neck 26 mm. Length of rowel box 18 mm. Span originally about 80 mm, (the sides now distorted).
D23 786036.

54.   Rowel spur. Identical to no 53. The terminal end of one side is missing. The rowel box is twisted and the rowel lost. The complete terminal has one stud attachment for a leather; also the small buckle, its frame with one square and one rounded side. Overall length (now distorted) 119 mm.
E42 786032.

Miscellaneous

55.   Eight petalled stud with rounded petals.
D21 796112.

56.   Iron canister with close fitting lid, lined with another tube. Made of milled iron sheet. Perforated with lead shot, seemingly air gun pellet. Milled iron, lack of corrosion and precise form indicate a modern date, nineteenth to twentieth century. Remains of illegible lettering.
E38 795141. Not illustrated.

57.   Hooked, spiked object.
E37 802432.

58.   Nails are found scattered throughout the site. They are mostly in poor condition and generally only identifiable under X-ray. Because such a large proportion are broken it was not considered helpful either to measure or count them. However two particularly large concentrations were excavated: 3.25 kg from D21 and 10 kg from D22. These were clearly associated with the stripping or collapse of the roof.

The large amount of uncatalogued ironwork was either in an extremely fragmentary condition or unidentifiable, even from X-rays.

The Slags *by Justine Bayley*

The total weight of slag (AML 811655) submitted for examination was only 2–3 kg.. A wide variety of origins were identified. A few pieces were analysed qualitatively by X-ray fluorescence but the majority were only examined as hand specimens. A full list of identifications is included with the excavation records.

The majority of the slag was produced in iron smelting operations. There was evidence of two different processes, in the iron-rich tap slag and the low-iron blast furnace slag. Most of the iron slag was of the former type, and this iron-rich slag was found in layers from all periods from the thirteenth century onwards (periods B–E), although mainly from medieval and Dissolution contexts. The low-iron type represents an improved technology as a higher proportion of the iron in the ore was recovered as metal, but the resulting slag has a higher free running temperature and so the process requires

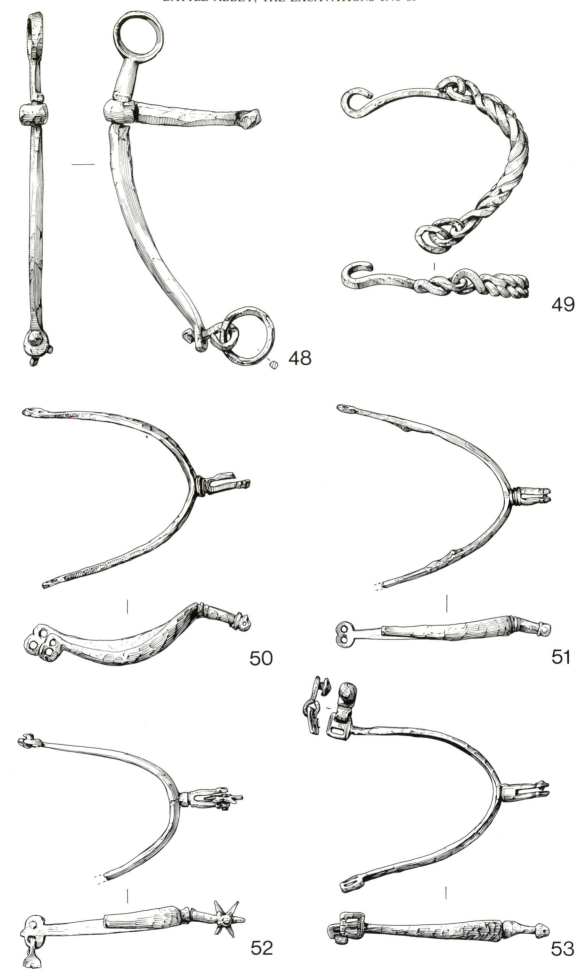

Figure 60   Battle Abbey. Iron objects nos. 48–53 ($\frac{1}{2}$)

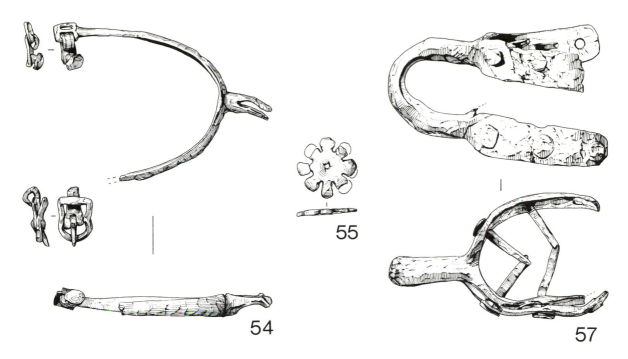

Figure 61   Battle Abbey. Iron objects nos. 54–57 ($\frac{1}{2}$)

higher furnace temperatures which were not obtainable until the post-medieval period. At Battle, it first appears in phase D24, and in a layer dating from the seventeenth century. The relatively small quantities of smelting slag found could be interpreted as imports to the site. Far larger amounts of slag would have been expected if the smelting was being done on the site itself. The Weald was well known as an iron-producing area in the sixteenth to eighteenth centuries (and earlier), while in the locality, there was a furnace at Beech in Netherfield and within Battle Park there was a mill and ironworks (Straker 1931, 325, 350–1). Local sources of iron slag, which might have been used for hard core or for road metalling, were thus available.

There were also a few examples suggesting the smithing of iron and the melting of other metals, both copper alloy and lead. This would probably have been at the Dissolution, although the copper-rich examples come from post-Dissolution contexts. The remainder of the slags are accidentally produced and might have been associated with the destruction of buildings.

Acknowledgements
I would like to thank John Cherry, John Clark, Sandy Heslop, Dr Barry Knight, Howard Nixon, Neil Stratford and Jim Thorn for their valuable comments on the small finds.

Stone Objects *by J.N. Hare*

The Inscribed Slates
The excavations produced eight inscribed fragments of slate, all of which came from phases D21 and D22, the Dissolution debris to the north of the reredorter. Seven of these fragments were of reused roof slates, and were of Norden slate from South Devon (*supra* Chapter III). Three of them still showed the hole by which the slate was hung. Some had small patches of fine mortar, such as would have been used to bed the slates, and two fragments show circular rust accretions such as could have resulted from contact with the head of the nail that held the slate below. The inscriptions consist of simple patterns of lines, letters and words and have been scratched to a very shallow depth, so that the precise meaning is often unclear. Most of them seem to represent graffiti with no clear meaning: an individual word or letter rather than anything coherent. They seem most suitably interpreted as the produce of doodling by one of those involved in the post-Dissolution clearance, using the roof debris that lay at hand.

One inscribed slate was, however, very different from these reused roof slates. This was from a different source from all the other medieval slates, which were from South Devon, and had been finely finished for use as a writing and music slate, with smoothly finished edges meeting at a right-angled corner and with smooth flat surfaces on either side. On one side the slate had been engraved with the ruled lines of the music stave. Three of the staves possessed their full width of five lines, and another had been broken so that fragments of only three of the lines survived. The surviving portion of the slate is 82 by 68 mm, the longer surviving dimension being originally horizontal. The inscription is on the opposite face to the staves and seems to be virtually complete except for one small breakage. It seems to have been written after the slate had been broken, for the inscription follows the line of the break rather than the axis of the original slate. It seems to be an account of payments for five items, including for clouting of a pair of boots (2d), for ink (½d) and for making of the King William table (½d). There are also traces of an underlying inscription which follows the top (or bottom) edge of the original slate and so is at right-angles to the later wording. Apart from the inscription, the presence of this fragment of music slate in the same context (D22) as the pegs from the musical instruments is of interest.

There seems nothing in the handwriting of any of the inscriptions to make a Dissolution date for them improbable.

The Whetstones and Honestones

Six whetstones or honestones were found during the excavations. These were examined and identified by *Mr D.T. Moore* of the British Museum (Natural History). There were no examples from medieval contexts but four came from Dissolution ones, from the main rubbish build-up to the north of the reredorter in D21 and D22. Items in the latter context could be of monastic or Dissolution date.

Of the Dissolution whetstones, three were of Norwegian ragstone, which was the most common source of such objects on English medieval sites (Moore 1978, 64–7). This corresponds to Ellis type 1A(i) (Ellis 1969). Like the evidence from Bayham (Streeten, 1983) the Battle evidence does not support the view that the use of this material had greatly declined on English sites after *c.* 1300 (Ellis 1969, 182). Of the three micaceous sandstones, one came from a Dissolution context and was probably of Pennant grit, a sandstone from the base of the upper coal measures on the Bristol coalfield. The other two examples come from modern topsoil.

Two of the examples of Norwegian ragstone, possess a complete cross-section of the finished whetstone, although they are incomplete in length. Both examples have a needle sharpening groove running part of their length. Their association in the same contexts with the parchment prickers may be significant.

1. Whetstone of micaceous sandstone. Similar to nineteenth-century scythestone from Telacre quarry, Flint. Coal measures sandstone. (In two pieces, 220 mm long and up to 45 mm in diameter).
E47 811668.
2. Honestone of micaceous sandstone of unknown provenance, perhaps of coal measures sandstone. (Dimensions 80 x 45 x 25 mm).
E47 811669.
3. Whetstone of Norwegian ragstone (Eidsborg, Telemark, Norway). A small fragment (50 x 15 x 10 mm).
D22 811671.
4. Whetstone of micaceous sandstone (probably Pennant Grit, Bristol coalfield). A small fragment with broken perforation (18 x 13 x 10 mm).
D21 811672.
5. Whetstone of Norwegian ragstone (probably Blautstein). Small rectangular bar with needle sharpening groove (77 x 19 x 10 mm).
D22 811670.
6. Whetstone of Norwegian ragstone (probably Hardstein). Similar shape to no. 5 and also possessing a groove (80 x 15 x 12 mm).
D21 811675.
7. An elongated water-worn siltstone pebble from the main Dissolution rubbish dump. This is not a local material and might have been used as a burnisher or hone (94 x 45 x 115 mm).
D22 811674.

The Clay Tobacco Pipes

Altogether 137 fragments of clay tobacco pipe were found during the main excavations and in those on the dormitory floor, of which the vast majority consisted of unidentifiable stem fragments. They have all been examined by *Mr D.R. Atkinson.* His comments have been lodged with the site records, and have provided the basis for this summary, which concentrates on the marked bowls and pieces, and with the general dating of the materials.

The largest number of fragments seem to derive from the period *c.* 1690–*c.* 1750 although there was a substantial scatter, mainly of stem pieces from within the period *c.* 1750–*c.* 1900. The former period was one when most of the monastic buildings in this area were being, or had just been, destroyed. The pipe fragments probably both represent late use of the buildings, as with a group from the dormitory (trench C, which was adjacent to a fireplace) and their destruction, as with the group from the robbing of the northern reredorter wall (R VI F165). Both of these groups date from the period *c.* 1720–*c.* 1750.

There were no finds of early seventeenth-century date. From late in the century came a bowl of A and O (Atkinson and Oswald, 1969) London type 18 (phase E35). There were also several plain stems all probably of late seventeenth-century date.

Most of the marked fragments are of early eighteenth-century date. Four have a crown moulded at each side of the base, A and O London type 25 (phases D23, E38, E47, F49). This is a London form of marking in the first half of the century, but examples occur in Kent, Surrey and Sussex (Atkinson, 1977). Two fragments have the initials T/H moulded sideways (phases E38 and F49). Thomas Harman of Lewes (1697–1781) worked *c.* 1720–60. Such mouldings are widely distributed in Sussex mainly south and east of Lewes. One piece with initials T/W upright, A and O type 22 (phase E42) would date from *c.* 1690–*c.* 1710, and a possible maker would be Thomas Whitewood of Hastings (*fl.* 1693–1710, buried 1711). Similar examples are known from elsewhere in East Sussex. One bowl has the initials T/W sideways, A and O type 25, *c.* 1720 (phase D23); although this is an early example of the type, it is probably too late for Thomas Whitewood, but no other Sussex maker is recorded with the same initials. Two pieces have a crowned E/G moulded sideways. One is of A and O type 22, *c.* 1690–*c.* 1710 (phase E47) and the other A and O type 25, *c.* 1720 (phase E39), and are probably the work of a London maker. One bowl had a moulded Royal Arms (Atkinson and Oswald, 1980) with the initials I/P and of A and O type 25, *c.* 1740–*c.* 1760 (phase F49). These initials have not hitherto been found on such 'Royal Arms' bowls. It may possibly be the work of John Pain of Petworth (married 1733) though only plain bowls of his have so far been recorded. This is an early example of an English decorated bowl and the design is more usually found on the slightly later type, A and O type 27. A plain bowl and various unmarked stems also probably date from this period.

There were no marked fragments from the second half of the eighteenth century and only two pieces of decorated bowl of later date, viz. *c.* 1820–*c.* 1840 (phase E42). There were a large number of fragments of pipe stem from the period *c.* 1750–*c.* 1900, but after the earlier date such stems cannot be dated with any certainty at all.

Chapter XI

Coins and Jettons

by Marion M. Archibald

Some of the coins and jettons are in very worn, corroded or fragmentary condition and so full classification has not been possible in all cases. The dates of deposition suggested for the coins are based principally on the evidence from hoards in which coins of comparable period of issue, denomination, weight and condition (before corrosion) have been included; some allowance has been made for the possible bias in favour of coins in better condition in hoards. These dates should be understood as the dates at which the coins were last in active circulation for most of them were, as will be discussed below, found in an undoubted Dissolution context. The dates ascribed to the jettons are those currently accepted, some of them noted on the find envelopes by the late Mr S.E. Rigold who examined a number of the coins and jettons shortly after they were excavated. The possible significance of the discrepancy in the date of the coins and the date of the jettons in the Dissolution layers on their likely period of issue is discussed below.

Coins
1. Edward I–II, period *c.* 1300–10.
Penny. Class X, later style. Canterbury mint.
Weight: 0.47g :7.2gr) Deposition: early fifteenth century.
D 22 801997
2. Hartard, Lord of Schoneck, 1316–50.
Sterling. Lise (Château de Lissem, near Trier) mint.
Obverse: hARS DNS DE SONEC. Crowned bust facing.
Reverse: MOn ETA DEL ISE. English sterling type, long cross with three pellets in each angle.
Weight: 0.62g (9.5gr). Deposition: *c.* 1350.
(c.f. Chautard 1871, No. 437.)
This coin has been bent double. Hartard's issue belongs to the generally later group of Continental sterling imitations which bear a crowned bust of the type issued by his neighbour John the Blind of Luxembourg. Hartard was charged by the Emperor, Louis of Bavaria, in 1341, with issuing coins of bad alloy. Although such sterling imitations were officially proscribed from currency in England, occasional examples are found in hoards and as site-finds.
D 24 796221
3. Edward III, 1327–77.
Halfpenny. Second Coinage, 1335–43. London mint.
Weight: 0.47g (7.2gr). Deposition: *c.* 1375–1400.
D 21 796217.
4. Edward III, 1327–77.

Penny. Florin Coinage, 1344–51. London mint.
Weight: 0.61g (9.4gr). Deposition: *c.* 1450.
D 20 785991.
5. Edward III, 1327–77.
Halfpenny. Florin Coinage, 1344–51. London mint.
Weight: 0.62g (9.5gr). Deposition: *c.* 1350–75.
D 21 796212.
6. Edward III, 1327–77.
Halfgroat. Pre-Treaty Coinage, Series C, 1351–2. London mint.
Weight: 2.14g (33.0gr). Deposition: *c.* 1360–75.
D 22 796214.
7. Edward III, 1327–77.
Halfgroat. Pre-Treaty Coinage, Series C, 1351–2. London mint.
Weight: 2.15g (33.1gr). Deposition: *c.* 1425–40
D 22 802006.
8. Edward III, 1327–77.
Halfgroat. Pre-Treaty Coinage, Series C, 1351–2. London mint.
Weight: 2.09g (32.2gr). Deposition: *c.* 1425.
D 22 796192.
9. Edward III, 1327–77.
Halfgroat. Pre-Treaty Coinage, Series E 1354–5. London mint.
Weight: 2.30g (35.5gr). Deposition: *c.* 1375.
D 21 796216.
10. Edward III, 1327–77.
Penny. Post-Treaty Coinage, 1369–77. London mint.
Weight: 0.84g (12.8gr). Deposition: *c.* 1425.
D 22 796191.
11. Edward III, 1327–77.
Penny. Period of issue uncertain. York mint.
Weight: 0.92g (14.2gr). Deposition: *c.* 1425
D 22 796215
12. Edward III or Richard II (probably the former)
Penny. Period of issue uncertain. York mint.
Weight: 0.69g (10.6gr). Deposition: *c.* 1450.
D 22 796197.
13. Amadeus VI, Count of Savoy, Italy, 1343–83.
Viennesi escucellati.
Weight: 0.57g (8.8gr). Deposition: *c.* 1400
(*cf Corpus Nummorum Italicorum* Casa Savoia vol 1, Rome, 1910, 28, No. 62) except Battle coin has trefoil stops. Owing to the acute shortage of small change in England there was an influx of small base foreign coins which served as halfpence, although their currency was officially proscribed. They are first mentioned in the official English records after the arrival of the Venetian fleet in 1400 and were nicknamed 'galyhalpens' (Spufford 1963, 132–9).

The majority of the coins which reached England in this way were Venetian soldini. From time to time other Italian and indeed Low Countries' coins were used and this half-penny sized coin clearly falls into the same category. It is only slightly worn and probably arrived with the first wave of 'galyhalpens' around 1400.
D 22 796215.

14. Henry V, 1413–22.
Penny. Type C. London mint (?).
Weight: 0.36g (5.5gr). Deposition: *c.* 1500.
D 22 796198.

15. Henry V, 1413–22.
Penny. Type G. London mint.
Weight: 0.79g (12.2gr) Deposition: *c.* 1430–40.
D 22 802000

16. Henry V, 1413–22.
Penny. Period of issue uncertain. York mint (?).
Weight 0.61g (9.4gr). Deposition: *c.* 1500
D 22 796196

17. Henry VI, 1st Reign, 1422–61.
Groat. Annulet Issue, 1422–7. Calais mint.
Weight: 1.88g (29.0gr, fragment only). Deposition: *c.* 1450–60.
D 21 802002.

18. Henry VI, 1st Reign, 1422–61.
Halfpenny. Annulet Issue, 1422–7. London mint.
Weight: 0.22g (3.4gr). Deposition: *c.* 1430–40.
D22 796187.

19. Henry VI, 1st Reign, 1422–61.
Halfpenny. Annulet/Rosette-Mascle Issue. Calais mint.
Weight 0.36g (5.5gr). Deposition: *c.* 1430–40.
D22 796193.

20. Edward IV, 1st Reign, 1461–70.
Groat. Light Coinage, initial mark rose, trefoil on breast, eye after TAS, Type Vc/b, 1465.
Weight: 2.55g (39.3gr). Deposition: *c.* 1500.
D 22 801992.

21. Edward IV, 1st Reign, 1461–70.
Penny. Light Coinage, Type VIII, trefoils by neck, 1467–8. Durham mint.
Weight: 0.58g (9.0gr). Depositions: *c.* 1500.
D 22 796194.

22. Edward IV, 1st Reign, 1461–70.
Groat. Light Coinage. Type VIII, lis by neck, 1467–8. London mint.
Weight: 2.71g (41.8gr). Deposition: *c.* 1475–1500.
D 22 801996.

23. Edward IV, 1st Reign, 1461–70.
Irish penny.
Weight: 0.35g (5.4gr). Deposition: *c.* 1475–1500.
D22 801989.

24. Edward IV, 2nd Reign, 1471–83.
Penny. Initial mark pierced cross but sub-type uncertain. York mint.
Weight: 0.35g (4.5gr, broken). Deposition: *c.* 1500.
D 22 801991.

25. Currency forgery of penny of Edward IV. Blundered legends, D in the centre of reverse. Copying Durham or Dublin mint.
Weight: 0.50g (7.7gr). Deposition: late fifteenth century.
Although giving the superficial appearance of having

been clipped, like many late fifteenth-century forgeries this piece was almost certainly struck on a flan too small for the dies. This matched the genuine coins in circulation, most of which were in poor or clipped condition. It appears to have seen little circulation before being deposited.
D 22 796188.

26. Charles the Bold, Duke of Burgundy, 1467–74. Double patard for Flanders, 1467–74.
Weight: 2.53g (39.0gr). Deposition: *c.* 1500–10 (Gelder and Hoc, 1960, No. 23–3). As a result of the monetary agreement between Edward IV and his brother-in-law, Charles the Bold, in 1469, the English groat and the double patard issued in the various Burgundian territories were declared to be equivalents and permitted to circulate freely in the possessions of both parties (Spufford 1964, 110–7). Double patards are occasionally found as site-finds and in hoards e.g. the Hartford, Hunts., hoard (Archibald & Kent 1974, 147) buried in *c.* 1509.
D 22 796195

27. Alfonso V of Portugal, 1438–81.
Chinfram. Lisbon mint.
Weight: 0.97g (14.9gr). Deposition: *c.* 1500
(Reis 1956, pl. 26, No. 21)
These coins occasionally occur in English finds e.g. the Hartford Hunts, hoard buried in *c.* 1509 (see in No. 26 above). Estimating the possible duration in circulation is difficult since the exact dates of issue of the different series of chinframs has not been established. As this coin is in somewhat better condition than those in the Hartford hoard, it is likely to have been deposited a little earlier.
D 22 801994

28. Elizabeth I, 1558–1603.
Three-halfpence, 1567. Initial mark coronet. London mint.
Weight: 0.54g (8.3gr). Deposition: *c.* 1600.
D 23a 785990

29. Charles II, 1660–85.
Halfpenny, 1672, 3 or 5 (date illegible). London mint.
Weight: 5.40g (83.3gr). Deposition: mid-eighteenth century or later.
E 47 785988.

30. Currency forgery of halfpenny of George II, later eighteenth century.
Weight: 5.91g (91.2gr). Deposition: *c.* 1800
Most of these forgeries of coins of George II were made in the reign of his grandson because of the shortage of official copper coins. The counterfeiting of copper coins, unlike forgery of silver issues, was not a capital offence.
E 47 802004

31. George III, 1760–1820.
Halfpenny, 1773. London mint.
Weight: 8.64g (133.3gr). Deposition: before 1800.
K 10 796220.

32. George III, 1760–1820.
Penny, 1806. Soho, Birmingham.
Weight: 18.67g (288.1gr). Deposition: before 1860, but probably earlier.
E 47 796219.

33. George VI, 1936–52.

Threepence (nickel-brass), 1942. London mint.
Weight: 6.79g (104.8gr). Deposition: before c. 1945.
E 47 802003.

Jettons
All jettons are copper alloy unless stated.
34.   English sterling jetton.
As penny type XVb, c. 1325.
Obverse: Legend replaced by alternate pellet and
rosette, bust crowned.
Reverse: Cross fleury to edge with I between
double-slipped trefoils in place of legend in each
quarter, crown above leopard's head in each quar-
ter. Usual incomplete piercing from reverse centre.
Weight: 4.83g Diameter: 14 mm.
D 21 801999.
35.   English lead jetton, early to mid-fifteenth cen-
tury.
Obverse: Sacred Monogram IhC within border of
closely spaced, curved lines.
Reverse: Cross pattée with pellet-in-annulet in each
angle within borders as on obverse.
Weight: 0.51g. Diameter: 12 mm.
D 22 796199.
36.   English (?) lead jetton, possibly later fifteenth
century.
Details uncertain due to corrosion.
Weight: 0.72g. Diameter: 13 mm.
D 22 796190.
37.   French jetton, mid-fifteenth century.
Obverse: lis MARIA (rest of legend illegible),
crown with AVE on band.
Reverse: (illegible) RACIA, cross pattée within
cusped quatrefoil.
Weight: 3.63g Diameter: 28 mm.
D 30 796209.
38.   French jetton, later fifteenth century.
Obverse: +LE CONTE VRAI TROVVERES,
flower stops, shield of France ancient with eight
small cusps to inner circle, a trefoil in each.
Reverse: Cross fleur-de-lisée with quatrefoil in cen-
tre with fleur-de-lis in each angle, an m between two
small crosses at edge in each angle (one cross
omitted and one duplicated).
Weight: 3.83g. Diameter: 27mm
D22 796200.
39.   French jetton, late fifteenth century.
Obverse: +GETES SANS FALIR, star stops,
Agnus Dei.
Reverse: +AVE MARIA MATE, star stops, cross
pattée with a fleur-de-lis in each angle.
Weight: 4.77g Diameter: 26 mm.
D 22 796202.
40.   French jetton, late fifteenth century.
Obverse: +AVE MARIA CRACIA [SIC] CD, star
stop, shield of France modern, crown above.
Reverse: Cross fleur-de-lisée with quatrefoil in cen-
tre within fleur-de-lis pointed quatrefoil, three
broken annulets in each outer angle.
Weight: 11.84g. Diameter: 27 mm.
D 22 801993.
41.   German derivative of French jetton, late
fifteenth century.
Obverse: Illiterate legend:

+ANLCECICRIELOVRNN, shield of France
modern.
Reverse: Cross fleur-de-lisée within quatrefoil,
ermine tails at points, three pellets in each outer
angle.
Weight: 4.20g Diameter: 25 mm.
D 22 796206.
42.   French jetton, late fifteenth century.
Obverse: Illiterate legend: –SL (inverted) SLSLPA-
SA (illegible) SASL, some letters uncertain, shield
of France modern with cross between two trefoils
above.
Reverse: Illiterate legend: STERSISTSTSIEIS
(illegible) SMA, cross fleur-de-lisée within quatrefoil, small lis on each cusp.
Weight: 0.54g. Diameter: 23 mm.
E 42 796222.
43.   French jetton, possibly of German manufacture, c. 1500.
Obverse: X AVE MARIA GRACIA, annulet stops,
shield of France modern with three pellets at the top
and sides. Very rough style.
Reverse: Cross fleur-de-lisée with four annulets
around a central pellet in the centre, two As and two
Ms in opposing quarters within a quatrefoil, a rosette between two annulets in each outer angle.
Weight: 5.18g. Diameter: 29 mm.
D 22 802007
44.   German jetton. c. 1500.
Obverse: Star AVE MARIA GRACIA, triple
annulet stops, crown with trefoil between two
annulets on band.
Reverse: Cross fleur-de-lisée with rosette in centre
and an A in each angle, all within a quatrefoil with
an A in each outer angle.
Weight: 3.52g. Diameter: 27 mm.
D 22 801995.
45.   French jetton, c. 1500.
Obverse: Illiterate legend:
+SADASVPASVANSVAPSAMVAI, crown with
three mullets on band.
Reverse: Cross fleur-de-lisée with quatrefoil in cen-
tre and an A in each outer angle.
Weight: 2.09g. Diameter: 26 mm.
D 22 796201.
46.   French-type jetton, possibly of German manu-
facture, early sixteenth century.
Obverse: +GARDES VOVS DE MES COMP-
TER, shield of France ancient.
Reverse: +GETTES ENTENDES AV COMPTE,
France modern and Dauphine quartered.
Weight: 1.82g. Diameter: 30 mm.
D 22 796205.
47.   French-type jetton possibly of German manu-
facture, early sixteenth century.
Illiterate legends, too corroded to transliterate.
Obverse: Crowned(?) fleur-de-lis.
Reverse: Curved-sided lozenge with rosettes at cor-
ners; in centre, fleur-de-lis over uncertain motif.
Weight: 1.53g. Diameter: 25 mm.
D 22 796207.
48.   French jetton, early sixteenth century.
Too corroded to distinguish details of legend or type
except that obverse has shield of France modern.

Weight: 0.47g. Diameter: 20 mm.
D 22 796203.

49. German jetton, early sixteenth century.
Obverse: Illiterate legend: ORABVMIINDORP-
BVMPPIN, reichsapfel in cartouche.
Reverse: Illiterate legend: MAPOIVMPAVICM-
VOIDNOV, three crowns and three lis.
Weight: 1.13g. Diameter: 23 mm
D 22 796208.

50. German jetton, early sixteenth century.
Obverse: VOLGVE LA GALLEE DE FRANCE,
ship.
Reverse: VIVE LE BON ROI DE FRAN, crown
initial mark, lozenge of France ancient with a trefoil
between two annulets between each side and the
inner circle.
Weight: 1.50g. Diameter: 24 mm.
D 22 796204.

51. German jetton, early sixteenth century.
Obverse: Trefoil AVE MAR ( ) quatrefoil GRA-
CIA VD, shield of France modern. Very crude style.
Reverse: Cross fleur-de-lisée with four-petalled
flower in centre and at points of surrounding quatre-
foil.
Weight: 2.90g. Diameter: 27 mm.
D 21 802990.

52. German jetton, early sixteenth century.
Obverse: Illiterate legend: ( ) VTIIIMRGVS ( ),
star and triple-annulet stops, shield with dolphin
head and star in each half bendy.
Reverse: Legend replaced by alternate Ss and stars,
three fleur-de-lis and three groups of three annulets.
Weight: 1.04 g. Diameter: 20 mm.
D 22 801990.

53. German jetton, early sixteenth century.
Obverse: +AVE MRIA GRACIA ( ), moor's
head to right, head bound with a fillet.
Reverse: +AVE MARI, voided cross fleur-de-lisée
with fleur-de-lis in centre, a rosette in each cusp and
a small cross at each side of lis at cross ends.
Weight: 1.70g. Diameter: 20 mm.
D 22 801998.

54. German jetton, early sixteenth century.
Obverse: Illiterate legend: AVRARAVARAVAR-
AVARAVA ( ), lozenge shield of France ancient.
Reverse: Illiterate legend as on obverse, cross fleury
with fleur-de-lis in each angle.
Weight: 2.92g. Diameter: 28 mm.
D 34 802005.

55. German jetton, early sixteenth century.
Obverse: Illiterate legend:
NVNBINNN NV IVHNVNR, double annulet stops
in intervals of legend, reichsapfel in cartouche.
Reverse: Illiterate   legend:
BGNBGNSNGBVNGBNGN,
three fleur-de-lis and three crowns with three
annulets.
Weight: 1.47g. Diameter: 24 mm
D 22 796213.

56. German jetton, late sixteenth century. Hans
Krauwinckel of Nuremberg.
Obverse: HANS KRAVWINCKEL GOTESS, [sic]
three crowns and three fleur-de-lis around rosette, a
quatrefoil at each side of crown.

Reverse: RECHEN PFENIG NVRENBER, reichsapfel in cartouche with a quatrefoil at each side of
the three points.
Weight: 1.32g. Diameter: 25 mm.
E 42 785980.

57. German jetton, c. 1600.
Hans Krauwinckel of Nuremberg.
Obverse: HANNS KR(AVWIN)CKEL IN NV:,
reichsapfel in cartouche.
Reverse: (GOTES) SEGEN MACHT REC, three
crowns and three fleur-de-lis around rosette
Weight: 1.03g. Diameter: 22 mm.
D 23a 785987.

58. and 59. ? 'Home-made' jettons.
Weight: 3.88g. Diameter: 27 mm.
Weight: 4.84g. Diameter: 27 mm.
These two pieces were made in the same way:
hand-cut from sheet copper/bronze with the edge
slightly bevelled to one side. Although No. 58
especially is rather too corroded for much of the
original surface of one side to survive, they do not
appear to have had a design on either side. As they
are about the same size and aspect as jettons, they
were perhaps home-made substitutes when more
jettons were needed and supplies were not immediately available. Dating is difficult, but perhaps
c. 1500.
D 30 796211 and D 30 796210.

60. Re-used jetton.
Weight: 3.76g. Dimensions: 27 x 21 mm.
This late fifteenth-century French jetton of the Ave
Maria gracia plena type with France modern, cross
fleury reverse has been cut down to a round-
cornered rectangular shape, pierced with a 5 mm
hole in the centre and has two 2 mm iron pins for
attachment. Its purpose is uncertain, possibly some
sort of escutcheon plate. The date when the adaption was made is also uncertain.
D 22 793289.

61. Similar to No. 60 but not made from a coin or
jetton.
Weight: 3.39g (incrustions on reverse). Dimensions:
25 x 22 mm.
This irregularly ovoid object with its round hole and
two pins is very reminiscent of No. 60 although in
this case the piercing is towards the edge rather than
in the centre. Date uncertain.
D 22 796189.

62. Re-used jetton.
Weight: 3.19g. Diameter: 29 mm.
This piece is pierced and so dented that little of the
original type is visible. It looks like a jetton of c.
1500. It is pierced all over but while one hole at the
edge looks purposeful, the rest are of a different
character and appear accidental, the result of some
other process. Date and purpose of adaption uncertain.
D 22 802008

Note on the Coins and Jettons from Dissolution Contexts
Out of the total of sixty-one pieces (one non-
numismatic item, No. 61, excluded), twenty-six coins
and twenty-one jettons (including re-used jettons)

were found in secure Dissolution contexts (D20, 21 and 22). Of these no fewer than twenty-one coins and nineteen jettons came from a single phase. D 22. The coins present in the layers were as follows (foreign coins being counted in the reign of the contemporary English monarch):

Period of:–	D20	D21	D22	Total
Edward I–II	–	–	1	1
Edward III	1	3	6	10
Henry IV	–	–	1	1
Henry V	–	–	3	3
Henry VI	–	1	2	3
Edward IV	–	–	8	8
TOTAL	1	4	21	26

The tokens present were as follows:

	D20	D21	D22	Total
14th century	–	1	–	1
Early-mid-15th century	–	–	1	1
Late 15th century	–	–	6	6
c. 1500	–	–	4	4
Early 16th century	–	1	8	9
TOTAL		2	19	21

The coins present are not what would have been expected had they been taken from those in circulation at or shortly before the Dissolution in 1538. There are no coins struck after c. 1475, (the only possible exception being the forgery of Edward IV whose issue is difficult to date precisely). There are no representatives of the coins of Henry VII such as the half-groats of Canterbury and the sovereign-type pennies both of which were struck in huge quantities and are present in large numbers in contemporary hoards. Neither are there any coins of the earlier issues of Henry VIII. Hoards buried in the earlier part of the reign of Henry VIII include some pre-Tudor coins but the great majority were struck after 1485. It is scarcely conceivable, given the high level of mint-output between 1485 and 1538, that there should not be a single coin from that half-century of production present among a sample of twenty-six coins. Even allowing for the possibility that some hoards can be biased in favour of recent coins in good condition, it is unlikely that they consistently, and so grossly, underestimate the survival of medieval coins as would have to be the case if the coins from Battle were abstracted from currency in 1538. Furthermore the appearance and weight of the individual specimens does not suggest that they had

been in circulation as late as this. In general, their condition suggests that the most recent deposits among them were made c. 1500. Some are likely to have ceased to be current much earlier (cf the deposition dates for some of the coins of Edward III suggested above). The reduction in the standard weight of the silver coinage in 1464 caused most of the earlier heavier coins to disappear from circulation. In particular, the plentiful issues of Edward III which had continued to be present in large numbers in the currency into the fifteenth century are no longer found apart from the odd stray survivor in very poor condition, yet ten out of the twenty-six coins in the Battle Dissolution layer were of this period, some of them in fairly good condition. The coins in these Dissolution contexts therefore cannot have been a group of coins taken from currency at one particular time but probably represent losses, or abstractions from currency, made piece-meal throughout the fifteenth century, with the majority having last seen active circulation sometime in the period c. 1465–c. 1500. The coin-pattern would fit in with the suggestion that the Dissolution layers in this context are the result of a clear-out of possibly several different rooms which had included material from earlier periods.

The problem arises however that, if the currently accepted dates for the jettons present are followed, about half of them are datable to the early sixteenth century which would of course allow them to have been in use at or shortly before the Dissolution. It would be possible to argue that the jettons were, in the main, later than the coins and that some explanation for this might be sought in a change in use of the rooms concerned which involved the handling of jettons but not money or that the jettons were in use at the time of the Dissolution but the coins were, say, from a bag or bags of old coins which had somehow been deposited in those layers. The alternative which must at least be considered is that the period of currency of the coins and some of the jettons present was the same and that it is therefore necessary to look again at the dating of these jettons to see if they could not be of the later fifteenth century rather than of the early sixteenth century. In view of the difficulty in dating jettons this would seem a more acceptable possibility than to suggest, in the face of the overwhelming evidence of the coins, that the jettons are of the early sixteenth century and that despite their old and curiously mixed condition, the coins represent the state of the currency as late as the Dissolution.

Chapter XII

Animal and Plant Remains

by A. Locker
with contributions by N.J. Armes,
M.A. Girling, C.A. Keepax and
P.J. Paradine

Three thousand eight-hundred and seventy-seven mammal, bird and fish bones were examined from the 1978–80 excavations. Bone from recent layers (eighteenth century and after) was counted on site but was not kept for examination and has not been included in any of the calculations. Archaeologically the material studied falls into two main groups: the material from the monastic period and that from the post-Dissolution period, when the abbey site was used as a country house for the Browne family. The monastic period has been divided into three with the great rebuilding of the thirteenth century as the central division (period B). Period A represents monastic use before this, and period C that of the later Middle Ages. Period D represents the post-Dissolution use up to about 1700 and has been divided into the Dissolution layers to the north of the reredorter (D21–22), other phases in the reredorter area (D28–30) and those in the chapter house area (D20, 23a, 24–28). In the case of the latter the figures cannot be complete. The thick rubbish layer within the chapter house (D23) continued accumulating into the eighteenth century and the bone material was therefore discarded in 1978.

Only eighteen percent of the bone came from the monastic deposits (i.e. A, B and C). The reason for this is related to the change in use of the excavated area. In the pre-Dissolution period these areas were part of the inner court of the monks and being an integral part of their living quarters would have been kept relatively clear of debris. Significantly most of the bone from these periods came from two phases when the ground level was deliberately raised in parts of the reredorter area (B7 and C14). Later, after the Dissolution, when the abbey was converted into a country mansion, the focus of occupation changed and these areas became peripheral to the main house and so much more debris accumulated. It is fortunate that the Cellarers' Accounts from 1275 to 1513 can help compensate for the paucity of bone from the monastic period.

Summary tables have been included (pp. 187–8) to show the distribution of species for each division of the site and the measurements are those used by Jones *et. al.* (1976). The recorded measurements are housed in the Ancient Monuments' Laboratory, while detailed tables showing both the species and the anatomies recovered are available in a fuller version of the report (Ancient Monuments Laboratory Report number 3612).

The Mammals

The following species were identified, ox (*Bos sp.*) pig (*Sus sp.*), sheep (*Ovis sp.*), horse (*Equus sp.*), fallow deer (*Dama dama*), dog (*Canis sp.*), cat (*Felis sp.*), rabbit (*Oryctolagus cuniculus*), hare (*Lepus sp.*), badger (*Meles meles*), hedgehog (*Erinaceus europaeus*), rat (*Rattus sp.*), vole (*Arvicola sp.*), and house mouse (*Mus musculus*).

Since the amount of material from periods A, B and C is so small it would be unwise to regard any differences between them as significant (see tables). However the trend from all three periods seems to imply that numerically pig was the most important species (29%), followed by cattle (21%), and sheep (18%) respectively. In period D although pig is still common, ox and sheep appear more frequently, ox forming 21%, sheep 21%, and pig 15 or 16% depending on whether the whole individual from D23a is included. It is difficult to know whether this represents a decline in the importance of pig or a reflection of the changing use of these parts of the site.

Butchery marks were observed on the bones of species that were eaten, together with a high degree of fragmentation. In all periods the vertebrae of ox, sheep and pig were chopped axially, there seemed to be no difference in the mode of butchery between pre- and post-Dissolution deposits, although there may be too little material from the early periods for any differences to show.

The main limb bones of cattle were chopped across the shaft area and also at the proximal and distal ends. Astragali and calcanea were sometimes chopped axially, and with regard to the pelvis, chopmarks were observed about the acetabulum. Knifecuts on some limb bones and ribs may be evidence of the boning out of meat.

Sheep limb bones were also chopped about the proximal and distal ends and the shaft area. Three femora from the post-Dissolution period showed overlapping knifecuts encircling the midshaft area, the purpose of these is unclear, but similar cuts have been found on sheep humeri in other sixteenth-century deposits at Nonsuch Palace (Locker in prep), Baynards Castle circa 1520 (Armitage 1977, 148), and St. Mary's Ospringe (Wall 1980, 239). The horn core of a ram was sawn off at its base.

Butchery of pig was less well defined, possibly because the animals are usually slaughtered before full maturity and evidence of butchery may be less clear on porous bone. However chopmarks were found on the shafts of humeri and femora and on the mandible in the area of the alveoli of the first molar and across the incisive area. The proportion of pig mandibles appears to be high, especially in the post-Dissolution periods, and they are usually heavily fragmented. Two metatarsals of fallow deer from period C showed evidence of knifecuts, as did two metatarsals from period D, while two fragments of antler from period D had been sawn. None of the antlers from the site showed any evidence of having been removed from the skull, some had definitely been cast so it is possible that cast antlers were collected for working.

A calcaneum of a hare from period D was chopped, and a knifecut was noted on the shaft of a rabbit tibia also in period D, as were the following: the humerus of a dog with knifecuts on the distal end, knifecuts on a dog astragalus, and two possible knifecuts on a cat ilium. These knifecuts on dog and cat bones could be evidence of skinning.

Very few remains of horse were found and these were mostly loose teeth.

With regard to ageing, only in pig were there enough suitable fragments of mandible for any comment to be made. Excluding the whole individual from D23a thirty-three mandibles contained sufficient teeth to be aged, only five of these came from the monastic use of the site. Seventy-nine percent of these mandibles appear to be over two years old. The stage of eruption has been calculated using Silver's old data (1969, 299) which although the actual ages may be inaccurate should give some idea of the relative stages of eruption. The whole pig from D23a was female (Armitage pers. comm.) and had all its teeth fully erupted and in wear, indeed some teeth were quite heavily worn, and using Grant (1975, 440–450) a value of 50 was obtained. However when taken in conjunction with the state of epiphyseal fusion which was incomplete, an age of around three years is indicated (Silver 1969, 285), which might suggest that the food the animal was eating was particularly abrasive. A shallow grave had been dug in which the entire carcase was placed, no evidence of butchery was found. Two ribs showed healed fractures, and there was slight collapse of the last lumber and first sacral vertebrae. The cause of death is not evident, but, whatever it was, this animal was considered unsuitable for eating.

A number of immature and porous bones, representing calves and piglets, were also present in the post-Dissolution periods and according to the Cellarers' accounts calves, piglets, lambs and kids were also quite common in the monastic period (Cellarers' Accounts', 18), but there is no bone evidence for the latter two. The best part of a sucking pig was the skin and ears, and of hares and rabbits, the saddle or back (Stewart 1975, 100).

Rodent and canid gnawing was found on some bones in the post-Dissolution deposits, which may suggest these bones were not immediately disposed of, but remained lying around for a while where they were chewed by dogs and various rodents.

Up to the time of the Dissolution the monks were able to eat meat as part of the main meal three days a week out of fast seasons, fish or eggs forming part of the main meal on the other four days (Cellarers' Accounts, 18). Much of the meat and dairy produce came from the abbey's own manors, but purchases were also made from Battle market. The Abbey bought both live animals and carcasses as in 1275 when expenses include: for beef bought 73s 9d, six ox carcasses bought against the arrival of the king 40s, a bull and three heifers 18s, eighty sheep for the kitchen 66s 8d, mutton 115s 3d, pork 3s, and one lamb 6d. (ibid, 41). Cattle and pigs are listed in the stock totals according to age and sex. Much of the meat was probably dry salted. Another method, used was green salting in brine overnight (the meat would last for a few days in the summer or a few weeks in winter) while for longer keeping it was steeped in brine for several days and then hung in a dry and smoky atmosphere; for consumption this hard salt beef had to be simmered in water with hay or bran to get rid of some of the salt (Wilson 1973, 87).

Note of the purchase of rabbits is often made, these are usually included with the birds; until the seventeenth century the term rabbit was used for a young coney less than a year old, also known as rabbit suckers or rabbit runners depending on their stage of development, and were very well regarded for food (Wilson 1973, 83), whether the cellarers' accounts refer to rabbits in this sense is not clear.

The fallow deer was counted as the second most noble game after the red deer stag, and the hare the fourth after roe deer, both are found in pre- and post-Dissolution deposits, but are not mentioned in the accounts. Hares and coneys could also be coursed on foot as poor man's game (Wilson 1973, 83).

The fragments of badger from outside of the reredorter were in far poorer condition than contemporary bones. Perhaps these had lain around on the surface for some time before becoming incorporated into the deposit. The remains of cat and dog are probably those of household pets, and it is interesting to note that the small mammal remains are all from post-Dissolution deposits when this area was abandoned for habitation.

The Birds

Four hundred and ninety bird bones were found; of these only 8.5 percent came from the monastic use of the site. The majority of bone came from the outside of the reredorter in the post-Dissolution period. The species are tabulated in table 2.

The following species were identified; domestic fowl (Gallus sp.), goose (Anser sp.), mallard (Anas platyrhynchos), teal (Anas crecca), pigeon (Columba sp.), ?swan (Cygnus sp.), buzzard (Buteo buteo), goshawk (Accipiter gentilis), woodcock (Scolopax rusticola), lesser black-backed gull (Larus fiscus), raven (Corvus corax), crow (Corvus corone), rook (Corvus frugilegus), jackdaw (Corvus monedula), blackbird (Turdus merula), ?greenfinch (Carduelis chloris), chaffinch (Fringilla coelebs), snipe (Gallinago gallinago).

The most commonly occurring species in the monastic period are domestic fowl, goose and pigeon. Examination of the accounts does not seem to add many other species, but these three are regularly mentioned, and seem to have been bought in substantial numbers. Large numbers of pigeons were frequently purchased from the manor at Alciston. In 1395–6 the cellarer purchased 12 swans for 20s and 794 pairs of pigeons from the manor of Alciston for 44s 1d (*Cellarers' Accounts*, 92), and in 1378–9 a pair of pigeons cost 2d (ibid 74), the purchase of partridges and ducks is also mentioned. Some poultry was purchased from London. There are some rather unspecific references to other birds that were bought, as in 1369–70, 'for cocks, hens, capons, chickens, geese and other birds pertaining to poultry bought this year £8 15s' (ibid, 62). In the 1319–20 account there is a reference to rabbits and birds bought for 32s 9d (ibid, 49).

In the post-Dissolution period both the numbers and the variety of species increase: many would have been eaten including mallard, teal, woodcock, snipe, blackbird, greenfinch (most of which were found in D21 and 22). A great variety of birds is known to have been eaten in the sixteenth and seventeenth centuries. Many species are recorded from Nonsuch Palace (Locker, in prep) and were nearly all edible. Drummond and Wilbrahim (1958, 61) list the birds that were fashionable in the sixteenth century and Stewart (1975, 100) says that birds and game were served whole for guests to help themselves, the best pieces were wings of birds that scratched, thighs of birds that flew and the white meat of larger birds such as goose. Only old game birds were eaten in the seventeenth century as the young ones were considered indigestible.

In London, the Company of Poulters was set up in the thirteenth century and it may be from one of their shops in the Poultry, or Leadenhall, or Smithfield markets that the poultry from London came. The tariffs of the Company of Poulters from 1274 and 1634 suggest that swan was the most expensive bird. Of the small birds, blackbirds were the most expensive followed by larks. A number of other birds are also mentioned and those found at Battle Abbey include woodpigeon, snipe, gull, mallard, finches and 'greenbirds' (Wilson 1973, 118). These probably provided some variety in what would otherwise have appeared to have been a rather monotonous diet.

The corvids were probably scavengers living close to areas of habitation; the buzzard was similarly known as a scavenger, and was common in most of mainland Britain until the second half of the nineteenth century (Sharrock 1976, 106). The goshawk was probably used for hawking, and was flown at such birds as cranes, geese, pheasants and partridges. It was a bird alloted to a yeoman, (Wilson 1973, 117), so it was not regarded as of a very high status for hawking.

Thirteen examples of butchery were found on the bird bones; these were all on domestic fowl, pigeon and goose, only two chopmarks were found, the rest were knifecuts. Three cases of rodent gnawing were found from the post-Dissolution period – these bones may have been lying around on the surface for a while.

The Fish

Handpicking and selected sieving produced 877 fish bones; the latter method gives the optimum chance of recovery. The following species were identified; roker (*Raja clavata*), eel (*Anguilla anguilla*), conger eel *Conger conger*), herring (*Clupea harengus*), sprat (*Sprattus sprattus*), Cyprinidae, cod (*Gadus morhua*), haddock (*Melanogrammus aeglefinus*), whiting (*Merlangius merlangus*), ling (*Molva molva*), tub gurnard (*Trigla lucerna*), turbot (*Scopthalmus maximus*), plaice (*Pleuronectes platessa*), and flounder (*Platichthys flesus*).

Sixty-seven percent of the bone came from the post-Dissolution deposits.

All the fish could have been caught off the south coast of England except ling whose range does not extend farther south than the northern part of the North Sea. Cod were caught in deep water using lines, while closer to shore flounder are caught from the shoreline to depths of 55 metres, turbot from the shoreline to 80 metres and plaice from 0 to 200 metres. These would be caught with a combination of lines and shoreline traps which trap flatfish as they go inshore to feed at high tide. Whiting are found in depths of 30 to 100 metres and haddock from 40 to 300 metres, caught on lines and in nets. Herrings and sprats would have been seasonally netted catches. Conger eels are often found on rocky shores which give them shelter, and are caught on lines. Further information on the habitats of these fish can be found in Wheeler (1978).

From the cellarers' accounts, herring seem to have been the staple fish for the monks. These are described as being red or white depending on the curing process. White herring was traditionally gutted and washed as soon as it was caught, left in brine for a day, then drained and barrelled. Red herring after being cleaned and soaked in brine for a short period were strung by the head on wooden spits and hung in a special chimney to be smoked for twenty-four hours (Sass 1977, 44). These methods of preserving herring were developed mainly in the thirteenth century; the Dutch method of the fourteenth century which was adopted in Britain involved soaking in brine before being barrelled in salt. The exclusion of air was the important factor as this causes the fat to oxidise and the fish become rancid (Wilson 1973, 33).

The cellarers' accounts show that the herrings were purchased in barrels or lasts, in 1306–7 . . . lasts and a half of fresh and gutted herrings cost £20 2s ¼d (*Cellarers' Accounts*, 47) and in 1351–52 five lasts of herring cost £26 (Ibid, 56). Each year many thousands of herring were pickled, salted and dried for the storeroom. The lean young fish can be dried; this was practised in Scotland around 1240 (Wilson 1973, 33). This is presumably because they have a lower fat content while young and are therefore less likely to become rancid. The herring fleets visited the south coast each year following the shoals.

Sprats would also have been seasonally netted being common in inshore coastal waters, and in their first year would have been exploited as whitebait.

The other main fish recorded in the accounts are cod and mackerel (although we have no archaeological evidence for mackerel). Dried cod was referred to as milvell, mulwell, or melewell. The term stockfish also usually refers to dried cod or other cod-like fish. Other fish mentioned include salmon, lamprey (for which there is never any archaeological record since this fish has no skeleton), conger eel, eel, sturgeon, porpoise, and dolphin. According to Stewart (1975, 100) porpoise counted as a fish, and therefore might be eaten by the monks on a fish day, but by the late sixteenth century the eating of porpoise had gone out of fashion (Drummond and Wilbrahim 1958, 58).

The market sources for all these fish are quite varied: Hastings, Winchelsea, Pevensey and Rye were visited by the herring fleet, where the cellarer probably purchased fresh herrings to be cured for the storeroom. There are records of fresh fish being purchased at Winchelsea, Hastings and elsewhere in 1306–7 for £75 (*Cellarers' Accounts*, 47), also of saltfish bought from Winchelsea in 1351–52 for £12 (Ibid, 56) and in the same year a porpoise was bought from Dengemarsh for 13s 4d (Ibid, 56). Fish were also sold at the gates of the Abbey in Battle itself, although what fish were bought by the cellarer was not made clear. Plaice from Winchelsea and whiting from Rye were esteemed in the fourteenth century, appearing in a number of household accounts, including royal households (Wilson 1973, 33).

Another important market that supplied the monks, and no doubt was just as important to the Browne family, was London. This was probably the source of ling. Examples of the fish that were brought from London mentioned in the accounts are: in 1319–20 for 100 dried milwell bought at London 63s 4d, for the carriage of the same 3s (*Cellarers' Accounts*, 50) and in 1369–70 for red and white herrings, salmon, sturgeon and others bought in London by the treasurer £14 9s (Ibid, 63). In the later fourteenth century, the accounts record frequent debts to London fishmongers, some of which were sepcifically for the purchase of fish.

The monks also owned some fish ponds (presumably those still surviving to the south of the abbey) and a weir at Peppering Eye, where fish could be caught and served fresh at table (ibid, 17). In 1275 at a cost of 2d the large fish pond was breached against the arrival of the King (ibid 42). Much was known about the maintenance of fishponds in the medieval period in Britain and although there is no evidence as to what was kept in the Battle fishponds, in Prior More's fishponds in Worcester in the sixteenth century (Hickling 1971, 119) the ponds were stocked with eels, tench, pike, bream, perch and roach. From the fish bone evidence the only fish likely to have been kept in these ponds are eels and possibly the cyprinid from the post-Dissolution deposits. Eels may also have been trapped in eel bucks (wicker baskets) stretched across the weir (Wheeler 1979, 61) or in free standing bucks. Baskets called fyke nets can also be laid in tidal areas as illustrated by Tesch (1977, 277). In the accounts of 1369 the purchase of both fresh and salt eels was made. (*Cellarers' Accounts*, 63). No specific mention is made of the tub gurnard which consistently appears in most deposits, although these are not especially favoured for food they are quite edible and were probably caught accidentally with other fish.

Some comparisons of size were made against modern reference specimens of known size and weight, but these proved to be unremarkable. Only two examples of knifecuts were found, both from the outside of the reredorter, on a cod post temporal and on a flounder inteahaemal. Two haddock cleithra from periods B and C were swollen, however this occurs so frequently with haddock as to be almost a normal condition.

I would like to thank Mr A Wheeler (BMNH) for all his help and for use of his reference collection.

General Remarks

Having presented the distribution of species recovered in Tables 1–3 this report has tended to focus on the importance of the species rather than their relative importance in the pre- and post-Dissolution periods. This is for two reasons, firstly as previously mentioned the change in the position of the deposits relative to the occupation area after the Dissolution makes comparison between the two from the aspect of faunal remains irrelevant. Secondly although the rule of St. Benedict forbade the eating of the meat of quadrupeds except in times of sickness, this rule was progressively relaxed after 1216 (Wilson 1973, 26). Although the ordinary monk may have eaten relatively frugally they were allowed to eat meat and the Abbot's household and their guests of varying importance must have feasted on quite luxurious items at certain times. So there is no reason to believe that all possible food sources were not exploited during the monastic use of the site. The cellarers' accounts are a testament to this, the exploiting of the manors, the purchase of goods from local markets, and the bringing of goods from London by sea down the coast, this being quicker than across the Weald. The goods were brought to Rye by ship and then by road using hired carters to Battle, or by river craft up the Brede as far as it was navigable (*Cellarers' Accounts*, 22).

If one accepts that the monks made the full use of their own manors and many other markets little change should be expected when after the Dissolution the Abbey became the country house of the Brownes; they would now receive stock and crops from similar sources. The Brownes, their guests and servants would represent the same varying degrees of status as the monks, their employees, the Abbot and his guests, so the information from the cellarers' accounts is useful for both, indeed little could have been said about the food consumed at the Abbey before the Dissolution had the accounts not been available.

BATTLE ABBEY TABLE 1
THE MAMMALS

	Period					Total	
	A	B	C	D(CH)	D(ER)	D(R)	
Cattle	8	18	54	77	303	68	528
Pig	16	31	65	102	206	31	451
Sheep	3	20	45	63	299	81	511
Horse	–	2	3	–	5	1	11
Dog	–	–	4	–	18	18	40
Cat	–	–	1	1	8	9	19
Rabbit	–	1	2	1	38	14	56
Hare	–	1	–	–	–	3	4
Badger	–	–	–	–	5	–	5
Hedgehog	–	–	–	1	–	–	1
Rat	–	–	–	1	3	–	4
Vole	–	–	–	2	1	–	3
Housemouse	–	–	–	–	11	–	11
Small mammal	–	–	–	3	1	–	4
Unidentifiable	8	48	54	99	452	153	814
Frog	–	–	–	–	–	12	12
Worked bone	–	–	–	–	1	–	1
Total	35	121	230	354	1374	390	2504

BATTLE ABBEY TABLE 2
BIRDS

	Period					Total	
	A	B	C	D(CH)	D(ER)	D(R)	
Domestic Fowl	–	4	9	9	42	8	72
Goose	1	1	10	–	38	7	57
Mallard	–	–	–	–	1	–	1
Teal	–	–	–	–	1	–	1
Pigeon	–	2	1	–	25	44	72
? Swan	–	–	–	–	1	–	1
Buzzard	–	–	–	–	9	–	9
Goshawk	–	–	–	–	1	–	1
Woodcock	–	–	–	–	9	–	9
Lesser b-backed gull	–	–	–	–	2	–	2
Raven	–	–	–	–	6	–	6
Crow	–	–	1	–	–	–	1
Rook	–	–	–	–	1	–	1
Jackdaw	–	–	1	–	11	–	12
Blackbird	–	–	–	2	1	–	3
? Greenfinch	–	–	–	–	2	–	2
Chaffinch	–	–	–	–	1	–	1
Snipe	–	–	–	–	1	–	1
? Crane	–	–	–	–	–	1	1
Wader	–	–	–	–	1	–	1
Corvid	–	–	–	–	1	–	1
Unidentifiable	–	2	10	10	173	40	235
Total	1	9	32	21	327	100	490

BATTLE ABBEY TABLE 3
FISH

	Period					Total	
	A	B	C	D(CH)	D(ER)	D(R)	
Roker	–	–	–	–	2	–	2
Eel	1	–	–	–	3	42	46
Conger eel	1	–	1	1	4	–	7
Herring	–	–	–	–	6	19	25
Sprat	–	–	–	–	5	–	5
Cyprinid	–	–	–	–	1	–	1
Cod	5	–	1	6	12	1	25
Haddock	2	1	1	2	2	–	8
Whiting	5	–	–	1	5	3	14
Ling	1	–	–	2	–	–	3
Tub gurnard	3	–	4	–	12	–	19
Turbot	–	–	–	–	1	–	1
Plaice	24	–	1	1	4	–	30
Flounder	–	–	–	–	1	–	1
Flatfish	3	–	–	1	5	1	10
Gadoid	–	1	1	3	4	–	9
Unidentifiable	227	3	10	92	132	217	681
Total	272	5	19	109	199	283	887

Tables 1–4: Key
A = Period A, Norman.
B = Period B, the great rebuilding of the thirteenth century.
C = Period C, the abbey in the later Middle Ages.
D(CH) = Chapter House Area (inc. the whole pig from 23a), D20, 23a, 24, 25, 26, 27, 28.
D(ER) = Reredorter Exterior, D21, 22.
D(R) = Reredorter, D30, 31, 33, 34.

Molluscs
by Nigel J. Armes

Molluscs from Battle Abbey sent to the Ancient Monuments Laboratory were identified and a minimum count was based upon shell apices. In addition shell fragments of oysters were recorded by the excavators on site, but these might over-represent the number of individuals. The totals of molluscs for each phase are given in Table 4. Two categories of species were present; the discarded shells of edible marine molluscs and several native terrestrial snails.

Molluscs first make a regular appearance in the cellarers' accounts in the fifteenth century, for example, the 1420–21 account reads; 'And as for ostres, berdys, welkeys and muskleys bought by the cellarer 9s 2d.' (*Cellarers' Accounts*, 110). The evidence from the excavations indicates that oysters, mussels and to a lesser extent cockles, were eaten prior to this period. No record is given in the cellarers' accounts of whether the shellfish was obtained locally or from fishing-port markets.

Only nineteen percent of the total shell was from the monastic phases of the site, a figure which reflects the post-Dissolution change in use of the reredorter and its environs. Evidence from the excavations indicates that the area underwent a period of decay during the Dissolution period, with accumulations of soil, discarded materials and rubbish. This change is borne out in the shell data; prior to the Dissolution, most of the shell was from edible species, while in the post-Dissolution phases edible species were still evident, (with an increase in the numbers of whelks), but there was also a component of small, typically calcareous grassland snails such as *Helicella caperata* and *H. itali* (calcicole species typical of short sward dry grassland), *Oxychilus* sp. (found in grasslands, cellars and derelict buildings) and *Cochlicopa lubricella* (characteristic of dry grassland) all of which might have invaded after the area had become neglected.

Shells of *Helix aspersa*, the common garden snail, were present in all phases apart from phase A. This snail is commonly found around human habitations as it has an affinity for the moist shady conditions provided by walls, water drainage systems and heaped refuse. Although this snail is edible and was eaten in Britain long before the Roman snail *H. pomotia* was introduced into southern England, there is no indication in the accounts as to whether this species was eaten at Battle Abbey. Evidence that they could have been eaten is threefold: they are present in appreciable numbers in the pre-Dissolution phases and are not, therefore, simply indicative of post-Dissolution decay; only large shells were present suggesting human selection and most of the shells were intact arguing against bird kills. The snail, however, would probably have occurred naturally in the area.

No significance can be attached to the presence of *Ceciloides acicula* in the post-Dissolution phases as this medieval introduction is a subterranean species which can burrow to depths of up to two metres (Evans 1972).

TABLE 4   SUMMARY OF BATTLE ABBEY MOLLUSC COUNTS

Species	Period					
	A	B	C	D(CH)	D(ER)	D(R)
Ostrea edulis L.	22	128	298	435	1124	433
Mytilus edulis L.		11	2		10	5
Buccinum undatum (L.)			1	10		3
Pecten maximus (L.)					1	
Cerastoderma edule (L.)		1		2		1
Helix aspersa Muller		14	16	9	49	8
Helicella caperata (Montagu)				18		
Helicella itali (L.)					5	
Oxychilus sp.				19		
Cochlicopa lubricella (Porro)				8		
Ceciloides acicula (Muller)				62		
CRUSTACEA *Carcinus maenus*					1	
TOTAL	22	154	317	501	1190	450

The Insect Remains

During conservation of two jettons from the primary filling of the main reredorter drain, beetle fragments preserved by metal corrosion products were observed on the surface of the metal and were examined by *Dr M.A. Girling* of the Ancient Monuments Laboratory (Girling 1981). On one jetton was a fragment of a Ptinidae, a small beetle usually found in foodstores, refuse and wood, which is often a household pest. The other jetton had fragments of a Staphylinidae, a widespread family of predators. Further identification was impossible because corrosion products obscurred the surface features.

The Charcoal
by C.A. Keepax

Sixty charcoal fragments were examined of which sixteen were recovered from sediment samples and the remainder were recovered on site during the excavation. This small quantity makes generalisations difficult, particularly since most phases produced isolated examples or none at all. A few comments are made here, the fuller text appears in Keepax (1984).

The burnt area below the pre-monastic soil line produced oak charcoal. In phase A5, the pre-thirteenth century layers in the reredorted area, oak appears to have been the most consistent find in the seven samples, but beech, *Prunus* sp. (cf ? blackthorn), ash, cf hawthorne type, subfamily apple/pear, hazel and/or alder and birch were found. The seven samples from D22, the Dissolution rubbish dump in the reredorter area, produced a different assemblage. Here, birch appears to have been most common, and other charcoal present included hazel and/or alder, oak, beech, willow or poplar, ash and possibly holly.

Seeds
by P.J. Paradine

Seeds from the following samples were analysed.

No.	Layer	Phase	Notes
7	RII 833	A5	Earliest fill of storm-water ditch (pre-13th. C).
10	P F410	pre-AO	Hearth overlain by pre-monastic land surface AO, date unknown.
13	L F324	D24	Fill of storm-water drain.
14	RII 841	A5	? Land surface, pre-monastic pre-13th. C.
15	Q 567	AO	Pre-monastic turf or soil line.
16	RI 859	A5	Ground surface before construction of reredorter.
17	RIII 230	D22	Main post-Dissolution rubbish dump at the junction of the dormitory and reredorter range.

TABLE 5   BATTLE ABBEY SEED SPECIES LIST

	Date	Pre-monastic		Pre-13th. cent.			16th. cent.	
	Sample No.	10	15	7	14	16	17	13
Agropyron repens	(Couch grass)	–	–	–	–	–	1	–
Ajuga reptans	(Bugle)	1	–	–	–	–	–	–
Calluna vulgaris	(Heather)	–	9	1	25	12	–	2
Cerastium sp.	(Mouse-eared-chickweed)	–	–	–	–	1	–	–
Chenopodium album	(Fat hen)	–	–	–	–	7	–	–
Cymbalaria muralis	(Kenilworth ivy)	–	–	–	1	–	–	–
Euphorbia helioscopia	(Sun spurge)	–	–	–	–	1	–	–
Gentianella amara	(Autumn felwort)	–	6	2	1	3	–	3
Glechoma hederacea	(Ale-hoof, Ground ivy)	–	–	–	–	3	–	–
Hydroscyamus niger	(Henbane)	–	–	–	–	1	–	–
Matricaria inodera	(Scentless mayweed)	–	–	–	1	–	–	–
Medicago arabica	(Spotted meddick)	–	–	–	–	1	–	–
Odonites verna	(Bartsia)	–	–	–	1	–	–	–
Phluem sp.	(Timothy)	–	–	–	–	1	–	–
Prunus domestica	(Plum)	–	–	–	–	–	?	–
Rubus sp.	(Blackberry)	–	–	7	–	12	–	–
Rumex acetocella	(Sheep's sorrel)	–	–	–	–	1	–	–
Sambucus nigra	(Elderberry)	–	–	2	–	28	5	22
Secale cereale	(Rye)	–	–	–	–	1	7	–
Sonchus asper	(Sow-thistle)	–	–	–	–	–	1	–
Stachys sylvatica	(Hedge woundwort)	–	–	–	–	15	1	–
Triticum turgidum	(Wheat)	–	–	–	–	–	6	–
Triticum sp.		–	–	–	–	–	1	–
Urtica dioica	(Stinging nettle)	–	–	–	–	5	1	–

Acknowedgements
The flotation and sorting of the soil samples was carried out by students in the archaeology group of Peter Symonds' College, Winchester under the supervision of John Bradfield of the Winchester City Archaeologist's Office. We are grateful to them and to K.E. Qualmann, the City Archaeologist who enabled this to be done.

Chapter XIII

Conclusion

Inevitably excavations on part of a well-known site are likely to build on and develop a framework that has already been established by previous scholars. But while the monastic plan still remains essentially that shown by Brakspear, the excavations have considerably deepened our understanding of the development of the monastery and its site. Occasionally new evidence has corrected earlier interpretations. It is now clear that the Norman monastic buildings were smaller than has hitherto been understood, that they did not extend far down the hill-side and that the round-headed arches of the reredorter drain do not belong to this period. It was in the thirteenth century that the monastic buildings were greatly extended, but this expansion did not see the replacement of the existing chapter house by a new building further east as Brakspear had suggested. It is now clear that the chapter house was extensively remodelled and that it was one of the first buildings to be rebuilt, but it maintained the plan of the Norman building until the Dissolution. The excavations have also clarified the situation to the east of the parlour, where the plan of the porch has been established and where Building Z now provides a much more likely position for the infirmary.

The excavations have also high-lighted points that were known before. They have reinforced our understanding of a problem bequeathed by the Conqueror to his new foundation: its hill-top site. We can now more fully appreciate the nature of the battlefield slope, the magnitude of the building works, and the unusual character of the reredorter operation. The excavations and further study of the standing buildings have reinforced our understanding of the scale of the thirteenth century rebuilding. For within little more than a century, almost a complete new monastery had been built: there was now a remodelled chapter house, new east, south and west ranges around the cloisters, a new eastern arm to the church, a new kitchen, and major work in the outer court. Moreover, during this century, the scale of the rebuilding became much more ambitious: the chapter house had retained its existing plan, but the dormitory range and the new eastern arm of the church represent massive enlargements of the existing buildings.

The scale of such works has implications both for the history of the abbey and for the architectural history of this part of south-east England. Professor Searle has written of the pressure of royal demands for money as an argument for the abbey revising the management of its estates in the thirteenth century,

but should not the pressures of these great building works have been equal or greater? The rebuilding of the monastery ran parallel to the transformation of the abbey's administrative and economic policies and no-where perhaps was this clearer than during the dynamic abbacy of Ralph of Coventry (1235–61). This probably saw the construction of the new dormitory range and part of the abbot's house, while it was also to see the abbey taking a much more active role in estate administration: buying up land in the *Leuga* and in Kent and East Sussex, and developing new types of records (Searle 1974, 113, 143, 144 and 147). The new abbey buildings may provide us with a further reason for seeing Ralph as one of the great administrator abbots of the period.

For much of the thirteenth century, Battle must have been a centre of major building work, but we know little about its architectural influence in the area around. Unfortunately the extensive destruction at Battle has been paralleled by that of thirteenth-century work elsewhere. Neighbouring Robertsbridge Abbey has been largely destroyed, while Bayham Abbey has only in recent years been receiving the attention it so richly deserves, and the lesser monasteries seem to have fared even worse.

The scale of the thirteenth-century building works meant that little further expansion of the buildings was necessary in the later Middle Ages. The excavations have shown, however, that work continued, albeit at a reduced scale: a new drainage system was introduced, existing buildings were renovated, a new building was added and the south transept apse was replaced. These changes may now be added to those that were already known from the surviving buildings: a new claustral range, a new hall and chamber block in the abbots' range, a new covered passageway in the outer court, and additions to the gatehouse range. All these would seem to be a product of about the last century and a half of the abbey's existence.

The excavations produced an extensive series of finds. The establishment of a datable sequence has allowed a study of the changing character and marketing of pottery and roof tiles from the late eleventh and twelfth centuries onwards, with groups from the late eleventh century, the mid-third of the thirteenth century, the early fifteenth century, the Dissolution and the seventeenth century. Since some of the contexts may be dated independently of the pottery, the dating of the Rye wares has been pushed back and the chronology of other local fabrics has been refined. The use of brick in this part of Sussex may also now be pushed back into the thirteenth century. Study of the floor tiles and roof tiles has shown the presence of later medieval re-roofing and re-flooring in the eastern range.

The finds have also produced information about the lost buildings elsewhere on the site, in the architectural details from the cloisters, the painted window glass, and the decorated floor tiles. Given that much of the abbey and particularly the abbey church is now destroyed and that excavation of the latter's eastern area is unlikely to produce much in the way of destructional debris, a great deal of the available evidence for its details will lie on the peripheries of the site as in the excavated reredorter area or in the Dissolution dumps in the outer court. Only further work will help to establish, for example, the significance for the abbey as a whole of the preponderance of late thirteenth-century window glass and the general absence of fourteenth-century material from excavated glass that had evidently come from several buildings.

The largest collection of finds came from Dissolution contexts and particularly from the rubbish dump outside the reredorter. This provides us with an extensive range of the sort of items that were around at the Dissolution: building and domestic debris, but also the remnants of the monastic life of prayers, of books and writing, and of music. But it also provides us with a cautionary reminder of the problems of dating material from Dissolution contexts. For as the coin evidence shows, material thrown out at the Dissolution may have dated from, and even been out of circulation, long before.

As on so many monastic sites, activity did not cease with the Dissolution. But although Battle Abbey now became the centre of a nobleman's household, the focus of the site had shifted. The area of the excavations had once been the heart of the monastic life, but now the centre had moved to the former monastic outer court and the excavated area was to find a new but much lower-grade existence as a farm or service area. Here, after a period of decay and in some cases of destruction, new buildings were constructed and old ones brought into service again. But even this use was to cease, and a second period of destruction was to follow in about 1700. Parts of the excavated areas were to witness short-lived periods of activity, and the dormitory itself was to undergo a final period of use in the early nineteenth century when for a time it became converted into stables, thus providing the last significant group of excavated finds, the horse furnishings. But essentially, by the eighteenth century the role of this area had become one of inactivity, and subsequently the ruins of the Conqueror's great foundation were to protrude from parkland, wasteland or ornamental gardens.

Appendix A:
A Group of Architectural Fragments in the Outer Court.

Four main groups of architectural fragments survive at the Abbey: that in the Common Room of the dormitory range (with an unknown provenance); a group of window and tracery fragments, probably from Brakspear's work and from the frater (left lying on the ground to the east of the parlour); the finds from the present excavations; and a recently rediscovered group considered in this appendix. The last three groups are now stored in the site stone store in two of the undercrofts of the cellarers' or guest range.

This last group was found in the medieval passageway from the abbots' range to the undercrofts of the cellarer, that now lies under the nineteenth-century library. It included a rich variety of architectural material whose importance deserves consideration. We have no direct evidence as to its source, but circumstantial evidence suggests that the material was derived from Brakspear's work in the outer court during the early 1930's. It had clearly been deliberately placed here on a pile of coal ash on one side of a narrow and what was to be a little-used passage. At the other end of the passage is the boiler of the house, and the material's deposition in this position may reflect changes in the fuel used and in the role of the passage that were consequent on the restoration of the abbots' range after its gutting by fire in 1931. Sir Harold Brakspear was the architect responsible for this restoration and he also carried out other work in the outer court: clearance of material from on top of the vaults of the cellarers' range and from the northern exterior of Sir Anthony Browne's new wing, repairs to the vaulting, and some work on the southern side of the range. All this can be established from photographs and drawings in the Brakspear papers (photographs and Battle folder).

For work in this area the passageway would have been a close and safe place of deposit. Moreover, the Brakspear papers include a drawing of the two paired capitals of Sussex marble in the group, in the same hand as the other record drawings, the work of F.G. Jones the clerk of works (Brakspear papers, Battle folder, and O.S. Brakspear pers. com.). They are described as 'Purbeck (sic) Marble Caps. Discovered'. The evidence suggests therefore that these finds may be ascribed to Brakspear's work, and since it seems unlikely that they would have been brought all the way from the claustral area, that they derived from his work around and on the cellarers' range.

In the light of this analysis, the architectural material could have derived from two sources: from the debris of Sir Anthony Browne's range, which itself had probably reused monastic material; or from the Dissolution debris that had been piled up to the north of the range in order to level the courtyard. This rubble may still be seen blocking the windows of the passageway and its ultimate source lay in the destruction of the abbey church and the adjacent buildings (*supra* p. 14).

Material such as this will need to be part of any subsequent and more detailed study of the architectural development of the abbey and the range of items has therefore been summarised. The fragments were washed and numbered (C.S. 700–746).

There is little clearly Romanesque material: a cushion capital, a moulding with chevron ornament and the interesting upper half of a respond(?) capital. The latter is in sandstone with a double scallop shape, decorated with scalloped leaves and leaf stems that flank a central 'dove' motif. A date of *c*. 1120–1150 seems likely. (C.S. 710)(plate 26).

Two double capitals of Sussex marble would seem to have ultimately derived from Walter de Luci's new cloisters built prior to his death in 1171 (*supra* **p**. 69). The water-leaf capital (C.S. 702) is identical in design to that from the excavations (figure 13, no. 6). The other (C.S. 701) provides a third extant design for the capitals of these cloisters. A broken base for a pair of columns such as would have supported these capitals was also present (C.S. 706 & 707)(plate 27). This, with its rather upright moulding and fluted leaf-spurs to the corner, seems a direct copy of Tournai marble bases. It is of Purbeck or Midhurst marble and not of the local Sussex variety that was used for the capitals. It should belong either to the cloisters themselves or to a similar and contemporary programme of work. A voussoir of approximately the same date (C.S. 718) may also have been derived from these cloisters.

There is also a group of keel-shaped mouldings in Caen stone, such as are familiar from the chapter house debris (*supra* p. 73), and which do not survive on any remaining buildings at Battle. The chapter house would therefore seem to be their likely source.

There is a substantial quantity of later thirteenth- or fourteenth-century work, of tracery, voussoirs and capitals. Most of this is not paralleled by the work of the dormitory range and seems to belong to a later period of construction. Sources in the church, frater or cloisters would seem to be likely. A fragment of the panelling of a purbeck marble tomb chest is also present (C.S. 700).

Plate 26   Fragment of a Romanesque capital (C.S.710: appendix A)

Plate 27   Marble base (C.S. 706 & 707: appendix A)

The fragments of post-Dissolution date include a cornice in Caen stone with a clearly classical design of about the second half of the sixteenth century, (C.S. 723) and part of the heraldic achievement of Sir Anthony Browne, the first lay owner of Battle (C.S. 721). The latter was also in Caen stone and consists of the lower part of the shield, including the arms of Nevill, Monthermer and Montacute brought by his mother Lucy Neville, and those of Browne, FitzAlan and Maltravers. It had presumably adorned Sir Anthony's new range.

The monastic material thus appears to be varied in date and provenance. At the Dissolution, the north range of Walter de Luci's cloisters may still have survived for we have no evidence of any rebuilding such as had evidently occurred in all the other ranges. If this indeed survived, then all the material of monastic date could have come from the chapter house, the church and the adjacent north claustral range; all these, moreover, were areas that were evidently destroyed after the Dissolution.

Acknowledgements:
I am grateful to Mr. R. Halsey for his comments on this material and to Mr. G.E. Elliott for his analysis of the heraldry.

Appendix B:
Other Recent Work at Battle Abbey

by J.G. and V.J. Coad, and J.N. Hare

The excavations of 1978–80 represent only part of the work carried out at Battle since its acquisition by the Department of Environment in 1976. Where trenches have been cut, the work has been observed and recorded or carried out under archaeological supervision. The records are being placed with the excavation archives and a summary is included here. Where relevant, the findings of such work have been included in the main report. This appendix summarises the work done between the start of the excavations in 1978 and June 1984.

The evident need to replace Brakspear's temporary 1930's protection for the dormitory subvault has led to a series of small scale studies and cuttings in this area. In 1979 a series of eight small trenches were cut into the dormitory floor to establish the nature of the layers and whether any parts of the tiled floor survived. The findings of these excavations have been incorporated into the main text. No evidence of the tiled floor survived. When the floor was re-covered and drainage incorporated in 1984, this was done without disturbing any archaeological levels.

In 1982 a small 1.5 m wide trench was cut to the north of the external stairway on the east side of the dormitory in order to establish the nature of the layers here and to see whether there were any surviving medieval levels associated with the foot of the steps. This showed that there was no indication of any such surviving medieval surface and, in the north-west corner of the trench, undisturbed natural lay only 0.06 m from the pre-excavation ground level. This lack of any substantial build-up may be a result of the Duchess of Cleveland's removal of destruction debris outside the Common Room (*supra* p. 42). The construction trench for the dormitory wall with a presumed width of 90 cm from the east face was cut into natural from 0.06 m from the pre-excavation ground level and its base had not been reached at 0.6 m from the surface. Its fill contained fragments of building debris, stone, tile, mortar, slate, brick, plaster and Sussex marble together with fragments of charcoal, glass and pottery. It should be noted, however, that the edge of the excavation trench bisected the doorway to the staircase and did not therefore extend to the wall itself. It seems highly probable that this deep feature represents the construction trench. The foundations of the staircase tower used a different technique. Mortar and stone footings extended 0.85 – 0.89 m beyond the wall itself at a depth of 0.53 to 0.6 m below the surface. The excavations did not

include the junction of the tower and the dormitory wall, but they do not suggest any reason why the two should be of different dates. The distinctive foundations are probably a product of the same problems as were found in the reredorter. The cutting of the necessary deep foundation trench for the dormitory wall had itself created an area of instability for the slighter buildings that were to abut the range. Thus the foundations of the reredorter footings were widened over the trench (*supra* p. 34) and here a broad foundation raft was laid. A modern drainage cut ran down the eastern side of the trench.

In 1982 a small 0.3 m wide trench was cut to the east of the third column from the south on the east side of the Common Room as part of an examination of the stability of the column. On the north side the natural yellow clay was reached at 0.08 m and on the south side at 0.11 m. A tile had been used in the levelling for the base of the column.

In 1984 a cutting for a new drain was made to the west of the dormitory along the line of the existing drain so that damage, and in consequence information, was minimised. A short section of a stone-lined drain was found, some 1.6m long and similar to those from the early fifteenth-century drainage system in the excavated area. The drain ran down the slope parallel to the dormitory. There was no evidence of the precinct wall but the trench was shallow and often in disturbed ground so that this cannot be treated as having any significance. The trench ran eastwards along the terrace path south of the reredorter and in what seemed to be a made-up ground consisting of clay and gravel. There was no evidence of the drain flowing south from a rainwater system (*supra* p. 37) but the trench may not have been deep enough for this to show.

On the eastern side a shallow surface drain was installed parallel to the dormitory range. Excavation for this did not go below the existing topsoil level, but at the bottom of the slope a small catch-pit was excavated and a drain laid parallel to the north wall of the reredorter. The catch-pit excavation recovered a small quantity of finds, including a few fragments of medieval painted window glass. The drain itself was held in the topsoil.

In 1982 a gas pipe trench, 0.45 m wide, was cut from the entrance in the precinct wall east of the court house to the west front of the abbots' range. At both ends the ground was too disturbed for anything to be learnt from the section. The intervening 23 m running southwards 1 m west of the hedge was examined, drawn and photographed. The cutting of the trench had uncovered a substantial stone wall in orange mortar with a width of 1.7 m and with an additional adjacent wall of compacted rubble for another 0.8 m. It ran parallel to the court house and 9.5 m south from it, and appeared 0.20 m below the surface (figure 2). It was similar in character to other medieval walls at Battle. It was evidently part of a substantial building and may have been associated with the range that preceded and lay to the east of the present gatehouse. To the south of the wall was about 2 m of mortar debris with the natural lying about 0.5 m below the surface. The layers and the natural began to dip sharply at about 23 m south of the court house, and at 24.5 m the natural fell below the 1 m deep trench.

Acknowledgements
The excavations in the dormitory floor were directed by Mark Taylor and those to the east of the dormitory by Vivienne Coad.

Bibliography

Unpublished Sources for the History of Battle Abbey
The extensive surviving medieval records of Battle have been widely dispersed since the Dissolution, with the largest group now in America at the Henry Huntington Library in California (H.H.L.), and with other material scattered in several English repositories. Information about the medieval records and about the later documentation is provided in Thorpe (1835), Swift (1934 and 1937), Brent (1973) and Searle (1974). Too much survives for a complete study of the surviving documentation to have been a realistic prospect. Attention was therefore concentrated on those sources which seemed to offer the greatest potential for the history of the conventual buildings and particularly for those within the excavated areas. Those examined are listed below. The American material was examined in the microfilm copies of the East Sussex Record Office (E.S.R.O.) and in the photostats in the Beveridge collection of the Department of Palaeography and Diplomatic, of the University of Durham (Durham). I am grateful to the archivists in Lewes and Durham as well as to the staff of the Public Record Office, the British Library and the Bodleian, for their assistance.

The two main Battle chronicles have recently been edited in a new edition by Professor Searle (*Chronicle*). The shorter chronicles and annals are in Bodleian Library, Rawlinson B 150 (part printed in Bémont 1884), and in B.L. Cottonian MS Nero D.ii.

Obedientary rolls: all the central abbey accounts and all the cellarers' accounts were examined but the Sacrists', Treasurers' and Almoners' accounts were merely sampled. Accounts have been dated by the closing Michaelmas, and run for the whole year unless otherwise stated.

Abbey accounts: 1347 (H.H.L./B.A. vol 80 ff. 48–9); 1352 (H.H.L./B.A. vol 80 f. 61); 1358 (H.H.L. vol 81 f. 3–4); 1365 (H.H.L./B.A. vol. 81 ff. 33–4); 1366 (E.S.R.O. Add. Mss. 4901); 1382 H.H.L./B.A. vol. 83 ff. 48–50); 1383 (H.H.L./B.A. vol. 82 ff. 23–4); 1394 (P.R.O./S.C.6/ 1251/1); 1479 (H.H.L. /B.A. vol. 90 ff. 29–32); 1500 (P.R.O. SC6/ Hen VII 1874); 1509 (H.H.L./B.A. vol. 92 ff 2–); 1514 (H.H.L./B.A. vol. 92 ff. 35–41; Undated accounts are H.H.L./B.A. vol. 92 ff. 69–71; P.R.O. SC6/ Hen VII 861, Hen VII 1838 and Hen VII 1875; and E.S.R.O. Add. Mss. 4900. The H.H.L. accounts were examined in the Durham photostats.

Cellarers' Accounts. Most are printed in translation in *Cellarers' Accounts*, and those that are only summarised there were examined in the Durham photostats.

The treasurers' Accounts in H.H.L. are in E.S.R.O. microfilm XA/3/20, and that for 1501 is H.H.L./B.A. 128.

The Sacrists' Accounts are in E.S.R.O. XA/3/21 and those for 1518 and 1521 are E.S.R.O. T.201 and BAT 17.

The Almoners' accounts are in E.S.R.O. microfilm X.A. 3/20 and that for 1520 is H.H.L. BA 208.

P.R.O. E.315/56 contains a rental and customary of Battle for 1429–30.

The site since the Dissolution. The grant to Sir Anthony Browne is E.S.R.O. BAT 269. The stewards' accounts for 1657–1710 are in H.H.L. and are on microfilm E.S.R.O. XA 3/13. The accounts for Sir Whistler Webster (1757–67) are E.S.R.O. 2751, and the accounts for work done for Sir Godfrey Webster in 1818–21 in E.S.R.O. BAT 17. Early maps of the site (c. 1720's and 1811) are in E.S.R.O. BAT 4421 f.12 and BAT 4435. Grimm's fine series of drawings of the abbey in 1783 are B.L. Add. Mss. 5670 nos. 64 and 72–88, Aubrey's notes on the buildings are in *Chronologia Architectonica* (Bodleian Lib. Ms. top. gen. C25 f.154). The printed details for the 1902 sale are in E.S.R.O. BAT 4511. A set of drawings of the abbey in 1791 by J. Carter is in B.L. Add. Mss. 29930, ff. 34–9 and 29943 f.58.

Sir Harold Brakspear's papers are now in the possession of Mr. O.S. Brakspear, to whom I am very grateful both for allowing me to consult and use these records and for sorting out the Battle material for me. The main Battle folder comprises plans, elevations and drawings; both working drawings and those prepared for possible publication. These drawings are the work of Brakspear himself and of F.G. Jones his clerk of works. A second group of drawings is mainly associated with the restoration of the abbots' range. There are groups of photographs, but no systematic photographic coverage. Letters (Battle Files) from 1933–6 and a notebook of 1933 were also consulted.

Published Works, Unpublished Theses and Ancient Monuments Laboratory Reports.
(The place of publication is London, unless otherwise stated. Periodicals have been abbreviated according to the C.B.A. recommendations, Council for British Archaeology, *Signposts for Archaeological Publication*, 1979.)

d'Allemagne H R 1968 *Decorative Antique Ironwork*, New York.

Ames H S 1975 A note on the recent excavations at Camber Castle *Post-Medieval Archaeol* 9, 233–6.

Amis P 1968 Some domestic vessels of southern Britain: a social and technical analysis. *Journal of Ceramic History* 2, Stafford, 1–35.

Anglo-Saxon Chronicle translated Garmonsway, G N 1972, Dent.

Annals of Winchester, Annales Monastici II, Rolls Series XXXVI ed Luard H R, 1865.

Anon 1874 Paving tiles from Frittenden Church. *Archaeol Cantiana* 9, 203.

Archibald M M and Kent J P C 1974 The 1964 hoard from Hartford, Huntingdonshire. In Stewart I, Problems of the Early Coinage of Henry VII. *Numismatic Chron.* XIV, 144

Armitage K H, Pearce J E and Vince A G 1981 Early medieval roof tiles from London. *Antiq J* 61, 359–362.

Armitage P L 1977 *Report on the mammalian remains from Baynard's Castle, Blackfriars, London.* Unpublished PhD Thesis University of London.

Atkinson D R & Oswald A 1969 London Clay tobacco pipes. *J Brit Archaeol Ass.* 32.

Atkinson D R 1977 *Sussex Clay tobacco pipes.* Eastbourne.

Austen E 1946 *Brede: the story of a Sussex Parish.* Rye.

Baart J et al. 1973 *Oppgravingen in Amsterdam,* Amsterdam.

Baker D 1971 Excavations at Elstow Abbey, Bedfordshire. *Bedfordshire Archaeol. J.* 6, 55–64.

Baines J M 1980 *Sussex Pottery.* Brighton: Fisher.

Barrelet J 1953 *La Verrerie en France.* Paris.

Barton K J 1963 Worthing Museum notes for 1961. *Sussex Archaeol Collect* 101, 20–34.

Barton K J & Holden E W 1967 Excavations at Michelham Priory. *Sussex Archaeol Collect* 105, 1–12.

Barton K J 1979 *Medieval Sussex Pottery.* Chichester: Phillimore.

Bayley J 1979 Skeletons found in the Chapter House at Battle. Ancient Monuments Laboratory: Report no. 2907

Bayley J 1980 Skeletal remains seen on a visit to Battle Abbey, August 1980. Ancient Monuments Laboratory: Report no. 3249.

Bedwin O 1975 The excavation of the Church of St Nicholas, Angmering, 1974. *Sussex Archaeol Collect* 113, 16–34.

Bedwin O 1976 The excavation of Ardingly fulling mill. *Post-medieval Archaeol* 10, 34–64.

Behrens L B 1937 *Battle Abbey under Thirty-Nine Kings.* London, St. Catherine Press.

Bémont C 1884 *Simon de Montfort.* Paris.

Beresford G 1974 The Medieval Manor of Penhallam, Jacobstow, Cornwall. *Medieval Archaeol* XVIII, 90–145.

Biddle M (forthcoming) ed. *Winchester Studies* VII pt II, Medieval Small Finds.

Biddle M 1965 Excavations at Winchester, 1964 third interim report. *Antiq J* 45, 230.

Biddle M and Kjølbye-Biddle B 1981 England's premier abbey: the medieval Chapter house of St Alban's Abbey, and its excavation in 1978. *Hertfordshire's Past,* 11.

Bilson J 1895 On the discovery of some remains of the chapter house of Beverley Minster. *Archaeologia* 54, 425–32.

Blair J et al. 1980 A transitional cloister arcade at Haughmond Abbey, Shropshire. *Medieval Archaeol* 24, 210–3.

Boston F 1977 Pottery Query (letter) *Vole* 3, 54.

Boyson A P 1900 On some encaustic tiles and other objects recently discovered at Lewes Priory. *Sussex Archaeol Collect* 43, 214–220.

Brakspear H 1907 The Cistercian Abbey of Stanley, Wiltshire. *Archaeologia* 60, 493–516.

Brakspear H 1916a The dorter range at Worcester. *Archaeologia* 67, 189–204.

Brakspear H 1916 *Proc. Soc. of Antiq.* London 28, 245–50.

Brakspear H 1931 Battle Abbey. *Antiq J* 11, 166–8.

Brakspear H 1933 The Abbot's House of Battle. *Archaeologia* 83, 139–166.

Brakspear H 1937 Battle Abbey, in *Victoria County History, Sussex* IX, 102–5.

Brandon P F 1972 Cereal yields on the Sussex estates of Battle Abbey during the later Middle Ages, *Econ Hist Rev,* 2nd ser 25, 403–420.

Brent J A 1968 Alciston Manor in the later Middle Ages. *Sussex Archaeol Collect* 106, 89–102.

Brent J A 1973 *A catalogue of the Battle Abbey Estate Archives.* Lewes, East Sussex County Council.

Brown R A, Colvin H M and Taylor A J 1963 *The History of the King's Works* I and II. H.M.S.O.

Brown R.A. 1981 The Battle of Hastings, in ed. Brown, R A, *Proceedings of the Battle Conference on Anglo-Norman Studies* III 1980, 1–21. Woodbridge. The Boydell Press.

Cal Pat Rl 1338–40 *Calendar of Patent Rolls, Edward III, 1338–40.* London 1898 H.M.S.O.

Cartulariam Abbathiae de Rievalle, ed. Atkinson, J.C. Surtees Society, 83, 1887 (1889).

Caviness M H C 1981 *The Windows of Christ Church Cathedral, Canterbury.* Corpus Vitrearum Medii Aevi Great Britain Vol II, British Academy.

Cellarers' Accounts eds. Searle E. and Ross B, available in two editions as The *Cellarers' Rolls of Battle Abbey, 1275–1513,* Sussex Record Society, 65, 1967; and *The Accounts of the Cellarers of Battle Abbey, 1275–1513,* Sydney University Press, 1967. (identical paginations)

Celoria F and West H W H 1967 A standard specification for tiles in 1477. *J Brit Ceramic Soc* 4.2, 217–20.

Charleston R J 1964 Medieval and later Glass, in Cunliffe B *Winchester Excavations 1949–60* I, 145–151. Winchester, City of Winchester Museums and Libraries Committee.

Charleston R J 1975 The Glass, in Platt C and Coleman-Smith R *Excavations in Medieval Southampton, 1953–1969* 2, The Finds, 204–226. Leicester, Leicester University Press.

Charleston R J 1979 Some aspects of 17th century Glass found in England, *Annales of the International Association for the History of Glass,* 283–297, Liège.

Charleston R J 1980 Vessel Glass, in Christie P M and Coad J G, Excavations at Denny Abbey, *Archaeol J* 137, 138–279.

Charleston R J 1981 Glass of the High Medieval Period (12th–15th century) *Bulletin of the International Association for the History of Glass* 8, 65–76.

Charleston R J 1983 The Vessel Glass, in Streeten (1983) 112–116.

Chautard J 1871 *Imitations des monnaies au type esterlin.* Nancy.

Cherry J 1979 Post-Medieval Britain in 1978. *Post-Medieval Archaeol* 13, 273–84.

Chronicle Searle E ed. *The Chronicle of Battle Abbey.* Oxford, Clarendon Press 1980.

Clapham A W 1955 *English Romanesque Architecture after the Conquest.* Oxford, University Press.

[Cleveland 1877] Anon [Duchess of Cleveland], *History of Battle Abbey.* London, private printing.

Clifton-Taylor A 1972 *The Pattern of English Building*. Faber.

Coad J G 1984 Battle Abbey and the Battle of Hastings. H.M.S.O.

Colvin H M *et al.* **1982** The History of the Kings' Works, IV, 1485–1660, part II. H.M.S.O.

Cook G H 1965 *Letters to Cromwell at the suppression of the monasteries*. Baker.

Cooper W D 1850 *The History of Winchelsea*. London and Hastings.

Corpus Nummorum Italicorum 1910, vol 1 Casa Savoia, Rome.

Cowdrey H E J 1969 Bishop Ermenfrid of Sion and the penitential ordinance following the battle of Hastings. *J Ecclesiastical Hist*, 20, 225–42.

Dawson G J 1976 Montague Close excavations 1969–73: Part I–A general survey. *Research Vol. Surrey Archaeol Soc*. 3, 37–58.

Dent J 1962 *The Quest for Nonsuch*. Hutchinson.

Diderot D 1763 *Encyclopédie ou Dictionnaire Raisonné des Sciences, des Arts et des Métiers*. Paris, Braisson etc. 1751–1777.

Draper S & Martin D 1968 The local brick-making industry. *Recologea Papers* 2.5, 54–8.

Drummond J C & Wilbrahim A 1958 *The Englishman's Food*. Cape.

Drury G D 1948 The use of Purbeck Marble in Medieval Times *Proc Dorset Natur Hist Archaeol Soc* 70, 74–98.

Drury P J 1974 Chelmsford Dominican Priory: The Excavation of the Reredorter, 1973. *Essex Archaeol and Hist*, 6, 40–81.

Drury P J 1977 Brick and tile, in F Williams, *Excavations at Pleshey Castle* 82–124. Brit. Archaeol. Rep. 42.

Drury P J 1979 Techniques of decoration and their distribution, in *Synopses of contributions presented to the Cambridge Tile Seminar, November 1978* ed. P.J. Drury, 9–11. Chelmsford.

Dugdale W 1846 *Monasticon Anglicanum* III. Bohn.

Dulley A J F 1967 Excavations at Pevensey, Sussex. *Medieval Archaeol* 11, 209–32.

Dunning G C 1945 An imported pitcher of the Norman period found at Dover. *Antiq J* 25, 153–4.

Dunning G C 1952 A lead ingot at Rievaulx Abbey. *Antiq J*. 32, 199–202.

Dunning G C 1960 The finial, in G B Leach, Excavations at Hen Blas, Coleshill Fawr, Nr Flint: Second Report, *Flintshire Hist Soc Publ* 18, 30–3.

Dunning G C 1961 Medieval chimney-pots, in *Studies in Building History* ed. E M Jope, 78–93. Odhams.

Dunning G C 1968 Medieval pottery roof ventilators and finials at Aardenburg, Zeeland, and post-medieval finials at Deventer, Overijssel. *Berichten van de Rijksdienst voor het Oudheidkundig Bodemonderzoek* 18, 209–25.

Dunning G C 1972 Medieval pottery louver from Winchester, *Antiq J* 52, 346–9.

Dunning G C 1974 Other finials, water pipe and louver, in M R McCarthy, The medieval kilns on Nash Hill, Lacock, Wiltshire. *Wiltshire Archaeol Natur Hist Mag*, 69, 128–31.

Durham B 1978 Archaeological Investigations at St Aldates, Oxford. *Oxoniensia* XLII, 83–202.

Eames E S 1980 *Catalogue of Medieval Lead-Glazed Earthenware Tiles in the Department of Medieval and Later Antiquities, British Museum* 2 vols. British Museum.

D'Elboux R H 1944 *Surveys of the Manors of Robertsbridge, Sussex and Michelmersh, Hampshire and The Demesne Lands of Halden in Rolvenden, Kent 1567–1570*. Sussex Record Soc. 47.

Ellis S E 1969 The petrography and provenance of Anglo-Saxon and medieval English hone stones, with notes on some other hones. *Bull. of British Museum (Natural History)*.

Ellison M *et. al.* **1979** The excavations of a 17th century Pit at the Black Gate, Newcastle-Upon-Tyne, 1975. *Post-Medieval Archaeol* 13, 153–181.

English Romanesque Art 1066–1200, 1984 Exhibition Catalogue. Arts Council of Great Britain, London.

Evans A 1942 Battle Abbey at the Dissolution: expenses, *Huntington Library Quarterly* VI, 53–102.

Evans J G 1972 *Land Snails in Archaeology* Seminar Press.

Evans K J 1969 The Maison Dieu, Arundel. *Sussex Archaeol Collect*. 107, 65–76.

Farmer P G 1979 *An Introduction to Scarborough Ware and a Re-assessment of Knight Jugs*. Hove; private publication.

Figg W 1850 Sussex Tiles. *Sussex Archaeol Collect* 3, 229.

Fingerlin I 1971 *Gürtel des Höhen und Späten Mittelalters*. Deutscher kunst verlag, Munich and Berlin.

Fletcher A 1975 *A county community in peace and war: Sussex 1600–1660*. Longman.

Fletcher J M and Tapper M C 1984 Medieval Artefacts and Structures dated by Dendrochronology. *Medieval Archaeol*, 28, 112–32.

Freke D J 1977–8 Excavations in Church Street, Seaford 1976. *Sussex Archaeol Collect* 116, 198–224.

Freke D J 1979 The excavation of an early sixteenth century pottery kiln at Lower Parrock, Hartfield, East Sussex, 1977. *Post-Medieval Archaeol* 13, 79–125.

Fry D K 1976 Anglo-Saxon lyre tuning pegs from Whitby, N. Yorkshire. *Medieval Archaeol* 20, 137–9.

Gaskell Brown C 1979 *Plymouth Excavations: Castle Street, the Pottery*. Plymouth Museum Archaeological Series No. 1.

Gay V 1887 *Glossaire Archaeologique du moyen Age et de la Renaissance*, Paris.

Geddes J 1983 Recently Discovered Romanesque Sculpture in South-East England, in ed. Thompson F H, *Studies in Medieval Sculpture*. Society of Antiquaries, Occasional Papers III.

Gelder, H Enno van & Hoc, Marcel 1960 Les Monnaies des Pays-Bas, bourguignons et espagnols, 1434–1713, Amsterdam.

Gem R 1981 The Romanesque rebuilding of Westminster Abbey, in ed. Brown R A, *Proceedings of the Battle Conference on Anglo-Norman Studies III* 1980, 33–60. Woodbridge. The Boydell Press.

Gilyard-Beer R 1958 *Abbeys* H.M.S.O.

Girling M A 1981 *Insect remains from Battle Abbey Coins*. Ancient Monuments Laboratory Report no 3376.

Godfrey W H and Salzman L F 1951 *Sussex Views*, Sussex Record Society.

Graham R 1929 The Monastery of Battle. In her *English Ecclesiastical Studies.* S.P.C.K. 188–208.

Grant A 1975 The use of tooth wear as a guide to the age of domestic animals, in *Excavations at Portchester Castle, I, Roman,* B V Cunliffe. 440–450. Society of Antiquaries Research Report.

Greenaway F 1972 Introduction. In S Moorhouse, Medieval distilling apparatus of glass and pottery. *Medieval Archaeol* 16, 79–88.

Greene P 1974 Norton Priory. *Current Archaeol* 43, 246–50.

Hadfield J 1981 The excavation of a medieval pottery kiln at Barnett's Mead, Ringmer, East Sussex. *Sussex Archaeol Collect* 119, 89–106.

Harbottle B & Salway P 1964 Excavations at Newminster Abbey, Northumberland. *Archaeol Aeliana* 42, 85–171.

Harden D B 1970 Medieval Glass in the West. *Proceedings of the VIIIth International Congress on Glass* 1968, 97–111. Sheffield, Society of Glass Technology.

Hare J N 1976 *Lord & Tenant in Wiltshire, c. 1380–c. 1520* Unpublished PhD thesis, London University.

Hare J N 1981 The Buildings of Battle Abbey in ed. Brown R A, *Proceedings of the Battle Conference on Anglo-Norman Studies* III 1980, 78–95. Woodbridge. The Boydell Press.

Hare J.N. forthcoming The monks as landlords, in eds. Barron C and Harper-Bill C, *The Church in Society in the Century before the Reformation.* Woodbridge. The Boydell Press.

Harmer J 1981 The use of Clay at Ashburnham Brickworks. *Sussex Industrial History* 11, 14–21.

Hawthorne J G & Smith C S eds. 1963 *Theophilus, On Diverse Arts.* Chicago.

Henig M 1974 in Tatton-Brown T, Excavations at the Custom House Site, City of London. *London Middlesex Archaeol Soc* 25, 117–219.

Heslop T A 1980 An ivory fragment from Battle Abbey. *Antiq J* LX pt II, 341–342.

Hickling C F 1971–2 Prior More's Fishponds. *Medieval Archaeol* 15–16, 118–123.

Hinton D A 1977 Excavations at Beaulieu Abbey, 1977. *Proc. Hampshire Field Club Archaeol Soc* 34, 47–52.

Hirst S M, Walsh D A, Wright S M 1983 *Bordesley Abbey* II. Brit Archaeol Rep.

Hohler C 1941 Medieval paving tiles in Buckinghamshire. *Rec. Buckinghamshire* 14, 1–49.

Hohler C 1942 Medieval paving tiles in Buckinghamshire (concluded). *Rec. Buckinghamshire* 14, 99–132.

Holden E W 1965 Slate Roofing in medieval Sussex. *Sussex Archaeol Collect* 103, 67–78.

Holling F W 1971 A preliminary note on the Pottery Industry of the Hampshire-Surrey Borders. *Surrey Archaeol Collect* 68, 57–87.

Holling F W 1977 Reflections on Tudor Green. *Post-Medieval Archaeol* 11, 61–66.

Holt M 1970 Early brick-making in Sussex. *Sussex Notes and Queries* 17.5, 164–5.

Homan W M 1940 *Winchelsea: the founding of a thirteenth-century town.* Privately published typescript.

Hope W H St John & Brakspear H 1906 The Cistercian Abbey of Beaulieu in the county of Southampton. *Archaeol J* 63, 82–186.

Hope W St John & Fowler J T 1903 Recent discoveries in the cloister of Durham Abbey. *Archaeologia* 58, 437–42.

Horton M C 1983 Floor Tiles. In Streeten 1983.

Hugo T 1857 Notes on a collection of Pilgrims signs. *Archaeologia* XXXVIII, 128–134.

Hume N I 1968 A find of Elizabethan ale glasses. *The Connoisseur* December 1968, 259–261.

Hume N I 1962 Tudor and Early Stuart glasses found in London. *The Connoisseur* August 1962, 269–73.

Hume N I 1957 Medieval Bottles from London. *The Connoisseur* March 1957, 104–8.

Hume N I 1956 A century of London Glass Bottles 1580–1680. *The Connoisseur Year Book*, 98–103.

Hurst J G 1974 Sixteenth and seventeenth century imported pottery from the Saintonge. In Evison V I *et al.* eds. *Medieval Pottery from Excavations*, 221–55. Baker.

Hurst J G 1977a Discussion of Pottery, in Neal D S, Excavations at the Palace of Kings Langley, Hertfordshire 1974–1976. *Medieval Archaeol* 21, 155–7.

Hurst J G 1977b Spanish pottery imported into medieval Britain. *Medieval Archaeol* 21, 68–105.

Hutchinson M E 1982 Identification of a Gemstone from Battle Abbey, East Sussex. *Ancient Monuments Lab Report* 3585

Johns C N 1970 *Criccieth Castle* H.M.S.O.

Jones R T, Wall S M, Locker A M, Coy J & Maltby M 1976 Ancient Monuments Laboratory, DOE, Computer Based Osteometry, Data Capture User Manual (1) Ancient Monuments Laboratory Report no 3342.

Jope E M & Dunning G C 1954 The use of blue slate for roofing in Medieval England. *Antiq J* 34, 209–217.

Jope E M 1964 The Saxon building-stone industry in southern and Midland England. *Medieval Archaeol* VIII, 91–118.

Kauffmann C M 1975 *Romanesque Manuscripts.* Harvey Miller.

Keen L & Thackray D 1974 A fourteenth-century mosaic tile pavement with line-impressed decoration from Icklingham. *Proc Suffolk Inst Archaeol* 33, 153–67.

Keepax C A 1984 Identfication of charcoal samples from Battle Abbey. Interim Report. Ancient Monuments Laboratory Report Series No. 4314.

Kelly D B 1972 An early Tudor kiln at Hareplain, Biddenden. *Archaeol Cantiana* 87, 159–76.

Kent J P C 1968 Excavations at the motte and bailey castle of South Mimms, Herts, 1960–1967. *Bull Barnet and Dist Local Hist Soc* 15, n.p.

Kenyon G H 1967 *The Glass Industry of the Weald.* Leicester, Leicester University Press.

Kerr J 1983 The Window Glass in Streeten 1983, 56–70.

Knight B 1983, Researches in Medieval Window Lead, *J Brit Soc Master Glass Painters* 18, 49–51.

Knowles D 1959 *The Religious Orders in England* III. Cambridge, The University Press.

Knowles D 1963 *The Monastic Orders in England.* Cambridge, The University Press, 2nd ed.

Knowles J A 1932 A History of the York School of Glass painting. *Journal of the British Society of*

Master Glass Painters IV no 4, Oct 1932.

Knowles J A 1930 Ancient leads for windows and the methods of their manufacture. *Journal of the British Society of Master Glass Painters III, 133–139.*

Lafond J 1953 Le vitrail en Normandie de 1250 à 1300. *Bulletin Monumental* CXI, 317–357.

Lane A 1960 *A Guide to the Collection of Tiles: Victoria and Albert Museum.* H.M.S.O.

Lawson G 1978 Medieval tuning pegs from Whitby, N. Yorkshire. *Medieval Archaeol* 22, 139–41.

Lawson G 1980 *Stringed Musical Instruments: artefacts in the archaeology of Western Europe.* Unpublished PhD thesis, Cambridge University.

Legge W H 1902 The forest of the Broyle and the parks of Ringmer. *The Reliquary* 73–86.

Leland J *Itinerary*, ed. Toulmin Smith, L. 5 vol. 1906–8. Bell.

Lelong C 1977 Recherches sur l'abbatiale de Marmoutier à l'epoque Romane. *Académie des Inscriptions de Belles Lettres 1976,* 704–734.

Lelong C 1979 Aperçus complementaires sur le plan de l'eglise abbatiale de Marmoutier au 11ᵐᵉ siècle. *Bulletin Monumental.* 137, 241–7.

Lemmon C H 1961–2 Finds and fieldwork: examination of a medieval site on Tower Hill Farm. *Trans. Battle and Dist. Hist. Soc.* 11, 28–29.

Leslie K 1971 The Ashburnham Brickworks 1840–1968. *Sussex Industrial History* I, 2–22.

Letters and Papers Henry VIII *Letters and Papers Foreign and Domestic of the Reign of Henry VIII.* H.M.S.O.

Lipski L L 1970 Delftware. In Moorhouse S, Finds from Basing House, Hampshire *c.* 1540–1645: Part One. *Post-Medieval Archaeol* 4, 70–3.

Lloyd N 1925 *A History of English Brickwork.* London and New York: Montgomery.

Lloyd N 1934 *A History of English Brickwork* (Abridged edn.). London; Montgomery.

LMMC 1940 Ward Perkins J B, *London Museum Medieval Catalogue.* H.M.S.O.

Lower M A 1859 A medieval pottery at Hastings, *Sussex Archaeol Collect* 11, 229–30.

Lower M A 1859 A medieval pottery at Hastings. *Sussex Archaeol Collect* 11, 229–30.

Macpherson-Grant N C 1978 The Pottery. In Bennet P *et al.* Some minor excavations undertaken by the Canterbury Archaeological Trust. *Archaeol Cantiana* 94, 174–90.

Manning R B 1968 Anthony Browne, 1st Viscount Montague: the influence in county politics of an Elizabethan Catholic Nobleman. *Sussex Archaeol Collect,* 105, 103–112.

Manning R B 1969 *Religion and Society in Elizabethan Sussex.* Leicester, University Press.

Marshall C J 1924 A medieval pottery kiln discovered at Cheam. *Surrey Archaeol Collect* 35, 79–97.

Martin D 1973 *Hastings Augustinian Priory.* Hastings Area Archaeological Papers, 2.

Martin D & King A 1975 Finds from Period II: Building materials. In A King, A medieval town house in German Street, Winchelsea. *Sussex Archaeol Collect* 113, 136–8.

Martin D 1978 [Anon]: *Historic Buildings in Eastern Sussex* 1.2 Rape of Hastings Archit. Survey.

Martin D n.d. *Glottenham Manor* unpublished typescript.

Martin W 1902 A forgotten industry; pottery at Ringmer. *Sussex Archaeol Collect* 45, 128–32.

Mawer A & Stenton F M 1969 *The Place-names of Sussex.*

Moore D T 1978 The petrography and archaeology of English hone stones. *J. of Archaeol Sci* 5, 61–73.

Moore J W 1974 Hastings town and parks: new archaeological finds. *Sussex Archaeol Collect* 112, 167–72.

Moorhouse S 1971 Finds from Basing House, Hampshire, *c.* 1540–1645, part II. *Post-Medieval Archaeol* 5, 35–76.

Moorhouse S 1972 Medieval distilling apparatus of glass and pottery. *Medieval Archaeol* 16, 79–121.

Moorhouse S 1979 Tudor Green: some further thoughts. *Medieval Ceramics* 3, 53–61.

Morgan N J 1983 *The Medieval Painted Glass of Lincoln Cathedral.* Corpus Vitrearum Medii Aevi Great Britain, occasional paper III, British Academy.

Murray J W 1965 The origins of some Medieval Roofing Slates from Sussex. *Sussex Archaeol Collect* 103, 79–82.

Musson R 1955 A thirteenth century dwelling at Bramble Bottom, Eastbourne. *Sussex Archaeol Collect* 93, 157–70.

Mynard D C 1974 Excavations at Bradwell Priory. *Milton Keynes J Archaeol Hist* 3, 31–66.

Myres J N L 1935 The medieval pottery at Bodiam Castle. *Sussex Archaeol Collect* 76, 222–30.

Nairn I and Pevsner N 1965 *Sussex: Buildings of England.* Harmondsworth Penguin.

Nelson S 1981 A group of pottery waster material from Kingston. *London Archaeol* 4.4, 96–102.

Newton E F & Bibbings E 1960 Seventeenth century pottery sites at Harlow, Essex. *Essex Archaeol Society Trans.* 25, 358–77.

Newton R G (forthcoming) *Lead cames and bulging windows.*

Norton E C 1974 The medieval paving tiles of Winchester College, *Proc. Hampshire Field Club Archaeol Soc* 31, 23–41.

Norton E C 1981 Review article: The British Museum collection of medieval tiles, *J. British Archaeol Ass* 134, 107–9.

Norton E C & Horton M C 1981 A Parisian workshop at Canterbury. A late thirteenth-century tile pavement in the Corona Chapel, and the origins of Tyler Hill. *J British Archaeol Ass* 134, 59–80.

Oakley G E & Hunter J 1979 The Glass. In Williams J J, *St Peter's Street, Northampton Excavations 1973–1976,* 295–302. Northampton, Northampton Development Corporation.

Orton C R 1975 Quantitative pottery studies: some progress, problems and prospects. *Science and Archaeology* 16, 30–35.

Orton C R 1982 The excavation of a late medieval/transitional pottery kiln at Cheam, Surrey. *Surrey Archaeol Collect* 73, 49–92 and microfiche.

O'Shea E W 1979 Pottery. In Westley B, Medieval finds from Denton (2). *Sussex Archaeol Collect* 117, 239.

Peacock D P S 1971 Petrography of certain coarse

pottery. In Cunliffe B *Excavations at Fishbourne* Society of Antiquaries Research Report 27, 225–9.

Peacock D P S 1977 Ceramics in Roman and Medieval Archaeology. In Peacock D P S ed. *Pottery and Early Commerce* 21–33. London, New York, San Francisco: Academic Press.

Peers C & Ralegh Radford C A 1943 The Saxon Monastery of Whitby. *Archaeologia* 89, 27–88.

Pevsner N 1953 *Durham: The Buildings of England.* Harmonsworth, Penguin.

Pichon, Baron J 1879 *Catalogue des Objets de Curiosité.* Paris.

Platt C & Coleman-Smith R 1975 *Excavations in Medieval Southampton.* 2 vols. Leicester, University Press.

Platt C 1976 *Archaeology in Medieval Southampton.* Southampton.

Ponsonby, Lord 1934 Monastic Paving tiles at . . . Shulbrede Priory, Lynchmere, *Sussex Archaeol Collect* 75 19–64.

Preston A E 1935 The demolition of Reading Abbey, *Berkshire Archaeol J* 39, 107–44.

Pryor S & Blockley K 1978 A seventeenth-century kiln site at Woolwich, *Post-Medieval Archaeol* 12, 30–85.

Raby F J E & Baillie Reynolds P K 1952 *Castle Acre Priory.* H.M.S.O. 2nd edn.

Raby F J E & Baillie Reynolds P K 1979 *Thetford Priory.* H.M.S.O.

Rademacher F 1933 *Die Deutschen Gläser des Mittelalters*, Berlin, Verlag für Kunstwissenschaft.

Rahtz P & Hirst S 1976 *Bordesley Abbey, Redditch. First report on excavations 1969–1973* British Archaeol. Rep.

Registrum Malmesburiense ed. Brewer J S and Martin C T, Rolls Series 72. 2 vol. 1879–80

Reis P B 1956 *Precario das Moedas Portuguesas de 1140 a 1640*, Lisbon.

Rhodes M R 1980 A pair of late medieval spectacles from Trig Lane site. *London Archaeologist* IV, I, 23–25.

Rigold S E 1968 The floor tiles, in Philp B, *Excavations at Faversham, 1965* 44–50. Kent Archaeol Research Groups Counc. Research Rep. 1.

Rigold S E 1974 *Bayham Abbey.* H.M.S.O.

Rigold S E 1977 Two common species of medieval seal matrix. *Antiq J* LVII, pt II, 324–9.

Rites of Durham ed. Raine J, Surtees Society, 107 (1903).

Ross T 1860 Medieval Pottery at Hastings. *Sussex Archaeol Collect* 12, 268.

Rudling D R 1976 Excavations in Winding Street, Hastings 1975. *Sussex Archaeol Collect* 114, 164–175.

Salzmann L F 1907 The abbey of Battle. In *Victoria County History: Sussex* II, 52–6.

Salzmann L F 1923 *English Industries of the Middle Ages.* Oxford: Clarendon Press.

Salzmann L F 1935 Excavations at Robertsbridge Abbey, *Sussex Notes and Queries* 5.7, 206–8.

Salzmann L F 1952 (and 1967) *Building in England down to 1540.* Oxford: University Press.

Sass L 1977 *To the Queen's Taste, Elizabethan Feasts and Recipes.* John Murray, London.

Schütte S 1976 Mittelalterliches Glas aus Göttingen *Zeitschrift fur Archäology des Mittelalters* Jahrg 4, 101 ff.

Searle E & Ross B 1967 *Accounts of the cellarers of Battle Abbey, 1275–1513* Sydney: University Press; and Sussex Record Soc. 65. (see *Cellarers' Accounts*)

Searle E 1974 *Lordship and Community, Battle Abbey and its Banlieu, 1066–1538.* Toronto, Pontifical Institute of Medieval Studies.

Searle E 1980 Introduction to *Chronicle.*

Selwood E B & Durrance E M 1982 The Devonian Rocks. In Durrance E M and Laming D J C eds. *The Geology of Devon.* Exeter: The University.

Sharpe E 1861 The collective architectural history of the foregoing buildings as indicated by their mouldings. In Willis R *et. al. The Architectural History of Chichester Cathedral.*

Sharrock J T R 1976 *The Atlas for Breeding Birds in Britain and Ireland.* British Trust for Ornithology, Irish Wildlife Conservancy.

Sherlock D forthcoming *St Augustine's Canterbury*, excavation report.

Silver I A 1969 The ageing of Domestic Animals, in *Science and Archaeology* ed. Brothwell D and Higgs E, 283–302. Thames and Hudson.

Simpson W D 1942 Herstmonceux Castle, *Archaeol J.* 99 110–22.

Slater W 1857 Etchingham Church. *Sussex Archaeol Collect.* 9, 340–60.

Stewart K 1975 with **P and M Michael** *Cooking and Eating, a pictorial history with receipes*, Hart Davis, Macgibbon.

Smith R 1627 *The life of the Lady Magdalene, Viscountess Montague.* In ed. Southern A C *An Elizabethan recusant house.* London and Glasgow. Sands and Co. 1954.

Spufford P 1963 Continental coins in late medieval England. *British Numismatic Jnl* XXXII, 127–139.

Spufford P 1964 Burgundian double patards in late medieval England. *British Numismatic Jnl* xxxiii, 110–17.

Straker E 1931 *Wealden Iron.* Bell 1931; reprinted David and Charles, Newton Abbot 1969.

Streeten A D F 1980 Potters, kilns and markets in medieval Sussex: a preliminary study. In Freke D J ed. The Archaeology of Sussex Pottery. *Sussex Archaeol Collect* 118, 105–17.

Streeten A D F 1981 Craft and Industry: medieval and later potters in south-east England, in Howard H and Morris E *Production Distribution: a ceramic viewpoint* 323–45. British Archaeological Report Internat. Ser. 120.

Streeten A D F 1982 Textural analysis: an approach to the characterisation of sand-tempered ceramics. In Freestone I *et al.* eds. *Current Research in Ceramics: Thin Section Studies* 123–134. British Museum Occasional Paper 32.

Streeten A D F 1983 *Bayham Abbey Sussex Archaeological Society Monograph* 2.

Streeten A D F forthcoming a. The Pottery. In Stevens L, *Excavations at Michelham Priory.*

Streeten A D F forthcoming b. Fabric analysis and regional comparison. In Canterbury Archaeological Trust report, *Excavations within the Canterbury Cathedral Precincts*

Stuttgart 1977 Catalogue *Die Zeit der Staufer*, Wurtemburgisches Landesmuseum.

Summerson J 1945 *Georgian London*. London: Pleiades

Swift E 1934 Obedientary and other accounts of Battle Abbey in the Huntington Library, *Bull Inst. Hist. Research* 12, 83–101.

Swift E 1937 The obedientary rolls of Battle Abbey, *Sussex Archaeol Collect.* 78, 37–62.

Tait H 1967 Glass with Chequered Spiral-trail Decoration. *Journal of Glass Studies* IX, 94–112.

Tester P J 1974 Excavations at Boxley Abbey. *Archaeol. Cantiana* 88, 129–158.

Tesch F W 1977 *The Eel*, ed. Greenwood P. English edition, Chapman and Hall.

Thomas-Stamford 1910 *Sussex in the Great Civil War & Interregnum 1642–1660* Chiswick Press

Thompson A H 1953 *Netley Abbey*. H.M.S.O.

Thompson R 1978 The roof tiles. In Walker J S F, Excavations at Quilter's Vault, Southampton, *Proc Hampshire Field Club Archaeol Soc* 35, 205.

Thorn J C 1979 The Camera in Area 10. In Andrews D D and Milne G eds. *Wharram: a study of settlement on the Yorkshire wolds, Volume 1, Domestic Settlement, 1: Areas 10 and 6* 55–66. Soc. Medieval Archaeol. Monograph 8.

Thorpe T 1835 *Descriptive Catalogue of the Original Charters etc . . . constituting the Muniments of Battle Abbey . . .* London.

Thorpe W A 1929 *A History of English and Irish Glass* I and II. The Medici Society.

Thorpe W A 1961 *English Glass* 3rd edn. A and C Black.

Torrington Diaries C. Bruyn Andrews ed., *The Torrington Diaries, concerning the tours through England and Wales of the Hon. John Byng (later fifth viscount Torrington), between 1791 and 1794.* I Eyre and Spottiswoode 1934.

Turner E 1865 Battel Abbey, *Sussex Archaeol Collect* 17.

Urry W 1967 *Canterbury under the Angevin kings*. Athlone Press.

Valor Eccl. Valor Ecclesiasticus. London: Record Commission, 1810.

VCH 1907 *Victoria County History: Sussex* 2.

VCH 1912 *Victoria County History: Hampshire 5*

VCH 1932 *Victoria County History: Kent 3*.

VCH 1937 *Victoria County History: Sussex 9*.

VCH 1940 *Victoria County History: Sussex 7*.

[Vidler] 1841 *A native [–Vidler], Gleanings respecting Battel and its Abbey*. Battle: F W Ticehurst.

Vidler L A 1932 Floor tiles and kilns near the site of St Bartholomew's Hospital, Rye. *Sussex Archaeol Collect* 73, 83–101.

Vidler L A 1933 Medieval pottery and kilns found at Rye. *Sussex Archaeol Collect* 74, 44–64.

Vidler L A 1936 Medieval pottery, tiles and kilns found at Rye. *Sussex Archaeol Collect* 77, 107–118.

Vince A 1982 Medieval and post-medieval Spanish pottery from the City of London. In Freestone I *et al.* eds. *Current Research in Ceramics: Thin-Section Studies*, 135–44. British Museum Occasional Paper 32.

Viollet-le-Duc M 1864 *Dictionnaire Raisonné de l'Architecture*, vol 7, Paris.

Walcott M E C 1866 The conventual arrangements of Battle Abbey. *Trans. Royal Instit. British Architects* (1865–6), 161–172.

Walker J W 1926 The Priory of St Mary Magdalene of Monk Bretton, *Yorks Archaeol Soc*, extra vol V.

Wall S M 1980 The animal bones from the excavation of the hospital of St Mary Ospringe. *Archaeol Cantiana* XCVI, 227–26.

Ward Perkins J B 1937 English medieval embossed tiles, *Archaeol J.* 94, 128–53.

Warneke J 1912 Mittelalterliche schulgeräte in Museum zum Lubeck. *Zeitschrift fur Geschichte der Erziehung und Unterrichts II*, 227–50.

Webb G 1956 *Architecture in Britain: the Middle Ages*. Harmondsworth: Penguin.

Westlake N H J 1881–1884 *A History of Design in Painted Glass* I–II. Parker and Co.

Whittingham S 1979 *A thirteenth century portrait gallery at Salisbury Cathedral*. Salisbury: Friends of . . . Cathedral.

Wheeler A 1978 *Key to the Fishes of Northern Europe*. F Warne.

Wheeler A 1979 *The Tidal Thames*. Routledge and Kegan Paul.

Willis R 1869 *The architectural history of the conventual buildings of the monastery of Christ Church in Canterbury*. Kent Archaeol Soc.

Wilson C A 1973 *Food and Drink in Britain*. Constable.

Wilson D M & Hurst D G 1962–3 Medieval Britain in 1961. *Medieval Archaeol* 6–7, 306–49.

Wilson D M & Hurst D G 1964 Medieval Britain in 1962–3. *Medieval Archaeol* 8, 231–99.

Williams J H 1979 *St Peters, Northampton*. Northampton Development Corporation.

Wood E 1982 A sixteenth-century Glasshouse at Knightons, Alford, Surrey, *Surrey Archaeol Collect* LXXIII, 1–47.

Wood M 1965 *The English Medieval House*. Phoenix House.

Woodward G W O 1966 *The Dissolution of the Monasteries*. Blandford Press.

Youings J 1971 *The Dissolution of the Monasteries*. Allen and Unwin.

Zastrow O 1978 *L'Oreficieria in Lombardia*, Milan.

Zigrosser C 1955 *Ars Medica*. Philadelphia, Philadelphia Museum of Art.

Index